Welcome to Wok World

Unlock EVERY Secret of Cooking Through 500 AMAZING Wok Recipes
(Unlock Cooking, Book 2)

Annie Kate

Copyright: Published in the United States by ANNIE KATE / © ANNIE KATE
Published on November 19, 2016

All rights reserved. No part of this publication may be reproduced, stored in retrieval system, copied in any form or by any means, electronic, mechanical, photocopying, recording or otherwise transmitted without written permission from the publisher. Please do not participate in or encourage piracy of this material in any way. You must not circulate this book in any format. ANNIE KATE does not control or direct users' actions and is not responsible for the information or content shared, harm and/or actions of the book readers.

In accordance with the U.S. Copyright Act of 1976, the scanning, uploading and electronic sharing of any part of this book without the permission of the publisher constitute unlawful piracy and theft of the author's intellectual property. If you would like to use material from the book (other than just simply for reviewing the book), prior permission must be obtained by contacting the author at contact@smallpassion.com

Thank you for your support of the author's rights.

Contents

Contents 5

Introduction 7

Chapter 1: How To Use A Wok 11

   Select A Right Wok 12

   Season Your New Wok 13

   Take Care Of Your Wok After Seasoning 13

Chapter 2: How To Cook With A Wok In Different Ways 15

   Start With Stir-Frying 16

   It's Easy To Steam With A Wok 17

   Don't Miss Your Wok When Deep-Frying 17

Chapter 3: Beef Recipes 19

Chapter 4: Chicken Recipes 65

   Chicken Noodles 66

   More Chicken Recipes 74

Chapter 5: Chinese Recipes 173

Chapter 6: Fish and Seafood 186

   Crab 187

   Fish 196

   Shrimp 201

Chapter 7: Italian Recipes 262

Chapter 8: Noodles Recipes 267

Chapter 9: Pork and Lamp Recipes 284

Chapter 10: Rice Dishes 325

Chapter 11: Soups 348

Chapter 12: Thai Recipes *355*
Chapter 13: Vegetarian Recipes *369*
Chapter 14: More Wok Recipes *386*
Conclusion *537*
An Awesome Free Gift For You *538*

Introduction

***

Wok Cooking - Siprit Of Chinese Cuisine

Chinese cuisine enjoys high fame throughout the world. It's famous not only for being delicious but also for being eye-catching and nutritious. When cooking, Chinese people often make use of various fresh ingredients, therefore, every Chinese dish is a harmonious combination of smells, flavors and colors. It's the combination that brings you a feeling that you're enjoying a colorful picture not a normal dish.

In general, to retain colors and nutrients of foods, we keep them fresh and eat them without cooking. Chinese people are different. They can preserve food's color and nutritional value even after cooking. Their secret is nothing but cooking in really high temperature and in a quick time. To cook well, they pay a particular attention to the complex process and equipment involved. They use special equipment called "Wok".

The first Woks seem to age from the Han dynasty (from 206 BCE to 200 CE). Since then, Wok has played such an important role in the everyday life of the Chinese. Nowadays, because of its amazing benefits, Wok appears not only in Chinese family kitchens but also in kitchens of many countries all around the world. Those benefits of Wok are listed below:

- ✓ **Healthy advantages**: Wok is a frying pan but its curved shape changes the way the food is cooked. It is healthier than a standard frying pan because of its high heat retention and the need for little cooking oil. Also, since the food can be pushed up the sides of the Wok, excess oil can drain off before it is served. Unlike standard frying pans, the high sides of a Wok allow large amounts of food to be stirred at the same time without the food soaking up oil sitting in the bottom of the pan.
- ✓ **More food:** Another benefit of a Wok, as compared to a standard frying pan, is a larger usable cooking area. Because of the high edges, more food can be put into a Wok. This means you can more easily cook greater quantities and have delectable leftovers for the next day's meals. This also helps with keeping your kitchen clean — less pans and utensils and less chance of spills onto the stove.

- ✓ **Limits Fat Content:** When stir-frying foods, you only need a minimal amount of oil due to the high heat used in this cooking method. You can even replace the fat with broth to lower the final fat content of your meal even more. You'll want to include at least a small amount of fat, either from the oil used to stir-fry your food or in the form of meat or nuts because otherwise you won't be able to absorb all of the fat-soluble vitamins from the vegetables in the dish.
- ✓ **Helps Minimize Nutrient Losses:** Long cooking times increase the loss of heat-sensitive vitamins such as vitamin B and vitamin C. Quickly stir-frying vegetables in a small amount of oil helps minimize these losses. Although the high temperatures used will still cause some nutrient losses, these will be less than if you grilled, baked or roasted your vegetables. Typically, the meat or hardier vegetable (whatever takes the longest to cook) is put into the very hot oil at the bottom of the Wok and stir-fried until it is about halfway cooked. It is then pushed up the sides of the Wok while the next ingredients, tender vegetables or delicate seafood, are added. While the last ingredient is being cooked, the first ingredients are remained at a much slower rate, which keeps them from overcooking.
- ✓ **Various cooking techniques:** Despite being a perfect pan to use for great-tasting stir-fries, the Wok has so much more potential Woks are used in a range of different Chinese cooking techniques, including stir frying, steaming, pan frying, deep frying, poaching, boiling, braising, searing, stewing, making soup, smoking and roasting nuts. It's also used to prepare some Thai and Italian dishes.

To me, Wok cooking method is too good to be ignored. Although I'm not a Chinese person, Wok cooking attracts me like a magnet. It's the reason why I tirelessly found out about it during many years and then wrote this book. **"Welcome to Wok World"** is the book taking me much more time than any other books I published before. It's also the book of which I'm proud most. It contains 500 recipes of Wok cooking method, all of which were made with love from bottom of my heart. These recipes are divided into some following parts:

- ✓ *Chapter 1: How to Use a Wok*
- ✓ *Chapter 2: How To Cook With A Wok In Different Ways*
- ✓ *Chapter 3: Beef Recipes*
- ✓ *Chapter 4: Chicken Recipes*
- ✓ *Chapter 5: Chinese Recipes*
- ✓ *Chapter 6: Fish and Seafood*
- ✓ *Chapter 7: Italian Recipes*
- ✓ *Chapter 8: Noodles Recipes*

- ✓ Chapter 9: Pork and Lamp Recipes
- ✓ Chapter 10: Rice Dishes
- ✓ Chapter 11: Soups
- ✓ Chapter 12: Thai Recipes
- ✓ Chapter 13: Vegetarian Recipes
- ✓ Chapter 14: More Wok Recipes

In addition to providing you with **500 AMAZING recipes**, I'll show you how to use a Wok to cook in many different ways including: stir-frying, stewing, deep frying and so much more. Now, you don't need to pay a lot of money to go to Chinese restaurants anymore. Also, you don't have to worry about the quality of delivered food anymore. Right after following some first recipes, you totally can prepare for your whole family a great meal which contains spirit of Asian tradition.

At the bottom line, I want to share a little thing with you - my dear friends: Cooking is like painting and writing a song. It may be difficult even challenging at the beginning. However, you can totally master it if you spend on it enough time, love and effort. Believe in me, you will receive a lot of wonderful things in return. Good luck!

Remember that:

"Cooking is like snow skiing: If you don't fall at least 10 times, then you're not skiing hard enough" - Guy Fieri

Chapter 1: How To Use A Wok

***

Select A Right Wok

Wok is considered a versatile pan for cooking. It can be used for various cooking methods including: stir-frying, deep frying, steaming, indoor-smoking and so much more. But as with most things, not all Woks are created equal. They come in a dizzying array of sizes, shapes, metals, and handle arrangements. Luckily for all of us, the best Woks also happen to be on the inexpensive end of the scale.

Here are some things you need to consider if wanting to choose a suitable Wok:

- ✓ **Material:** Woks are typically made from three materials: stainless steel, cast iron, and carbon steel. You shouldn't choose stainless steel ones because they are so heavy. In addition, they often require a long time to heat and cool, and often have food stick to them. Cast iron is better, but it can be fragile and take a long time to heat. A carbon steel Wok is best option for a Wok because it heats evenly, is durable, and doesn't cost as much as other materials. Like cast iron, carbon steel needs to be seasoned before using and then given special care to maintain its coating. This pan will become naturally nonstick over time and will last a lifetime. Avoid nonstick Woks. Most if not all nonstick coatings are not supposed to be heated to a very high temperature, but all stir-fry cooking happens at a high temperature.
- ✓ **Shape:** When choosing a Wok, you need to pay special attention to the bottom. Woks come in a two bottom styles: round- and flat-bottomed. Round-bottomed Woks are traditional to Chinese cooking, but they don't work well on most of our Western stovetops. For both gas and electric ranges, a flat-bottomed Wok is the way to go. This style keeps the pan stable as you cook. Moreover, the pan is brought into direct contact with the high heat. Therefore, cooking will be quicker and easier.
- ✓ **Handle:** Let's choose Woks with a long, heat-resistant wood handle on one side and a small looped handle on opposite side. This arrangement is easiest for handling the work during stir-frying and then lifting the Wok off the stove afterwards.
- ✓ **Size:** Woks come in a variety of sizes. For home use, Woks come in a variety of sizes from 12 to 18 inches. One that measures 14 inches in diameter is big enough for most families, as this gives plenty of room for all of the ingredients, and the tumbling/tossing action of stir frying

Season Your New Wok

Before using a new carbon steel or cast iron Wok for the first time, you have to season it in order to form a protective, nonstick and rust resistant surface.

Here's a traditional Chinese method:
- ✓ **Wash the new Wok**: It's necessary to scrub your Wok away before you season it. Avoid using factory oil when seasoning your new Wok in order to protect the metal and keep Wok from rusting. Thoroughly scrub the Wok inside and out using a steel scrubbing pad and dish soap. Rinse with hot water.
- ✓ **Dry the Wok**: The next step is drying your Wok. Set the clean Wok over low heat and let it dry for 1 to 2 minutes, until no water remains. Otherwise it can and will rust
- ✓ **Heat the Wok**: Woks always need to be preheated when being seasoned. Turn on a stove burner with pretty high temperature. The Wok is hot enough when droplets of water evaporate within 1 to 2 seconds of. At that time, you know that the Wok is heated and ready for stir-frying. After heating the Wok for about a minute, add the oil if you're going to stir fry or deep - fry
- ✓ **Pull Wok off the heat and add oil**: Pull the Wok off the heat and add 2 tablespoons of oil. Pick up the pan and carefully swirl it to coat the bottom and sides. If the Wok smokes wildly the moment you add the oil you've overheated the Wok. Remove the Wok from the heat and let it cool for a few minutes. When it's cool enough to handle carefully remove the oil with paper towels, wash the Wok, and start again.

Take Care Of Your Wok After Seasoning

There are some thing you need to take care of after seasoning your new Wok:
- ✓ **New Woks are hungry for fat**: A new Wok will soak up any fat you give it. You don't have to worry about it because soaking fat helps develop the seasoning on the new Wok. Let's cook anything that uses fat: stir-fries, deep-fat frying, cooking bacon and so on.
- ✓ **Things to avoid**: As I mentioned before, it's necessary to cook some dishe that use fat. In other words, you need to avoid steaming, boiling, or poaching in your new work. Also avoid cooking with any acid such as tomatoes, vinegar, and lemons. These things are fine once you've been using your Wok for a while, but can damage the delicate seasoning on the newly-seasoned Wok.
- ✓ **The teenage Wok:** Woks go through an adolescent stage before they develop the deep patina and nonstick coating of a well-used Wok. During this stage, the seasoning can look splotchy, feel

gummy, or develop rust spots, especially if you live somewhere humid or go a few weeks between uses.
✓ **Watch for Color Change:** The color of the Wok will gradually change from shiny new silver to mottled light yellow-brown. You may possibly see some blue, bright yellow, or even black colors; this is fine. (With some Woks there will be no change. Every pan will react differently). The Wok will also start to look smoother.

Chapter 2: How To Cook With A Wok In Different Ways

***

Start With Stir-Frying

Wok can be used to cook in many ways. The most common way is stir-frying. So here are some additional tips for you when stir-frying:

- ✓ **Preheat** the Wok before adding oil. You'll know it's hot enough when a bead of water evaporates within seconds of contact. Drizzle the oil down the side of the hot Wok, swirling to coat the entire surface.
- ✓ **Cold oil**: It's better to use cold oil such as peanut oil (smokes at 410°F) or canola oil. Because of their high smoke points, they can take the heat without burning. Olive oil (325°F) and butter (350°F), both of which can't withstand the high heat required for a Wok, should be avoided. Once you add your oil, work quickly, as stir-frying isn't about taking it slow and low.
- ✓ **Reduce Heat**: Reduce the heat to medium and stir-fry the aromatics for 15 to 20 minutes. Smear the aromatics up the sides of the Wok all the way to the edge. If the mixture becomes too dry, add an additional tablespoon of oil as needed.
- ✓ **Prepared ingredients:** Make sure that your ingredients are cut into uniform-size pieces before cooking because stir-frying is quick and you're throwing things in the pan one after the. Speaking of chopping, make sure all your ingredients are more or less the same size. A hunk of red pepper is going to take way longer to cook than a tiny minced onion. If you cut everything roughly the same size, it will all cook at about the same rate. Bite-sized pieces work best so you won't have to use a knife while eating.
- ✓ **Blanching first**: Give hard veggies such as carrots, broccoli and potatoes a head start by blanching them before stir-frying. You need to pay attention to your veggies before tossing them into the pan. Cook thicker and harder vegetables first, since they take longer.
- ✓ **Dry before cooking:** Dry vegetable, shrimp and scallops well before adding to the Wok. Even slightly damp ingredients will alter the Wok' temperature, turn down the volume on the sizzling sound that ingredients make in oil, and cause your food to steam instead of sear.
- ✓ **Order of cooing ingredients:** If your stir fry contains meat such as chicken and fish, cook them first. Then remove and set them aside on a plate when they're about 80 per cent done. Later, when your vegetables are done, just add your meat back in for the final heating. This will prevent the meat from getting over-cooked, and it will retain the flavor of your meat and not having everything in your stir fry tasting exactly the same.

- ✓ **Keep moving:** The key to stir fry is to keep it moving. Stir your ingredients continually in the pan with a wooden spatula. Veggies will need more tossing than meat, however.

It's Easy To Steam With A Wok

Steamer is a method of cooking using steam. Food steamed is healthier because of being cooked without oil. Here are some things you need to take care when use Wok to steam:

- ✓ Use a steamer basket or rack. When you use your Wok for steaming, you need to add a basket or rack to hold the food above the water. You should choose a bamboo steamer basket. Using a bamboo steamer basket is that its lid actually absorbs excess moisture inside the Wok, so it doesn't drip back down over the food and make it soggy. Place the vegetables, dumplings, or other food that you're steaming in a single layer in the basket or rack, so they'll all be steamed evenly

- ✓ Remember to bring the water in the Wok all the times to a boil before putting food in the steamer. The food in your steamer basket or on the rack should sit above the water, so it doesn't get overcooked. You don't have to use water to steam in your Wok. Any translucent, light liquid, such as broth, stock, wine, or juice, can work.

- ✓ Take care when adding and removing food because the temperature of steam is really high. You should use retriever tongs for safe and easy transfer.

- ✓ If you use a newly seasoned carbon-steel Wok, steaming may remove the Wok's thin patina. Simply season your Wok if this happens.

Don't Miss Your Wok When Deep-Frying

Deep-frying in a Wok is ideal because its concave shape requires less oil than a regular pot, and the roominess of the Wok lets you fry more food at one time without crowding, which means frying in fewer batches. Here are some tips for deep-frying in a Wok:

- ✓ **Heat your Wok:** Always heat your Wok until a drop of water evaporates upon contact before adding the oil. A well-heated Wok prevents ingredients from sticking and gives them a good sear.
- ✓ **Add oil to the Wok**: For deep frying, it's better to use inexpensive, flavorless oil with a high smoke point such as: canola, peanut, and safflower You can also use clean animal fats, such as lard or duck

fat, but they tend to cost much more. And remember to never fill the Wok more than halfway with oil.
- ✓ **Heat the oil:** Use a deep-fry/candy thermometer to monitor the oil temperature. It's the easiest way to determine that the oil is hot enough.
- ✓ **Prepared food:** Make sure that all of the pieces that you add to the oil are the same size, so they'll cook evenly. It's also important to dry all of the food thoroughly before adding it to the oil or battering it and placing it in the oil because moisture will make the oil spatter.
- ✓ **Be careful when adding food**. After the oil is properly heated, you can begin to add food into the Wok. Moisture causes oil to spatter, so thoroughly dry the food to be fried. Therefore, you have to be careful when adding food. Don't crowd the Wok with too many ingredients, which will reduce the temperature of the pan and cause the food to steam
- ✓ **Using skimmer:** Wooden chopsticks are handy for adding ingredients to the oil, but I prefer to use a metal skimmer or strainer (spider) to remove several pieces of fried food at a time.

Chapter 3: Beef Recipes

***

Asian Beef Noodle Stirfry

"Noodle bowls and stirfrys are soooo easy to be creative with."

Servings: 10 | **Time**: 30m

Ingredients

- 2 lb beef strips (or sliced steak)
- 2 cup beef broth
- 4 cup mixed vegetables
- 2 green onions (sliced)
- 1 lb spaghettini noodles
- 4 tbsp teriyaki sauce
- 2 tbsp peanut butter
- 3 tbsp sesame oil
- 3 tbsp soya sauce
- 1/2 cup unsalted cashews

Directions

1. Saute beef strips in sesame oil and soya sauce.
2. Then after add the beef broth, peanut butter and teriyaki sauce and bring to a simmer.
3. Add the spaghettini noodles and vegetables. Cover and simmer for about 10-12 minutes.
4. Keep stiring frequently.
5. Season with salt & pepper.
6. Top with cashews and sliced green onions.
7. Serve & Enjoy!!!

Basic Marinade for Chicken or Beef Slices for Stir fry Veggies

"This marination is good for all veggies stir fry. So easy and delicious. ."

Servings: 2 | **Time**: 30m

Ingredients

- 1 chicken breast cut into strips
- 1/2 tbsp dark soy sauce (I used vegetarian mashroom oyster)
- 1/2 tsp tapioca starch/corn starch
- 1 tsp sesame oil
- 1/2 tsp sugar
- 1/2 tsp chicken broth powder (option)
- 1/2 tbsp cooking oil.
- 1 cup cooking oil for stir fry

Directions

1. Cut chicken breast into long strips.
2. Place chicken strips into a container box. And add all ingredients into it.
3. Stir it well. We can use it after at least 15 minutes after marinating. Or you could also put them into the fridge.
4. After 15 minutes or more, add chicken strips marinated into frying pan with so much oil. Don't stir it until chicken lil bit stiff, so it will have a straight shape.
5. Stir it well. Cook chicken until colour changed to pale. Around 5 - 10 min. Separate chicken and oil, so now we are ready to use stir fry chicken for mix all kind of veggie stir fries.
6. Hmm.. it is really yummy !!

Beef & Bok Choy Stir Fry

Servings: 4

Ingredients

- 2 tbsp soy sauce
- 2 tbsp rice vinegar
- 1 tbsp peanut butter
- 1 tbsp honey
- 2 garlic cloves, minced
- 1 Coarse salt and ground pepper

- 1 lb skirt steak, thinly sliced crosswise
- 1 tbsp cornstarch
- 1 tsp vegetable oil
- 1 large head bok choy, cut 1 inch thick crosswise
- 4 medium carrots, halved lengthwise, thinly sliced on bias
- 1 Cooked rice, for serving
- 1/4 cup peanuts, chopped

Directions

1. In a small bowl, mix soy sauce, vinegar, peanut butter, honey, and garlic; season with pepper.
2. In a bowl, toss steak with cornstarch; season with salt and pepper. In a large nonstick skillet with a lid, heat oil over medium-high. Add 1/2 of steak; cook, tossing, until browned, 1 to 2 minutes. Transfer to a plate; repeat with remaining steak.
3. To skillet, add soy mixture, bok choy, and carrots. Cover and cook, tossing occasionally until tender, about 5 minutes. Return steak to skillet; cook until heated through, about 5 minutes. Serve over rice; sprinkle with peanuts.

Beef and Broccoli Stir-fry

"A zesty vegetable stir-fry is a delight for the eyes as well as the taste buds. No time to cook? No worries! Busy weeknights are no match for this beef and broccoli stir-fry. So put away that takeout menu and make weeknight dinner even easier by using a pre-cut beef for stir-fry, unless you already have some lean beef on hand. Toss in fresh broccoli, bean sprouts, and freshly minced ginger for a distinct Asian flavor. "

Servings: 4 | **Prep**: 15m | **Cook**: 10m

Ingredients

- 1 pound pre-cut beef for stir-fry
- 2 garlic cloves, smashed
- 1 tablespoon minced fresh ginger
- 2 tablespoons soy sauce
- 1 bunch broccoli (about 1 lb.)

- 2 tablespoons vegetable oil
- 1/2 cup water
- 1 1/2 cups beef broth
- 2 tablespoons cornstarch
- 1 cup fresh mung bean sprouts

Directions

1. Combine beef, garlic, ginger and soy sauce in a bowl and let stand.
2. Wash broccoli thoroughly and cut into florets. Trim and peel stems and cut into 1/4-inch thick slices.
3. Heat 1 Tbsp. oil in a large nonstick skillet or Wok over high heat, add broccoli florets and stems, then stir-fry for 2 minutes. Add 1/2 cup water and stir until water evaporates. Transfer broccoli to a plate.
4. Add remaining oil to pan, add beef mixture and stir-fry for 3 minutes. Stir together broth and cornstarch, add to meat and stir-fry until sauce is thickened, about 3 minutes longer. Add broccoli and bean sprouts, then cook, stirring, until heated through, about 2 minutes.

Beef Lo Mein

"I couldn't find a good lo mein recipe on here, so I'm posting mine. I made it this week and my roommate and I agreed that it was possibly the best that we've ever had."

Servings: 4 | **Prep**: 15m | **Cook**: 25m | **Ready In**: 40m

Ingredients

- 1 (8 ounce) package spaghetti
- 1 teaspoon dark sesame oil
- 1 tablespoon peanut oil
- 4 cloves garlic, minced
- 1 tablespoon minced fresh ginger root
- 4 cups mixed vegetables
- 1 pound flank steak, thinly sliced
- 3 tablespoons reduced-sodium soy sauce

- 2 tablespoons brown sugar
- 1 tablespoon oyster sauce
- 1 tablespoon Asian chile paste with garlic

Directions

1. Bring a large pot of lightly salted water to a boil. Cook spaghetti in the boiling water until cooked through but firm to the bite, about 12 minutes; drain and transfer to a large bowl. Drizzle sesame oil over the spaghetti; toss to coat. Place a plate atop the bowl to keep the noodles warm.
2. Heat peanut oil in a Wok or large skillet over medium-high heat. Cook and stir garlic and ginger in hot oil until fragrant, about 30 seconds. Add mixed vegetables to the skillet; cook and stir until slightly tender, about 3 minutes. Stir flank steak into the vegetable mixture; cook and stir until the beef is cooked through, about 5 minutes.
3. Mix soy sauce, brown sugar, oyster sauce, and chile paste together in a small bowl; pour over the spaghetti. Dump spaghetti and sauce mixture into the Wok with the vegetables and steak; cook and stir until the spaghetti is hot, 2 to 3 minutes.

Cook's Note:

- I added a small package of sliced mushrooms, a shredded broccoli, carrots, cabbage mix (coleslaw mix) and snap peas, but you can pretty much add whatever veggies you like. About 4 to 5 cups of veggies is a good amount.

Tip

- Aluminum foil helps keep food moist, ensures it cooks evenly, keeps leftovers fresh, and makes clean-up easy.

Beef Noodle Stir Fry

"Nice noodle dish."

***Servings**: 4 | **Cook**: 30m*

Ingredients

- 400 grams egg noodles
- 4 tbsp olive oil
- 2 tbsp ginger
- 4 garlic cloves
- 3 limes
- 5 tbsp soy sauce
- 3 tbsp honey
- 300 grams sirloin steak
- 2 bell peppers

Directions

1. Cook noodles according to the package directions.
2. Fry the green bell pepper, ginger, and the garlic with the olive oil in a pan.
3. Add the beef, soy sauce, and the juice of the limes to the pan.
4. Add the cooked noodles to the pan.
5. Mix well, add honey.
6. Serve.

Beef Stir Fry W Rice

Servings: 6 /**Time**: 1h

Ingredients

- 1/2 lb Beef stew meat
- 1 bunch broccoli
- 1 packages stir fry veggies
- 1/2 cup worcestershire sauce
- 1/2 cup soy sauce
- 1 dash soy sauce

Directions

1. Mix & Marinate beef tips in soy sauce for 30 minutes
2. Add meat to Wok & add the Worcestershire sauce leaving the meat to cook for 30minutes on med-low heat
3. Add broccoli & stir fry veggies
4. Throw a few dashes of soy & mix, cook for 20-25 minutes on med heat
5. Boil rice for 20 minutes
6. Add rice to bowl & top w stir fry then add soy as u like

Beef-and-Brussels Sprouts Stir-fry

"A ripping-hot skillet works as well as a Wok to sear food fast. Just be sure to use one that can take the heat, preferably cast-iron or a large, heavy-bottomed stainless. Feel free to substitute any cruciferous vegetable cut into even pieces in place of Brussels sprouts, from broccoli and cauliflower to cabbage and bok choy."

Servings: 4

Ingredients

- 1/2 pound flank steak
- 1/4 teaspoon salt
- 1/8 teaspoon freshly ground pepper
- 2 tablespoons peanut oil, divided
- 1/2 cup beef broth or water
- 1 tablespoon light brown sugar
- 2 tablespoons soy sauce
- 2 teaspoons fresh lime juice
- 1/2 teaspoon cornstarch
- 12 ounces fresh Brussels sprouts, trimmed and halved
- 1 red jalapeño or red serrano pepper, sliced
- 1 tablespoon grated fresh ginger
- 2 garlic cloves, thinly sliced
- 1/4 cup chopped fresh mint
- Hot cooked rice

Directions

1. Cut steak diagonally across the grain into thin strips. Sprinkle with salt and pepper.
2. Stir-fry steak, in 2 batches, in 1 Tbsp. hot oil in a large cast-iron or stainless-steel skillet over high heat 2 to 3 minutes or until meat is no longer pink. Transfer to a plate, and wipe skillet clean.
3. Whisk together beef broth and next 4 ingredients in a small bowl until smooth.
4. Stir-fry Brussels sprouts in remaining 1 Tbsp. hot oil over high heat 2 minutes or until lightly browned. Add jalapeño pepper, ginger, and garlic, and stir-fry 1 minute. Pour soy sauce mixture over Brussels sprouts, and bring mixture to a boil. Cook, stirring often, 3 to 4 minutes or until sprouts are tender. Stir in mint and steak. Serve over rice.

Beef and Vegetable Stir-Fry

"This easy stir-fry dinner calls for strips of top round steak, fresh asparagus, and classic stir-fry seasonings and vegetables. By cooking your favorite takeout dishes at home, you'll save both money and calories. See our full collection of stir-fry recipes for more dinner ideas."

Servings: 4 | **Prep**: 25m | **Cook**: 25m

Ingredients

- 1 pound fresh asparagus
- 12 ounces top round steak, cut into thin strips
- 3 tablespoons all-purpose flour
- 1/4 cup lite soy sauce
- 1/4 cup water
- 2 garlic cloves, minced
- 1 tablespoon dark sesame oil, divided
- 1 tablespoon hoisin sauce
- 1/4 teaspoon dried crushed red pepper
- 4 small carrots, cut diagonally into 1/4-inch-thick slices
- 1 small red bell pepper, cut into thin strips
- 1/2 cup sliced fresh mushrooms
- 5 green onions, cut into 1-inch pieces
- 2 cups hot cooked rice

Directions

1. Snap off tough ends of asparagus; cut spears into 1-inch pieces, and set aside.
2. Dredge steak in flour; set aside.
3. Stir together soy sauce, 1/4 cup water, garlic, 1 teaspoon sesame oil, hoisin sauce, and crushed red pepper.
4. Heat remaining 2 teaspoons oil in a large skillet or Wok over medium-high heat 2 minutes. Add beef and carrot, and stir-fry 4 minutes. Add soy sauce mixture, and stir-fry 1 minute. Add asparagus, bell pepper, mushrooms, and green onions, and stir-fry 3 minutes. Serve over rice.
5. Vegetable Stir-fry: Omit round steak and flour, and stir-fry vegetables as directed above.

Beef and Watermelon Stir-fry

"This is inspired by a hot pepper beef recipe by Grace Young."

Servings: 4-6 | **Hands-on:** 25m | **Total time:** 55m

Ingredients

- 1 pound sirloin strip steak, cut into thin strips
- 3 garlic cloves, minced
- 2 teaspoons cornstarch
- 2 teaspoons cold water
- 2 teaspoons lite soy sauce
- 1 1/2 teaspoons sesame oil
- 2 tablespoons dry white wine
- 2 tablespoons hot water
- 2 tablespoons hoisin sauce
- 1 teaspoon kosher salt
- 1/2 teaspoon ground black pepper
- 2 tablespoons canola oil, divided
- 1 medium-size sweet onion, halved and sliced
- 12 ounces fresh sugar snap peas
- 1 teaspoon grated fresh ginger
- 1/2 teaspoon dried crushed red pepper

- 16 ounces watermelon, rind removed and cut into sticks (about 2 cups)
- 2 cups hot cooked rice

Directions

1. Toss together first 6 ingredients and 1 Tbsp wine. Let stand 30 minutes. Meanwhile, stir together hot water, hoisin, and remaining 1 Tbsp. wine.
2. Remove beef from marinade, discarding marinade. Sprinkle with salt and black pepper; cook half of beef in 1 1/2 tsp. hot canola oil in a large skillet over high heat, without stirring, 45 seconds or until browned; turn beef, and cook 30 seconds or until browned. Transfer to a warm plate. Repeat with remaining 1 1/2 tsp. oil and beef.
3. Stir-fry onion in remaining 1 Tbsp. hot canola oil in skillet over medium-high heat 2 minutes or until tender. Add sugar snap peas, ginger, and crushed red pepper; stir-fry 2 minutes. Add beef and hoisin mixture; stir-fry 1 minute or until slightly thickened. Remove from heat. Stir in watermelon. Add salt, black pepper, and red pepper to taste. Serve immediately with hot cooked rice.

Crispy Ginger Beef

"This recipe is so much better than take out! Serve it with homemade fried rice or plain rice. If you like spicy, just add more chili pepper flakes!"

Servings: 5 | **Prep**: 25m | **Cook**: 20m | **Ready In**: 45m

Ingredients

- 3/4 cup cornstarch
- 1/2 cup water
- 2 eggs
- 1 pound flank steak, cut into thin strips
- 1/2 cup canola oil, or as needed
- 1 large carrot, cut into matchstick-size pieces
- 1 green bell pepper, cut into matchstick-size pieces
- 1 red bell pepper, cut into matchstick-size pieces

- 3 green onions, chopped
- 1/4 cup minced fresh ginger root
- 5 garlic cloves, minced
- 1/2 cup white sugar
- 1/4 cup rice vinegar
- 3 tablespoons soy sauce
- 1 tablespoon sesame oil
- 1 tablespoon red pepper flakes, or to taste

Directions

1. Place cornstarch in a large bowl; gradually whisk in water until smooth. Whisk eggs into cornstarch mixture; toss steak strips in mixture to coat.
2. Pour canola oil into Wok 1-inch deep; heat oil over high heat until hot but not smoking. Place 1/4 of the beef strips into hot oil; separate strips with a fork. Cook, stirring frequently, until coating is crisp and golden, about 3 minutes. Remove beef to drain on paper towels; repeat with remaining beef.
3. Drain off all but 1 tablespoon oil; cook and stir carrot, green bell pepper, red bell pepper, green onions, ginger, and garlic over high heat until lightly browned but still crisp, about 3 minutes.
4. Whisk sugar, rice vinegar, soy sauce, sesame oil, and red pepper together in a small bowl. Pour sauce mixture over vegetables in Wok; bring mixture to a boil. Stir beef back into vegetable mixture; cook and stir just until heated through, about 3 minutes.

Cook's Note:

- This is the original recipe but I like to add about 1/4 cup of teriyaki sauce as a variation. I also like to add sesame oil to the oil when I fry the beef.

Editors' Note:

- The nutrition data for this recipe includes the full amount of the coating ingredients. The actual amount of the coating consumed will vary. We have determined the nutritional value of oil for frying based on a retention value of 10% after cooking. The exact amount will vary depending on cooking time and temperature, ingredient density, and the specific type of oil used.

Emerald Stir-Fry with Beef

Servings: 4 | **Prep**: 30m | **Cook**: 12m | **Ready In**: 42m

Ingredients

- 1/4 cup mirin or semisweet white wine, like Riesling
- 1/4 cup orange juice
- 1/4 cup low-sodium soy sauce
- 2 tablespoons rice vinegar
- 1/4 teaspoon red pepper flakes
- 1/4 cup water
- 2 tablespoons canola oil
- 8 ounces beef round tip steak, sliced 1/4-inch thick
- 3 cloves garlic, minced
- 2 cups fresh snow peas (6 ounces)
- 1 large bunch broccoli (1 1/4 pounds) trimmed and cut into small florets
- 1 bunch asparagus (1 pound), trimmed and sliced on diagonal into 2-inch pieces
- 2 cups (8 ounces) frozen shelled edamame
- 1 1/2 teaspoons cornstarch dissolved in 1/4 cup warm water
- 1 teaspoon sesame oil

Directions

1. Combine mirin or white wine, orange juice, soy sauce, rice vinegar, red pepper flakes and water in a small bowl.
2. In a large Wok or very large (14-inch) saute pan, heat 1 tablespoon of oil over medium-high heat. Add the beef and cook, stirring, until just browned, about 2 minutes. Transfer the beef to a plate. Heat the remaining tablespoon of oil over medium heat and cook garlic until fragrant, about 30 seconds. Add snow peas, broccoli, asparagus and edamame, raise heat to medium-high, and cook for 3 minutes until vegetables are slightly softened. Add the mirin-soy mixture and cook, stirring, until edamame are cooked and asparagus is crisp-tender, about 4 minutes. Add the beef and dissolved cornstarch and stir to incorporate. Cook until mixture

thickens slightly and beef is heated through, an additional 2 minutes. Drizzle with sesame oil and serve.

Erika's Ginger Beef

"Despite the prep work, this dish isn't too hard to make and it tastes amazing. Add more or less ginger and chiles to suit your taste. This is best served over rice."

Servings*: 6 | **Prep**: 20m | **Cook**: 25m | **Ready In**: 45m*

Ingredients

- 1/2 pounds beef top round steak, cut into thin slices
- 2 eggs, beaten
- 1 cup cornstarch
- 1/2 cup water
- 1 cup oil for frying, or as needed
- 1 tablespoon sesame oil
- 2 carrots, cut into matchstick-size pieces
- 1 green onion, chopped
- 5 tablespoons minced fresh ginger root
- 5 cloves garlic, chopped
- 1/4 cup soy sauce
- 2 tablespoons white vinegar
- 1/2 cup white sugar
- 1/4 teaspoon red pepper flakes
- 1 tablespoon sesame seeds, or as needed

Directions

1. Stir beef and eggs together in a bowl. Whisk cornstarch and water together; stir into beef mixture.
2. Pour oil 2 to 3 inches deep in a Wok; heat to 350 degrees F (175 degrees C). Cook beef strips in oil, working in batches, until brown and crisp, about 4 minutes; remove to drain and keep warm. Repeat with remaining beef.
3. Heat sesame oil in a large nonstick skillet over medium high heat; stir in carrots, green onion, ginger, and garlic. Cook and stir until

vegetables begin to soften, about 5 minutes. Stir soy sauce, white vinegar, sugar, and red pepper flakes into vegetable mixture; bring to a boil. Stir beef strips into vegetables; sprinkle with sesame seeds.Footnotes

Cook's Note:

- It is easier to slice beef thinly when it is partially frozen.
- Red bell peppers are nice in this dish, too. Add more carrot and green onion if you like.

Editor's Note:

- The nutrition data for this recipe includes the full amount of the coating ingredients. The actual amount of the coating consumed will vary. We have determined the nutritional value of oil for frying based on a retention value of 10% after cooking. The exact amount will vary depending on cooking time and temperature, ingredient density, and the specific type of oil used.

Essanaye's Sesame Beef Stir Fry

"Very good stir-fry. A little on the sweet side. Cook in a large Wok on medium-high heat. Marinating overnight is good, but not necessary."

***Servings**: 6 | **Prep**: 25m | **Cook**: 15m | **Ready In**: 40m*

Ingredients

- 1/2 cup soy sauce
- 1/2 cup white sugar
- 1/3 cup rice wine vinegar
- 1/3 cup minced garlic
- 1 tablespoon sesame seeds
- 1 pound round steak, thinly sliced
- 1/4 cup peanut oil
- 2 cups 1-inch sliced asparagus
- 1 cup sliced fresh mushrooms, or more to taste

- 1 sweet onion, chopped
- 1 red bell pepper, sliced
- 1 bunch green onions, chopped into 1-inch pieces
- 1 cup whole cashews
- 1 tablespoon sesame seeds
- 1 tablespoon cornstarch (optional)
- 1 tablespoon water (optional)
- 1 tablespoon sesame seeds

Directions

1. Whisk soy sauce, sugar, rice wine vinegar, garlic, and 1 tablespoon sesame seeds in a bowl; pour into a resealable plastic bag. Add beef, coat with marinade, squeeze out excess air, and seal bag. Marinate beef in the refrigerator overnight.
2. Heat peanut oil in a Wok or large skillet over medium-high heat; cook and stir beef and marinade until beef is well-browned, about 5 minutes. Stir in asparagus, mushrooms, onion, bell pepper, and green onions; cook and stir until vegetables begin to soften, 3 to 4 minutes. Add cashews and 1 tablespoon sesame seeds; continue cooking until vegetables are tender, 2 to 3 minutes more.
3. Mix cornstarch and water in a small bowl; stir into beef stir fry until sauce is thickened, about 3 minutes. Sprinkle with remaining 1 tablespoon sesame seeds.

Cook's Note

- If you don't plan on consuming the entire batch the first meal, I suggest you omit the cashews altogether, or add them to each plate when served. They will turn soggy and not be very appealing the second day.

Tip

- Aluminum foil helps keep food moist, ensures it cooks evenly, keeps leftovers fresh, and makes clean-up easy.

Five Spice Beef and Pepper Stir-Fry

Servings: 4 | *Prep*: 10m | *Cook*: 20m | *Ready In*: 30m

Ingredients

- Jasmine rice or short grain white rice, 1 to 1 1/2 cups, prepared to package directions
- 2 cups beef broth or stock, paper container or canned
- 2 tablespoons Wok or clear oil, 1 turn of the pan
- 1 1/2 pounds beef sirloin or beef tenderloin tips, trimmed, placed in the freezer for 5 to 10 minutes then thinly sliced
- 2 green bell peppers, seeded and diced into 1-inch pieces
- 1 medium onion, diced
- 1/2 cup dry cooking sherry
- 2 tablespoons dark soy sauce, eyeball the amount (recommended: Tamari)
- 2 tablespoons cornstarch
- 1 teaspoon Chinese five-spice powder, found on Asian foods aisle of market
- Cracked black pepper
- 3 scallions, thinly sliced on an angle, for garnish
- 1/2 cup smoked whole almonds, available on snack aisle, for garnish

Directions

1. Boil water for rice and prepare to package directions.
2. Place beef broth in a small pot over low heat to warm the liquid.
3. Heat a Wok shaped skillet or pan over high heat. Add oil (it will smoke) and meat bits. Stir-fry meat 3 minutes and remove from pan or move off to the side of the Wok. Return pan to heat and add peppers and onions. Stir-fry veggies 2 minutes. Add meat back to the pan. Add sherry and stir fry until liquid almost evaporates about 1 minute. Add soy sauce to the pan. Dissolve cornstarch with a ladle of warm beef broth. Add beef broth to the pan, then add cornstarch combined with broth, the five-spice powder and black pepper. Stir sauce until it thickens enough to coat the back of a spoon. Adjust seasonings. Add more soy or salt if necessary. Remove stir-fry from heat. Fill dinner bowls with beef stir-fry and top with a scoop of rice. Scoop rice with ice cream scoop to get a rounded ball. By placing rice on top of stir-fry, rice will stay firm and not soak up too much sauce. Garnish with chopped scallions and smoked almonds.

Five-Spice Orange Beef and Broccoli

"Orange rind and five-spice powder perfume the dish with sweet notes that are countered by a hit of red pepper heat. Decrease the pepper for kids or folks who prefer to walk on the mild side."

Servings: 4 | **Hands-on**: 20m | **Total time**: 20m

Ingredients

- 1 pound flank steak, trimmed
- 3/4 teaspoon five-spice powder
- 3/4 teaspoon black pepper
- 1/4 teaspoon kosher salt
- 2 tablespoons peanut oil, divided
- 2 cups small broccoli florets
- 1 1/2 cups vertically sliced onion
- 8 (1-inch) strips orange rind
- 4 garlic cloves, thinly sliced
- 1/2 cup unsalted beef stock
- 3 tablespoons orange juice
- 3 tablespoons hoisin sauce
- 1 tablespoon lower-sodium soy sauce
- 2 teaspoons rice vinegar
- 1 teaspoon cornstarch
- 3/4 teaspoon crushed red pepper
- 1 (8.8-ounce) package precooked white rice
- 1/2 cup sliced green onions
- 2 tablespoons toasted sesame seeds

Preparation

1. Sprinkle steak evenly with five-spice powder, black pepper, and salt. Heat a large Wok or skillet over high heat. Add 1 tablespoon oil to pan; swirl to coat. Add steak; cook 4 minutes on each side or until browned. Remove steak from pan; let stand 5 minutes. Cut steak across grain into thin slices.
2. Return pan to high heat. Add remaining 1 tablespoon oil; swirl. Add broccoli, onion, rind, and garlic; stir-fry 3 minutes or until lightly

browned. Combine stock and next 6 ingredients (through red pepper) in a bowl, stirring with a whisk. Add stock mixture to pan; cook 1 minute or until slightly thickened.
3. Spoon 1/2 cup rice onto each of 4 plates; top each serving with 3/4 cup broccoli mixture and 3 ounces beef. Sprinkle evenly with green onions and sesame seeds.

Korean Beef Stir-Fry

*Servings: 4 | **Prep**: 5m | **Cook**: 6m | **Ready In**: 11m*

Ingredients

- 2 tablespoons soy sauce
- 2 tablespoons rice wine or dry white wine
- 1 teaspoon Asian sesame oil
- 3 cloves garlic, finely chopped
- 1 pound flank steak, sliced thin against the grain
- 1 tablespoon vegetable oil
- 4 scallions, white and light green parts, finely chopped
- 1 tablespoon sesame seeds

Directions

1. Whisk soy sauce, rice wine, sesame oil and garlic in a large bowl. Add flank steak and toss to coat. Let stand 10 minutes.
2. In large nonstick skillet or Wok over high heat, warm oil until hot. Add flank steak and cook, stirring often, until it loses its pink color, 2 to 3 minutes. Stir in scallions and sesame seeds, stir-fry for 1 minute longer and serve.

Korean Sesame Beef with Lettuce Wraps

"Based on the classic Korean barbecue dish bulgogi, this recipe offers savory-sweet-garlicky beef wrapped in lettuce leaves with rice and kimchi."

Servings: 4

Ingredients

- 3/4 pound flank steak, trimmed
- 1/3 cup thinly sliced green onions, divided
- 1 tablespoon sugar
- 2 tablespoons low-sodium soy sauce
- 1 tablespoon minced garlic
- 1 teaspoon dark sesame oil
- 2 tablespoons canola oil, divided
- 1 tablespoon toasted sesame seeds
- 4 cups hot cooked short-grain rice
- 1 cup kimchi
- 16 red leaf lettuce leaves

Directions

1. Cut steak across grain into 1/4-inch slices; cut slices into 1/2-inch-wide strips. Cut strips into 3-inch-long pieces. Combine steak pieces, 1/4 cup onions, sugar, soy sauce, garlic, and sesame oil.
2. Heat a 14-inch Wok over high heat. Add 1 tablespoon canola oil to Wok, swirling to coat. Add half of steak mixture to Wok; stir-fry 2 minutes or until lightly browned. Spoon cooked steak mixture into a bowl. Repeat procedure with remaining 1 tablespoon canola oil and remaining steak mixture. Sprinkle with remaining onions and sesame seeds. Spoon 1/4 cup rice, about 2 tablespoons steak mixture, and 1 tablespoon kimchi onto each lettuce leaf; roll up. Serve immediately.

Low Calorie Soy Sauce Cauliflower And Ground Beef Stir Fry

"another go to recipe for lighter, cleaner eating. great way to get your veggies without compromising taste:)"

Servings: 3 | *Cook*: 20m

Ingredients

- 1/2 oz chopped carrots
- 9 oz chopped cauliflower
- 1/2 chopped peppers-i like green yellow and red
- 2 tbsp soy sauce
- 1/2 onion chopped
- 1/2 lb lean ground beef
- 1 seasoning to taste
- 1 tsp hot sauce
- 1 tbsp Brown sugar

Directions

1. in seperate pans, Brown beef, onion, peppers and boil carrots and cauliflower until tender but still keeping a little crunch
2. once beef is brown and veggies are cooked, add veggies to meat pan
3. combine rest of ingredients to beef pot and stir until warm and flavors are well married
4. season to taste and enjoy

Macaroni With Pan Fried Smoked Beef Sausage And Stirfry Veg

"I had just got back home from work, starving and only had about 10 minutes before my telemundo show started. So, i needed to fix something great and fast, and viola!"

Servings: 2 | **Time:** 10m

Ingredients

- 1/2 cup macaroni
- 3 medium smoked beef sausages
- 2 medium carrots, thinly cut
- 1 medium Green pepper
- 2 teaspoons of garlic
- 1 medium onion, chopped

- salt
- 2 teaspoons of mixed herbs
- 2 tablespoons of tomato sauce
- 1 tablespoon of sweet chilli
- 1 cup water
- cooking oil
- grated chedder cheese

Directions

1. Boil the macaroni with a pinch of salt and 1 teaspoon of cooking oil for about 7 minutes, or until cooked to your liking. When ready, set aside.
2. Cut the sausages into smaller pieces. Use 1 teaspoon or so of the cooking oil to pan fry them. Add sweet chilli and fry for about 3 minutes. When done, set aside
3. Use about 2 teaspoons or so of cooking oil to fry the vegetables. Add a pinch of salt, the garlic, the tomato sauce and the mixed herbs for taste. Fry for about 3-5 minutes, depending on how crunchy or soft you like your veggies.
4. Plate your food. Mix your macaroni with the sausages, then add the vegetables. Grate the cheese on top, as desired

Marinated Beef Vegetable Stir Fry & Rice

Servings: 1 | Time: 30m

Ingredients

- 1/4 onion, chopped
- 2 cup marinated beef
- 1 1/2 bunch cilantro
- 1/2 each bell pepper
- 1 1/4 head cauliflower
- 7 mushrooms
- 1 cup white rice
- 1/4 stick butter
- 1/3 lemon
- 3 dash soy sauce

Directions

1. Add butter to pan and cook sliced marinated beef (short ribs) and stir cook for 3 mins
2. Take beef out and add onions, bell peppers, cauliflower, mushrooms, and any other chopped vegetables to the pan. Stir for 3 mins.
3. Once the vegetables are crunchy but cooked, add the beef back in and stir, adding salt and pepper as needed.
4. Serve with a side of rice and a slice of fresh lemon.

Mike's, Everybody In The Pool! Beef Stir Fry

"When you find yourself with excess leftover vegetables that need to be used, dethaw some beef, chicken or seafood and throw them in your Wok and serve with some warm fluffy white rice and soy sauce. This dish is always a hit in our family!"

Servings: 4 | **Cook**: 30m

Ingredients

Steak And Steak Marinade And Veggies

- 1 lb Tenderloin Or Sirloin Beef [sliced against grain in thin strips]
- 1 tbsp Chinese Chili Sauce
- 1 tsp Worchestershire Sauce
- 1/4 tsp Chinese Five Spice
- 1 tsp Red Pepper Flakes
- 2 tbsp Sweet And Sour Sauce
- 2 tbsp Light Soy Sauce
- 1 tbsp Sirarcha Sauce
- 1 tbsp Minced Ginger [heaping]
- 2 tbsp Minced Garlic
- 1 tbsp Oyster Sauce [optional]
- 2 box 32 oz Beef Broth [you will not need all]
- 1 packages 1 oz Sun Bird Beef & Brocoli Seasoning [this adds a nice caramel color]
- 1/4 tsp Black Pepper

- 2 tbsp Cornstarch
- 3 tbsp Sesame Oil Or Wok Oil
- 1/2 White Onions [cut in strips]
- 1/2 Red Or Yellow Bell Peppers
- 1/2 cup Each Sliced Chives And Carrot Strips
- 1 can Baby Corn And Bamboo
- 1/2 Green Bell Peppers
- 1 can Water Chestnuts
- 2 Crowns Of Brocoli
- 2 cup Snap Peas

Rice

- 4 cup Water
- 2 cup White Rice

Directions

1. Place your dethawed Sirloin or Tenderloin in the freezer for a half an hour. This will make it much easier to slice in thin strips.
2. Fill a bowl with 2 cups beef broth and all marinade seasonings except for the Cornstarch or Sesame Oil and mix together.
3. Slice beef in thin strips across the grain and place in bowl to marinate in fridge for 1 hour. Stir occasionally.
4. Place all vegetables in a large pot and fill with 1" - 1 1/2" of water, 1 tsp garlic powder and a little salt. Bring to a boil and turn to lower heat. Steam vegetables for 8 to 10 minutes or until brocoli looks somewhat soft. Stir occasionally. Don't over steam. You'll want a slight snap to your veggies. Drain and set to the side.
5. Mix 2 tbs cornstarch with 4 tbs water and set to the side.
6. In a large Wok, pour in 3 tbs Sesame Oil and heat. Then add beef and all marinade.
7. Cook on high for 10 minutes stirring constantly bit keep lid on add much as possible.
8. If some or most of your marinade has dissipated, add 1 additional cup of your beef broth and quickly allow it to heat up.
9. You'll want to start your rice at the same time as your veggies and cook your beef last.
10. Once almost completely cooked, add half of your Cornstarch and mix it in to your marinade fast. Hopefully your marinade will be slightly thicker and will be able to adhere to your veggies when you're ready for them. You will know almost immediately. If not, add the other half of your Cornstarch mixture and stir quickly. If you find it's now too thick, add additional broth a little at a time

and stir quickly. You don't want to overcook your meat. You will also want enough marinade to slightly coat your veggies as well.
11. Now add all of your steamed veggies to the Wok and stir quickly. Cook for an additional 3 minutes stirring regularly.
12. Remove from heat and serve atop rice, with soy sauce and chopsticks. If cooking with Sesame Oil, there's really no need for Sesame Seeds to garnish your dish with.
13. Since I have two super picky eaters in the house, I was unable to put baby corn, water chestnuts, bamboo or snap peas in this specific dish but you certainly can!
14. For the rice, prepare it the way the manufacture recommends. Usually, you'll rinse your rice until the water isn't cloudy then bring 1 cup of rice to 2 cups of water to a boil and turn down. Keep lid on tight for 15 minutes and do not stir. Remove from heat and let it stand with the lid on for 5 more minutes undisturbed.

Mild Thai Beef with a Tangerine Sauce

"This is a very tasty dish that is perfect for people, like myself, who don't enjoy spicy Thai restaurant food. "

Servings: 4 | **Prep**: 20m | **Cook**: 25m | **Ready In**: 45m

Ingredients

- 1 (8 ounce) package dry Chinese noodles
- 1/4 cup hoisin sauce
- 1/4 cup dry sherry
- 1 teaspoon tangerine zest
- 1/4 teaspoon ground ginger
- 4 teaspoons vegetable oil
- 1 pound flank beef steak, cut diagonally into
- 2 inch strips 2 teaspoons vegetable oil
- 1/2 small butternut squash - peeled, seeded, and thinly sliced
- 1 cup sliced fresh mushrooms
- 1 large red onion, cut into
- 2 inch strips
- 3 cups cabbage, thinly sliced
- 1 tangerine, sectioned and seeded

Directions

1. Fill a large pot with lightly salted water and bring to a rolling boil over high heat. Once the water is boiling, stir in the noodles, and return to a boil. Cook the pasta uncovered, stirring occasionally, until the pasta has cooked through, but is still firm to the bite, about 5 minutes. Drain, rinse, and set aside.
2. Whisk together the hoisin sauce, sherry, tangerine zest, and ground ginger in a small bowl.
3. Heat 2 teaspoons vegetable oil in a large Wok or skillet over high heat. Add one half of the beef slices to the pan; cook, stirring constantly, until the meat is nicely browned, 2 to 3 minutes. Remove meat to a platter with a slotted spoon. Repeat with the remaining beef.
4. Heat the remaining 2 teaspoons of oil in the pan. Stir in the butternut squash, mushrooms, and onion. Cook, stirring constantly, until vegetables are crisp-tender and slightly brown on the edges, 5 to 7 minutes. Add the cabbage, and cook and stir until slightly wilted, about 2 additional minutes.
5. Reduce the heat to medium. Stir the cooked beef, tangerine sections, and hoisin mixture into the vegetables. Cook until heated through, 2 to 3 minutes. Serve over Chinese noodles.

Cook's Notes

- If desired, garnish with flaked, unsweetened coconut and additional tangerine sections.
- Beef broth can be substituted for the sherry.
- Stir in the watercress and bean sprouts, and continue to simmer until tender yet still crisp, about 10 minutes more. Mix in the tofu, cover, and simmer 5 minutes more.

My Hot Beef Stir Fry

"It is lovely and catches your breath"

Servings: 2 | *Time*: 5m

Ingredients

- 400 grams sirloin beef or frying steak cut into 5mm 1/4 inch slices
- 1 tbsp Corn Flour / Corn Startch
- 2 tbsp olive oil or veg oil
- 1 piece 1 inch Root Ginger, peeled and grated
- 300 grams thin sliced veg. ie carrot,Onion,or Shallots green beans, red cabbage ,loose corn, pak choy Courgette some or all.
- 1 pinch 1/4 tsp Chilli powder
- 1 dash of light soy sauce to taste
- 1 For The Marinade
- 1 tbsp Dark Soy sauce
- 1 tbsp light soy sauce
- 1 tbsp Rice Wine
- 2 pinch Black Pepper

Directions

1. Mix all the Marinade ingredients together in a large bowl, then add the beef strips and stir to coat
2. Cover the bowl with cling film and set aside for 20 minutes. Then remove from marinade and dust the pieces of beef in the corn flour
3. Heat a Wok on high heat when it starts to smoke add half the oil. Add the ginger and chilli flakes and fry for a secound or two.
4. Then add your mix of veg and stir in, add a little drop of water to help with the steaming the veg. Cook for 1-2 minutes and transfer to a plate.
5. Put the Wok back over the heat, and add the remaining oil.
6. Add the beef let settle for a few secounds then stir the beef in the Wok for 1-2 minutes.
7. Tip back in the veg and stir in with the beef and mix together for a further 1-2 minutes. Season further, to taste with light soy sauce and black pepper.
8. Serve immediatley .Enjoy with some fried Rice or Noodles .

Orange Beef and Broccoli Stir-fry

Servings: 4 | Prep: 5m | Cook: 10m | Ready In: 15m

Ingredients

- 1/4 cup low-sodium beef broth or water
- 1 tablespoon soy sauce
- 1 tablespoon lemon juice
- 2 teaspoons cornstarch
- 1 tablespoon vegetable oil
- 1 pound top round London broil, cut into strips
- 1 (10 oz.) package frozen broccoli spears, thawed and patted dry
- 1 tablespoon grated orange zest
- 1/4 cup fresh orange juice
- Salt and pepper

Directions

1. Whisk together broth, soy sauce, lemon juice and cornstarch in a bowl; set aside.
2. Warm oil in a Wok or large skillet over medium-high heat until hot. Add beef, turn heat to high and cook, stirring constantly, until no longer pink, 2 to 3 minutes.
3. Add broccoli and cook, stirring, until warmed through, about 2 minutes.
4. Stir in reserved sauce, orange zest and juice. Cook, stirring constantly, until sauce is thickened, about 2 minutes. Season with salt and pepper.

Orange Peel Beef

"I came up with this by attempting to duplicate a dish at a local Chinese restaurant. An Asian friend told me that Asian chefs often use baking soda as a meat tenderizer. My family thinks it tastes even better than the original."

Servings: 6 | **Prep**: 25m | **Cook**: 6m | **Ready In**: 1h30m

Ingredients

- 1 1/2 pounds beef top sirloin, thinly sliced
- 1 tablespoon low-sodium soy sauce
- 1 tablespoon cornstarch
- 1 teaspoon dark sesame oil

- 1/2 teaspoon baking soda
- 1 tablespoon low-sodium soy sauce
- 2 tablespoons frozen orange juice concentrate, thawed
- 1 tablespoon rice vinegar
- 1 teaspoon dark sesame oil
- 1 tablespoon brown sugar
- 1 teaspoon cornstarch
- 1 tablespoon peanut oil
- 3 cloves garlic, minced
- 1 tablespoon minced fresh ginger root
- 1 tablespoon finely shredded orange zest
- 1/4 teaspoon red pepper flakes

Directions

1. Combine the beef, 1 tablespoon of soy sauce, 1 tablespoon cornstarch, 1 teaspoon sesame oil, and baking soda in a bowl and mix thoroughly. Cover and refrigerate 1 to 3 hours.
2. Heat peanut oil in a Wok or large, nonstick skillet over high heat. Stir in garlic, ginger, orange zest, and red pepper flakes, and cook until the garlic begins to brown, 20 to 30 seconds. Add the beef; cook and stir until the beef begins to brown and crisp, about 5 minutes. Whisk together 1 tablespoon soy sauce, orange juice concentrate, rice vinegar, 1 teaspoon sesame oil, brown sugar, and 1 teaspoon cornstarch in a small bowl. Stir into the beef, and cook until the sauce has thickened and turned clear, about 30 seconds.

Rice Noodles with Beef

*Servings: 6 | **Prep**: 20m | **Cook**: 10m | **Ready In**: 30m*

Ingredients

- 1 (8 oz.) package pad Thai rice-stick noodles
- 1 (1 lb.) bag frozen Asian stir-fry vegetables
- 2 cloves garlic, minced
- 1-inch piece fresh ginger, peeled and grated
- 1 1/2 tablespoons soy sauce
- 1 tablespoon red curry paste

- 1 tablespoon rice wine vinegar
- 2 tablespoons lime juice
- 5 tablespoons peanut oil
- 1 pound beef sirloin or flank steak, sliced 1/4-inch thick
- 1 red bell pepper, sliced into 1/4-inch strips
- 6 scallions, sliced (1 cup)
- 1/2 pound bean sprouts (2 cups), optional
- 1/2 cup roasted, unsalted peanuts, chopped (3 oz.), optional

Directions

1. Soak rice noodles in cold water for 15 minutes; drain. Add to a pot of boiling water and cook for 5 minutes. Drain again and set aside.
2. Rinse Asian vegetables in a colander briefly with cold water; let drain thoroughly. In a small bowl, stir together garlic, ginger, soy sauce, curry paste, vinegar, lime juice and 2 Tbsp. peanut oil; set aside.
3. In a large, nonstick skillet, heat 1 Tbsp. peanut oil over medium-high heat. Add half of beef and stir-fry for 4 minutes. Transfer to a plate. Repeat process with 1 Tbsp. oil and remaining beef. Keep beef warm. Wipe out pan; add remaining 1 Tbsp. oil and red pepper, then stir-fry for 2 minutes. Add scallions and reserved Asian vegetables and cook for 3 minutes.
4. Add reserved sauce to skillet; cook for 1 minute. Add beef and cooked noodles and toss thoroughly to combine with sauce.
5. Serve noodles in bowls with bean sprouts and peanuts, if desired.

Shaking Beef

"In Vietnam, this classic--named for how the meat is tossed in the pan--is usually made with tough, overcooked beef cuts. For his version, which has been on the Slanted Door's menu since 1995, Charles uses grass-fed filet mignon. On an electric stove, use a flat-bottomed Wok or pan so the cooking surface gets as hot as possible. On gas, use a Wok ring to nestle the Wok down into the flames."

Servings: 4-6 | **Total time**: 2h45m

Ingredients

- 1 1/2 pounds filet mignon, trimmed of excess fat and cut into 1-in. cubes
- 1 tablespoon plus 1 tsp. sugar, divided
- 1 teaspoon kosher salt
- 1 teaspoon pepper
- 7 tablespoons canola oil, divided
- 2 tablespoons rice vinegar
- 2 tablespoons mirin
- 1 tablespoon soy sauce
- 2 teaspoons dark soy sauce*
- 1/2 teaspoon Vietnamese or Thai fish sauce
- 1 cup thinly sliced red onion
- 3 green onions, ends trimmed, onions cut into 1-in. lengths
- 1 tablespoon finely chopped garlic
- 1 tablespoon unsalted butter
- 1 bunch watercress, tough stems removed
- Spicy Lime Dipping Sauce

Directions

1. Mix beef with 1 tsp. sugar, the salt, pepper, and 1 tbsp. oil in a bowl. Let marinate at room temperature 2 hours.
2. Whisk together remaining 1 tbsp. sugar, the vinegar, mirin, soy sauces, and fish sauce until sugar has dissolved.
3. Divide meat into 2 equal portions. Heat a large Wok or a large (not nonstick) frying pan over high heat until very hot but not smoking. The metal will have a matte look and a drop of water flicked onto its surface should evaporate on contact.
4. Add 3 tbsp. oil to Wok and heat until shimmering but not smoking. Add half the beef in a single layer and sear until a brown crust forms underneath, about 30 seconds. Flip cubes and cook 30 seconds on second side.
5. Add half each of red and green onions and cook, stirring, about 30 seconds. Add half the soy sauce mixture and shake Wok to coat beef. Add half each of garlic and butter and shake Wok to distribute evenly. Transfer to a bowl and keep warm.
6. Wipe Wok clean and return to high heat. Repeat steps 4 and 5 with remaining 3 tbsp. oil, beef, red and green onions, sauce mixture, garlic, and butter.
7. Arrange watercress on a platter; top with beef and vegetables. Serve with sauce.

1. *Dark soy sauce is thicker, darker, and less salty than regular soy; find it at Asian markets and well-stocked grocery stores.

Sichuan Water Boiled Beef

Servings: 4 | **Prep**: 35m | **Inactive**: 30m | **Cook**: 10m | **Ready In**: 1h15m

Ingredients

For the marinade and beef:

- 2 teaspoons rice wine
- 1 tablespoon light soy sauce
- 3 tablespoons cornstarch
- 1 pound beef loin strip steak (or fish fillets, or chicken breasts, or pork loin)
- For the garnish:
- 5 tablespoons corn oil, divided
- 2 tablespoons Sichuan peppercorns (available in Chinese markets)
- 1/2 cup dry small red chili
- For the vegetables:
- 1/4 pound Chinese celery (or celery)
- 1/4 pound Chinese leeks (or leeks or scallions)
- 1/4 pound stem lettuce, romaine lettuce heart (or napa cabbage)
- 2 tablespoons corn oil
- 1 tablespoon chopped scallion

Ingredients to cook beef:

- 1/4 cup corn oil
- 1 tablespoon fresh ginger, minced
- 2 tablespoons chopped scallion
- 1/4 cup hot chili sauce, Chinese (or Chinese hot bean paste)
- 3 tablespoons rice wine
- 3 tablespoons light soy sauce
- 2 cups chicken or beef stock

Directions

To marinate beef:

1. Mix rice wine and soy sauce in a large bowl and add cornstarch gradually while whisking constantly. Slice beef into thin pieces and place into bowl with marinade stirring to coat. Let marinate for at least 30 minutes.
2. Prepare garnish by heating 1 tablespoon of the oil in a saute pan, reserving the other 4 tablespoons. Add the Sichuan peppercorn and dry chili and cook until the chili turns dark red. (Do not allow it to turn black.) Remove the cooked peppercorn and chili to a cutting board and use the side a large chef's knife blade to smash it. Then chop it into pieces and transfer to a small dish. Keep the saute pan handy for the final touches.
3. Prepare vegetables by washing and cutting celery, leeks, and lettuce into 3-inch lengths. Heat the 2 tablespoons of corn oil in a Wok, add scallions and stir once. Add the celery, leeks, and lettuce and stir-fry for 20 seconds over high heat. Remove and place in a large shallow serving bowl.
4. To cook beef, heat the 1/4 cup corn oil in the Wok and add ginger, scallion, and chili sauce. Cook until the oil turns red from the chili. Add wine, soy sauce and stock. When the mixture begins to boil, add marinated beef and gently stir to cook. As soon as beef is completely cooked, remove from Wok and place beef over vegetables in serving bowl and pour sauce from Wok over it.
5. Heat the remaining 1/4 cup of oil for the garnish in the saute pan, and when it begins to smoke slightly, pour the oil over the Sichuan peppercorns and chili in the small dish.
6. Serve everything immediately.

Speedy Beef Stir-Fry

Servings: 4 | *Time*: 20m

Ingredients

- 400 grams Beef, thinly sliced
- 1 large red capsicum, sliced
- 1 large brown onion, thin wedges
- 3 cup Shredded cabbage

- 200 grams Udon noodle
- 1/2 tsp Bi-carb soda
- 1 Sprinkle of chilli flakes
- 1 Sea salt &cracked black pepper to taste
- 1 (MARINADE/SAUCE)
- 1 cup Soy sauce
- 2 tsp Minced garlic
- 3 tsp Minced ginger
- 1 tbsp Honey
- 1 tbsp Minced lemon grass
- 1 tbsp Sesame oil

Directions

1. Sprinkle bi-carb over beef and mix well (to tenderise). Set aside for 10 minutes.
2. In another bowl get your marinade ready. Rinse beef and throw into marinade.
3. Prepare veggies and set aside (onions separate to other veggies)Prepare veggies and set aside (onions separate to other veggies).
4. When you are ready heat Wok, add a little oil and fry beef in batches until browned and set aside.
5. Clean Wok and fry onions. Set aside with beef.
6. Stir-fry remaining veggies until starting to soften.
7. Add remaining sauce, noodles, beef and onion and heat through. Serve with a sprinkle of chilli flakes, cracked salt and black pepper. Yum!

Spicy Beef and Bell Pepper Stir-Fry

"Fans of quick and easy will love this asian-inspired stir-fry dish. Beef, bell pepper and rice get a dip in a spicy sauce and a sprinkle of toasted sesame seeds"

***Servings**: 4 | **Total time**: 20m*

Ingredients

- 1 tablespoon canola oil
- 12 ounces flank steak, cut diagonally across the grain into thin slices
- 1 red bell pepper, cut into thin strips
- 1 yellow bell pepper, cut into thin strips
- 3 tablespoons lower-sodium soy sauce
- 1 1/2 tablespoons rice wine vinegar
- 1 tablespoon minced peeled fresh ginger
- 2 teaspoons chili garlic sauce (such as Lee Kum Kee)
- 4 green onions, cut into 2-inch pieces
- 2 teaspoons toasted sesame seeds

Directions

1. Heat a large nonstick skillet over medium-high heat. Add oil to pan; swirl to coat. Add steak to pan; cook 2 minutes, searing on one side. Add bell peppers; cook 2 minutes or until beef loses its pink color, stirring constantly. Remove beef mixture from pan.
2. Add soy sauce, vinegar, ginger, and chili garlic sauce to pan; bring to a boil. Cook 1 minute or until slightly thickened. Add beef mixture and green onions to pan; toss well to coat. Sprinkle with sesame seeds.

Spicy Beef and Kimchi Stew

" This recipe is high in sodium (due to the soy sauce and the kimchi), so if high blood pressure is a concern for you, omit the soy sauce, which will bring the sodium down about 200 milligrams."

Servings: 4 | **Prep**: 15m | **Cook**: 1h12m | **Ready In**: 1h27mm

Ingredients

- 1 1/2 pounds boneless chuck roast or beef tenderloin, cut into 1 1/2-inch chunks
- 2 large garlic cloves, minced (about 1 tablespoon)
- 1 tablespoon peeled minced fresh ginger
- 3/4 cup water

- 2 tablespoons low-sodium soy sauce
- 2 tablespoons sugar or mirin
- 2 cups chopped jarred kimchi
- 1 tablespoon sesame oil
- 1 tablespoon sesame seeds, toasted, for garnish
- 2 tablespoons chopped scallions for garnish
- 3 cups cooked rice

Directions

1. Turn the heat to high under a large skillet that can later be covered. Add the beef cubes a few at a time and brown well, adjusting the heat so the meat browns but does not burn and turning beef to brown on all sides; this will take about 10 minutes. Remove the meat to a plate when it is done, and turn the heat to low.
2. Add garlic and ginger to the pan and cook, stirring occasionally, until the garlic colors, about 2 minutes. Add the water, then the soy sauce and either sugar or mirin. Add the meat and bring to a boil; cover, reduce heat, and simmer.
3. Adjust the heat so the mixture simmers steadily but not violently and cook, stirring occasionally, until the meat is tender, 50 minutes, depending on the cut you used (tenderloin cooks much faster than chuck). Add the kimchi, and cook 10 minutes or until heated through. (You can prepare the dish several hours in advance up to this point. Cover and set aside until you're ready to eat, then reheat; or cover and refrigerate overnight before reheating.)
4. Uncover, then taste and adjust seasoning. Stir in sesame oil, sprinkle with sesame seeds and scallions, and serve immediately over cooked rice.

Spicy Beef Filet in Oyster Sauce

"My good friend Lin gave me a recipe for beef in oyster sauce, I misread the amount of black pepper called for in her recipe, and the result was fantastic! I especially like the recipe because no soy sauce is used. My husband likes to eat them with the leftover sliced uncooked onion to bring out the sweetness of the oyster sauce."

Servings: 4 | **Prep**: 15m | **Cook**: 10m | **Ready In**: 35m

Ingredients

- 1 teaspoon vegetable oil
- 1 teaspoon oyster sauce
- 1/2 teaspoon cornstarch
- 3/4 pound beef tenderloin, cut into 1/4 inch strips
- 1 teaspoon water
- 1 teaspoon cornstarch
- 2 tablespoons oyster sauce
- 1 teaspoon sugar
- 1 teaspoon black pepper
- 1 tablespoon vegetable oil
- 1/2 onion, thinly sliced

Directions

1. Stir together 1 teaspoon vegetable oil, 1 teaspoon oyster sauce, and 1/2 teaspoon cornstarch in a bowl. Add beef and toss to coat. Marinate in the refrigerator 30 to 45 minutes. Remove from the refrigerator 10 minutes before cooking.
2. Stir together water, 1 teaspoon cornstarch, 2 tablespoons oyster sauce, and pepper in a small bowl; set aside. Heat 1 tablespoon vegetable oil in a large skillet over high heat. Stir in onion, and cook until it beings to brown on the edges, about 1 minute. Add the beef, and continue cooking and stirring until the beef is just slightly pink, about 5 minutes. Pour in the sauce; cook and stir until the sauce has thickened and turned translucent, about 1 minute more.

Spicy Orange Beef

Servings: 4 | *Prep*: 10m | *Cook*: 20m | *Ready In*: 30m

Ingredients

- 1/3 cup cornstarch
- 1/2 teaspoon kosher salt
- 1 1/4 pounds beef steak, thinly sliced across the grain and cut into 2-by-1/3-inch strips

- 6 tablespoons vegetable oil
- 1 tablespoon sesame oil
- 1 clove garlic, minced
- 1 1/2 teaspoons minced fresh ginger, optional
- 7 small dried red chiles or
- 1/2 teaspoon chili powder
- 1/2 cup orange juice
- 2 tablespoons orange marmalade
- 1 tablespoon soy sauce
- 1 tablespoon rice wine vinegar
- 4 cups cooked white rice, for serving

Directions

1. In a large bowl, whisk together cornstarch and salt. Add beef; toss to coat. Shake off any excess.
2. In a large skillet, heat 3 Tbsp. oil over medium-high heat. Add half of beef and fry until browned on all sides, about 5 minutes. Using a slotted spoon, transfer beef to a colander. Wipe any browned bits from skillet, and repeat using remaining 3 Tbsp. vegetable oil and second batch of beef. Wipe out skillet.
3. Add sesame oil, garlic and ginger (if using) to skillet and cook for 1 minute over medium heat. Stir in chiles, orange juice, marmalade, soy sauce and vinegar and cook over medium-high heat until slightly syrupy, about 4 minutes. Reduce heat to medium and stir in beef to coat with orange sauce. Heat through, 2 minutes.
4. Serve beef and sauce over rice.

Spicy Tangerine Beef

Servings: 4-6 | *Prep*: 20m | *Inactive*: 20m | *Cook*: 5m | *Ready In*: 42m

Ingredients

- 3 tablespoons soy sauce
- 1 tablespoon cornstarch
- 1 pound flank steak or tri-tip, cut in thin strips on the bias
- 2 tablespoons dry sherry
- 2 tablespoons hoisin sauce

- 2 tablespoons honey
- 1 tablespoon chili sauce
- 2 tablespoons soy sauce
- 1/4 cup freshly squeezed tangerine juice
- 3 tablespoons canola oil
- 2 tablespoons minced fresh ginger
- 3 scallions, chopped
- 1/4 tangerine, zested
- 2 tablespoons toasted sesame seeds

Directions

1. In a resealable plastic bag combine the soy sauce and cornstarch and mix well. Add beef, cover, and let marinate for 20 minutes in the refrigerator.
2. Whisk together the sherry, hoisin, honey, chili sauce, soy sauce, and tangerine juice until completely combined.
3. In large pan or Wok, heat oil on high. Add the ginger and beef and cook for 2 to 3 minutes. Then add sauce mixture and cook for another 2 minutes on medium heat until sauce thickens. Serve on warm platter, garnish with scallions, tangerine zest and sesame seeds.

Stir Fry Bulgogi Beef PorkLamb

"easy korean fish in 15 minutes"

Servings: 6 | **Cook**: 15m

Ingredients

- 6 fried egg
- 6 bowl of cooked rice
- 6 small beancurd puff option
- 4 medium onion
- 4 red chili pepeer
- 1 cup bulgogi sauce ready to used store bought
- DIY BULGOGI SAUCE
- 1 tbsp each honey , soy sauce and rice wine

- 1 small grated pear and 1tbsp ginger and 1 clove or garlic
- THINLY SLICED MEAT OPTION
- 400 grams thinly sliced beef /pork/lamb

Directions

1. Fried eggs set aside
2. Cooked rice set aside
3. Marinate meat
4. For diy bulgogi sauce just mix all ingredient ,or used stored bought ready to use bulgogi sauce
5. marinate thinly slice beef /pork/lamb for minimum 10 minutes with bulgogi sauce
6. Stir fry
7. in pan with 2 tbsp of oil stir fry onion together with marinated sliced meat for 3 minute
8. add beancurd puff and red chili pepper and stir fry for another 2 minute then off heat and serve
9. Serve stir fry bulgogi pork as it is or
10. Serving option stir fry bulgogi pork and fried egg with white rice

Stir-Fried Beef with Broccoli and Bell Peppers

"Make an easy Asian-inspired meal for dinner tonight."

Servings: 6

Ingredients

- 1 pound flank steak, trimmed
- 2 tablespoons low-sodium soy sauce
- 1 teaspoon minced garlic
- 1/2 teaspoon freshly ground black pepper
- 3 1/2 tablespoons water, divided
- 2 tablespoons oyster sauce
- 1/4 teaspoon crushed red pepper
- 3/4 pound broccoli
- 2 tablespoons canola oil, divided
- 1 large red bell pepper, halved, seeded, and cut into 1-inch pieces (about 1 1/2 cups)
- 4 cups hot cooked long-grain rice

Directions

1. Cut steak in half lengthwise. Cut each half across the grain into 1/8-inch-thick slices. Combine beef, soy sauce, garlic, and black pepper; toss well. Cover and refrigerate 30 minutes.
2. Combine 1 1/2 tablespoons water, oyster sauce, and crushed red pepper in a small bowl; set aside.
3. Cut broccoli into florets. Peel broccoli stems; cut stems diagonally into 1/4-inch-thick slices.
4. Heat 1 tablespoon canola oil in a large nonstick skillet over medium-high heat. Add beef mixture to skillet; cook 3 minutes or until beef is browned, stirring constantly. Remove from heat. Transfer beef mixture to a bowl.
5. Heat the remaining 1 tablespoon canola oil in pan over medium-high heat. Add broccoli; cook 2 minutes, stirring constantly. Add the remaining 2 tablespoons water; cook 1 minute, stirring constantly. Add bell pepper; cook 30 seconds, stirring constantly. Return beef mixture to pan. Stir in the oyster sauce mixture; cook until thoroughly heated. Serve over rice.

Stir-Fried Beef with Clementines

*Servings: 4 | **Prep**: 15m | **Cook**: 6m*

Ingredients

- 12 ounces flank steak, thinly sliced against the grain
- 3 tablespoons soy sauce
- 3 tablespoons rice wine
- 1 tablespoon cornstarch
- 1 tablespoon sriracha or other hot sauce
- 1/4 cup orange juice
- 2 tablespoons vegetable oil
- 3 scallions, white and light green parts, chopped
- 1 tablespoon finely chopped fresh ginger
- 2 cloves garlic, minced
- 6 ounces snow peas, trimmed
- 4 clementines, peeled and sectioned
- Cooked brown rice, optional

Directions

1. Combine steak, 1 Tbsp. soy sauce, 1 Tbsp. rice wine and 2 tsp. cornstarch in a bowl. In a separate bowl, whisk together sriracha and orange juice with remaining 2 Tbsp. soy sauce, 2 Tbsp. rice wine and 1 tsp. cornstarch.
2. Warm 1 Tbsp. vegetable oil in a large skillet over medium-high heat. Add steak and stir-fry until it loses most of its pink color, 1 to 2 minutes. Transfer to a bowl. Add remaining oil to pan, then add scallions, ginger and garlic and cook, stirring, for 30 seconds. Add snow peas and clementines and cook, stirring, for 1 to 2 minutes.
3. Return steak to skillet along with orange juice mixture. Stir-fry until sauce thickens, 30 seconds to 1 minute. Serve immediately, with brown rice, if desired.

Stir-Fried Rice Noodles with Beef and Spinach

"Your family will love this Stir-Fried Rice Noodle with Beef and Spinach recipe. One online reviwer claims, "Super easy to make in a snap!"

Servings: 4 | ***Total time***: 24m

Ingredients

- 6 ounces uncooked wide rice sticks (rice-flour noodles)
- 1 tablespoon canola oil
- 1 cup thinly sliced green onions
- 2/3 pound top sirloin steak, cut into thin strips
- 2 cups sliced shiitake mushroom caps
- 2 garlic cloves, finely minced
- 1 (6-ounce) bag washed baby spinach
- 2 tablespoons rice vinegar
- 1 tablespoon fresh lime juice
- 3 tablespoons lower-sodium soy sauce
- 2 teaspoons grated peeled fresh ginger
- 2 teaspoons Sriracha (hot chile sauce)
- 1 tablespoon dark sesame oil
- 1/4 teaspoon salt
- 2 teaspoons sesame seeds, toasted

Directions

1. Cook noodles according to package directions, omitting salt and fat. Drain and rinse under cold water; drain.
2. Heat a large skillet or Wok over high heat. Add canola oil to pan; swirl to coat. Add onions and steak; stir-fry 1 minute. Add mushrooms and garlic; stir-fry 1 minute. Add spinach; stir-fry 1 minute or until greens wilt.
3. Combine rice vinegar and the next 4 ingredients (through Sriracha) in a small bowl, stirring with a whisk. Add vinegar mixture to steak mixture; cook 30 seconds, stirring constantly. Stir in noodles, sesame oil, and salt; cook for 1 minute or until noodles are thoroughly heated, tossing to combine. Sprinkle with sesame seeds.

Stir-Fry Beef with Sugar Snap Peas

"I prefer this over any takeout! So quick and flavorful!"

Servings: 6 | **Cook**: 30m

Ingredients

- 6 tbsp low sodium soy sauce
- 4 tbsp rice wine (saki)
- 2 tbsp brown sugar
- 1 tsp corn starch
- 2 tbsp vegetable oil
- 1 tbsp fresh grated ginger root
- 1 tbsp fresh grated garlic
- 1 lb beef steak
- 1 lb fresh sugar snap peas

Directions

1. In a small bowl, combine first 4 ingredients. Set aside.
2. Thinly slice steak. Partially freezing the steak will make it easier to slice thinly. I usually use a chuck flatiron steak, but have also used a round steak or sirloin steak. Use whatever you prefer.

3. Clean and stem the sugar snap peas. You can use snow peas if you prefer.
4. Heat oil in Wok or skillet over medium high heat. Stir-fry ginger and garlic for 30 seconds. Add the steak and stir-fry 2-3 minutes or until evenly browned. Add the sugar snap peas and stir-fry for 2 minutes.
5. Add the soy sauce mixture and bring to boil stirring constantly. Lower heat and simmer until sauce is slightly thickened.
6. Serve immediately over brown or white rice

Super-Simple, Super-Spicy Mongolian Beef

"This is a great-tasting recipe that is easy to prepare ahead and takes minutes to actually cook it! Serve with rice and veggie side for a nice family dinner!"

Servings: 4 | **Prep**: 15m | **Cook**: 6m | **Ready In**: 1h 21m

Ingredients

- 1/4 cup soy sauce
- 1 tablespoon hoisin sauce
- 1 tablespoon sesame oil
- 2 teaspoons white sugar
- 1 tablespoon minced garlic
- 1 tablespoon red pepper flakes (optional)
- 1 pound beef flank steak, thinly sliced
- 1 tablespoon peanut oil
- 2 large green onions, thinly sliced

Directions

1. Whisk together soy sauce, hoisin sauce, sesame oil, sugar, garlic, and red pepper flakes in a bowl. Toss beef with marinade, cover, and refrigerate 1 hour to overnight.
2. Heat peanut oil in a Wok or large, nonstick skillet over high heat. Add the green onions, and cook for 5 to 10 seconds before stirring in the beef. Cook and stir until the beef is no longer pink and is beginning to brown, about 5 minutes.

Sweet and sour beef noodles

Servings: 2 | Cook: 15 m

Ingredients

- 1 tablespoon vegetable oil
- 180g stir-fry beef slices
- 290g stir-fry vegetables
- 300ml sweet and sour sauce
- 300g pack straight-to-Wok medium noodles (we like Amoy)
- Create a shoppi

Directions

1. Heat 1 tablespoon vegetable oil in a Wok or large frying pan over a high heat. When hot, add 180g stir-fry beef slices and stir-fry for 2-3 minutes, until browned. Remove the beef and set aside.
2. Add 290g stir-fry vegetables and stir-fry for 2-3 minutes, then stir in 300ml sweet and sour sauce. Add a 300g pack straight-to-Wok medium noodles and the seared beef and toss for a few minutes to heat through. Season to taste with salt and freshly ground black pepper.
3. Divide between bowls and serve with soy sauce to drizzle over, if you like.

Three-Pepper Beef

"This beef stir-fry gets its color and crunch from a variety of bell peppers. Serve over rice."

Servings: 4

Ingredients

Sauce:

- 2 1/2 teaspoons cornstarch, divided
- 1 teaspoon sugar, divided
- 1/2 teaspoon salt
- 1 pound flank steak, trimmed and thinly sliced across the grain
- 1/4 cup low-salt beef broth
- 3 tablespoons low-sodium soy sauce
- 1 teaspoon freshly ground black pepper
- 1 teaspoon vegetable oil
- 1/4 cup thinly sliced green onions
- 1 teaspoon minced peeled fresh ginger
- 1 garlic clove, minced
- 1 cup sugar snap peas, trimmed
- 1 1/4 cups cubed red bell pepper
- 1 1/4 cups cubed yellow bell pepper
- 1 1/4 cups cubed green bell pepper

Directions

1. Combine 1/2 teaspoon cornstarch, 1/2 teaspoon sugar, salt, and flank steak in a medium bowl; toss to coat. Set aside.
2. Combine 2 teaspoons cornstarch, 1/2 teaspoon sugar, broth, soy sauce, and black pepper, stirring with a whisk until sugar dissolves; set aside.
3. Heat oil in a Wok or large nonstick skillet over medium-high heat. Add the green onions, ginger, and garlic; stir-fry 10 seconds. Add beef mixture; stir-fry 3 minutes or until done. Remove the beef mixture from pan; cover and keep warm. Add peas and bell peppers to pan; stir-fry 4 minutes or until crisp-tender. Add beef and broth mixture to pan; cook 2 minutes or until thickened, stirring constantly.

Chapter 4: Chicken Recipes

***

Chicken Noodles

***

Chicken and Rice Noodle Stir Fry

"I've been experimenting with my new Wok and think this meal came out pretty good and is relatively easy. Sorry for not providing exact measurements, I just eyeballed everything, adding a dash of this and a little of that."

Servings: 4 | **Prep**: 15m | **Cook**: 20m | **Ready In**: 35m

Ingredients

- 1 large skinless, boneless chicken breast, cut in bite-sized pieces
- 1 pinch garlic powder, or to taste
- 1 pinch onion powder, or to taste freshly ground black pepper to taste
- 1 (8 ounce) package dried rice noodles
- 4 cups hot water, or as needed
- 3 tablespoons vegetable oil, divided
- 4 cloves garlic, minced
- 1 onion, chopped
- 1 green bell pepper, chopped
- 1/2 cup white cooking wine, or to taste
- 1/4 cup soy sauce, or to taste
- 2 tablespoons teriyaki sauce, or to taste
- 1 (6 ounce) can sweet baby corn, drained
- 3 green onions, chopped

Directions

1. Sprinkle chicken with garlic powder, onion powder, and black pepper.
2. Soak rice noodles in a bowl with hot water until softened, about 10 minutes; drain and cut noodles in half with scissors.

3. Heat 1 1/2 tablespoons vegetable oil in a Wok or large skillet over medium-high heat; cook and stir garlic in the hot oil until fragrant, about 1 minute. Add onion and green bell pepper; cook, stirring constantly, until onion and pepper are softened, about 5 minutes. Add remaining 1 1/2 tablespoons vegetable oil; cook and stir chicken into onion mixture until chicken is no longer pink in the center, 5 to 7 minutes.
4. Stir wine, soy sauce, and teriyaki sauce into chicken mixture; simmer until liquid is slightly reduced, about 3 minutes. Add baby corn and green onions; toss to evenly coat with sauce. Mix rice noodles into stir fry mixture; toss to coat. Cook and stir until heated through, about 2 more minutes.

Chicken Stirfry with Chow Mein Noodles

"Stirfry comes together quickly and easily and you can prep it all ahead of time so it's great for a healthy weeknight meal"

Servings: 4 | **Time**: 45m

Ingredients

- 1 red onion - sliced
- 8 oz button or cremini mushrooms - thinly sliced
- 1 red pepper - sliced
- 1 yellow pepper - thinly sliced
- 2 celery stalks - thinly sliced on an angle
- 1 head broccoli - chopped into med-large florets
- 200 grams snow peas or snap peas - strings removed
- 5 clove garlic - chopped or crushed
- 1 thumb sized piece of ginger - grated
- 1 packages blue dragon stirfry sauce (or your favorite)
- 1 tbsp hoisin sauce
- 2 tbsp soy sauce + more to taste (as needed)
- 1 tsp sesame oil
- 1 packages fresh chow mein noodles

Directions

1. Get all the veggies washed and prepped. Group the veggies in bowls in the order you will add them to your skillet/Wok (see photo). Cube chicken and place in a ziplock bag.
2. Add hoisin sauce, soy sauce and sesame oil and about a half tsp of the garlic and ginger to the chicken and let it marinate for at least half an hour
3. Bring a medium pot of water to a boil and add chow mein noodles. Keep an eye on them and use a fork to help break them up gently.
4. Bring a large skillet or Wok to med-high heat and pour the contents of the chicken bag in. Sautee the chicken until just cooked through. Remove to a bowl and keep warm.
5. Turn heat up to high and let your skillet/Wok heat up again. Once it's super hot, start adding your veggies. Remember to keep them moving! Mushroom and onions first for about 5 mins. Then add peppers and celery for another 5 minutes. Finally, add broccoli, snow peas, garlic and ginger and about 1/4 cup water. Cover to let the broccoli soften a bit.
6. Your noodles should be softened by now - strain them.
7. Turn off heat but leave your skillet/Wok on the burner. Add noodles, stirfry sauce and chicken back to the pan and mix it all together (I find tongs easiest). Add more soy sauce if needed - as desired.
8. Enjoy!!

Chinese chicken stir fry with egg noodles

"healthy and easy"

Servings: 2 | **Cook**: 15m

Ingredients

- 2 marinated chicken breast fillet
- 2 clove garlic
- 1 ginger
- 1 celery
- 1 spring onion
- 1 red and orange pepper
- 1 red onion

- 1 chilli, deseeded
- 1 tin chopped tomatoes

Directions

1. fry chicken in 1tsp oil
2. boil egg noodle in separate pan, 6 mins, drain and rest.
3. while chicken cooks chop, spring onions, peppers, onion, chilli and garlic and ginger
4. add ginger and garlic to chicken
5. add red onion, red and orange peppers, celery, chilli, reduce heat and simmer for 10 mibs
6. add pepper and seasoning
7. add drained chopped tomatoes
8. add noodles, stir and serve

Hong Kong Style Noodles with Chicken and Vegetables

*Servings: 4-6 | Prep: 20m | **Inactive**: 1h | **Cook**: 15m | **Ready In:** 1h35m*

Ingredients

- 1/4 cup soy sauce, divided
- 2 tablespoons minced ginger
- 1 tablespoons minced garlic
- 2 tablespoons chili garlic paste
- 4 tablespoons cornstarch, divided
- 2 cups chicken breast, cut 1/4-inch slices, skinless
- 16 ounces chow mein noodles
- 1/2 cup canola oil
- 1 cup 1/8-inch julienne white onion
- 1/2 cup 1/4-inch strips red bell pepper
- 1 cup 1/4-inch sticks cut carrot
- 1 cup 1/2-inch bias cut celery
- 1/2 cup 1/2-inch strips shiitake mushrooms
- 3/4 cup 1/2-inch strips snow peas
- 1 cup mung bean sprouts
- 3 tablespoons hoisin sauce
- 1/4 teaspoon sesame oil

- 1 1/2 cups low-sodium chicken stock
- 1/2 cup strips green onions

Directions

1. In a re-sealable plastic bag add, 3 tablespoons soy sauce, ginger, garlic, chili garlic paste, 2 tablespoons cornstarch and mix thoroughly, then add chicken and marinate for 1 hour.
2. In a medium stock pot boil water and cook chow mein noodles until al dente, remove and shock in ice bath, shake dry and toss with 2 tablespoons oil to keep from sticking.
3. In a large saute pan or Wok, heat 2 tablespoons oil to almost smoke point and add chicken, separating each peace upon entry. Cook until browned on all sides. Remove and hold warm.
4. In same Wok, add 2 tablespoons oil. Heat until almost the smoke point, then add the onions, bell peppers, carrots and celery., Saute for 2 minutes then add mushrooms, peas and bean sprouts. Cook for 1 minute, then add chicken saute for 1 minute, add hoisin, 3 tablespoons soy sauce and sesame oil, toss and remove.
5. Heat a 12-inch nonstick saute pan, add 3 tablespoons oil, heat to almost smoke point, and add chilled chow mein noodles. Cook on one side until crispy light golden brown. Flip noodles and another 2 tablespoons of oil and cook other side. When done, remove and let drain on paper towels, while holding warm.
6. Mix 2 tablespoons cornstarch and chicken stock, and deglaze hot Wok with mixture and let reduce by one-third.
7. Place noodles on a rimmed serving platter, top with chicken and vegetable saute, and pour chicken reduction over top. Garnish with green onions.

Nessa's Chicken Noodle Stir Fry

"Quick easy meal after a long day."

Servings: 4 | **Cook**: 30m

Ingredients

- 4 Chicken Breasts
- 1 Onion

- 1 Bell Peppers (Red, Green& Yellow)
- 1 Spring Onions
- 1 packages Mushrooms (Pack)
- 2 clove Garlic
- 1 tbsp Ginger
- 1/2 cup Soy Sauce
- 1 tbsp Lemon Juice
- 1 Salt & Pepper To Taste
- 1 Egg Noodles

Directions

1. Boil egg noodles with a pinch of salt until cooked. Add half of the soy sauce and allow to sit
2. (While noodles are boiling) Cut Chicken Breast into strips
3. Cut all vegetables to your liking.
4. Heat Vegetable Oil in a deep pan and add chicken, garlic, salt and pepper. Fry until cooked
5. Add vegetables and cook until cooked
6. Add Cooked Egg Noodles and the rest of the soy sauce plus lemon. (I like to add a table spoon of sweet chilli sauce aswell)
7. Serve and Enjoy :)))

Spicy Thai Chicken Noodle Wok

"So yummy and tasty!"

Servings: *2 |* ***Ready In****: 20m*

Ingredients

- 110 grams noodles
- 200 grams vegetables
- 2 chicken breasts marinated in honey
- 1/2 cup sweet chili sauce
- 1/2 cup soya sauce

Directions

1. Cut chicken breasts to pieces.
2. Fry chicken and vegetables in a pan.
3. Put noodles in boiled water for few minutes.
4. Add noodles to the pan.
5. Add soya sauce and sweet chili sauce and mix all together.
6. Enjoy your meal!

Stir-fried chicken and noodles in plum sauce

Servings: 2 | Cook: 20 m

Ingredients

- 300g chicken strips
- 2 tsps sunflower oil
- A handful baby corn
- 2 pak choi, sliced
- 150g pack straight-to-Wok egg noodles
- 3 tbsp plum sauce

Directions

1. Stir-fry the chicken strips in sunflower oil until browned.
2. Add a handful of baby corn and the pak choi. Stir-fry for 2 minutes with a dash of water, then add the egg noodles, plum sauce and water.
3. Toss until the noodles are piping hot.

Thai Chicken and Noodle Curry

"Thai Chicken and Noodle Curry is your go-to recipe when you need a chicken and noodle fix--with a kick. The secret ingredient in Thai Chicken and Noodle Curry is the curry paste, originally from Malaysia and now popular all over northern Thailand. It keeps in the fridge for months, and once you have it, you can whip up this recipe any time. Use the larger amount if you like heat."

Servings: 4-6 | Total time: 45m

Ingredients

- 10 ounce wide rice noodles
- 2 teaspoons vegetable oil
- 2 tablespoons minced garlic
- 1/4 cup minced shallots
- 12 ounces boned, skinned chicken breast, thinly sliced crosswise
- 1 1/2 tablespoons panang curry paste, such as Mae Ploy brand*
- 1 can (14 oz.) coconut milk, divided
- 1 tablespoon sugar
- 1 tablespoon lime juice
- 1 tablespoon reduced-sodium soy sauce
- 1 tablespoon Thai or Vietnamese fish sauce
- 1/2 cup sliced green onions
- 1/2 cup cilantro leaves and small sprigs
- 1/2 cup Thai basil* leaves and small sprigs
- 1 lime, cut into wedges

Directions

1. Bring a medium pot of water to a boil. Add noodles and cook until softened, about 4 minutes. Drain and rinse with cold water. Set aside.
2. Heat oil in a Wok or large frying pan over high heat. Add garlic and shallots and cook until fragrant, about 30 seconds. Add chicken, curry paste, and half the coconut milk. Stir well to dissolve paste and boil until liquid is slightly reduced, about 5 minutes. Stir in remaining coconut milk, the sugar, lime juice, soy sauce, and fish sauce, then bring to a boil. Reduce heat and simmer until liquid is slightly thicker, 2 to 3 minutes more.
3. Add noodles, toss to coat, and cook a few minutes until hot, stirring often. Pour mixture into a serving bowl. Sprinkle with green onions, cilantro, and basil. Serve with lime wedges.
- *Find in grocery stores' Asian foods aisle, at Asian markets, or on amazon.com. Use regular basil if Thai isn't available.

More Chicken Recipes

***

Barbecued Chinese Chicken Lettuce Wraps

Servings: 4 | ***Prep***: 15 m | ***Cook***: 10 m | ***Ready In:*** 25 m

Ingredients

- 2 cups, 4 handfuls, fresh shiitake mushrooms
- 1/3 to 1 1/2 pounds thin cut chicken breast or chicken tenders
- 2 tablespoons light colored oil, such as vegetable oil or peanut oil
- Coarse salt and coarse black pepper
- 3 cloves garlic, chopped
- 1 inch ginger root, finely chopped or grated, optional
- 1 orange, zested
- 1/2 red bell pepper, diced small
- 1 small tin, 6 to 8 ounces, sliced water chestnuts, drained and chopped
- 3 scallions, chopped
- 3 tablespoons hoisin, Chinese barbecue sauce, available on Asian foods aisle of market
- 1/2 large head iceberg lettuce, core removed, head quartered
- Wedges of navel orange -- platter garnish

Directions

1. Remove tough stems from mushrooms and brush with damp towel to clean, Slice mushrooms. Chop chicken into small pieces.
2. Preheat a large skillet or Wok to high.
3. Add oil to hot pan. Add chicken to the pan and sear meat by stir frying a minute or 2. Add mushrooms and cook another minute or two. Add salt and pepper to season, then garlic and ginger. Cook a minute more. Grate zest into pan, add bell pepper bits, chopped water chestnuts and scallions. Cook another minute, continuing to stir fry mixture. Add hoisin Chinese barbecue sauce and toss to coat

the mixture evenly. Transfer the hot chopped barbecued chicken to serving platter and pile the quartered wedges of crisp iceberg lettuce along side. Add wedged oranges to platter to garnish. To eat, pile spoonfuls into lettuce leaves, wrapping lettuce around fillings and squeeze an orange wedge over.

Basil, Chicken, and Veggies in Coconut-Curry Sauce

"Forget takeout! Basil, Chicken, and Veggies in Coconut-Curry Sauce delivers one of the best Asian-inspired recipes--complete with tasty ingredients you can easily find at your local grocery store."

***Servings**: 4-6 | **Prep**: 17m | **Cook**: 10m | **Ready In**: 27m*

Ingredients

- 1 (14-ounce) can coconut milk
- 2 teaspoons curry powder
- 1 tablespoon cornstarch
- 1 tablespoon brown sugar
- 1/2 teaspoon sea salt
- 3 tablespoons peanut oil or canola oil, divided
- 1 pound boneless chicken breasts, cut into thin strips
- 1 red bell pepper, seeded and chopped
- 1 pound small green beans
- 1 tablespoon minced fresh ginger
- 1/4 cup fresh basil leaves, slivered
- 3/4 cup whole, salted cashews, toasted
- Hot cooked rice
- Sriracha
- Garnish: fresh basil leaves

Directions

1. Whisk together first 5 ingredients in a small bowl; set aside.
2. Heat Wok over high heat until a few drops of water evaporate immediately. Swirl 2 tablespoons oil in pan to coat. (If using a nonstick skillet, heat oil over medium-high heat.) Add chicken,

and cook 2 to 3 minutes on each side or until lightly browned. Remove from pan; cover and keep warm.

3. Heat remaining 1 tablespoon oil in Wok over high heat (medium-high, if using a nonstick skillet). Add bell pepper, green beans, and ginger; stir-fry 3 to 4 minutes.

4. Whisk reserved sauce mixture, and add to Wok with vegetables. Cook 1 minute or until sauce thickens. Stir in slivered basil and reserved chicken. Sprinkle with cashews; serve with hot cooked rice and sriracha. Garnish, if desired.

Broccoli and Chicken Stir-Fried Rice

"Chicken and rice dishes are common family meals. This one gives new life to leftover grilled chicken. Slightly browning the broccoli deepens the taste of the dish."

Servings: 4

Ingredients

- 1 1/2 tablespoons canola oil
- 8 cups broccoli florets (about 2 bunches)
- 2 cups vertically sliced onion (about 1)
- 1/2 cup fat-free, less-sodium chicken broth, divided
- 2 cups cooked long-grain rice
- 1 tablespoon minced garlic
- 2 teaspoons minced peeled fresh ginger
- 1/2 teaspoon crushed red pepper
- 2 Hoisin and Lime-Marinated Grilled Chicken breast halves, thinly sliced
- 2 tablespoons low-sodium soy sauce
- 2 tablespoons oyster sauce
- 1 tablespoon rice wine vinegar
- 1 teaspoon cornstarch
- 1/4 teaspoon salt

Directions

1. Heat canola oil in a large nonstick skillet over medium-high heat. Add broccoli and onion; sauté for 5 minutes. Add 1/4 cup broth; cover and cook for 3 minutes. Remove broccoli mixture from pan.
2. Place pan over medium-high heat. Add rice; cook 5 minutes, stirring occasionally. Add broccoli mixture, garlic, ginger, pepper, and chicken; toss well.
3. Combine remaining 1/4 cup broth, soy sauce, oyster sauce, vinegar, and cornstarch; add to pan. Bring to a boil; cook 1 minute. Stir in salt.

Buffalo Chicken Stir Fry

"This is one of my new healthy recipes. 620 calories total. 155 calories per serving"

Servings: 4 | **Cook**: 20m

Ingredients

- 4 tbsp Light country crock butter spread
- 1/2 Onion (chopped)
- 4 Buffalo chicken sausage links
- 1 bunch Broccoli
- 1 Cauliflower
- 1 bunch Asparagus
- 1 cup Fresh spinach
- 1 as needed Adobo
- 1 as needed Garlic powder

Directions

1. Chop broccoli, cauliflower, and asparagus
2. Steam vegetables in water
3. In separate pan, heat yogurt butter and sauté chopped onions.
4. Add 4 links of chopped buffalo chicken sausage (thin and trim brand)
5. Add steamed vegetables and add spinach
6. Sprinkle adobo and garlic powder to taste

Buo-luo Ji Sweet and Sour Chicken

*Servings: 2-4 | **Prep**: 25m | **Cook**: 10m | **Ready In**: 35m*

Ingredients

Sweet and Sour Sauce:

- 1/2 cup pineapple juice
- 1 tablespoon cornstarch
- 1 tablespoon ketchup
- 1 tablespoon light soy sauce
- 1 tablespoon brown sugar
- 1 tablespoon rice vinegar
- 1 tablespoon Shaohsing rice wine

Chicken:

- 2 tablespoons cornstarch
- 1 large egg white
- 1 pound chicken thighs, deboned, de-skinned, sliced into 1 1/2-inch cubes
- 1 pinch sea salt
- 1 pinch ground white pepper
- 2 1/8 cups peanut or vegetable oil, for frying
- 1 tablespoon freshly grated ginger
- 2 cloves garlic, minced
- 1 green pepper, deseeded and sliced into 1-inch chunks
- 1 red pepper, deseeded and sliced into 1-inch chunks
- 1/2 cup cubed fresh pineapple
- 1 scallion, finely sliced into rounds, for garnish, optional
- Serving suggestion: jasmine rice

Directions

1. For the sweet and sour sauce: Mix together the pineapple juice, cornstarch, ketchup, soy sauce, sugar, vinegar and rice wine in a sauce jug.

2. For the chicken: Mix together the cornstarch and egg whites in a bowl to make a "batter", adding a tablespoon of cold water to thin out if necessary. Toss the chicken pieces into the batter and sprinkle with the salt and white pepper. Mix well and set aside.
3. Heat the oil in a Wok to 350 degrees F. Add the chicken pieces and cook until golden brown (this helps to seal in the chicken juices) and cooked through, 3 minutes. Turn the heat off and be extra careful - pour the chicken and hot oil into a stainless-steel colander set over a heatproof bowl to collect the excess oil. Set aside 1 tablespoon of the oil, and discard the rest. Drain the chicken well and set aside.
4. Reheat the Wok until smoking and add the reserved oil. Add the ginger and garlic and stir for a few seconds. Add the peppers and cook for less than 1 minute, and then add the pineapple. Pour in the sweet and sour sauce and bring to a boil. Cook until the sauce is reduced and sticky, 1 to 2 minutes, and then toss in the cooked chicken pieces and stir well for 1 minute. Transfer to a serving plate and garnish with scallions. Serve with rice.

Cajun Chicken and Okra Stir-Fry

Servings: 4

Ingredients

- 2 tsp olive oil
- 1 lb skinless boneless chicken, cut to bite-size
- 1/4 tsp salt
- 1/4 tsp pepper
- 2 tsp cajun seasoning
- 1 green bell pepper, chopped
- 1 red bell pepper, chopped
- 1 onion, chopped
- 4 garlic cloves, minced
- 1 cup okra, cut to 1/2 inch pieces
- 1 can (14 1/2 oz) diced tomatoes with jalapenos
- 1 tsp oregano

Directions

1. Season chicken with salt, pepper and cajun seasoning, stir-fry in 1 tsp oil until cooked through. Transfer chicken to plate and set aside.
2. Stir fry peppers, onion, and garlic until tender. Add okra and stir-fry until tender (the onions should be translucent at this point).
3. Return chicken to pan and add tomatoes and oregano. Bring to a boil and reduce heat to simmer for about 5 minutes, until mixture is slightly thickened.

Cashew Chicken Stir Fry

"A healthy and delightful one dish meal. Low sodium soy sauce can be used."

Servings: 4 | Prep: 25m | Cook: 15m | Ready In: 40

Ingredients

- 4 skinless, boneless chicken breast halves, cut into bite-size pieces
- 1 tablespoon Cajun seasoning blend (such as Tony Chachere's®), or to taste
- 1 1/4 cups chicken broth
- 1 tablespoon cornstarch
- 4 teaspoons soy sauce, divided
- 2 tablespoons olive oil, divided
- 2 cups shredded cabbage
- 25 sugar snap peas, chopped
- 10 small spears fresh asparagus, trimmed and cut into bite-size pieces
- 3 stalks celery, chopped
- 1/2 red bell pepper, cut into thin strips
- 2 green onions, chopped
- 1 (8 ounce) can sliced bamboo shoots, drained
- 1/2 cup cashews
- 1 pinch paprika, or to taste (optional)

Directions

1. Sprinkle chicken pieces with Cajun seasoning.

2. Whisk chicken broth, cornstarch, and 3 teaspoons soy sauce together in a bowl until completely blended.
3. Heat 1 tablespoon olive oil in a deep frying pan or Wok over high heat. Cook and stir chicken in hot oil until cooked through, 6 to 10 minutes. Remove chicken from pan and drain any accumulated liquids.
4. Heat remaining 1 tablespoon olive oil in the frying pan or Wok over high heat. Stir fry cabbage, snap peas, asparagus, celery, red bell pepper, green onions, and bamboo shoots for 1 minute. Stir in 1 teaspoon soy sauce. Continue cooking until vegetables are tender but still crisp, about 3 minutes.
5. Stir chicken into cabbage mixture. Pour chicken broth mixture over chicken mixture, reduce heat to medium, and simmer until sauce thickens, about 1 minute. Reduce heat to low; add cashews and cook until heated through, 1 minute. Sprinkle with paprika.

Cashew Chicken stirfry with goji berries

"Low carb high vitamins"

Servings*: 4 | **Time***: m

Ingredients

- 4 large chicken breasts, boneless and skinless
- 2 cup chicken broth
- 1/4 tsp salt
- 1/2 cup dried goji berries
- 1 stick butter
- 1 cup cashew nuts
- 16 oz broccoli
- 1 tsp granulated garlic powder
- 1/4 cup water
- 3 tbsp arrowroot powder

Directions

1. Melt butter add garlic and salt put into pan

2. Cut the chicken into bite sized pieces. Stir fry in butter till done. Then add chicken broth. Add goji berries, cashews, and broccoli. Simmer 5-7 minutes till broccoli is tender.
3. Mix arrowroot powder with quarter cup of water add to chicken stir till thickened
4. Let sit 5 minutes serve hope you enjoy!

Cheaters Chicken Stir Fry

Ingredients

- 1 lb Chicken Breast
- 4 cup Raw Rice
- 1 packages Frozen Stir Fry Mix
- 1 Soy Sauce
- 1 Garlic Powder & Pepper

Directions

1. Rinse Chicken breast & cube into small pieces. Season to taste with pepper & garlic powder. Start cooking in a separate skillet on medium heat. Cook all the way through. Once it's completely cooked add to the stir fry mixture.
2. Empty your favorite bag of stir fry mix into Wok or non stick pan. Start cooking on medium - high heat. Stir frequently.
3. Rinse raw rice & place into rice steamer. If you don't have a steamer, cook rice the old fashioned way on the stove.
4. Once rice is done the stir fry mix should be fully cooked. Serve over the rice with a splash of soy sauce if you like. Enjoy!

Cheesy chicken and potato stir fry

"So me and my fiancé were trying to figure out what we were going to make for dinner we were running out of options lol but had a some chicken breast and the rest is history"

Servings: 6 | **Time**: 45m

Ingredients

- 4 boneless chicken breast
- 2 tablespoons garlic powder
- 1 chopped onion
- 1 tablespoon minced garlic
- to taste Salt and pepper
- 1 tablespoon adobo
- 1 cup sweet corn
- 1 cup broccoli florets
- 2 cups shredded cheddar cheese
- 3-4 potatoes

Directions

1. Cut all 4 chicken breast into cubes season with garlic powder adobo and salt and pepper and set aside
2. Then chop 3 potatoes into cubes and 1 onion.
3. Next you will add your minced garlic and chopped potato into a frying pan with a little bit of oil and allow it to cook down some. Once you've done that, add your potatoes and chicken to the frying pan and a little bit of water and cover tightly.
4. Allow the chicken and potatoes to cook for 30 minutes on a low to medium heat, then you stir in your cup of corn and cup of broccoli. Allow it to cook for an additional 10 minutes and than cover with cheddar cheese cover again and allow the cheese to melt! ▢
5. Pair with any side of your choice and enjoy

Chicken & Vegetable Stir Fry

Servings: 6 | *Time:* 30m

Ingredients

- 3 large Chicken Breasts
- 2 large Bell Pepper
- 1 cup Fresh Broccoli
- 1 1/2 cup Fresh Bean Sprouts

- 2 cup Kikkoman Stir Fry Sauce
- 4 cup Cooked Rice (2 cups uncooked)
- 1 Garlic Salt
- 1 Black Pepper

Directions

1. Thinly slice chicken breasts. Add to Wok or large skillet. Cook on medium until thoroughly cooked. During this time, thinly slice bell peppers.
2. Once chicken is cooked add garlic salt, pepper, and broccoli. Simmer on medium for five minutes.
3. Add bell peppers, stir fry sauce, and bean sprouts. Cook until vegetables are tender.
4. Serve on white or brown rice and enjoy!

Chicken and asparagus stir fry

"I had chicken and asparagus with nothing else for a casserole so this it was the outcome :) loved it"

Ingredients

- 4 chicken breasts
- 1 packages frozen asparagus
- 6 Brown or white rice
- 1 worcestershire sauce
- 1 Italian seasoning

Directions

1. Put skillet on with a little olive oil on med
2. Cut up chicken into small/ med slices. Cut asparagus stocks into 3 pieces. Put into preheated skillet with sauce and seasoning
3. Make rice accordingly. I made about 6 servings

Chicken And Asparagus Stirfry

Ingredients

- 1 lb Boneless skinless chicken thighs cut into 1 inch pieces
- 2 tbsp Soy sauce
- 1 tsp Cornstarch
- 2 clove Garlic thinly sliced
- 3 tbsp Canola oil
- 1 lb Asparagus trimmed and sliced on an angle into 2 inch pieces
- 1 bunch Lettuce cord and chopped
- 3 cup Cooked rice
- 1 bunch Mint leaves for garnish

Directions

1. In medium bowl toss chicken with 1 tablespoon soy sauce the cornstarch and half of the garlic let marinade
2. In large skillet or Wok heat 1 tablespoon oil over medium hi heat add remaining garlic and cook stirring until fragrant about 30 seconds
3. Add asparagus and 1 teaspoon water cook stirring until crisp and tender about two minutes transfer into a bowl
4. In the same skillet heat the remaining oil add the chicken in a single layer cook without stirring until browned on the bottom about two minutes then cook stirring until cooked through about one minute more
5. Stir in lettuce and cook until just wilted about 30 seconds
6. Stir in asparagus and the remaining tablespoon of soy sauce served with rice and garnish with mint

Chicken and Basil Stir-Fry

"Thai basil adds an anise nuance, and cinnamon basil contributes notes of spice to this quick chicken stir-fry; however, other basil varieties work well too. Serve with hot cooked rice. Asian fish sauce is available in most supermarkets and in Asian grocery stores."

Servings: 3-4

Ingredients

- 1 pound boned, skinned chicken breast halves
- 1 tablespoon vegetable oil
- 1 tablespoon minced garlic
- 1 tablespoon minced fresh ginger
- 1/4 teaspoon hot chili flakes
- 2/3 cup fat-skimmed chicken broth
- 1 tablespoon Asian fish sauce (nuoc mam or nam pla) or soy sauce
- 2 teaspoons cornstarch
- 3 cups lightly packed fresh basil leaves (see notes), rinsed
- Salt

Directions

1. Rinse chicken and pat dry. Cut crosswise into 1/8-inch-thick strips 2 to 3 inches long.
2. Place a 10- to 12-inch nonstick frying pan over high heat; when hot, add oil, garlic, ginger, chili flakes, and the chicken. Stir often until chicken is no longer pink in the center (cut to test), 3 to 4 minutes.
3. In a small bowl, mix broth, fish sauce, and cornstarch until smooth. Add to pan and stir until sauce is boiling, about 1 minute. Add basil leaves and stir just until barely wilted, about 30 seconds. Add salt to taste and pour into a serving bowl.

Chicken and Bok Choy Stir-Fry

"This simple chicken and bok choy stir-fry is a colorful and nutritious Asian-inspired meal. Seve with steamed white rice"

Servings: 4 | **Prep**: 15m | **Other**: 10m

Ingredients

- This recipe goes with Perfectly Cooked White Rice
- 1 tablespoon canola oil
- 4 6-ounce boneless, skinless chicken breasts, cut into 1-inch pieces
- Kosher salt and black pepper

- 4 heads baby bok choy, quartered lengthwise
- 1/4 cup low-sodium soy sauce
- 1/4 cup store-bought barbecue sauce
- 4 scallions, thinly sliced

Directions

1. Heat the oil in a large skillet over medium-high heat. Season the chicken with 1/4 teaspoon each salt and pepper and cook, tossing occasionally, until browned and cooked through, 4 to 6 minutes. Transfer to a plate.
2. Add the bok choy and 1/4 cup water to the skillet. Cover and cook until the bok choy is just tender, 3 to 4 minutes.
3. In a small bowl, combine the soy sauce, barbecue sauce, and scallions. Add to the skillet and bring to a boil. Return the chicken to the skillet and cook, tossing, until heated through, 1 to 2 minutes.

Chicken And Green Bean Stir Fry

"This is a great recipe my husband, kids, and parents love this recipe..."

Servings: 6 | **Time**: 35m

Ingredients

- Ingredients
- 1 1/2 lb chicken breasts
- 1 1/4 lb Green beans
- 2 tbsp cooking oil
- Marinade
- 3 tbsp soy sauce
- 2 tbsp dry sherry
- 1 clove garlic
- Sauce
- 2 tbsp brown sugar
- 1 tbsp cornstarch
- 1 tbsp apple cider vinegar
- 6 tbsp soy sauce
- 1 clove garlic

- 2 tbsp dry sherry
- 3 tbsp hoisin sauce

Directions

1. Clean and cut green beans. Then add the oil. Cook green bean at medium high heat.
2. As your cooking the green beans , start making the marinade.
3. Clean and cut the chicken into 1/2 inch squares. After the chicken is cut add the chicken to the marinade.
4. Well the chicken is marinade, start making the sauce. By mixing all the sauce ingredients. Save this till the chicken is done cooking.
5. Check the green bean to see if there ready. If th.ey are remove them from the pot and add the chicken and cook in till that is ready.
6. After the chicken is ready add the green beans back into pot and add the sauce.
7. Cook at medium heat till the sauce is ready.
8. Then I make some steamed white rice. Dinner is ready.

Chicken And Leek Stir Fry

Servings: 4

Ingredients

- 2 chicken breast
- 1 Tbsp garlic or to taste
- 1 leek chopped
- 6 rashers bacon sliced
- 1 1/2 cup mushrooms
- 3/4 cup peas
- 250 ml cream
- 400 g pasta

Directions

1. Cook pasta
2. Brown chicken and set aside

3. Fry leek, garlic and bacon until brown and add mushrooms
4. Add chicken and peas, mix well until peas are thawed
5. Add cream and let simmer until sauce thickens slightly
6. Add cooked pasta mix well then serve

Chicken and Mushrooms, Zucchini Stir Fry With(Szechuan Stir-Fry Sauce)

Ingredients

- 1 lb Skinless Boneless Chicken Thighs
- 1 1/2 cup Slice mushrooms
- 1/2 Dice Onions
- 4 garlic cloves
- 3 Zucchini
- 1/4 cup cooking oil

Directions

1. Dice your boneless, skinless chicken. Slice zucchinis, Dice onions, Slice mushrooms , minced garlic.
2. Add cooking to the pan add dice chicken. Cooking chicken for 10 minutes. Remove chicken from Wok.or frying pan.. Add 2 tablespoons oil add onions, zucchinis., mushrooms, garlic. Stir fry for 10 to 15 minutes or done. You want that freshness and crispy ness. Add Szechuan Stir-Fry Sauce Eat over steam rice.

Chicken and Mustard Green Stir-fry

"This is very good, not difficult and contains pretty common ingredients. If you love that slight pepper taste of mustard greens, you will like this. Of course you can use other greens, or even baby bok choy if it's your preference. One of the things that make this recipe good, is it is easily changeable. Spinach works good also, my wife likes it that way not being a mustard green fan."

Servings: 6 | **Time**: 15m

Ingredients

- chicken
- 6 boneless, skinless chicken thighs (no reason you could not use breasts)
- 1 tablespoon corn starch
- 1/2 teaspoon salt
- as needed ground black pepper
- sauce
- 1/2 cup vegetable, mushroom or chicken stock
- 1 tablespoon corn starch
- 1 tablespoon oyster sauce
- 1 tablespoon light soy sauce
- 1-2 teaspoon hot sauce (use the amount you like)
- 1-2 teaspoon garlic powder
- stir-fry
- 1 tablespoon oil (I like peanut oil, but use what you like)
- 1 tablespoon white cooking wine, rice wine, broth what ever you have
- 1-2 inch fresh ginger (use what you like)
- 4-5 fresh mushrooms. Shiitaki are awesome, but baby bello or button work fine
- 2 large scallions
- 1 large bunch greens

Directions

1. Clean chicken, Debone and remove skin, or buy already prepared.
2. Cut your chicken into 1-2 inch pieces
3. Put chicken in a bowl, salt and pepper, add corn starch.
4. Mix chicken to combine all ingredients. Set aside.
5. Mix all sauce ingredients in a separate bowl, set aside.
6. Clean your ginger, and cut into coins (rounds). I like ginger so I use a 2 inch piece
7. Cut the thicker stems from your greens, into 1/2-3/4 inch pieces, we will cook these a tad longer from the leaves.
8. Slice the leaves, I usually cut them in about 2 inch lengths across. Do them how you may like them. Sorry, the picture didn't turn out.
9. Slice your mushrooms to a size you like. I like larger pieces myself.
10. Slice your scallions (green onions) into small slices, forgot to take a picture, but it isn't hard, just cut across the onions into about 1/4 inch lengths.

11. Put large skillet, Wok or stir-fry pan on medium high heat. Add oil, let it heat up.
12. Put ginger into oil, stir-fry about 1/2 to 1 minute until you can smell it. Add chicken, give it a quick stir. Let it sit for a minute. Stir it for another minute, add wine/broth, stir for 1 more minute.
13. Now stir the chicken about 4-5 times a minute, until it gets opaque, then add the sauce. Stir all the time now, bring sauce to a boil.
14. I like to turn down the heat to medium at this point because I burn stuff, your choice, add stems from the greens, stir 1 minute
15. Add mushrooms stir 2 more minutes, then add the leaves. Stir for about 2 minutes until the greens wilt.
16. Add green onions save some for garnish if you desire, I don't, I just add them all, but that is just me. Stir for 1 minute.
17. Serve. You can eat it as is or with rice or over noodles.

Chicken and Snow Peas

"A simple, tasty, and quick version of a popular Chinese Style recipe."

Servings: 6 | ***Prep***: 15m | ***Cook***: 15m | ***Ready In***: 30m

Ingredients

- 1 cup chicken broth
- 3 tablespoons soy sauce
- 1 tablespoon cornstarch
- 1 tablespoon ground ginger
- 2 tablespoons vegetable oil
- 4 large skinless, boneless chicken breast halves, cubed
- 2 cloves garlic, minced
- 1 1/2 cups sliced fresh mushrooms
- 2 (8 ounce) cans sliced water chestnuts, drained
- 3 cups snow peas
- 1 tablespoon sesame seeds

Directions

1. Whisk the chicken broth, soy sauce, cornstarch, and ginger together in a small bowl; reserve.

2. Heat oil in a large skillet or Wok. Cook and stir chicken and garlic in the oil until chicken is cooked through, 8 to 10 minutes. Stir in mushrooms, water chestnuts, and reserved chicken broth mixture. Cook until sauce begins to thicken, 3 to 5 minutes.
3. Stir snow peas into the pan and cook until tender, 3 to 5 minutes. Transfer to a platter and sprinkle with sesame seeds before serving.

Chicken and Veggies stir fry

"Quick snack from leftover marinated chicken.."

Servings: 4 | **Time**: 20m

Ingredients

- 200 grams boneless chicken
- 2 tbsp dried mixed herbs
- 1 capcicum
- 1 yellow bell pepper
- 1 red bell pepper
- 1 onion
- 1 tbsp lemon juice
- 1 salt and pepper
- 1 grams spring onion
- 1/2 tbsp olive oil

Directions

1. Cut the boneless chicken into small bite size pieces.
2. Put the chicken in a bowl and marinate it with salt and pepper as per taste, one tablespoon of the mixed herbs, 1/2 tablespoon olive oil and all of the lemon juice.
3. Mix and keep aside for an hour or two.
4. In the meantime dice the veggies in almost the same size as the chicken. Chop the spring onion.
5. Stir fry the veggies in a pan with one tablespoon olive oil for 2 to 3 minutes. Sprinkle mixed herbs and salt and pepper to taste. Take out the veggies from the pan after 3 minutes.

6. Stir fry the chicken with some olive in a pan till the chicken is cooked. This may take 4-6 minutes.
7. When the chicken is cooked, toss the veggies in the pan with the chicken, give it a final toss so that all the flavours come together and turn off the heat.
8. Garnish with chopped spring onion and serve hot with Mint chutney or any sauce of your choice.

Chicken Asparagus Lemon Stir Fry

"Found this recipe and loved it. Low carb and healthy. We add some soy sauce to the chicken before cooking and used olive oil spray. My husband and daughter loved it also."

Servings: 4 | **Time**: 30m

Ingredients

- 2 lb boneless skinless chicken breast
- 1/2 cup low sodium chicken broth
- 2 tbsp reduced sodium soy sauce
- 2 tsp cornstarch
- 2 tbsp water
- 1 tbsp olive oil, extra virgin
- 6 clove garlic chopped
- 3 tbsp fresh lemon juice
- 1 salt and pepper to taste

Directions

- Cut chicken into one inch cubes and salt. One bowl combine chicken broth and soy sauce. Another bowl combine cornstarch and water. Heat skillet over medium heat add 1 tsp. Oil Cook asparagus 3-4 minutes then add garlic, Cook until golden brown. Remove and set aside. Cook chicken until brown and cooked through, remove and set aside. Add soy sauce mixture and bring to a boil, add lemon juice and cornstarch mixture, mix well. Bring to a simmer and add chicken and asparagus mix well and serve.

Chicken Fried Rice with Vegetables

"Why call for take out from your favorite Chinese restaurant when you can make this quick and easy chicken fried rice recipe at home? Use leftover rice and frozen vegetables to make this rice dish even easier."

Servings: 4 | **Prep**: 7m | **Cook**: 15m | **Ready In**: 22m

Ingredients

- 1/2 (12 oz.) chicken breast, chopped
- 2 tablespoons soy sauce
- 2 teaspoons sesame oil
- 1/4 cup vegetable oil
- 3/4 cup chopped onion
- 1/2 (10 oz.) package frozen mixed vegetables, thawed
- 4 cups cooked white rice
- 3 eggs
- Kosher salt
- Black pepper

Directions

1. In a medium bowl, toss chicken with soy sauce and sesame oil. Cover and marinate at room temperature for 10 minutes.
2. Heat a large nonstick skillet over medium-high heat. Add chicken and marinade and stir-fry until chicken is cooked through, 3 to 4 minutes. Transfer chicken to a plate; set aside. Add vegetable oil to skillet and heat over medium heat. Add onion and cook for 3 minutes. Stir in vegetables and cook for 1 minute. Increase heat to medium-high, stir in rice until incorporated and cooked through, 3 minutes.
3. Using a wooden spoon, form a well in mixture. Add eggs and scramble within well just until soft. Then break apart and mix into rice; season with salt and pepper. Let cook undisturbed until a golden crust forms, about 1 minute. Turn rice with a spatula and cook other side. Repeat 2 or 3 times until rice is uniformly golden. Add chicken and stir to combine. Serve warm.

Chicken Fried Rice

"This recipe uses leftover rice from Stuffed Peppers."

Servings: 4 | **Prep**: 10m | **Cook**: 15m

Ingredients

- 1 pound boneless, skinless chicken breast, cut into 1-inch pieces
- 1/4 cup low-sodium soy sauce
- 3 tablespoons vegetable oil
- 1 onion, halved and sliced
- 1 pound frozen stir-fry vegetables, thawed, patted dry
- 2 cloves garlic, minced
- 2 tablespoons grated fresh ginger
- 2 cups cooked brown rice from Stuffed Peppers

Directions

1. Toss chicken with 1 Tbsp. soy sauce. Place a large skillet over high heat. Add 1 Tbsp. oil, then onion; stir-fry until onion starts to brown, about 1 minute. Add chicken; stir-fry until cooked through, 5 to 6 minutes. Transfer mixture to a bowl. Add 1 Tbsp. oil to skillet. Stir-fry vegetables for 2 minutes. Transfer to bowl with chicken.
2. Add 1 Tbsp. oil, garlic and ginger to skillet; stir-fry for 30 seconds. Add rice; cook for 2 minutes. Add chicken, vegetables and remaining soy sauce; cook 1 minute longer. Serve immediately.

Chicken Hearts Stir Fry with Bean Sprouts and Carrots

"Just a simple way to cook a chicken hearts. Bon appétit!"

Servings: 2 | **Time**: 30m

Ingredients

- 1 lb chicken hearts
- 2 white onions, chopped
- 1 tbsp butter
- 1 tbsp vegetable oil
- 1 inch ginger, sliced vertically
- 175 g bean sprouts
- 1 carrot, sliced
- 3 cloves garlic
- 2 chili peppers
- 1/2 tsp salt
- 1/2 tsp pepper
- 2 tbsp soy sauce
- 1 tbsp vinegar
- 3 leaves lamb's lettuce for garnishing

Directions

1. Wok the onion, garlic, ginger and carrots in the butter and oil until the onion and carrots just starts to soften.
2. Add the chicken hearts and stir fry until just cooked.
3. Add the bean sprouts and stir fry for about 2-3 minutes.
4. Stir in the salt, pepper, chili pepper, vinegar and soy sauce, then allow to bubble away for about 3 minutes.
5. Remove from the flame and garnish it with lamb's lettuce. Serve while it's warm.

Chicken Stir Fry I

Ingredients

- 2 chicken breasts; trimmed and sliced thin on bias
- 1/4 red onion; julienne
- 1/3 yellow bell pepper; julienne
- 1/3 green bell pepper; julienne
- 1 cup sherry
- 1/4 cup sesame oil
- 1/4 cup ponzu (lime soy sauce)
- 1 tbsp garlic paste
- 1 tbsp lemongrass paste

- 2 tbsp cornstarch
- 1/2 cup cold water
- 1 vegetable oil; as needed

Directions

1. Combine sherry, sesame oil, ponzu, garlic, and lemongrass. Whisk together.
2. Heat enough vegetable oil to cover bottom of large saute pan, or Wok. Before oil starts to smoke, add chicken.
3. When chicken is 90% cooked, add veggies.
4. When veggies and chicken are nearly finished, add sauce. Bring to boil.
5. Seperately, whisk cornstarch and cold water.
6. Add cornstarch slurry to pan while whisking or tossing to avoid clumping.
7. Variations; Coconut milk, basil, parsely, cilantro, scallions, leeks, ramps, caramelized onions, jalapeños, shallots, celery, bacon, corn, zucchini, bamboo shoots, noodles, mirin, sake, Sriracha, tamari, plum sauce, brown sugar, cayenne, crushed pepper flakes, thai basil or chile, water chestnut, pork, beef, shrimp, lemon

Chicken Stir-Fry with Peanut Sauce

"Save time, money, and calories by making this simple stir-fry in the comfort of your own kitchen. Want more for later? Try doubling the batch of peanut sauce and using it as a dip for grilled chicken kebabs tomorrow night!"

Servings: 4

Ingredients

- 2 teaspoons dark sesame oil, divided
- 1 pound chicken cutlets, trimmed
- 2 cups broccoli florets
- 1 large red bell pepper, sliced
- 1/4 cup light coconut milk
- 2 tablespoons lower-sodium soy sauce
- 2 tablespoons creamy peanut butter

- 1 tablespoon Sriracha
- 2 teaspoons grated lime rind
- 1 tablespoon lime juice
- 1/4 teaspoon ground ginger
- 1/4 teaspoon ground cumin
- 1/4 cup unsalted cashews

Directions

1. Heat a Wok or large skillet over high heat. Add 1 teaspoon oil; swirl to coat. Add chicken; cook 1 minute on each side. Remove chicken from pan; cut into thin slices. Add broccoli and bell pepper to pan; stir-fry 4 minutes or until vegetables are lightly browned.
2. Reduce heat to medium-high. Combine remaining 1 teaspoon oil, coconut milk, and next 7 ingredients (through cumin) in a small bowl, stirring with a whisk. Add chicken and coconut milk mixture to pan; cook 30 seconds. Sprinkle evenly with cashews.

Chicken Stir-Fry II

Servings: 4 | *Prep*: 10m | *Cook*: 20m | *Ready In*: 30m

Ingredients

- 2 tablespoons dark sesame oil, divided
- 2 garlic cloves, finely minced
- 2 pounds chicken breasts, skinless and boneless
- 1 head broccoli, stems removed
- 1 dozen mushrooms, sliced
- 3 carrots, peeled and julienned
- 1/4 pound green beans, diced
- 1 head bok choy, chopped
- 2 to 3 tablespoons teriyaki sauce

Directions

1. Heat 1 tablespoon oil in a saute pan over medium heat. Add garlic and stir. Place the chicken in the pan and brown 4 minutes on each side. Remove from pan, slice into strips, set aside.
2. Heat remaining tablespoon of oil in a Wok over high heat. Add the vegetables and teriyaki sauce. Stir-fry quickly until the vegetables begin to soften. Add the chicken strips, combine well and continue to cook for 2 to 3 minutes. Serve immediately.

Chicken with peanuts stir fry

"Good Asian taste of food"

Servings: 2 |**Time**: 30m

Ingredients

- 300 grams of slices chicken
- 1/2 of each red and yellow sweet peppers cut chuck
- 1/2 chuck cut onion
- 3 stripes of green onion cut 2 cm long
- 1/4 cup of roasted peanuts
- 2 stripes of cut salary
- 1 tbsp spoon of oyster sauce
- 1 tsp spoon of chicken stock powder
- 1 tsp spoon of sugar
- 1 tsp spoon of light soy sauce
- 2 tbsp spoon of oil

Directions

1. In the heating pan pour in oil add chicken fry till cook
2. Add onion and sweet peppers
3. Add peanuts and add oyster sauce, light soy sauce, sugar and chicken stock powder keep frying to get all the flavours in the chickens
4. Add green onion and salary stir in for 3 minutes

Chicken with Snap Peas and Shiitakes

Servings: 4 | **Prep**:1h | **Cook**: 10m | **Ready In**: 1h10m

Ingredients

- 6 chicken thighs
- 1 tablespoon sesame oil
- 1/2 cup oyster sauce
- 2 tablespoons cornstarch
- 2 tablespoon minced garlic, divided
- 2 tablespoon minced ginger, divided
- 1/2 pound snap peas, blanched
- 1/2 cup canola oil
- 4 sliced scallions, separate green and white
- 1/2 cup chicken stock (if canned, use low sodium)
- 2 cups sliced shiitakes
- Salt and black pepper to taste

Directions

- Marinate chicken in sesame oil, oyster sauce, cornstarch, 1 tablespoon garlic and 1 tablespoon ginger for 30 minutes. Blanch snap peas al dente in hot salted water followed by an iced bath. Keep the peas crisp. In a hot Wok, coat bottom with oil and add remaining 1 tablespoon of garlic, 1 tablespoon of ginger and white scallions. Stir quickly to avoid burning. Season chicken and brown. After about 8 minutes, add chicken stock and reduce by half. Add mushrooms quickly stir for 1 minute. Add peas just to heat up and serve. Check for seasoning. Garnish with fresh cracked black pepper. Serve with rice.

Chicken, Cashew, and Red Pepper Stir-Fry

"This chicken stir-fry dish balances salty, sweet, tangy, and spicy ingredients. Spoon it alongside a quick rice pilaf for the perfect meal."

Servings: 4 | **Prep**: 30m

Ingredients

- 3 3/4 teaspoons cornstarch, divided
- 2 tablespoons low-sodium soy sauce, divided
- 2 teaspoons dry sherry
- 1 teaspoon rice wine vinegar
- 3/4 teaspoon sugar
- 1/2 teaspoon hot pepper sauce (such as Tabasco)
- 1 pound chicken breast tenders, cut lengthwise into thin strips
- 1/2 cup coarsely chopped unsalted cashews
- 2 tablespoons canola oil
- 2 cups julienne-cut red bell pepper (about 1 large)
- 1 teaspoon minced garlic
- 1/2 teaspoon minced peeled fresh ginger
- 3 tablespoons thinly sliced green onions

Directions

1. Combine 1 teaspoon cornstarch, 1 tablespoon soy sauce, and next 4 ingredients (through hot pepper sauce) in a small bowl; stir with a whisk.
2. Combine remaining 2 3/4 teaspoons cornstarch, remaining 1 tablespoon soy sauce, and chicken in a medium bowl; toss well to coat.
3. Heat a large nonstick skillet over medium-high heat. Add cashews to pan; cook 3 minutes or until lightly toasted, stirring frequently. Remove from pan.
4. Add oil to pan, swirling to coat. Add chicken mixture to pan; sauté 2 minutes or until lightly browned. Remove chicken from pan; place in a bowl. Add bell pepper to pan; sauté 2 minutes, stirring occasionally. Add garlic and ginger; cook 30 seconds. Add chicken and cornstarch mixture to pan; cook 1 minute or until sauce is slightly thick. Sprinkle with cashews and green onions.
5. Quick rice pilaf: Cook 1 (10-ounce) package frozen white rice (such as Birds Eye SteamFresh) according to package directions. Combine cooked rice, 2 tablespoons drained chopped water chestnuts, 1/2 teaspoon crushed red pepper, 1/4 teaspoon salt, and 1/4 teaspoon freshly ground black pepper.

Chicken, Snow Pea, and Cashew Fried Rice

"Great recipe on a budget."

Servings: 4 | **Prep**: 15m | **Cook**: 8m | **Ready In**: 23m

Ingredients

- 1 pound skinless, boneless chicken breasts, cut into thin strips
- 1/4 cup teriyaki sauce, divided
- 3 tablespoons vegetable oil, divided
- 3 scallions, thinly sliced
- 2 cloves garlic, minced
- 1 tablespoon minced fresh ginger root
- 8 ounces snow peas, trimmed
- 1/4 cup low-sodium chicken broth
- 4 cups cooked white rice
- 3 tablespoons chopped roasted cashews

Directions

1. Combine chicken and 2 tablespoons teriyaki sauce in a bowl. Heat 1 1/2 tablespoons vegetable oil in a large skillet or Wok over high heat. Add chicken; cook and stir until no longer pink in the center, 3 to 5 minutes. Transfer to a separate bowl.
2. Stir scallions, garlic, ginger, and remaining vegetable oil into skillet until fragrant, about 1 minute. Stir in snow peas and chicken broth; cover and cook until tender; 2 to 3 minutes.
3. Stir rice, cooked chicken, and remaining teriyaki sauce into skillet; cook and stir until rice is heated through, 2 to 3 minutes. Sprinkle with cashews.

Chicken-and-Cabbage Fried Rice

"One-dish meals make weeknight dinner a breeze, and Chicken-and-Cabbage Fried Rice is no exception. This family meal is ready in only 30 minutes."

Servings: 4 | **Prep**: 20m | **Cook**: 10m

Ingredients

- 5 tablespoons vegetable oil
- 2 1/2 cups cored and chopped napa cabbage (about 1/4 small head)
- 1 medium onion, coarsely chopped
- 4 scallions, chopped, white and green parts separated (about 1 cup total)
- 2 teaspoons grated fresh ginger
- 2 cloves garlic, finely chopped
- 5 cups cooked brown or white rice
- 3 large eggs, lightly beaten
- 3 tablespoons low-sodium soy sauce
- 2 cups shredded cooked boneless, skinless chicken, from a rotisserie bird (about 8 oz.)

Directions

1. Warm 2 Tbsp. oil in a Wok or large nonstick skillet over medium-high heat until oil is shimmering. Add cabbage, onion and white parts of scallions and stir-fry for 30 seconds. Add ginger and garlic to skillet, toss to combine with cabbage mixture and stir-fry for an additional 15 to 20 seconds. Transfer to a wide, shallow bowl or plate.
2. Warm remaining 3 Tbsp. oil in same skillet. Add rice, mix to coat with oil and spread out in pan (but don't press flat). Let rice cook undisturbed for 2 minutes, then stir. Let cook undisturbed 1 minute longer, then push to edges of pan. Add eggs to center of pan and stir to scramble. Break eggs into pieces and stir into rice.
3. Drizzle soy sauce over rice, add chicken and stir to combine well. Cook for 1 to 2 minutes longer to warm through. Stir in cabbage mixture and half of scallion greens and continue cooking and stirring until warmed through, about 1 minute. Sprinkle with remaining scallion greens and serve.

Chicken-Cashew Stir-Fry

"This classic chicken stir-fry combines both sweet and hot Asian flavors. Cashews give it crunch. You can use this recipe as a base and vary the *ingredients as you like."*

Servings: 6

Ingredients

- 1/2 cup fat-free, less-sodium chicken broth
- 3 tablespoons oyster sauce (such as Kame)
- 1 1/2 tablespoons cornstarch
- 1 1/2 tablespoons honey
- 1 tablespoon low-sodium soy sauce
- 2 teaspoons rice or white wine vinegar
- 1/2 teaspoon salt
- 2 tablespoons oil, divided
- 1 cup chopped green onions, divided
- 1 small onion, cut into 8 wedges
- 1 cup (3 x 1/4-inch) julienne-cut red bell pepper
- 1/2 cup diagonally sliced carrot
- 1 cup sliced mushrooms
- 1 cup snow peas
- 1 pound skinned, boned chicken thighs, cut into bite-size pieces
- 1/4 cup canned pineapple chunks in juice, drained
- 1/3 cup cashews
- 1/2 to 1 teaspoon crushed red pepper
- 6 cups hot cooked long-grain rice

Directions

1. Combine first 7 ingredients in a small bowl; set aside.
2. Heat 1 tablespoon oil in a stir-fry pan or Wok over medium-high heat. Add 1/2 cup green onions and onion wedges; stir-fry 1 minute. Add bell pepper and carrot; stir-fry 2 minutes. Add mushrooms and peas; stir-fry 2 minutes. Remove vegetable mixture from pan. Keep warm.
3. Heat 1 tablespoon oil in pan over medium-high heat. Add chicken; stir-fry 5 minutes. Add broth mixture, vegetable mixture, pineapple, cashews, and crushed red pepper; bring to a boil, and cook 1 minute or until thick. Stir in 1/2 cup green onions. Serve with rice.

Chicken-Edamame Stir-Fry

Servings: 4 | *Prep*: 15m | *Cook*: 21m | *Ready In*: 36m

Ingredients

- 2 tablespoons cornstarch
- 1/2 teaspoon salt
- 1/4 teaspoon pepper
- 1 pound boneless, skinless chicken breasts, cut into 1/2-inch-thick strips
- 2 tablespoons vegetable oil
- 1 red onion, thinly sliced
- 2 cloves garlic, thinly sliced
- 3 cups finely shredded savoy cabbage
- 1 1/2 cups thawed frozen shelled edamame
- 2 tablespoons hoisin sauce
- 1/3 cup chopped fresh cilantro
- 2 cups cooked brown or white rice

Directions

1. Stir together cornstarch, salt and pepper in a medium bowl. Add chicken and toss to coat. Warm oil in a large nonstick skillet over medium high heat. Place chicken in skillet and cook, stirring, about 5 minutes, until lightly browned. With a slotted spoon, transfer chicken to a plate.
2. Return skillet to heat, add red onion and garlic and cook, stirring, until softened, about 3 minutes. Stir in cabbage, edamame and 1/2 cup water and cook, stirring, about 8 minutes, or until edamame are cooked through.
3. Stir in reserved chicken and hoisin sauce and cook, stirring, about 3 to 5 minutes, or until warmed through. Remove skillet from heat, stir in cilantro, and serve hot on top of rice.

Chicken-Orange Stir-Fry

"Mandarin oranges and apricot preserves add a fruity sweetness to this veggie-packed chicken stir fry recipe."

Servings: 4

Ingredients

- 1 (11-ounce) can mandarin oranges in light syrup, undrained
- 1/3 cup thawed orange juice concentrate, undiluted
- 2 tablespoons low-sodium soy sauce
- 1 tablespoon minced peeled fresh ginger
- 1 1/2 teaspoons apricot preserves
- 1/2 teaspoon dark sesame oil
- 1/8 teaspoon chili oil (optional)
- 1 garlic clove, minced
- 1/2 pound skinned, boned chicken breasts, cut into bite-size pieces
- 1 1/2 teaspoons canola or vegetable oil
- 1 cup (1-inch) diagonally sliced asparagus (about 4 ounces)
- 1/2 cup (3-inch) julienne-cut red bell pepper
- 1/2 cup (3-inch) julienne-cut zucchini (about 1 small)
- 1/2 cup (3-inch) julienne-cut carrot (about 1 medium)
- 1/2 cup snow peas
- 1/2 cup diagonally sliced celery
- 1/2 pound green beans, trimmed and diagonally sliced
- 1 (8-ounce) package presliced mushrooms
- 1 1/2 teaspoons cornstarch
- 3 cups hot cooked rice
- 2 tablespoons slivered almonds, toasted

Directions

1. Drain oranges in a colander over a bowl, reserving syrup.
2. Combine juice concentrate and the next 6 ingredients (concentrate through garlic) in a bowl, stirring with a whisk. Add chicken; cover and marinate in refrigerator 1 hour.
3. Heat canola oil in a stir-fry pan or Wok over medium-high heat. Add asparagus and the next 6 ingredients (asparagus through green beans); stir-fry for 6 minutes or until crisp-tender. Add mushrooms, and stir-fry for 2 minutes. Remove vegetable mixture from pan. Add chicken mixture to pan, and stir-fry for 4 minutes or until chicken is done. Return vegetable mixture to pan. Combine reserved syrup and cornstarch in a small bowl, stirring well with a

whisk. Add syrup mixture to pan, and cook for 1 minute or until slightly thick. Stir in oranges. Serve over rice and almonds.

Chicken-Peanut Chow Mein

"Chow mein noodles are often labeled chuka soba. If you can't find them in the Asian section of the supermarket, substitute spaghetti or linguine. Chop and measure ingredients while you wait for water to boil."

Servings: 4

Ingredients

- 1 cup precut matchstick-cut carrot
- 1 cup snow peas, trimmed
- 2 (6-ounce) packages chow mein noodles
- 1 tablespoon dark sesame oil, divided
- 1/2 pound skinless, boneless chicken breast
- 3 tablespoons low-sodium soy sauce, divided
- 3/4 cup fat-free, less-sodium chicken broth
- 2 tablespoons oyster sauce
- 1 teaspoon sugar
- 1/4 teaspoon crushed red pepper
- 1 cup presliced mushrooms
- 2 teaspoons bottled fresh ground ginger (such as Spice World)
- 1 cup (1-inch) sliced green onions
- 2 tablespoons dry-roasted peanuts, coarsely chopped

Directions

1. Cook carrots, snow peas, and noodles in boiling water 3 minutes; drain.
2. Heat 2 teaspoons oil in a large nonstick skillet over medium-high heat. Cut chicken crosswise into thin strips. Add chicken and 1 tablespoon soy sauce to pan; stir-fry 3 minutes. Remove chicken from pan; keep warm.
3. Combine remaining 2 tablespoons soy sauce, broth, oyster sauce, sugar, and pepper, stirring well. Heat remaining 1 teaspoon oil over medium-high heat. Add mushrooms and ginger to pan; stir-fry for 3

minutes. Add broth mixture, and cook for 1 minute. Add noodle mixture and chicken to pan; cook 1 minute, tossing to combine. Sprinkle with onions and peanuts.

Chili Mango Chicken Stir-fry

"If you can't find Mango, peaches are a good substitute"

Servings: 4

Ingredients

- 1 lb boneless skinless chicken, thinly sliced
- 2 Tbsp dry sherry, divided
- 2 tsp soy sauce, low sodium
- 2 tsp cornstarch, divided
- 1 tsp salt, divided
- 1/3 cup chicken broth, low sodium
- 1 Tbsp sriracha
- 1 Tbsp peanut oil (substitute sesame oil if needed)
- 3 quarter size pieces of ginger root (peeled and smashed)
- 2 cups green bell peppers, chopped
- 1 cup red bell peppers, chopped
- 1 large mango, 1/2 inch slices

Directions

1. Mix: 1 Tbsp sherry, 2 tsp soy sauce, 1 1/2 tsp cornstarch, 1/2 tsp salt. Coat chicken and set aside
2. Mix: chicken broth, sriracha, 1 Tbsp sherry, 1/2 tsp cornstarch. Set aside
3. Heat skillet or Wok over high heat. Add oil, then ginger - stir-fry until fragrant
4. Add chicken, cook until no pink remains but chicken should not be done
5. Add bell peppers and 1/2 tsp salt, let cook 1-2 minutes
6. Stir broth and add to Wok stir-fry 1-2 minutes or until chicken is cooked through
7. Remove from heat mix with mango

China Sun Chicken

"This sweet and savory dish is prepared Wok-style. You can substitute the chicken for pork if you like. Serve it over rice. I hope you enjoy!"

Servings: 3 | **Prep**: 25m | **Cook**: 15m | **Ready In**: 40m

Ingredients

- 2 tablespoons vegetable oil
- 1 pound skinless, boneless chicken breast halves - cut into 1/2 inch pieces
- 2 carrots, julienned
- 2 cloves garlic, pressed
- 1 teaspoon ground ginger
- 4 shallots, chopped
- 1 bell pepper, slivered
- 1 (20 ounce) can pineapple chunks in natural juice, liquid drained and reserved
- 1/2 cup water
- 2 tablespoons soy sauce
- 1 tablespoon cornstarch
- 1 teaspoon white vinegar
- 1/2 teaspoon red pepper flakes

Directions

1. Heat the oil in a Wok or large skillet over medium-high heat; cook the chicken and carrots in the hot oil until the chicken is no longer pink in the center and the carrots are tender, about 5 minutes. Stir in the garlic and ginger; cook another 1 minute. Add the shallots and bell pepper; cook another 1 minute.
2. Whisk together 3 tablespoons of the reserved liquid from the canned pineapple chunks along with the pineapple chunks, the water, soy sauce, cornstarch, vinegar, and pepper flakes; stir into the chicken and vegetable mixture and bring to a boil, stirring until the sauce thickens.

Crispy Kung Pao Chicken

"This is an easy recipe. The chicken is extra crispy with out being greasy and the sauce is excellent. Serve with hot cooked white rice."

***Servings**: 2 | **Prep**: 35m | **Cook**: 10m | **Ready In**: 45m*

Ingredients

- 1 quart vegetable oil for frying
- 1/2 pound chicken tenders, cut into bite-size pieces
- 1 egg, beaten
- 1 cup panko (Japanese bread crumbs)
- 1 tablespoon vegetable oil
- 2 cloves garlic, minced
- 1 tablespoon minced fresh ginger
- 3 tablespoons chopped green onion
- 2 teaspoons red pepper flakes
- 6 tablespoons soy sauce
- 6 tablespoons rice vinegar
- 2 tablespoons brown sugar
- 1 tablespoon cornstarch
- 2 tablespoons water
- 1/3 cup dry roasted peanuts

Directions

1. Heat 1 quart of vegetable oil in a deep-fryer or electric skillet to 375 degrees F (190 degrees C).
2. Toss chicken with beaten egg in a bowl until coated. Place the panko in a shallow dish, then drop the egg coated chicken pieces into the panko one at a time, and roll to coat; set aside.
3. Deep fry the chicken pieces in the hot oil until golden brown on all sides, 4 to 5 minutes. Remove the chicken to drain on a paper towel, and keep warm.
4. Heat 1 tablespoon of vegetable oil in a Wok over high heat. Stir in garlic, ginger, green onion, and red pepper flakes. Cook and stir until the garlic and ginger begin to turn golden brown, then pour in the soy sauce, rice vinegar, and brown sugar. Bring to a boil. Dissolve cornstarch in water, then stir into the boiling sauce to thicken. Cook and stir until the sauce clears, about 45 seconds.

5. Toss the fried chicken with the sauce and peanuts in the Wok to serve.

Editor's Note

- We have determined the nutritional value of oil for frying based on a retention value of 10% after cooking. The exact amount may vary depending on cook time and temperature, ingredient density, and the specific type of oil used.
- The nutrition data for this recipe includes information for the full amount of the breading ingredients. The actual amount consumed will vary.

Easy Breezy Chicken, Carrots and Long Green Beans Stir Fry

"Cooking times may vary depending on equipment used. If for some reason, your sauce seizes up and becomes lumpy, add an ounce of water and keep stirring."

Servings: 3 | **Time**: 30m

Ingredients

- 3 pieces chicken meat
- 1 tablespoon butter
- 1 white onion, chopped
- 1 slice orange bell pepper, chopped
- 2 chili peppers
- 2 carrots, sliced in vertical positions
- 1 pound long green beans
- 2 tablespoon soy sauce
- 1/2 cup water
- 3 cloves garlic, minced
- 1 teaspoon salt and pepper

Directions

1. Heat Wok or large frying pan on medium high heat (3-5 minutes) until a drop of water sizzles.
2. Add the 1 tablespoon of butter, swirl to coat pan, add garlic and onions, stir fry for 30 seconds. Mix 1 teaspoon of salt and pepper.
3. Add chicken and spread the pieces out, allow the meat to sear for 30 seconds and then stir fry until no longer pink on the outside (2-3 minutes).
4. Add carrots and green beans and stir fry for a minute.
5. Add soy sauce and water to the stir-fry (1-2 minutes), bubbly, and everything is heated through.
6. Transfer to a serving bowl and serve immediately.

Easy Chicken Veggie Stir Fry

"Veggie hating family devoured this! I used about a handful of green beans and handful of bean sprouts."

Servings: 4 | *Time*: 30m

Ingredients

- 1/4 green pepper
- 1 lb cubed chicken breast
- 1 can water chesnuts
- green beans
- 1 packages microwave steamed broccoli
- 2 green onions
- 1 packages asian rice dry mix
- 2 packages ramen noodles
- 2 tbsp vegetable oil
- soy sauce
- bean sprouts
- 1 cup water

Directions

1. Chop water chestnuts into med. chunks or slices. Put aside
2. Chop green pepper into small chunks. Put aside

3. Chop green beans into inch sections. Put aside.
4. Slice green onions.
5. Cook chicken in med. skillet.
6. Mash ramen in their packets then brown in large skillet with oil.
7. Add onions and peppers.
8. Add asian rice packet, water, and soy sauce. Cook out water.
9. Steam broccoli as directed on package.
10. Add water chestnuts and bean sprouts. Saute
11. Add broccoli and chicken
12. Add soy sauce to taste and enjoy!

Egyptian Mashi Cosa (Stuffed Squash) With Chicken Vegetable Stir Fry

"Changing up the rhythm in healthy eating, I turned my meal around to get my nutritional intake with some variety."

Servings: 4 | **Time**: 45m

Ingredients

Stir fry

- 1 cup Mushrooms diced
- 200 grams Diced chicken breast

Stuffed squash

- 8 small Italian zucchini (about 6 inches in length)
- 1 cup Short grain rice
- 20 grams Chopped fresh dill
- 2 clove of garlic minced
- 2 tbsp Tomato paste
- 20 grams Chopped fresh corriander
- 20 grams Chopped fresh parsley
- 2 bullion cubes (chicken or vegetable)
- 4 cup boiling water

Directions

1. Divide squash evenly in half trying to keep all a uniform size. Cut the tips off the end so they can stand.
2. Core the middle of the squash with a vegetable peeler, being careful to not go through the bottom or the sides.
3. Mix together in a bowl the rinced rice, herbs, tomato paste, garlic and salt.
4. Stuff each zucchini with the rice mixture generously
5. Waste not what not, set aside the cores of the zucchini for the stir fry.
6. Stand the stuffed zucchini in a medium size sauce pan evenly, making sure you get a good fit. If loose they will tip over.
7. Boil the water with bullion cubes, pour the broth over the stuffed zucchinis until just over the top. Any not covered well will cook just fine.
8. Bring pan to a boil and reduce heat to simmer about 20 minutes. Until broth is absorbed and rice cooked.
9. In a frying pan add the diced chicken, zucchini cores and mushrooms seasoning to taste. Stir fry until cooked about 10 minutes.

Emeril's Chicken Stir-Fry with Green Beans

***Servings**: 4 | **Prep**: 15m | **Inactive**: 10m | **Cook**: 8m | **Ready In**: 33m*

Ingredients

- 6 ounces boneless, skinless chicken breasts, very thinly sliced 1/8-inch thick
- 3 tablespoons soy sauce
- 3/4 teaspoon Asian spice blend
- 1/4 cup vegetable oil
- 1/2 pound green beans, stem ends trimmed, cut into 3-inch lengths
- 1 tablespoon minced garlic
- 1/4 cup roughly chopped cashews
- 2 tablespoons hoisin sauce
- 1 teaspoon sesame oil
- 1 tablespoon lightly toasted white sesame seeds
- 1 1/2 teaspoons roasted garlic-red pepper sauce (recommended: Sriracha)

- 1/4 teaspoon red pepper flakes
- Chopped green onions, for garnish

Directions

1. In a bowl, combine the chicken, 4 1/2 teaspoons of the soy sauce, and Asian spice blend. Toss to coat and let sit for 10 minutes.
2. In a large Wok or saute pan, heat the oil over high heat. Add the chicken and stirring constantly, cook until brown, 1 to 2 minutes. Add the beans and stir-fry until wrinkled, stirring, about 2 to 3 minutes. Add the garlic and cook, stirring, for 10 seconds. Add the cashews, hoisin, remaining 3 teaspoons of soy sauce, sesame oil, sesame seeds, red pepper sauce and red pepper flakes. Stir to coat, and cook for 1 minute. Remove from the heat and serve immediately, over white or basmati rice. Garnish with green onions.

Fiery Pepper Chicken

"This chicken dish is straight from the Szechuan province of China and it is hot! It is known in China as Chong Qing Lazi Ji. Unfortunately, substituting black peppercorns for Szechuan will not taste right."

Servings: 4 | **Prep**: 20m | **Cook**: 15m | **Ready In**: 35m

Ingredients

- 1 teaspoon Chinese cooking wine
- 1/2 teaspoon salt
- 1/2 pound boneless chicken, cut into 1/2 inch cubes
- 1/4 cup cornstarch, or as needed
- 3 cups peanut oil for frying
- 4 cloves garlic, minced
- 1 tablespoon minced fresh ginger root
- 2 green onions, julienned
- 2 long, green chilies - cut into 1/2-inch pieces
- 2 cups dried chilies, chopped
- 2 tablespoons Szechuan peppercorns

- 2 teaspoons soy sauce
- 2 teaspoons Chinese cooking wine
- 1/2 teaspoon white sugar
- 1/2 teaspoon salt

Directions

1. Stir together 1 teaspoon cooking wine and 1/2 teaspoon salt in a bowl; add the chicken and stir to coat. Allow to marinate 2 to 3 minutes. Place the marinated chicken in a large, sealable plastic bag with the cornstarch and shake to coat.
2. Heat the peanut oil in a Wok or large skillet over high heat. Fry the chicken in the oil until it begins to crisp around the edges, 7 to 10 minutes. Remove the chicken to a paper towel-lined plate to drain. Reserve 2 tablespoons of the oil, discarding the rest.
3. Reheat the reserved oil in the Wok over medium-high heat; cook and stir the garlic, ginger, and green onions in the oil until fragrant, about 1 minute. Add the green chilies, crushed dried chilies, and Szechuan peppercorns; continue frying about 20 seconds more. Return the chicken to the Wok; stir in the soy sauce, 2 teaspoons cooking wine, sugar, and 1/2 teaspoon salt until thoroughly combined. Remove from heat and serve immediately.

Ginger Chicken with Cashews

"Inspired by some other stir-fry experiments, this is an attempt to recreate a Chinese takeout favorite from a restaurant I no longer live close to. Other veggies can be added as you like."

Servings: 6 | **Prep**: 25m | **Cook**: 15m | **Ready In**: 40m

Ingredients

- 1/2 cups chicken broth
- 1/2 cup soy sauce
- 1 tablespoon cornstarch
- 3/4 teaspoon ground ginger
- 3/4 teaspoon brown sugar
- 1/4 cup cornstarch

- 1/2 teaspoons ground ginger
- 1/4 teaspoon curry powder
- 2 pounds skinless, boneless chicken breast meat - cut into cubes
- 3 tablespoons extra-virgin olive oil
- 1 tablespoon sesame oil
- 3 green onions, chopped
- 1 bell pepper, chopped
- 1 teaspoon sesame seeds
- 1/2 cup cashews

Directions

1. Whisk together the chicken broth, soy sauce, 1 tablespoon cornstarch, 3/4 teaspoon ground ginger, and brown sugar in a bowl.
2. Combine 1/4 cup cornstarch, 1 1/2 teaspoons ground ginger, and curry powder in a large, sealable plastic bag and shake to mix. Add the chicken to the bag and toss until well coated.
3. Heat the olive oil and sesame oil in a Wok or large skillet over high heat. Cook and stir the chicken in the hot oil until golden brown, 3 to 5 minutes. Add the green onions and bell pepper to the pan, cooking another 2 to 3 minutes. Stir the sauce mixture into the chicken and vegetable mixture; reduce heat to medium. Sprinkle sesame seeds over the dish and bring to a boil; allow to boil until the sauce thickens, 3 to 5 minutes. Remove from heat; add cashews and toss to serve.

Hainanese Chicken Rice

Servings: 4-6 | **Prep**: 10m | **Cook**: 2h | **Ready In**: 2h10m

Ingredients

Chile Sauce:

- 2 to 3 tablespoons freshly squeezed lemon juice
- 2 tablespoons chopped fresh red chiles
- 5 cloves garlic, chopped
- Salt

Chicken and Rice:

- 1 (2-pound) chicken
- 1 scallion, cut into 1-inch pieces
- 4 slices fresh, peeled ginger
- 6 tablespoon vegetable oil or olive oil
- 6 to 8 cloves garlic, finely chopped
- 4 cups long-grain uncooked rice
- 1 teaspoon fine salt

Directions

1. Make the Chile Sauce: Combine all the ingredients in a bowl, mix well, and season with salt, to taste. Set aside
2. Make the Chicken and Rice: Bring a large pot of salted water to a boil (enough water to immerse the chicken). Stuff the cavity of the chicken with the scallion and ginger. Add the chicken to the boiling water, breast side-down. Lower the heat to a simmer just under boiling point and cook, covered, until just cooked through, about 40 minutes.
3. Transfer the chicken to an ice water bath for about 5 to 6 minutes. (This is to arrest the cooking and will make the chicken skin crisp.) Drain. De-bone the chicken and cut into bite-sized pieces. Reserve the chicken stock, and keep hot.
4. Heat the oil in a Wok or saucepan over high heat. Add the garlic and stir-fry until fragrant. Add the rice and stir-fry for 1 to 2 minutes. Add enough of the hot reserved chicken soup to reach 1/2- inch above the top of the rice. Bring to the boil, add the salt, and lower the heat to low. When steam holes form in the rice, cover the Wok, and steam until cooked, about 30 minutes.
5. Whisk 1/4 cup of the hot chicken stock into the chile sauce.
6. Arrange the rice and poached chicken on a platter and drizzle with the chile sauce.

Herb Crusted Chicken over Vegetable Stir Fry

Ingredients

- 200 grams Chicken breast
- 5 Basil leaves, minced
- Fresh parsley, minced

- 1 cup cherry tomatoes
- 1 cup mushrooms, diced
- 200 grams long green beans
- 2 carrots, chopped

Directions

1. Cut fat off chicken breast and season with salt and pepper.
2. Heat a tbs of olive oil in a Wok and add the green beans and carrots. (They will need 30-45 mins to soften)
3. In the meantime mince the basil and parsley together. Cut the cherry timatoes in half.
4. Heat a skillet and add a tbs. of olive oil. Add the basil and parsley and cook for 2 minutes. Add the tomatoes. Cook for another 2 minutes. Add the chicken. Cover the skillet. Cook for 5-7 minutes on each side.
5. Add the mushrooms to the Wok while the chicken is cooking and season the vegetables in the Wok. I used chili flakes, salt and pepper.
6. When the mushrooma have softened and the chicken is cooked, serve.

Honey and Ginger Chicken

"This is a chicken stir-fry that has been adapted to the paleo diet, consisting of lean meat, fruit, and many vegetables."

***Servings**: 6 | **Prep**: 20m | **Cook**: 15m | **Ready In**: 35m*

Ingredients

- 2 tablespoons olive oil
- 2 large boneless, skinless chicken breasts, cubed
- 1/4 cup honey
- 2 tablespoons finely chopped ginger
- 2 red bell peppers, chopped
- 1 large onion, cut into 8 wedges
- 1 large head broccoli, cut into florets
- 1 cup peeled and cubed fresh pineapple

- 1/2 cup honey

Directions

1. Heat olive oil in a skillet or Wok over medium heat. Add chicken cubes, 1/4 cup honey, and ginger. Cook and stir until chicken is golden brown, about 10 minutes. Add bell peppers, onion, broccoli, pineapple, and remaining 1/2 cup honey. Cover and cook over medium-high heat until vegetables are tender, 5 to 10 minutes, stirring occasionally.

Tip

- Aluminum foil helps keep food moist, ensures it cooks evenly, keeps leftovers fresh, and makes clean-up easy.

Honey Cashew Chicken

Servings: 4 | Prep: 25m | Cook: 10m

Ingredients

- 1 tablespoon cornstarch
- 1 1/2 teaspoons honey
- 2 tablespoons soy sauce
- 6 tablespoons low-sodium chicken broth
- 2 tablespoons vegetable oil
- 1 medium onion, thinly sliced
- 3 cloves garlic, minced
- 1 tablespoon grated fresh ginger
- 1/2 teaspoon crushed red pepper
- 1 1/4 pounds boneless, skinless chicken breasts or thighs, cut into 3/4-inch dice
- 6 ounces snow peas, trimmed (about 2 cups)
- 1 large red bell pepper, seeded, cut into strips
- 1/2 cup unsalted cashews
- 2 teaspoons sesame oil, optional

Directions

1. In a small bowl, whisk 1 Tbsp. water with cornstarch until smooth. Whisk in honey, soy sauce and broth.
2. Warm oil in a large skillet over high heat. Add onion, garlic, ginger and crushed red pepper; cook for 30 seconds, stirring constantly.
3. Add chicken and stir-fry until opaque, 5 to 6 minutes. Add snow peas, bell pepper and cashews and continue stir-frying for 1 to 2 minutes. Stir reserved sauce and pour it into skillet. Cook for 1 to 2 minutes longer, stirring constantly, until sauce is bubbling and has thickened. Drizzle with sesame oil and serve over rice, if desired.

Honey Chicken Stir-fry

"Awesome dish- a bit fiddly and time consuming getting the chicken done right. But well worth it in the end. Great when you've got friends over- just up the ingredients for how many people are coming over. I promise they will be impressed!"

Servings: 4

Ingredients

- 500 grams Chicken thigh fillet, 2cm pieces
- 1 Egg white, lightly beaten
- 1 cup Flour
- 2 Brown onions, into wedges
- 1 Green capsicum, sliced
- 2 Carrots, into batons
- 100 g snow peas, trimmed
- 1/4 cup honey
- 1 tbsp Soy sauce
- 1 tsp Minced garlic
- 1/2 cup Macadamia, toasted
- 1 Vegetable oil to cook with

Directions

1. Toast macadamias in Wok until lightly browned and set aside.

2. Dip chicken pieces in egg white- then into flour to coat. Shake off excess.
3. Add 2 tablespoons oil in a hot Wok and stir fry chicken in batches until well browned and cooked through. Drain well in paper towel and set aside.
4. Add a little more oil to Wok and fry onion and garlic until onion is softening.
5. Now add carrot and capsicum and fry for 3 to 4 minutes, stirring constantly.
6. Add snow peas and soy. Cook (stirring) for further 2 minutes.
7. Now add your honey, toss until veggies are coated.
8. Add the chicken and toss to coat also.
9. Remove from heat, throw on your toasted macadamia, season and serve with boiled or fried rice. I usually put in the effort and whip up a cracking fried rice to go with this one.

Honey Teriyaki Chicken Stir Fry

Cook: 30m

Ingredients

- 4 tbsp sugar
- 3 tbsp honey
- 1 tbsp minced garlic
- 1/2 cup soy sauce
- 1/2 tsp sesame oil
- 2 tbsp sweet rice wine
- 1/3 cup water
- 1 pinch red pepper flakes
- 1/2 tbsp corn startch
- 1 tbsp water
- 1/2 tsp ginger
- 1 12oz bag fresh broccoli
- 1 bag bean sprouts
- 1 12oz. bag vegtable stir fry
- 1 lb boneless skineless chicken thighs
- 1/2 diced purple onion
- 1 tsp pepper
- 1 tsp salt

Directions

1. add all sauce ingredients to a small pot excluding (cornstarch & tbs water) bring to a simmer. taste for seasonings set aside
2. in a large Wok or skillet heat oil & add in diced onion on cook on med high heat about 2minutes. add in chicken salt, & pepper cook about 6minutes remove from pan & set aside. now add in veggies cook down about 7-8 minutes just till tender, add chicken back in and add sauce. cook another 5 minutes or so. make your corn starch slurry with water stir well add to mix stir cook till thickened about 2 minutes. enjoy!

Honey-Garlic Chicken & Sweet Pepper Stir-fry

"I'm a huge oriental food lover and was needing to figure out how to make my favorite stir-fry dish at home. I stumbled across this recipe and was blown away how easy it really is to make! My boyfriend and I have had this dish a zillion times and it never gets old."

Servings: 4 | **Cook**: 25m

Ingredients

Required

- 1 cup milk
- 3 tbsp cornstarch
- 1/3 cup reduced-sodium soy sauce
- 2 tbsp liquid honey
- 1 lb skinless chicken breast, cut into strips
- 3 clove garlic, minced
- 1/2 each sweet red, yellow, green & yellow pepper, cut into strips
- 2 tbsp butter or margarine, divided

Optional

- 2 tbsp rice vinegar (to flavor rice)

Directions

1. In a bowl, whisk a little milk into cornstarch to make a smooth paste. Whisk remaining milk, soy sauce & honey; set aside.
2. Heat Wok or large skillet over high heat. Add half of butter or margarine & swirl to coat. Add chicken & butter & stir-fry for 3 mins or until browned; transfer to a bowl
3. Add remaining butter or marj to pan then add sweet peppers. Stir-fry for 5 mins or until tender. Return chicken & juices to pan; reduce heat to medium.
4. Whisk milk mixture then pour into pan. Cook, stirring, for 5 mins or until chicken is no longer pink inside & sauce is thickened.
5. Optional: After rice is finished, evenly pour vinegar and fold into rice.

Hot & Sour Chicken & Pepper Stir-fry

"Tasty as hell :)"

Servings: 2 | **Cook**: 35m

Ingredients

- 100 grams Thai Jasmine Rice
- 1 tbsp Sesame Seeds
- 1 tsp Sunflower Oil
- 1 medium Yellow Pepper
- 1 medium Red Pepper
- 2 tsp Cornflour
- 2 tsp Soy Sauce
- 1 medium Lime
- 2 tbsp Clear Honey
- 1/2 medium Red Chili
- 4 medium Chicken Fillets

Directions

1. Place the rice in a saucepan with 300ml boiling water.
2. Bring to the boil, stir once, cover with a lid and reduce the heat to low.

3. Cook for 15 minutes, by which time the rice should have absorbed all the liquid and be perfectly cooked.
4. Dry fry the sesame seeds until toasted golden and set aside.
5. Squeeze as much juice from the lime as possible and set aside.
6. Slice and deseed the chilli and cut into small pieces.
7. Mix the cornflour and soy sauce together in a bowl, then add the honey, lime juice, chilli and sesame seeds plus 6 tablespoons of cold water.
8. Cut the chicken fillets in to chunks.
9. Cut up and deseed the yellow and red pepper.
10. Heat the oil in a frying pan, add the chicken chunks and peppers and stir-fry until the chicken is lightly browned and cooked through.
11. Add the sauce mixture to the frying pan.
12. Cook until the sauce has slightly thickened, making sure the chicken and peppers are well coated.
13. Serve with the rice.

Jerk Chicken Stir Fry

"This is just one way I enjoy my veggies. It's my version of stir fry without the sauce that's usually in it. It's healthier for me this way too :)"

Servings: *2* | **Time:** *25m*

Ingredients

- 6 oz Chicken breast, cubed
- 1 large Carrot
- 1 each Green and red bell pepper
- 1 stick Celery
- 1 tsp Jerk seasoning (or to personal taste)
- 2 tbsp Olive oil
- 1 Salt and pepper

Directions

1. Combine chicken with jerk seasoning and salt to taste. Cover and let marinate for 15 minutes.

2. Wash and slice vegetables. Any combination of vegetables work well. You just have to know how fast each cooks.
3. Heat oil in a nonstick skillet on medium heat. Add chicken and cook until center is no longer pink.
4. Add carrots and celery to the pan and cook for another 2 minutes. Then add the peppers and let cook for another 2 mins.
5. Season with more salt if needed and pepper to taste. Turn off heat and enjoy! Please note that cook times may vary for different vegetables. The result you want to get should be crisp tender vegetables and moist juicy chicken.

Joe's Fusion Chicken Pad Thai

"My girlfriend and I were craving pad Thai! So we looked at a few recipes and made our version. It is not exactly traditional pad Thai, so -- lo and behold -- the name!"

*Servings: 5 | **Prep**: 20m | **Cook**: 30m | **Ready In**: 50m*

Ingredients

- 1 pound boneless, skinless chicken breast halves, cut into bite-size pieces
- salt and ground black pepper to taste
- 3/4 cup white sugar
- 1 teaspoon ground cayenne pepper
- 3 tablespoons white wine vinegar
- 6 tablespoons fish sauce
- 1 tablespoon creamy peanut butter
- 1 tablespoon olive oil
- 5 cloves garlic, minced
- 4 large eggs, lightly beaten
- 1 (16 ounce) package pad Thai rice noodles
- 1/2 cup fresh bean sprouts
- 2 cups beef broth
- 1/2 cup chopped green onion

Directions

1. Bring a large pot of water to a boil.
2. Season chicken with salt and black pepper; set aside.
3. Whisk sugar, cayenne pepper, white wine vinegar, fish sauce, and peanut butter together in a bowl.
4. Coat the inside of a large skillet or Wok with olive oil and place over high heat.
5. Cook and stir chicken in the hot oil just until the meat is white outside but still pink inside, about 3 minutes.
6. Remove chicken and set aside in a bowl.
7. Lower the heat under the skillet to medium-low. Cook and stir garlic in the skillet until it becomes translucent, 1 to 2 minutes.
8. Cook and stir eggs into garlic until loosely cooked, 2 to 3 minutes.
9. Pour peanut sauce into the garlic and eggs, and stir to combine. Bring sauce to a simmer.
10. Stir rice noodles into the boiling water. Cook until noodles are still slightly tough, about 5 minutes.
11. Drain the noodles.
12. Return chicken to the skillet with eggs and sauce. Simmer until chicken is no longer pink in the center and the juices run clear, stirring frequently, 5 to 8 more minutes.
13. Stir bean sprouts, rice noodles. and beef broth into the skillet. Bring to a simmer, and cook until noodles are tender and most of the broth has been absorbed, about 10 minutes.
14. Sprinkle with green onions to serve..

Kickin' Chicken Stir Fry

"A great, easy stir fry with a good, spicy kick. This is a great way to stretch your protein while enjoying an awesome meal for two!"

Servings: 4 | **Prep**: 15m | **Cook**: 30m | **Ready In**: 45m

Ingredients

- 4 cups water
- 1/4 teaspoon salt
- 2 tablespoons butter
- 3 dried red chiles, broken into several pieces
- 2 cups uncooked white rice

- 1 tablespoon sesame oil
- 2 garlic cloves, minced
- 2 tablespoons soy sauce, divided
- 1 skinless, boneless chicken breast half, diced
- 1 teaspoon dried basil
- 1 teaspoon ground white pepper
- 1/2 teaspoon dry ground mustard
- 1 pinch ground tumeric
- 1 tablespoon butter
- 1/2 cups broccoli florets
- 1 cup diced green bell pepper
- 1 cup diced red bell pepper
- 1/2 cup diced onion
- 1 teaspoon lemon juice

Directions

1. Combine water, salt, 2 tablespoons butter, and red chili peppers in a pot over medium-high heat. Bring to a boil.
2. Stir in rice, cover, and lower heat to medium. Cook until rice is tender, 15 to 20 minutes, stirring occasionally.
3. Heat sesame oil in a skillet or Wok over medium heat. Cook and stir garlic until fragrant, about 1 minute; pour in half the soy sauce.
4. Cook and stir chicken, basil, white pepper, dry mustard, and turmeric with garlic until chicken is browned, no longer pink in the center, and juices run clear, 5 to 8 minutes.
5. Mix remaining soy sauce into chicken mixture.
6. Cook and stir 1 tablespoon butter with broccoli, green pepper, red pepper, and onion in a separate skillet until tender, about 10 minutes. Stir lemon juice into vegetables.
7. Toss vegetables with chicken.

Kung Po Chicken

*Servings: 2-4 | **Prep**: 10m | **Cook**: 10m | **Ready In**: 20m*

Ingredients

Sauce:

- 7 tablespoons cold vegetable stock
- 1 tablespoon cornstarch
- 1 tablespoon hoisin sauce
- 1 tablespoon ketchup
- 1 tablespoon light soy sauce
- 1 tablespoon Chinkiang black rice vinegar or balsamic vinegar
- 1 teaspoon chili sauce

Chicken:

- 2 skinless chicken breasts or 4 thighs, cut into 1/2-inch slices
- Salt and ground white pepper
- 1 tablespoon potato flour or cornstarch
- 1 tablespoon peanut oil
- 2 tablespoons Sichuan peppercorns
- 4 dried red chiles
- 1 tablespoon Shaohsing rice wine or dry sherry
- 1 red bell pepper, seeded and cut into chunks
- 2 scallions, chopped into 1-inch lengths
- Handful of dry-roasted cashews

Directions

1. For the sauce: Add the vegetable stock, cornstarch, hoisin sauce, ketchup, soy sauce, vinegar and chili sauce to a medium bowl and stir to combine.
2. For the chicken: Place the chicken in a bowl and sprinkle with salt and pepper. Add the potato flour or cornstarch and mix well to coat the chicken pieces.
3. Heat a Wok over high heat until it starts to smoke and then add the peanut oil. Add the Sichuan peppercorns and dried chiles and fry for a few seconds, then add the chicken pieces and stir-fry for 2 minutes. As the chicken begins to turn opaque, add the rice wine or dry sherry. Cook for an additional 2 minutes, then pour in the sauce.
4. Bring the mixture to a boil, add the red pepper and cook until the meat is cooked through and the sauce has thickened and become slightly sticky in consistency, another 2 minutes. Add the scallions and cook for 1 minute. Toss in the cashews, then transfer to a serving plate and serve immediately.

Leftover chicken stir fry

"I had leftover chicken...and I had so many sweet and sour packets"

Servings: 1 | **Time**: 20m

Ingredients

- 3 slice red pepper chopped
- 1 chicken breasts cooked
- cup broccoli chopped
- 1/4 cup onion, chopped
- soy sauce
- 1/2 cup sweet and sour sauce
- 1/2 cup angel hair pasta
- 3 tbsp vegetable oil

Directions

1. Medium skillet add vegatable oil broccoli, onions, and peppers.
2. Cook until broccoli is tender and onions are translucent. While that is cooking boil water for the angel hair pasta
3. Add soy sauce and chicken to the pan and let that simmer for a little bit while noodles are cooking
4. Before the angel hair pasta is all the way cooked drain the pasta than add to the skillet also add soy sauce
5. Let that also simmer for five minutes on medium. Than your done

Lemon Chicken

Servings: 4 | **Prep**: 10m | **Cook**: 15m | **Ready In**: 25m

Ingredients

- 1/2 pounds chicken breast or chicken tenders, cut into chunks
- 1/4 cup all-purpose unbleached flour

- Coarse salt
- 2 tablespoons Wok or vegetable oil, 2 turns of the pan (preferred brand: House of Tsang)
- 1 tablespoon (a splash) white or rice wine vinegar
- 1/2 cup chicken broth or stock
- 8 ounces (1 cup) prepared lemon curd
- 1/4 cup hot water
- 1 lemon, zested
- 2 scallions, thinly sliced or 20 blades fresh chives, finely chopped

Directions

1. Coat the chunked chicken lightly in flour, seasoned with a little salt. Heat a large skillet or a Wok-shaped nonstick pan over high heat. Stir fry chicken until golden, 3 or 4 minutes. Remove chicken from the pan and return pan to heat. Reduce heat to medium.
2. Add a splash of vinegar to the pan and let it evaporate. Add stock or broth to the pan and scrape up any drippings with a whisk. Thin curd by stirring in a little hot water. Add curd to broth and whisk to combine. Add chicken back to the pan and simmer for 1 to 2 minutes to thicken sauce and finish cooking chicken pieces through. Remove the pan from heat, add the scallions or chives and zest, and toss chicken pieces well to combine zest and scallions or chives evenly throughout the sauce. Serve with Special Rice, recipe follows.

Cook's Notes

- Wok oil infused with ginger and garlic is usually available on the International Foods aisle in many markets.
- Chicken broths and stocks are available in resealable paper containers, making storage of remaining product easy and on hand in the refrigerator; they are found in the soup aisle.
- Lemon curd is a sweet lemon spread available in most markets. It is on the jam/jelly aisle.

Mango Chicken over Rice

"This recipe, from Sunset reader Barbara Triplett of Neskowin, Oregon, is *especially good in summer, when Western mangoes are in season."*

Servings: 4 | **Total time**: 25m

Ingredients

- 1 tablespoon olive oil
- 1 pound boned, skinned chicken thighs, halved
- 1/4 teaspoon turmeric
- 1/4 teaspoon cayenne
- 1/4 teaspoon white pepper
- 1 large ripe mango, cut into 1-in. chunks
- 3 tablespoons lime juice
- 3 tablespoons Thai or Vietnamese fish sauce
- 4 green onions, sliced diagonally
- Steamed rice
- 2 tablespoons thinly sliced fresh basil leaves

Directions

1. Heat a Wok or large frying pan over high heat. Add oil and swirl to coat pan. Cook chicken with spices until browned, about 5 minutes. Add mango, lime juice, fish sauce, and half the onions and cook, stirring often, until mango starts to soften and release juices, about 3 minutes.
2. Serve over rice with remaining onions and basil sprinkled on top.

Minute Rice's Chicken Stir Fry

"I found this recipe on the back of a box of Minute Rice. It makes a large amount of food that stretches.

The pictured batch is made with venison (deer meat) and everyday run of the mill frozen mixed vegetables. I also used instant brown rice instead of white. This recipe is very versatile."

Servings: 4 | **Time**: 20m

Ingredients

- 1 lb Boneless, Skinless Chicken Pieces
- 1 tsp Garlic, minced
- 1 tbsp Cooking Oil
- 1/4 cup Water
- 1/4 cup Soy Sauce
- 1 tbsp Sugar
- 16 oz Package frozen stir fry vegetables
- 2 cup Uncooked White Rice

Directions

1. Cook and stir chicken and garlic in hot oil in large skillet on medium heat for 5 minutes. Cook till chicken is well done.
2. Add water, soy sauce, sugar, and vegetables then stir. Bring to a boil.
3. Stir in rice and cover. Remove from heat and let stand for 5 mins.

Mu Shu Chicken

Servings: 4-6 | ***Prep***: 1h40m | ***Inactive***: 20m | ***Cook***: 20m | ***Ready In***: 2h20m

Ingredients

- 1/3 cup hoisin sauce, plus more for serving
- 3 tablespoons low-sodium soy sauce
- 2 tablespoons mirin
- 1/2 tablespoons sesame oil
- 3 tablespoons peeled and minced fresh ginger
- 1 tablespoon minced garlic
- Kosher salt and freshly ground black pepper
- 1 pound boneless, skinless chicken thighs, sliced
- 3 tablespoons canola oil
- 1 red pepper, seeded, membrane removed, julienned
- 1/2 yellow onion, thinly sliced
- 1/2 medium head green cabbage, finely shredded
- 1/2 large head Napa cabbage, finely shredded
- 1/2 medium head purple cabbage, finely shredded

- 1/2 cup julienned carrots
- 1 cup sliced button mushrooms
- 1/4 cup shaved bamboo shoots, drained
- 1/4 cup sliced water chestnuts, drained
- 4 eggs, beaten
- 2 recipes Chinese Crepes with Scallions, recipe follows
- 3 tablespoons toasted black sesame seeds
- 1 small bunch scallions, finely shaved
- Fresh cilantro leaves, for serving, optional
- Sriracha, for serving, optional

Chinese Crepes with Scallions:

- 3/4 cup all-purpose flour
- 1/4 cup rice flour
- 1/2 teaspoon salt
- 1/8 teaspoon toasted sesame oil
- 2 eggs
- 2 scallions, finely sliced
- Nonstick cooking spray

Directions

1. Whisk the hoisin, soy, mirin, sesame oil, garlic and ginger in a mixing bowl. Season with salt and pepper. Add the sliced chicken and toss to coat evenly. Marinate the chicken, covered, at room temperature for 20 to 30 minutes.
2. Once 5 minutes of marinating time remains, heat a large Wok or skillet over high heat and add 2 tablespoons of the canola oil to heat. Using a slotted spoon, strain the chicken add to the very hot Wok or skillet. Cook, allowing it to brown, stirring occasionally, about 2 minutes. Add the red bell pepper and the onion slices, allowing them to soften, another minute. Next, add the cabbages and carrots and cook, stirring occasionally, until just browning, about 2 minutes. Push the chicken and vegetables to the side of the Wok and stir in the mushrooms, bamboo shoots and water chestnuts. Remove from the heat and set aside, keeping warm.
3. Place a nonstick skillet over medium heat and add the remaining 1 tablespoon canola oil. Add the beaten eggs to the skillet, allowing to scramble, 2 to 3 minutes. Once cooked, break up the eggs with a rubber spatula and add to the chicken. Toss to combine.
4. Spread about 1 tablespoon hoisin sauce on each Chinese Crepes with Scallions. Top with some mu shu chicken, sesame seeds and

scallions. Add cilantro leaves if desired. Roll up like a crepe and serve with Sriracha if desired.

Chinese Crepes with Scallions:

1. In a medium glass mixing bowl, whisk the flours, salt, 1 cup water, the sesame oil and eggs; the batter should be smooth and free of lumps.
2. Heat a crepe pan or 8-inch nonstick skillet over medium heat. Very lightly coat the skillet with nonstick cooking spray. Ladle in 1/4 cup of the batter. Gently rotate the skillet for a few seconds, swirling the batter to create a thin, even layer over the bottom. Add 1 to 2 tablespoons scallions to each pancake at this point. Cook the pancake until the underside is pale and just firmed up, about 1 minute.
3. Flip the pancake over and cook for another 30 seconds. Remove from the skillet and transfer to a plate and cover with a kitchen towel. Continue with the rest of the batter until all the pancakes have been made. Keep warm until ready to serve.

My Chinese Chicken Stir Fry With Mix Veg

"Too yummy!!!!"

Servings: 6 | **Time**: 20m

Ingredients

- 2 tbsp veg oil
- 1/2 tbsp Ginger shredded
- 4 cloves Garlic Crushed
- 4 Chicken Breasts cut cubed 1 inch
- 1/2 Onion chopped length wise
- 2 Carrots cut into strips
- 10 long beans left length wise
- 1/2 tsp Course salt
- 1/2 tsp White Pepper
- 3 sweet coloured sweet peppers chopped length wise
- 1 large Spring onion chopped length wise
- 1 bunch Bok Choy cut length wise

Sauce:

- 3 tbsp Oyster sauce
- 1 tbsp Soy Sauce
- 1 1/4 cup Chicken Stock
- 1 pinch salt
- 1 tsp Brown Sugar
- 1 tsp Rice wine vinegar
- 2 tsp Corn Starch or Corn Flour

Directions

1. Have all your veg prepared, and chicken .
2. Grate the ginger and crush the garlic.
3. Mix all the sauce ingredients in a bowl and mix, but leave out the corn starch at this stage. Set aside
4. In a deep Wok, or large deep fry pan, heat up the oil until hot. Add the ginger then garlic fry for about 6 seconds.
5. Then add the chicken and fry and keep turning and mixing, until the chicken turns white all over, about 5--6 minutes.
6. Add the onion, carrots, salt, pepper and green beans and fry for about 5 minutes stirring all the time.
7. Add the spring onion and sweet peppers, fry for 1 minute
8. Add the sauce, bring to boil, stirring all the time, then lower hear and simmer for 5 minutes. Add the cornstarch to a little water and add to the mixture. It should go thicker.
9. Add the bok choy, stir and serve with fried rice, steameed rice or noodles.

Myra's Basil Chicken Stir Fry

"This is easy and my kids love it. I've also made it with cubed pork from cheap pork chops. You can spice this dish up with crushed red pepper flakes. Serve over rice. Don't substitute dried basil, though! It has to be fresh! And though it sounds like a lot of basil, that makes the dish."

Servings: 6 | Prep: 10m | Cook: 15m | Ready In: 55m

Ingredients

- 1 tablespoon soy sauce
- 2 tablespoons water
- 1 tablespoon white sugar
- pounds skinless, boneless chicken breast halves, cut into small pieces
- 1 tablespoon vegetable oil
- 5 green onions, sliced
- 3 cloves garlic, chopped
- 3 tablespoons vegetable oil
- 2 (6 ounce) bags fresh baby spinach leaves
- 1 cup thinly sliced fresh basil

Directions

1. Combine soy sauce, water, and sugar in a bowl.
2. Marinate chicken in soy sauce mixture for 30 minutes.
3. Heat 1 tablespoon oil in a large skillet or Wok over medium heat.
4. Cook and stir green onions in oil for 1 minute. Add garlic and cook and stir for 1 minute. Transfer to a small bowl.
5. Pour 3 tablespoons oil into the skillet. Cook and stir chicken and marinade until chicken is no longer pink in the center and juices run clear, about 5 minutes.
6. Add spinach leaves to chicken. Cover for 4 minutes stirring occasionally.
7. Stir green onion mixture into chicken and spinach; cook to reheat onions, 1 to 2 minutes.
8. Stir in basil and cook until heated, 1 to 2 minutes. Serve!

Tip

- Aluminum foil helps keep food moist, ensures it cooks evenly, keeps leftovers fresh, and makes clean-up easy.

Panang Curry with Chicken

"Panang curry with chicken represents the diversity of Thailand's southern region. Panang refers to the island of Penang in Northern Malaysia bordering southern Thailand. Use 4 tablespoons curry paste from a fresh curry paste

recipe or 5 tablespoons pre-made curry paste if time does not permit making your own paste"

Servings: 4 | **Prep**: 15m | **Cook**: 20m | **Ready In**: 35m

Ingredients

- 5 tablespoons Panang curry paste
- cooking oil
- 4 cups coconut milk
- 2/3 pound skinless, boneless chicken breast, cubed
- 2 tablespoons palm sugar
- 2 tablespoons fish sauce, or to taste
- 6 kaffir lime leaves, torn
- 2 fresh red chile peppers, sliced
- 1/4 cup fresh Thai basil leaves

Directions

1. Fry the curry paste in the oil in a large skillet or Wok over medium heat until fragrant. Stir the coconut milk into the curry paste and bring to a boil. Add the chicken; cook and stir until the chicken is nearly cooked through, 10 to 15 minutes. Stir the palm sugar, fish sauce, and lime leaves into the mixture; simmer together for 5 minutes. Taste and adjust the saltiness by adding more fish sauce if necessary. Garnish with sliced red chile peppers and Thai basil leaves to serve.

Tip

- Aluminum foil helps keep food moist, ensures it cooks evenly, keeps leftovers fresh, and makes clean-up easy.

Pat's Broccoli and Chicken Stir-Fry

Servings: 4 | **Prep**: 10m | **Cook**: 10m | **Ready In**: 20m

Ingredients

- 2 tablespoons soy sauce
- 1 tablespoon orange juice
- 1 tablespoon light brown sugar
- 1 tablespoon rice wine vinegar
- 1/2 tablespoon cornstarch
- 1/2 tablespoon sesame oil
- 1/2 to 1 teaspoon red pepper flakes, or more if desired
- 1 tablespoon peanut oil, plus more as needed
- 1 pound boneless, skinless chicken thighs, cut into 1/2-inch pieces
- 2 tablespoons peeled and chopped fresh ginger
- 4 cloves garlic, minced
- 4 green onions, sliced
- 4 cups broccoli florets, pre-cooked
- Hot cooked rice, for serving

Directions

1. In a small bowl, whisk together the soy sauce, orange juice, light brown sugar, rice wine vinegar, cornstarch, sesame oil and red pepper flakes. Reserve.
2. Set a Wok over medium-high heat and coat with 1 tablespoon of the peanut oil. When the oil shimmers, add about half of the chicken thigh pieces. Stir-fry until the chicken is fully cooked through, 3 to 4 minutes. Transfer to a plate and repeat the process with the remaining chicken thighs.
3. Add enough peanut oil to the hot Wok to coat the bottom. Add the ginger, garlic and green onions and stir-fry until fragrant, about 1 minute. Add the chicken back to the Wok along with the broccoli florets and stir to warm through. Pour in the reserved sauce and stir until the sauce is thickened and bubbly, about 45 seconds. Transfer to a serving bowl and serve with rice.
4. From Food Network Kitchens; after further testing and to ensure the best results this recipe has been altered from what was in the actual episode.

Pineapple chicken stir fry kinda

"I had pineapple I had chicken I had stir fried vegetables so I found oh wait to cook it without actually stir frying it and that makes a chicken just fall apart *in your mouth"*

***Servings**: 4 | **Cook**: 5m*

Ingredients

- 4 each Chicken breast
- 1 can Pineapple
- 1 dash Soy sauce
- 1 dash Ground ginger
- 1/2 cup Brown sugar
- 1 cup White rice
- 1 can Stir fry vegetables
- 1 dash Sesame seed oil

Directions

1. Put chicken pineapple soy sauce brown sugar ginger in a slow cooker and cook for 6 hours on low
2. Cook your rice and stir fried vegetables with the sesame seed oil

Pineapple Chicken Stir Fry

***Servings**: 4 | **Time**: 40m*

Ingredients

- 1/4 pounds chicken breasts cut into strips
- 1/2 teaspoon salt
- 2 tablespoons vegetable oil
- 1 large red bell pepper cut into 1 inch pieces
- 6 green onions cut into 1 inch pieces
- 1 tablespoon minced fresh ginger root
- 1 cup Pace Citrus Pineapple Salsa

Directions

1. Season the chicken with the salt.
2. Heat 1 tablespoon oil in a 12 inch skillet over medium high heat. Add the pepper and green onions and stir fry for 3 minutes or until tender crisp. Add the ginger and stir fry for 30 seconds. Remove the vegetables from the skillet.
3. Heat the remaining oil in the skillet. Add the chicken and stir fry for 7 minutes or until cooked through. Return the vegetables to the skillet. Stir in the salsa and cook until the mixture is hot and bubbling.

Salt-Baked Chicken

"Traditionally, this recipe uses a whole chicken, marinated, wrapped in lotus leaves, immersed in a bed of hot rock salt in a Wok, and cooked on a stovetop. The modern convenience of an oven makes it much easier to control the cooking temperature. Allowing the chicken to stand at room temperature for an hour before cooking creates succulent results. The golden color of the roasted bird also represents wealth, and serving a whole chicken is thought to ensure good luck for the coming year. Garlic chives make a memorable garnish."

Servings: 8

Ingredients

- 2 1/2 cups boiling water
- 1 (1 x 2–inch) strip dried tangerine peel
- 1 (4.5- to 5-pound) roasting chicken
- 5 1/2 teaspoons coarse sea salt, divided
- 1/4 cup finely chopped shallots
- 2 tablespoons minced ginger
- 2 tablespoons Shaoxing (Chinese rice wine) or dry sherry
- 1 tablespoon low-sodium soy sauce
- 1 1/2 teaspoons sesame oil
- 1 teaspoon honey
- 2 green onions, cut into 1-inch pieces
- Cooking spray

Directions

1. Combine 2 1/2 cups boiling water and tangerine peel in a bowl; cover and let stand 30 minutes. Drain in a colander over a bowl, reserving liquid.
2. Remove and discard giblets and neck from chicken. Trim excess fat. Starting at neck cavity, loosen skin from breast and drumsticks by inserting fingers, gently pushing between skin and meat. Rub 1 tablespoon salt under skin; let stand 5 minutes. Rinse chicken under cold water; pat dry with paper towels. Place chicken on the rack of a roasting pan; let stand 1 hour at room temperature.
3. Preheat oven to 425°.
4. Transfer chicken to a work surface. Combine remaining 2 1/2 teaspoons salt, shallots, ginger, wine, soy sauce, oil, and honey in a small bowl. Rub 3 tablespoons shallot mixture inside cavity of chicken. Place onions and tangerine peel inside cavity. Rub remaining shallot mixture under loosened skin.
5. Place chicken, breast side up, on the rack of a roasting pan coated with cooking spray. Pour reserved tangerine soaking liquid into a shallow roasting pan; place rack in pan. Bake at 425° for 1 hour or until a meat thermometer registers 165° and skin has turned a dark golden brown color. Let stand 15 minutes. Discard skin, and slice.

Savory Chicken Veggies Stir Fry

"Actually this dish was out of my first plan and accidentally created. I added too much water from the first recipe, so I change the recipe to plan B ⍰ and tried to save it with another way. I boiled the rest of the veggies and add the egg for extra flavor. Voila!! Out of my desperate expectation, it turned out better! No, no, no... So good..!!!

(I was out of leek or chives, it would be nice if it was there)"

Ready In: 30m

Ingredients

- 1 onion, julienne cut
- 1 carrot, julienne cut
- few cuts of broccoli

- 1/2 Chicken breast, cube cut
- 2 cloves garlic
- 1 whole egg
- 1 tbs fish sauce
- 1 tbs oyster sauce
- 1 tbs honey
- 1 cup water
- Salt and pepper
- 1 stalk leek or chives

Directions

1. Cut and clean all of your veggies and your chicken.
2. Marinate your chicken using 1 tbs of fish sauce, 1 clove of minced garlic, a pinch of salt and pepper. Let it sit about 15-30 minutes. The longer the best.
3. Stir fry your chicken until become all white, and add a cup of water, season with oyster sauce and honey, check and fix the taste. If you like a deep flavor you could add a lil bit of grated ginger.
4. Add your onion, another clove of minced garlic, carrot, and broccoli.
5. Stir them until all combined. Boil them and close your pan with its lid, about 5 minutes or until the veggies become a bit soften.
6. Open the lid, cracks the egg over it and stir it quick, start from the yolk twisting to the outside, it helps to thick the soup and create soft lumps. The heat should be medium low.
7. Add chopped leek or chives, stir a bit, turn off the heat, and ready to be serve.

Shoyu Chicken Stir-Fry

"Did a Shoyu Chicken a couple of weeks ago and it was great so I've used the same marinate for this one. Definitely a keeper."

***Servings**: 4 | **Time**: 25m*

Ingredients

- 500 grams Chicken thigh fillets, sliced into strips

- 1 Shoyu marinade (see related recipe)
- 250 grams Udon noodles
- 1 bunch Baby bok choy, roughly chopped
- 400 grams Can baby corn spears, washed & sliced in half lengthways
- 1 Red capsicum (pepper), sliced
- 1 medium onion, into wedges
- 2 stick Green onion, sliced
- 1 Sesame oil for frying

Directions

1. Marinate chicken for at least an hour. Shoyu marinade recipe attached.
2. Heat oil in Wok on full blast. Fry onion until browned and set aside.
3. Stir fry chicken in batches and set aside with onion.
4. Clean Wok, then fry your veges for a few minutes until veges start to soften.
5. Add marinate liquid and and udon noodles. Cook through for 3 or 4 minutes. Don't forget you had raw chicken in marinate so cook through well.
6. Return chicken and onion to hear through and serve.

Sichuan-Style Stir-Fried Chicken With Peanuts

"Also known as kung pao chicken, this 5-Star Sichuan classic boasts multidimensional hot-sweet and salty-sour flavors. As one user review put it, "It is, hands-down, the best stir-fry chicken recipe I've ever tried." Serve this soon-to-be favorite with rice and a steamed vegetable."

Servings: 6

Ingredients

Marinade:

- 2 tablespoons low-sodium soy sauce
- 2 tablespoons rice wine or sake
- 1 teaspoon cornstarch

- 1 teaspoon dark sesame oil
- 1 1/2 pounds skinless, boneless chicken breasts, cut into bite-size pieces

Stir-Frying Oil:

- 2 tablespoons vegetable oil, divided

Sauce:

- 1/2 cup fat-free, less-sodium chicken broth
- 2 tablespoons sugar
- 2 1/2 tablespoons low-sodium soy sauce
- 2 tablespoons rice wine or sake
- 1 tablespoon Chinese black vinegar or Worcestershire sauce
- 1 1/4 teaspoons cornstarch
- 1 teaspoon dark sesame oil
- 2 tablespoons minced green onions
- 1 1/2 tablespoons minced peeled fresh ginger
- 1 1/2 tablespoons minced garlic (about 7 cloves)
- 1 teaspoon chile paste with garlic

Remaining Ingredients:

- 1 1/2 cups drained, sliced water chestnuts
- 1 cup (1/2-inch) sliced green onion tops
- 3/4 cup unsalted, dry-roasted peanuts
- 6 cups hot cooked long-grain rice

Directions

1. To prepare marinade, combine first 5 ingredients in a medium bowl; cover and chill 20 minutes.
2. Heat 1 tablespoon of the vegetable oil in a Wok or large nonstick skillet over medium-high heat. Add the chicken mixture; stir-fry 4 minutes or until chicken is done. Remove from pan; set aside.
3. To prepare sauce, combine broth and next 6 ingredients (broth through 1 teaspoon sesame oil); stir well with a whisk. Heat 1 tablespoon vegetable oil in pan. Add 2 tablespoons green onions, ginger, garlic, and chile paste, and stir-fry for 15 seconds. Add broth mixture, and cook 1 minute or until thick, stirring constantly.
4. Stir in cooked chicken, water chestnuts, sliced onion tops, and peanuts; cook for 1 minute or until thoroughly heated. Serve over rice.

Slutty Chicken Stir-Fry

"This is called slutty stir-fry because it's so EASY! Hey-ooooh! This recipe is a good way to use up some ingredients left over after making something else. For example, I made this with mostly leftover gumbo stuff, Spices that sit around in the cabinet and condiments that sit around in the fridge. As always, you can use many variations of ingredients for this and make it your own. When using spices, avoid using any kind of salts. Soy sauce is super salty by itself. Extra salt added is unnecessary and will be a bit too much."

Servings: 2 | ***Time***: 30m

Ingredients

- 2 boneless skinless chicken breasts
- 1/2 green pepper, diced large
- 3/4 cup onion, diced large
- 3 cloves garlic, minced
- 3/4 cup olive oil
- 4 Tbsp Soy sauce
- 3 Tbsp Worcestershire sauce
- 3 shakes Balsamic vinegar
- Ground ginger
- Ground mustard
- Garlic powder
- Red pepper flakes
- Black pepper
- White rice

Directions

1. Slice raw chicken, against the grain, in about 1/4 inch strips. Then cut the strips into about 2 inch pieces. In a preheated skillet with about 1/2 cup olive oil, add the chicken pieces, a few sprinkles of black pepper and some garlic powder. Cook until just about white.
2. Now add the green pepper, onion and garlic. Stir constantly till the onion pieces just begin to start turning translucent around the edges. Now add approximately 4 tbsp soy sauce, 3 tbsp Worcestershire sauce, about 3 shakes of balsamic vinegar and a

little more olive oil. (The liquid should appear like it's slightly too much and thin. It will reduce and thicken as you cook it. If you don't have enough the dish will be gummy and dry.) Add the rest of the spices using the ground ginger as the main spice. I use red pepper flakes for some kick. Also, ideally, sesame oil would be used instead of olive oil. But that shiz is expensive and pretty much only good for Asian food haha
3. "Stir-fry" the whole mixture together for about 5 minutes or so more. Serve over a bowl of cooked white rice and enjoy! The only thing missing is the white cardboard containers and a fortune cookie.

Spicy Chicken Stir-Fry

"Recipe taken from the recipe book "Chinese The essence of Asian cooking" by Linda Doeser"

***Servings**: 4*

Ingredients

- 1/2 tsp ground turmeric
- 1/2 tsp ground ginger
- 1 tsp salt
- 1 tsp ground black pepper
- 2 tsp ground cumin
- 1 tbsp ground coriander
- 1 tbsp caster sugar
- 450 grams boneless chicken breasts, skinned
- 1 bunch spring onions
- 2 red peppers, seeded
- 1 yellow pepper, seeded
- 175 grams courgettes
- 175 grams mangetouts or sugar snap peas
- 1 sunflower oil, for frying
- 1 tbsp lime juice
- 1 tbsp clear honey

Directions

1. Mix together the turmeric, ginger, salt, pepper, cumin, coriander and sugar in a bowl until well combined
2. Cut the chicken into bite-sized strips. Add to the spice mixture and stir to coat the chicken pieces thoroughly. Set aside.
3. Prepare the vegetables. Cut the spring onions and peppers into 5cm-long, thin strips. Cut the courgettes at a slight angle into thin rounds and top and tail the mangetouts or sugar snap peas.
4. Heat 30ml/2 tbsp of oil in a preheated Wok or large frying pan. Stir-fry the chicken in batches until cooked through and golden brown adding a little more oil if necessary. Remove from the pan and keep warm.
5. Add a little more oil to the pan and cook the spring onions, peppers and courgettes over a medium heat for about 8-10 minutes, until beginning to soften and turn golden. Add the mangetouts or sugar snap peas and cook for a further 2 minutes.
6. Return the chicken to the pan, with the lime juice and honey. Cook for 2 minutes. Serve immediately.

Spicy Chicken with Peppers and Basil

Servings: 4 | Prep: 15m | Cook: 24m | Ready In: 40m

Ingredients

- 2 cups jasmine rice, prepared to directions on the package
- 1 1/2 pounds boneless, skinless chicken breast
- 1 tablespoon (1 turn around the pan) Wok or light colored oil
- 1 tablespoon hot chile oil
- 1/2 to 1 teaspoon crushed red pepper flakes
- 1 small to medium onion, thinly sliced
- 2 red bell peppers, seeded and thinly sliced
- 4 cloves garlic, chopped
- 2 tablespoons (2 turns around the pan in thin stream or 2 splashes) fish sauce
- 20 leaves fresh sweet basil, torn
- Serving suggestion: Thai Salad with Peanut Dressing, recipe follows
- Thai Salad with Peanut Dressing:
- 3 tablespoons chunky style peanut butter
- 2 tablespoons light oil, vegetable or canola

- 1 tablespoon dark soy sauce, a splash
- 2 tablespoons (2 splashes) rice wine vinegar
- 1 teaspoon sugar
- 1/4 teaspoon (2 pinches) cayenne pepper
- 1 small head Iceberg lettuce, shredded
- 2 cups fresh bean spouts
- 2 carrots, grated or peeled into curls with a vegetable peeler

Directions

1. Place rice on the stovetop to cook.
2. Cut chicken on an angle across the breast into thin strips. Cut strips across into bite size pieces. Set chicken aside. Wash hands and cutting board.
3. When the rice is 6 or 7 minutes away from being done, begin your stir fry.
4. Heat a Wok, Wok shaped skillet, or large nonstick skillet over high heat. When the pan smokes, add Wok or light cooking oil, and hot chile oil. Sprinkle in crushed pepper flakes. Add chicken and stir fry 2 minutes. Add onions, red bell peppers, and garlic and stir-fry for 1 or 2 more minutes. Add fish sauce. Remove the pan from heat and add basil. Toss chicken dish until basil wilts.
5. Serve chicken and peppers with prepared rice, salad with peanut dressing.
6. Thai Salad with Peanut Dressing:
7. Heat peanut butter in microwave in a small microwave safe dish on high for 15 seconds to soften. Transfer peanut butter to a bowl. Whisk in oil, soy, vinegar, sugar, and cayenne pepper.
8. Pile lettuce, bean spouts, and carrots on a serving platter. Drizzle liberally with peanut dressing and serve.

Spinach Chicken Stir Fry

"Easy low carb high fat, minimum ingredient spinach chicken stir fry. It was so awesome, that the photo does it no justice. It can be served hot or cold!"

Servings: 2 | Time: 25m

Ingredients

- 500 g chicken breast- diced in small pieces
- 200 g spinach- diced
- 1 medium onion - diced
- 1 tbsp ginger garlic paste
- butter/olive oil
- 2 tbsp white vinegar
- to taste salt

Directions

1. Fry the chicken in butter, till brown. Add the ginger garlic paste.
2. Saute the onions with the chicken.
3. Add the washed spinach to the pan, and mix into the chicken. Cook with the lid closed, on low flame, till the spinach is done.
4. Add the vinegar and salt and stir, after turning off the heat.
5. Serve hot or cold!

Stir Fry Chicken Fajita

Ingredients

- 2 chicken breast
- 1/2 each crushed chilli, coriander powder, chicken powder, tikka masala, salt, garlic paste
- 1 slice can pineapple slice
- 1 tsp hot sauce
- 1 capsicum
- 1/2 onion
- 1 tomato deseeded
- 1 tsp lemon juice
- sauce
- 20 grams butter
- 60 grams fresh cream
- 1 tsp cayeene pepper
- 1 tsp garlic paste

Directions

1. Cut chicken breast intp thin strips
2. Mix all spices together, lemon juice, hot saucw and pineapple slice together and marinade for 2 hours
3. Cut the vegetables and set aside
4. Stir fry chicken, after 5 mins add vegetables and toss
5. When chicken is cook, lower the flame and add butter
6. Add garlic paste and cayeene pepper cook for 1 min
7. Add fresh cream and mix until the sauce becomes thick and consistent, add water if becomes too thick
8. I have garnish mine with thin strips of cheese, and served with fresh salsa

Stir Fry Eggplants with Chicken and Fresh Basil

"Easy way to cook eggplant - just stir fry. Healthy is another reason. You should try it.. ? "

Servings: 4 | **Time**: 30m

Ingredients

- 3 medium size eggplant cut into strips
- handful fresh basil
- 1 chicken breast cut into strips
- 3 cloves chopped garlic
- 1 cup cornstarch water
- 2 fresh chili peppers
- Oil
- For chicken marinade:
- 2 Tbsp dark soy sauce
- 1/2 tsp corn starch
- 1 Tbsp cooking oil
- 1 pinch sugar
- 1 pinch chicken broth powder
- 1 tsp sesame oil

Directions

1. Mix chicken strips with marination. Keep aside about 15 min.
2. Boil eggplant strips until medium soft. Then drain from excess water.
3. Pour oil into frying pan. No need to wait until the oil warms up. Put chicken in. Stir fry it until colour changes. Then remove chicken from excess oil.
4. Use rest of the oil from first stir fry. Pour a little bit oil to stir fry garlic. Stir fry until the smell come out. Drop boiled eggplants into pan and stir.
5. Continue put chicken into the pan and stir together.
6. Pour 1 cup corn starch water into the pan. Lastly add chilli and fresh basil. Serve it with rice.

Stir Fry Long Beans with Bell Pepper and Chicken Hearts

"A healthy easy breezy stir fry. Enjoy the meal!"

Servings: 2 | **Time**: 25m

Ingredients

- 1/2 lb chicken Hearts
- 1 white onion, sliced
- 1 tbsp butter
- 1 tbsp vegetable oil
- 175 g long beans
- 4 cloves garlic, chopped
- 1 inch ginger, chopped
- 2 tbsp soy sauce
- 1 bell pepper, sliced
- 1/2 tsp salt and pepper
- 1 chili pepper

Directions

1. Wok the onions, garlic, ginger and long beans in the butter and oil until all ingredients starts to soften.
2. Add the chicken hearts and continue stir frying until just cooked.

3. Stir in the salt and pepper, chili pepper, bell pepper and soy sauce, then allow to bubble away for about 3 minutes.
4. Remove from the flame and serve it while it's warm.

Stir Fry Mash-Up (Chicken & Veggies)

"Simple stir fry that can be altered according to what's on hand...it is good with beef too, be sure to cut diaganally across the grain to get tender beef, or use a tender cut like sirloin."

Servings: 4 | **Cook**: 1h

Ingredients

- 3 tsp sesame oil, or other oil suitable for high heat
- 2 clove garlic, crushed or grated
- 1/2 tsp grated ginger root (optional)
- 1 cup total combined assorted canned asian veggies such as water chestnuts, baby corn, bamboo shoots, straw mushrooms
- 3 cup total combined mixed fresh veggies of choice, such as bok choy, carrots, white onion, snow or sugar snap peas, bean sprouts, scallions, grape tomatoes, green cabbage, broccoli, red/orange bell peppers
- 4 tbsp stir fry sauce, add to taste
- chicken marinade
- 2 boneless skinless chicken breasts
- 2 tbsp low sodium soy sauce
- 1 tbsp dry white wine
- 1 tbsp oyster sauce or other stir fry sauce (teriyaki, etc)

Directions

1. Slice chicken, about 1/4" thickness, place in bowl with marinade ingredients, stir to coat and set aside
2. Cut fresh veggies into thin, evenly sized pieces, place in prep bowls
3. Heat oil in Wok until shimmering and nearly starting to smoke. Add garlic, ginger and chicken, stir fry until nearly cooked, then transfer to a clean dish and set aside

4. Add a bit more oil to Wok, add 2-3 types of firm veggies, (e.g. carrots & bok choy, water chestnuts & bamboo shoots), stir and toss for 1-3 minutes depending on desired "crispiness factor". Remove and set aside, repeat with remaining veggies
5. Add all heated veggies back to Wok, add chicken and any additional sauce desired, adding any delicate veggies such as bean sprouts, mushrooms, or tomatoes and stir fry for another 1-2 minutes until chicken is cooked and veggies are heated through
6. Thicken pan juices with corn starch if desired
7. Serve immediately with white or fried rice

Stir Fry Peppers With Marinated Chicken Slices

"I love my spicy peppers."

Servings*: 2 | **Time***: 30m

Ingredients

- 3 peppers (3 colours)
- 2 cloves chopped garlic
- 10 pcs cilantro
- 1 recipe basic chicken marinade (see my recipe list)
- 1 tbsp dark soy sauce
- 2 Thai chillis, sliced
- 1 tbsp cooking oil
- 2 tsp tapioca starch + 50 ml water
- 100 ml water
- Sesame seeds

Directions

1. Cut peppers into long nice strips. And I had stir fried chicken that I cooked before in the photo.
2. Check my recipe list for chicken marinade recipe.
3. Pour cooking oil into the frying pan. Add chopped garlic. Stir until a nice smell comes out.
4. Add peppers into the frying pan once garlic is ready.

5. After peppers softer or as a desired, add thai chili, soy sauce, chicken strips in it. Stir it well
6. Add water, cook until peppers are the softness you want.
7. Lastly add tapioca starch water and cilantro. Sprinkle with sesame. Serve it with rice or just like that ☺.. hmmm its soo yummy

Stir-Fried Chicken with Broccoli, Water Chestnuts and Peppers

Servings: 6 | Prep:30m | Cook: 10m | Ready In: 40m

Ingredients

- 3 tablespoons peanut oil
- 2 teaspoons minced garlic
- 2 teaspoons minced ginger
- 2 teaspoons minced green onion bottoms
- 1 1/2 pounds boneless, skinless chicken breasts, diced into 1-inch cubes
- 1 cup julienned red bell peppers
- 1/2 cup water chestnuts
- 3 cups blanched broccoli florets
- 1/4 cup soy sauce
- 2 teaspoons toasted sesame oil
- 3/4 cup chicken stock
- 4 teaspoons cornstarch slurry
- Salt and pepper
- Steamed rice, for serving

Directions

1. Set a Wok over high heat and add the peanut oil. Be sure to swirl the Wok to get the oil to coat most of the pan. Once the oil smokes, quickly add the garlic, ginger, green onions and chicken to the Wok. Saute, stirring continuously until the chicken in lightly browned, about 2 to 3 minutes. Add the red peppers and saute for another 1 minute. Add the water chestnuts and broccoli and saute for another minute. Add the soy sauce and sesame oil and reduce for 30

seconds. Add the chicken stock, slurry and season with salt and pepper. Use a paddle to toss the ingredients and be sure that the stock comes to a boil. Cook at a boil for 2 to 3 minutes, before serving over steamed rice.

Stir-fry Polynesian Chicken

***Servings**: 4 | **Cook**: 20m*

Ingredients

- 1 cup white rice
- 1 tbsp vegetable oil
- 2 Chicken breast
- 10 oz LA choy sweet and sour sauce
- 1 tbsp shari
- 10 green onions
- 1/4 cup slivered almonds
- 1 Red pepper
- 1/2 can pineapple chunks

Directions

1. Cook rice.
2. While rice is coming, heat oil in large skillet over medium heat.
3. Cut the chicken into 1 inch cubes and brown them in the skillet (about 5 minutes).
4. Pour in the sweet and sour sauce and the Shari. Cover and simmer for 8 minutes.
5. Add in the green onion, red pepper, almonds, and pineapple chunks.
6. Simmer for 2 to 3 more minutes. Serve over rice.

Sweet and Hot Pepper Chicken, Asian-Style

***Servings**: 6 | **Prep**: 20m | **Inactive**: 15m | **Cook**: 10m | **Ready In**: 45m*

Ingredients

- 1 tablespoon soy sauce
- 1/2 teaspoons dark soy sauce
- 1/2 teaspoons cornstarch
- 1/2 pounds boneless, skinless chicken breast, diced into 1-inch cubes
- 1/2 cup ketchup
- 1/4 cup chicken stock
- 1 tablespoon chili garlic sauce
- 2 teaspoons sugar
- 4 teaspoons vegetable oil
- 2 teaspoons minced ginger
- 2 teaspoons minced garlic
- 2 teaspoons minced green onion bottoms
- 10 dried red chiles
- 1 jalapeno, stemmed, seeded and thinly sliced
- 1 red bell pepper, stemmed, seeded and thinly sliced
- 1 cup sliced yellow onion
- 2 teaspoons toasted sesame seeds
- 1 teaspoon sesame oil
- 1 tablespoon chopped fresh cilantro leaves

Directions

1. In a medium bowl, combine the soy sauce, dark soy and cornstarch. Whisk to blend well, and add the chicken to the sauce. Toss to evenly coat the chicken and set aside for 15 to 20 minutes.
2. In a medium bowl, combine the ketchup, stock, chili garlic sauce and sugar. Stir to combine and set aside until ready to use. Place a Wok over high heat and add the vegetable oil to the pan. Swirl the Wok to be sure to coat well with the oil. Add the ginger, garlic, green onions, dried chilies and jalapenos to the Wok. Cook, stirring often until the garlic is fragrant and the chilies begin to brown, about 20 to 30 seconds. Add the chicken, bell peppers and onions to the pan and stir-fry until the chicken is no longer pink, about 4 to 5 minutes. Add the sauce to the pan and bring to a boil, being sure to toss well in order to coat all the chicken and vegetables evenly, about 1 to 2 minutes. Sprinkle the sesame seeds, sesame oil and cilantro into the pan and toss to combine. Remove from the heat and serve on a platter with steamed white rice.

Sweet and Sour Chicken

Servings: 6 | **Prep**: 25m | **Cook**: 8m | **Ready In**: 33m

Ingredients

- 1 tablespoon cornstarch
- 2 teaspoons ground white pepper
- 1 egg white
- 1 1/2 pounds boneless skinless chicken breasts, sliced into thin strips
- 1 tablespoon canola oil
- 1/4 cup low sodium soy sauce
- 2 tablespoons tomato paste
- 2 teaspoons sesame oil
- 1 tablespoon honey
- 1 tablespoon crushed garlic
- 2 tablespoon grated ginger
- 1/4 cup rice wine vinegar
- 1 tablespoon orange marmalade
- 1 (8-ounce) jar baby corn, drained
- 1 (8-ounce) can sliced bamboo shoots, drained
- 1 (8-ounce) can crushed pineapple, drained

Directions

1. In a large bowl, mix the cornstarch, white pepper, and egg whites. Add the chicken and toss until well coated.
2. Heat a large nonstick Wok until blazing hot. Coat the bottom of the pan with the canola oil. Add the chicken to the pan and move continuously to prevent chicken from sticking together. Saute for about 1 1/2 minutes. Once the chicken is cooked, remove from the Wok and keep warm.
3. Over high heat, add to the Wok the soy sauce, tomato paste, sesame oil, honey, garlic, ginger, vinegar, and marmalade. Lower heat and simmer for approximately 30 seconds to thicken. Add the baby corn and bamboo shoots and warm through.
4. Once sauce is thick and warm, whisk in the pineapple.

5. To serve, arrange chicken strips on a platter and pour the sauce over the chicken.

Sweet and Spicy Chicken Stir-fry

"I was craving Panda Express's Firecracker Chicken, so I decided to make my own!"

Servings: 3 | **Cook**: 15m

Ingredients

Main Dish

- 1 lb Boneless Chicken (cut into small pieces)
- 2 medium Bell Peppers (Yellow and Red; Julianned)
- 1/2 medium White Onion (Chopped)
- 3 small Serrano Chiles (Julianned)
- 1 tsp Salt
- 1 tsp Pepper
- 1 pinch Paprika
- 1 Prepared Steamed White Rice
- 1/4 cup Coconut Oil for cooking (adds a nice sweetness)
- 3 clove Garlic (smashed)

Sauce

- 1/3 cup Frank's Red Hot Buffalo Sauce
- 1/2 cup Brown Sugar
- 1 oz Water
- 1/2 tbsp Red Pepper Flakes
- 1 tsp Apple Cider Vinegar
- 1 dash Salt

Directions

1. Prepare vegetables (as in description) and set aside.
2. Prepare sauce by adding the necessary ingredients together and wisking it until you get a nice blend. Set Aside.
3. Over medium heat, fry the chicken pieces with the salt, pepper, and paprika.

4. When the chicken is about half way done, add the sauce into the pan with the chicken. Cover and let it simmer. The sauce will begin to thicken up after about 10-15 minutes.
5. Note: Make sure you stir the chicken every so often to get that nice thick coating around the chicken.
6. As the chicken and sauce are hooking up, fry your vegetables into a nice sautee along with the garlic. Set aside when onions are translucent.
7. When the chicken is cooked and the sauce has thickened, stir in the vegetables and allow the flavors to marry for a couple minutes.
8. Finished! Serve over a nice bed of white Steamed rice.

Sweet and Spicy Stir Fry with Chicken and Broccoli

"Spicy! I substituted chili powder for chili paste."

Servings: 4

Ingredients

- 3 c broccoli florets
- 1 T olive oil
- 12-14 oz chicken breasts, boneless and skinless, cut into strips
- 1/4 c green onions
- 4 cloves garlic, sliced
- 1 T hoisin sauce
- 1 T chili paste
- 1 T low-sodium soy sauce
- 1/2 tsp ground ginger
- 1/4 tsp red pepper flakes
- 1/2 tsp salt
- 1/2 tsp black pepper
- 2 T chicken broth

Directions

1. Steam broccoli until tender but firm.
2. In large skillet, heat oil. Saute chicken, onions and garlic until chicken no longer pink.

3. Stir in hoisin sauce, chili paste, soy sauce, ginger, red pepper flakes, salt and pepper. Stir in broth and simmer 2 min. Add in broccoli and gently toss until coated with chicken mixture.

Sweet & Sunny Mandarin Chicken Stir-Fry

"A light, quick, and tasty dinner for hot summer nights! (but yummy year round!)"

Servings: 6

Ingredients

- 3 box Perdue Honey Roasted Short Cuts (or 2.5 lbs cooked chicken strips)
- 1/2 vadallia onion, sliced in thin strips; optional or more if preferred
- 1/2 green bell pepper sliced in strips; s.a.a.
- 2 can 11 oz mandarin oranges, drained, reserving 3/4 cup juice
- 1/3 cup packed brown sugar
- 1/4 tsp ginger
- 1/4 tsp pepper, preferably white but black is fine.
- 1 tsp sesame oil
- 2 tbsp honey
- 1/2 tsp garlic salt, optional
- 1 tbsp oil ; i use olive but vegetable fine

Directions

1. heat oil over medium high heat in skillet, add veggies and cook about 5 minutes til tender crisp
2. lower to medium heat and stir in chicken, mandarin orange juice, brown sugar, honey, ginger, pepper, and sesame oil; cover and cook until liquid absorbed, about 10-15 minutes, stirring occasionally.
3. top with mandarin oranges and serve over white rice. *if you prefer the citrus liquid to have a more glaze-like consistency, drain into a saucepan, add about a tablespoon of cornstarch to a few teaspoons of the excess mandarin orange juice, and stir with a whisk to desired thickness. Pour over the chicken and enjoy!

Sweet-and-Spicy Chicken Stir-Fry

"Sweet-and-Spicy Chicken Stir-Fry is a quick and easy one-dish meal that will be be your family nex favorite dish. For extra heat to this chicken stir-fry, add more hot sauce, or use a lighter hand for milder flavor"

Servings: 4 | **Prep**: 10m | **Cook**: 10m | **Ready In**: 20m

Ingredients

- 1 small head cauliflower, cored, cut into small florets
- 2 tablespoons honey
- 2 tablespoons hot sauce such as sriracha
- 1/4 cup low-sodium chicken broth
- 1 teaspoon cornstarch
- 3 tablespoons soy sauce
- 3 tablespoons rice vinegar
- 3 tablespoons vegetable oil
- 1 pound boneless, skinless chicken breasts or thighs, cut into strips
- 2 cloves garlic, finely chopped
- 1 tablespoon finely chopped fresh ginger
- 3 scallions, white and pale green parts finely chopped, dark green parts sliced
- 2 cups cooked rice, optional

Directions

1. Place cauliflower in a dish, sprinkle with 2 Tbsp. water and microwave on high until tender, 3 to 4 minutes. In a small bowl, whisk together honey, hot sauce, broth, cornstarch, 2 Tbsp. soy sauce and 2 Tbsp. rice vinegar.
2. In a large skillet or Wok, warm 2 Tbsp. oil over high heat. In a bowl, toss chicken with remaining 1 Tbsp. soy sauce and 1 Tbsp. rice vinegar. Stir-fry until chicken is no longer pink. Transfer to a clean bowl.
3. Add remaining 1 Tbsp. oil to skillet. Stir-fry garlic, ginger and white and pale green parts of scallions until fragrant, about 30 seconds. Return chicken to skillet with cauliflower and sauce. Cook, stirring,

until sauce thickens, 2 to 3 minutes. Sprinkle dark green scallion bits on top. Serve on rice, if desired.

Sweet-Spicy Chicken and Vegetable Stir-Fry

"This colorful chicken and veggie stir-fry features a sweet-spicy sauce and a topping of dry-roasted peanuts, which add delicious crunch.

Servings: 4

Ingredients

- 3 tablespoons dark brown sugar
- 1 1/2 tablespoons lower-sodium soy sauce
- 1 tablespoon fish sauce
- 1 tablespoon rice vinegar
- 1 tablespoon sambal oelek
- 1 teaspoon dark sesame oil
- 3/4 teaspoon cornstarch
- 2 tablespoons canola oil, divided
- 1 pound skinless, boneless chicken breast, cut into bite-sized pieces
- 8 ounces sugar snap peas
- 1 red bell pepper, sliced
- 1/2 medium red onion, cut into thin wedges
- 1/4 cup sliced green onions
- 1/4 cup unsalted dry-roasted peanuts

Directions

1. Combine the first 7 ingredients, stirring well; set aside.
2. Heat a large Wok or large heavy skillet over high heat. Add 1 tablespoon canola oil to pan; swirl to coat. Add chicken; stir-fry 4 minutes or until browned and done. Remove chicken from Wok. Add remaining 1 tablespoon canola oil to Wok; swirl to coat. Add sugar snap peas, bell pepper, and red onion; stir-fry 3 minutes or until vegetables are crisp-tender. Stir in brown sugar mixture; cook 1 minute or until thickened. Stir in chicken; toss to coat. Sprinkle with green onions and peanuts.

Tea Smoked Chicken

Servings: 4 | *Prep*: 30m | *Inactive*: 4h30m | *Cook*: 16m | *Ready In*: 5h16m

Ingredients

- 1 tablespoon Szechuan peppercorns
- 1 teaspoon five-spice powder
- 2 tablespoons kosher salt
- 1 pound boneless skinless chicken thighs
- 1/4 cup white rice
- 3 tablespoon Chinese black tea
- 2 tablespoons brown sugar
- 1/4 cup plus 2 tablespoons Shao-sing wine or medium-dry sherry
- 2 tablespoons soy sauce, preferably dark (See Cook's Note)
- 1 tablespoon peeled and minced fresh ginger
- 2 teaspoons toasted sesame oil
- 5 scallions (white and green), thinly sliced
- 1/4 cup chopped peanuts
- 1/2 head iceberg lettuce
- Sriracha sauce or other Asian chili sauce, to taste
- Juice of 1/2 lime

Directions

1. Toast the Szechuan peppercorns in a dry skillet until fragrant, about 4 minutes. Cool slightly, and then crush in a spice grinder or mortar and pestle with the salt and five-spice powder until very fine. Rub seasoned salt all over the chicken thighs. Place in a bowl, cover with plastic wrap and refrigerate for at least 4 hours or preferably overnight.
2. Bring the chicken to room temperature about 30 minutes before cooking.
3. Line the bottom of a Wok, skillet or heavy pot with a double layer of aluminum foil. Mix the rice, tea and brown sugar together and mound on the foil. Set a steamer on top, and evenly space the chicken on the rack. Cover and cook over high heat. Hot smoke the chicken until smokey-brown colored and cooked through, about 12 minutes.
4. While the chicken cooks, whisk the Shao-sing wine or sherry, soy, ginger, and sesame together in a small saucepan. Bring to boil over

high heat, remove from heat and steep for 5 minutes. Brush over cooked chicken.
5. To serve: Dice the chicken into very small pieces. Toss with the scallions and peanuts in a medium bowl. Cut the lettuce leaves into 40 squares or triangular scoops. Place a drop of Sriracha on top of each lettuce cup, and top with about 2 teaspoons of the diced chicken. Squeeze lime juice over the top, and drizzle the remaining soy-ginger sauce over the chicken. Serve.
6. Cook's Note: Dark soy sauce is thicker and lightly sweeter tasting than other soys. It adds a depth of flavor that is great with the chicken. It can be found in Asian markets or supermarkets with a good Asian section.

Thai Fried Rice with Pineapple and Chicken

"This is a Bangkok street food style recipe which I snagged on a recent trip there. Serve and enjoy. Try a hollowed pineapple shell as a serving bowl."

*Servings: 6 | **Prep**: 10m | **Cook**: 20m | **Ready In**: 30m*

Ingredients

- 3 slices bacon, diced
- 3 shallots, sliced
- 4 ounces chicken breast, cut into small cubes
- 4 teaspoons curry powder, divided
- 3 egg yolks, beaten
- 1 teaspoon vegetable oil, or as needed (optional)
- 3 cups cooked jasmine rice
- 1 red Thai bird chile pepper, finely chopped
- 2 tablespoons whole cilantro leaves
- 1 tablespoon soy sauce
- 2 teaspoons fish sauce
- 1/2 teaspoon white sugar
- 4 ounces tiger prawns, peeled and deveined
- 1/4 cup chopped fresh pineapple
- 3 green onions, finely chopped

Directions

1. Place bacon in a Wok or large skillet; cook and stir over medium-high heat until crisp, about 10 minutes. Remove bacon with a slotted spoon and reserve bacon drippings in the Wok. Cook and stir shallots in bacon drippings over medium-high heat until fragrant and light brown, 1 to 2 minutes.
2. Stir chicken into shallots and cook without stirring until browned on one side, 45 seconds to 1 minute; stir. Continue cooking until chicken is browned, about 1 minute. Add 2 teaspoons curry powder; stir until chicken is coated.
3. Make a well in the center of chicken and pour oil into center of the well; add egg yolks. Cook and stir egg yolks until set, 1 to 2 minutes. Add rice and stir, breaking up rice.
4. Mix chile pepper, cilantro, soy sauce, remaining 2 teaspoons curry powder, fish sauce, and sugar into rice mixture; add shrimp and cook until shrimp is cooked through and pink, about 2 minutes. Fold pineapple, green onions, and bacon into rice mixture.

Footnotes

- Use fresh pineapple when available. Hollow out pineapple and serve it in the shell. Using day old cold rice from the fridge will work best. You can add most frozen vegetables to this for added goodness. It also works well with brown rice.

Thai Spicy Basil Chicken Fried Rice

"This is a staple of Thai cooking. Adjust the spices to your own tastes for a really great use for leftover rice!! I get the basil from a local Asian market. It has a different flavor than that of regular basil and makes all the difference in this recipe. It is fast and fairly easy to make, but requires constant stirring."

Servings: 6 | **Prep**: 30m | **Cook**: 10m | **Ready In**: 40m

Ingredients

- 3 tablespoons oyster sauce
- 2 tablespoons fish sauce
- 1 teaspoon white sugar

- 1/2 cup peanut oil for frying
- 4 cups cooked jasmine rice, chilled
- 6 large cloves garlic clove, crushed
- 2 serrano peppers, crushed
- 1 pound boneless, skinless chicken breast, cut into thin strips
- 1 red pepper, seeded and thinly sliced
- 1 onion, thinly sliced
- 2 cups sweet Thai basil
- 1 cucumber, sliced (optional)
- 1/2 cup cilantro sprigs (optional)

Directions

1. Whisk together the oyster sauce, fish sauce, and sugar in a bowl.
2. Heat the oil in a Wok over medium-high heat until the oil begins to smoke. Add the garlic and serrano peppers, stirring quickly. Stir in the chicken, bell pepper, onion and oyster sauce mixture; cook until the chicken is no longer pink. Raise heat to high and stir in the chilled rice; stir quickly until the sauce is blended with the rice. Use the back of a spoon to break up any rice sticking together.
3. Remove from heat and mix in the basil leaves. Garnish with sliced cucumber and cilantro as desired.

Tip

- Aluminum foil helps keep food moist, ensures it cooks evenly, keeps leftovers fresh, and makes clean-up easy.

Thai-Style Chicken Stir-Fry

"This had a good spicy/sweet flavor! I subbed chopped chestnuts for bean sprouts and adjusted the carbs (11 NC). I also used tamari sauce because I didn't have coconut aminos."

Servings: 4

Ingredients

- 1 lb chicken thighs, skin and bones removed
- 2 T fish sauce
- 1 T coconut aminos
- 2 small bell peppers, red, orange or yellow, sliced
- 2 medium spring onions, sliced
- 1 T fresh ginger, grated
- 2 garlic cloves, crushed
- 1 small hot chile pepper, seeded and minced
- 1/4 c coconut oil
- 2 c bean sprouts
- 1/4 c toasted nut butter
- 1 T lime juice
- salt and pepper
- 2 T fresh cilantro

Directions

1. Slice chicken into med. pieces and add fish sauce and coconut aminos. Marinate at least 1 hr.
2. In large pan, heat half of coconut oil. Add chicken and cook until browned. Remove from pan and set aside.
3. Grease pan with remaining oil. Add ginger, garlic and chile pepper. Cook 2-3 min., stirring constantly.
4. Add bell pepper and onion and season with salt and pepper, cook 5 min. Add bean sprouts and cook 1 min.
5. Add chicken, toasted nut butter, lime juice and combine well. Cook until chicken is heated through. Garnish with cilantro and season with more salt if needed.

Veggie Chicken Stir Fry

Ingredients

- about 1/2 a chicken cut up
- 3 carrots
- 1/2 cauliflower head
- 1/4 broccoli head
- 1 yellow zucchini
- 1 green zucchini

- 1/2 pepper
- 1 onion
- optional fresh garlic and fresh ginger
- soy sauce
- agave
- spices of your choice

Directions

1. Mix soy sauce and agave together
2. Pour over cut up chicken (great way to use the leftover gedempte chicken from pesach ;))
3. Mix and let marinate
4. Meanwhile chop up onions (you could add garlic and ginger too for a great kick)
5. Prepare the rest of your veggies by chopping them up to desired size (i like thin sticks for this dish)
6. Add oil and onions (together with fresh garlic and ginger if you added) to a pan and stir fry until onions are clear
7. Add veggies to the pan
8. I used the biggest pan we had but it was too small ;) i switched to the big skillet to fit them all in :)
9. Add a bit of soy sauce (i generally use a cup cuz im great at putting too much in ;) i managed this time to just drip in a bit)
10. Add desired spices. I put in salt, pepper, garlic, ginger..
11. I dont have it worked out to a science with which spices work well.. all i could say is that it came out delish however i would love to learn about spices and which are the best to add
12. Mix and stir and continue cooking until veggies are soft
13. Add in chicken (ours was already cooked, that's why its the last step here)
14. Mix it in and stir a bit
15. Let rest a bit on simmer/low/warm until ready to serve
16. Serve with rice, salad, or just eat plain.
17. Enjoy!

Wifey Chicken Stir-Fry I

"Filling up those Bellies one fork full at a time! This meal is so good it'll become a weekly favorite oh n did I mention soooooo easy!? Please do enjoy!"

Ingredients

- 1 lb Skinless boneless chicken tenders
- 1 bunch Broccoli
- 1 Onion
- 1 Green Bell pepper
- 1 Carrot
- 1 Red bell pepper
- 1 Stir Fry sauce
- 1 cup Rice
- 1 Salt
- 1 Pepper

Directions

1. Heat a teaspoon of olive oil in a large skillet or Wok if u have one
2. Drop in chicken and cook until no longer pink salt and pepper
3. Cut up all the veggies
4. Drop your veggie mix into the pan and cook until crispy and done to your liking
5. Pour in your stir fry sauce
6. Bring to a boil then turn down to a simmer
7. While that is simmering cook your rice and put it on the plate
8. Add your stir fry to the top of rice
9. Enjoy

Wifeys Chicken Stir Fry II

"Just a quick stir fry for a week ending meal! Enjoyyyy"

Servings: 4 | *Time*: 30m

Ingredients

- 4 each Skinless boneless chicken breast
- 2 Green bell pepper deseeded
- 2 Red bell pepper deseeded
- 2 Yellow bell pepper deseeded

- 2 Onions
- 1 dash Olive oil
- 1 Soy sauce

Directions

1. Swirl olive oil in a large skillet or Wok heat up
2. Chop up chicken and add to olive oil in pan
3. Cook chicken until no longer pink
4. Add cut up veggies to chicken
5. Sir to combine and cook until veggies are tender (add soy sauce I did not at this point we had some1 over 4 dinner who was not a fan of soy sauce)
6. While your veggies are cooking make your rice
7. After your rice is done lay on plate like a bed
8. Add your stir fry to the top of the rice
9. Dig in and enjoyyyy

Yuzu and Mirin Marinated Grilled Chicken Thighs with Chinese Vegetable Fried Rice

Servings: 4 | Prep: 15 | Inactive: 15m | Cook: 20m | Ready In: 50m

Ingredients

For the grilled chicken:

- 2 cups rice wine
- 1 cup sake
- 1 cup soy sauce
- 1 cup yuzu juice or ponzu
- 6 tablespoons sugar or honey, plus 1 tablespoon
- 1 (3 to 4-inch) piece fresh ginger, cut into coins
- 3/4 cup rice vinegar
- Pinch red pepper flakes
- 1/2 teaspoon salt plus extra salt and freshly ground black pepper
- 8 chicken thighs

For the fried rice:

- 1/4 cup peanut oil
- 3 cups cooked white rice
- 1/2 cup chopped green onions
- 2 teaspoons minced garlic
- 3 eggs
- 1 1/2 tablespoons soy sauce
- 2 tablespoons sesame oil
- 3 tablespoons finely chopped parsley leaves
- 2 cups stir-fry vegetables
- 1 tablespoon finely chopped parsley leaves

Directions

1. For the grilled chicken:
   In a large bowl combine all of the ingredients apart from the chicken thighs. Whisk to combine. Add chicken thighs and toss to coat. Marinate for 15 minutes. Preheat a grill to medium-high heat, and place chicken thighs directly onto grill. Cook on each side for 4 to 6 minutes. Remove from grill and keep warm on a plate covered with foil. Serve with Chinese Fried Rice.
2. For the Fried Rice:
   Heat the oil in the Wok. Toss in the rice until hot and golden. Stir in the green onions, garlic, eggs, soy sauce, sesame oil and parsley. Stir-fry for 2 minutes. Season with salt and pepper.

Chapter 5: Chinese Recipes

***

Chinese 5-Spice Salmon Stir-fry

"This isn't a genuine Chinese stir fry, it's the kind of thing you make up as you go along depending on what's in the fridge so add more pepper, less onion, cabbage instead of spinach, peanuts instead of cashews, noodles instead of rice. Make sure everything is ready in advance before you being cooking as it all happens very quickly once you get started."

Servings: 2 | **Time**: 20m

Ingredients

- 2 salmon steaks
- Sesame oil
- Chinese 5-spice
- 1 or 2 red or yellow peppers, sliced
- 1 or 2 red onions, finely sliced
- 1 or 2 carrots, peeled and cut into thin batons
- 1 knob fresh ginger, grated
- 1 or 2 cloves garlic, finely sliced
- 2 helpings cooked basmati rice
- 1 handful cashew nuts, roasted and salted
- 1 squirt of lemon grass paste, if you have it
- 1 tiny bit of shrimp paste, if you have it
- 2 handfuls baby spinach, roughly chopped
- Thai fish sauce
- 4-6 tablespoons soy sauce
- juice of half a lemon and wedges for serving
- fresh mint, chopped

Directions

1. Preheat the grill. Put the salmon steaks in a grill pan, I line it with foil to save washing up. Drizzle some sesame oil over the top and sprinkle generously with the 5-spice mixture. Place under a hot grill until crisp on the top and just cooked inside. This will only take 6 to 10 minutes.

2. Once the salmon is cooked, flake it into chunks and peel off and discard the skin, pour over a little shake of soy sauce and lemon juice and set aside.
3. Start to fry all the vegetables, if you have a Wok you can probably do them all in one go, in a frying pan it might be better to do them in batches. Don't fry for too long, everything needs to keep some crispness and texture. When the peppers are just beginning to char at the edges, add the ginger, garlic, lemon grass and shrimp paste. Stir until you can smell the fragrances, then tip the vegetables on to a plate.
4. Quickly return the pan to the heat and fry the cooked rice and the cashews, then return the vegetables to the pan, stir in the chopped spinach, add 2 or 3 teaspoons of fish sauce, depending on how much you like it, and 3 to 4 tablespoons of soy sauce. Stir until the spinach has wilted then add the salmon chunks and the juice of half a lemon. Taste. Add more soy sauce or lemon juice to taste.
5. Serve piled in bowls, topped with fresh mint.

Chinese Braised Zucchini

"Black bean sauce, ginger and thai chilies make this zucchini a perfect side dish to go along with any Chinese-style main dish. Add eggplant and snow peas served with a side of fried rice for an exotic weekday meal"

Servings: 4 | **Prep**: 30m | **Cook**: 20m | **Ready In**: 50m

Ingredients

- 2 tablespoons sesame oil
- 1 small yellow onion, diced
- 3 cloves garlic, minced
- 1 tablespoon Chinese black bean sauce
- 2 Thai chile peppers, seeded and chopped
- 4 zucchinis, cut into 1/2-inch slices
- 1 tablespoon minced fresh ginger root
- 1 tablespoon soy sauce
- 1/4 cup water

Directions

1. Heat the sesame oil in a Wok or large skillet over medium-high heat. Stir fry the onion and garlic in the hot oil until the onion begins to soften, about 2 minutes. Stir in the black bean sauce and chile peppers, and continue stir frying about 30 seconds to coat the onions with the black bean sauce.
2. Stir in the zucchini, ginger, soy sauce, and water. Cover, reduce the heat to medium-low, and cook for 15 minutes until the zucchini is soft, stirring occasionally.

'Chinese Buffet' Green Beans

"Every time my family and I go to a Chinese buffet we make a bee line for the green beans! This is a simple and tasty re-creation of that much loved side dish, goes well with any Asian meal. Make sure to slice the garlic, don't use a garlic press. Oyster sauce can be found in the Asian section of your grocery store, at an Asian grocery store, and online."

Servings: 6 | **Prep**: 15m | **Cook**: 10m | **Ready In**: 25m

Ingredients

- 1 tablespoon oil, peanut or sesame
- 2 cloves garlic, thinly sliced
- 1 pound fresh green beans, trimmed
- 1 tablespoon white sugar
- 2 tablespoons oyster sauce
- 2 teaspoons soy sauce

Directions

1. Heat peanut oil in a Wok or large skillet over medium-high heat. Stir in the garlic, and cook until the edges begin to brown, about 20 seconds. Add the green beans; cook and stir until the green beans begin to soften, about 5 minutes. Stir in the sugar, oyster sauce, and soy sauce. Continue cooking and stirring for several minutes until the beans have attained the desired degree of tenderness.

Chinese Stirfry Mother Sauce

Ingredients

- 5 clove garlic, smashed
- 1 piece of ginger, large chop
- 3 oz Chinese rice wine
- 3 Szechuan peppercorns
- 1/4 cup soy sauce
- 1 tbsp dark soy sauce
- 1 tbsp sesame oil
- 2 tbsp oyster sauce
- 1 tbsp white sugar
- 1 tsp white ground pepper

Directions

1. Add all the ingredient in a mason jar and let sit for a couple of days in the fridge. The longer, the better.
2. Strain before use.
3. Enjoy!

Chinese Tomato and Egg

"Tomato and egg served over rice is a Chinese staple. You can easily omit the pork to make this vegetarian. This recipe is from my mom, who grew up in Guangzhou."

Servings*: 6 | **Prep**: 15m | **Cook**: 20m | **Ready In**: 30m*

Ingredients

- 1/2 pound boneless pork loin, cut into thin strips
- 2 tablespoons soy sauce
- 1 tablespoon brandy
- 1 teaspoon white sugar
- 1 tablespoon cornstarch
- 4 eggs

- 2 teaspoons salt
- 1/2 cup canola oil, divided
- 8 large tomatoes, cut into chunks
- 1 teaspoon white sugar
- 2 bunches green onions, chopped

Directions

1. Mix together the pork, soy sauce, brandy, 1 teaspoon sugar, and cornstarch in a bowl, then cover with plastic wrap, and marinate in the refrigerator 4 to 6 hours.
2. Beat the eggs together with the salt, and set aside. Heat half of the oil in a Wok over medium-high heat. Pour in the eggs, and cook until they just begin to coagulate, but are still very raw. Remove from the Wok and set aside. Heat the remaining vegetable oil in the Wok over high heat. Stir in the tomatoes and remaining 1 teaspoon of sugar. Cover, and allow to simmer until the tomatoes have softened, about 7 minutes.
3. Mash the tomatoes until the mixture resembles a chunky soup. Stir in the marinated pork, and cook 3 to 4 minutes until the pork is no longer pink in the center. Gently fold in the eggs and green onions. Continue cooking uncovered 2 minutes more to cook the eggs.

Chinese-Style Whole Fried Black Bass over Wok-Sauteed Bok Choy, Ginger, and Spring Garlic

Servings: 4 | *Prep*: 10m | *Cook*: 15m | *Ready In*: 25m

Ingredients

- egetable oil, for frying
- 1 (2-pound) black bass
- 1 cup rice flour
- 1 cup cornstarch
- Salt and freshly ground black pepper
- 1/4 cup Essence, recipe follows
- 2 teaspoons five-spice powder
- 4 bunches spring garlic, sliced

- 4 small heads baby bok choy, split
- 1 teaspoon sesame oil
- 2 tablespoons rice wine vinegar
- Garlic chili sauce, store bought

Emeril's ESSENCE Creole Seasoning (also referred to as Bayou Blast):Emeril's ESSENCE Creole Seasoning (also referred to as Bayou Blast):

- 2 1/2 tablespoons paprika
- 2 tablespoons salt
- 2 tablespoons garlic powder
- 1 tablespoon black pepper
- 1 tablespoon onion powder
- 1 tablespoon cayenne pepper
- 1 tablespoon dried oregano
- 1 tablespoon dried thyme

Directions

1. Preheat the oil to 360 to 375 degrees F in a deep-fryer or Dutch oven.
2. Cut 4 or 5 (2-inch) slits into the skin of the bass. In a large bowl, combine the rice flour, cornstarch, salt, pepper, Essence and five-spice powder. Season the fish with salt and pepper and dredge in the flour mixture. Drop into the hot oil and fry for 8 to 10 minutes until the fish is golden brown and cooked through.
3. Heat a large Wok and add vegetable oil. When the oil is hot, add the spring garlic and bok choy. Cook for 4 to 5 minutes. Toss vegetables with the sesame oil and the rice wine vinegar.
4. Serve the fish on top of the sauteed vegetables with the garlic chili sauce on the side.

Emeril's ESSENCE Creole Seasoning (also referred to as Bayou Blast):Emeril's ESSENCE Creole Seasoning (also referred to as Bayou Blast):

Combine all ingredients thoroughly.

Ginger Garlic Broccoli Stirfry - Chinese Style

"Quick and easy siding or vegetarian main dish."

Servings: 2 | Time: 20m

Ingredients

- 1 Broccoli head, good for 2
- 1/2 garlic head (or to taste)
- 1 pinch minced ginger
- 2 Tbsp water
- 2 Tbsp Cooking oil
- 2 Tbsp soy sauce + (optional) oyster sauce
- 1 tsp cornstarch
- 1 tsp Sesame oil (optional)
- 1 tsp sugar (if no oyster sauce)

Directions

1. In Wok, heat cooking oil and sauté garlic and ginger until brownish.
2. Drop in sliced broccoli and sauté about 3-4 minutes. Test doneness with a fork. Make sure garlic & ginger are mixed in well. Remove from Wok, don't over cook the broccoli. It should still be bright green and crisp.
3. In same Wok, combine soy sauce, oyster sauce or sugar, water and corn starch. Stir until it thickens. Taste and ajust with water or sugar or soy sauce according to desired balance. Turn off heat.
4. Put back ginger garlic broccoli in Wok and toss to distribute sauce. Drizzle with sesame oil. Serve while hot.

Sesame Stir-Fried Chinese Greens

Servings: 6 | Prep: 10m | Cook: 3m | Ready In: 13m

Ingredients

- 2 teaspoons canola oil
- 2 pounds baby bok choy
- 2 tablespoons low-sodium soy sauce
- 1 tablespoon rice wine vinegar
- 2 teaspoons toasted sesame oil

- 1 tablespoon toasted sesame seeds

Directions

1. In a Wok or large frying pan heat the oil over high heat until very hot. Add the bok choy and stir-fry until they begin to soften slightly, 1 to 2 minutes. Add the soy sauce, vinegar and sesame oil and cook until just done, 1 to 2 minutes longer. Sprinkle with sesame seeds and serve.

Steamed Halibut Fillets, Chinese Style

Servings: 4 | *Prep*: 10m | *Inactive*: 30m | *Cook*: 12m | *Ready In*: 52m

Ingredients

- 1/2 cup thinly sliced scallion
- 1/4 cup soy sauce
- 2 tablespoons rice-wine vinegar (available at Asian markets) or white-wine vinegar
- 1 (1 1/2-inch) piece peeled fresh gingerroot, cut into very fine julienne strips
- 2 tablespoons vegetable oil
- 1 tablespoon Asian sesame oil, plus 1 teaspoon for drizzling the fish
- 2 teaspoons sugar
- 2 garlic cloves, minced and mashed to a paste with a pinch of salt
- 1/4 to 1/2 teaspoon dried hot red pepper flakes, or to taste
- 4 (6-ounce) Pacific halibut fillets, skinned

Directions

1. In a bowl, whisk together the scallions, soy sauce, vinegar, gingerroot, vegetable oil, 1 tablespoon of the sesame oil, sugar, garlic paste, and red pepper flakes. Season with salt and pepper, to taste. In a shallow dish, arrange the halibut fillets in 1 layer, pour the soy sauce mixture over them, and let the fish marinate, covered and chilled, for 30 minutes.

2. Arrange a steamer or baking rack in a wide deep kettle and add water to the kettle to reach just below the steamer rack. Put a plate, such as a glass pie plate, at least 1-inch smaller in diameter than the steamer on the rack and place the fish on top. Bring the water to a boil. Pour the marinade over the fish.
3. Steam the fish, covered, over the boiling water until it just flakes, about 12 minutes, and with oven mitts, remove the steamer from the Wok. Transfer the fillets carefully to a heated platter and drizzle them with the remaining 1 teaspoon sesame oil and the sauce remaining on the plate.

Stir-Fried Chinese Greens with Ginger, Oyster and Soy Sauce

Servings: 4-6

Ingredients

- 11 -14 ounces mixed Chinese greens -- bok choy, Chinese broccoli (gai larn), baby spinach
- 3 tablespoons walnut oil
- 1 tablespoon sesame oil
- 1/2 tablespoon thinly sliced ginger
- 4 scallions, finely shredded
- 2 tablespoons oyster sauce
- 1 tablespoon soy sauce
- 2 pinches of sugar
- juice of 1 lime
- salt and freshly ground black pepper

Directions

1. Remove any blemished outside stalks from the greens. Put the spinach to one side so that you can add it to the Wok or pan at the last minute, as it cooks very quickly. Prepare the rest of the Chinese greens; i normally cut the Chinese broccoli into strips and the bok choy into quarters. Plunge the greens into boiling water for about 1 1/2 minutes until just tender, and drain well.
2. Put the oil and the ginger into a very large, hot Wok or other suitable pan and cook for about 30 seconds. Add the scallions and

the rest of the ingredients apart from the seasoning. Stir, then add the spinach and toss so that everything is coated in sauce. The vegetables will sizzle and stir-fry. The oyster and soy sauce will reduce, just coating the greens. At this point season to taste. Stir-fry for a further minute and serve immediately.

Stir-Fry Cauliflower With Ketchup And Soy Sause - Chinese Dish

"in Europe and America, I find people normally boil cauliflowers as a part of sides. But you should have tried this kind...more"

Servings: 3 | ***Time***: 10m

Ingredients

- 1 each cauliflower
- 1 slice ginger
- 1 spring onion or leek
- 1 garlic

Directions

1. Put washed cauliflower in boiling water until water boils again
2. Chop some pieces of ginger garlic and leek or spring onion just for seasoning
3. Sunflower seed oil in the pan and put in prepared ginger garlic leek
4. Ketchup and soy sauce in. If your tomato sauce is thick, then put in some water. Choose chinese soy sauce marked as 酱油 or 生抽. Do not use japanese sushi sauce which is quite different.
5. Then cauliflower in. Keep fry until the pedicel parts become green
6. Then a simple nice chinese dish is done.

Tea Smoked Salmon with Chinese Long Bean Saute

***Servings**: 4 | **Prep**: 15m | **Cook**: 40m | **Ready In:** 55m*

Ingredients

For the Asian Smoked Salmon:

- 1 (2-pound) salmon fillet, center cut, skin removed
- 1/2 cup rice wine
- 1/2 cup water
- 1 tablespoon sugar
- 1 tablespoon salt
- 1/4 cup julienned ginger,
- 1 teaspoon toasted Szechwan peppercorns
- For the smoking mix:
- 1 cup long-grain rice
- 1 cup oolong tea or black lychee tea
- 1 cup orange peels

For long bean saute:

- 2 tablespoons canola oil
- 1 pound ground pork
- 2 tablespoons garlic
- 1/2 cup finely chopped white onion
- 2 pounds Chinese long beans
- 1 tablespoon soy sauce
- 1/2 cup chicken stock
- 1 tablespoon freshly grated ginger

Directions

1. Cut the salmon in 4 equal pieces and place into a shallow baking dish. In a bowl, mix together rice wine, water, sugar and salt, stir until dissolved. Add ginger and peppercorns to liquid. Pour mixture onto salmon and turn to coat. In the bottom of the smoker over high heat, place rice, tea, orange peels. Stir to combine. Place a rack into the smoker and lay the salmon pieces on top of the rack. When mixture starts to smolder, turn the heat down to medium and continue to smoke another 15 minutes.
2. In a large Wok over high heat, add canola oil. When the oil is hot but not smoking, add ground pork, garlic and white onions. Sauteed until the pork begins to lose its pink color, and add long beans, soy

sauce, chicken stock and ginger. Continue to cook for 2 to 3 minutes.
3. To plate: Place beans on the bottom of the plate and top with tea smoked salmon.

Chapter 6: Fish and Seafood

***

Crab

***

Asian Crab

Servings: 4 | **Prep**: 10m | *Cook*: 5m | **Ready In**: 15m

Ingredients

- 1/4 cup canola oil
- 1 pound Dungeness crab, in shell (or king crab, or shell on 1-pound (21/25 count) shrimp for substitute)
- 3 tablespoons hoisin sauce
- 1 tablespoon chile hot sauce (recommended: Sriracha)
- 3 tablespoons black bean garlic paste
- 1/4 cup white wine
- 1 teaspoon sesame oil
- 1 tablespoon sesame seeds, toasted
- 2 tablespoons green onions, sliced

Directions

1. In a large Wok, heat canola oil over medium-high heat.
2. Crack crab shells in multiple areas to allow sauce to enter shell without crab shells falling apart.
3. Add crab to oil and quickly saute for 1 to 3 minutes until crab is hot. Remove crab and drain oil.
4. Add hoisin, chile hot sauce, black bean paste, and white wine and heat until bubbling. Add crab, toss for 30 seconds. Add sesame oil, and toss for 15 seconds.
5. Remove to plate and garnish with sesame seeds and green onions.

Black Pepper Dungeness Crab

"Dungeness crab is a Pacific coast favorite. This peppery recipe gets an Asian twist with cilantro, green onions, and soy sauce. Serve with steamed white rice."

Servings: 4

Ingredients

- 1 tablespoon chopped fresh cilantro
- 1 1/2 tablespoons finely chopped garlic
- 1/3 cup minced green onions
- 1 teaspoon minced ginger
- 3/4 cup reduced-sodium or regular soy sauce
- 1/2 cup honey
- 3 cooked Dungeness crabs (4 3/4 to 5 1/2 lb. total), cleaned and cracked
- 1/4 cup peppercorns
- 3 tablespoons peanut oil or salad oil

Directions

1. In a large bowl, combine cilantro, garlic, onions, ginger, soy, and honey. Add crab pieces. Cover and chill 15 minutes to 1 hour, turning crab often.
2. Coarsely grind pepper in a coffee grinder or crush with a rolling pin.
3. Pour oil into a 14-inch Wok or 6- to 8-quart pan over medium-high heat. Pour crab, marinade, and 1 1/2 tablespoons pepper into Wok. Stir often until crab is steaming hot, about 5 minutes.
4. Sprinkle remaining pepper over crab and mix well. Ladle crab and juices into bowls.

Note

- Sharon Tobin starts with live crabs that she catches. If you start with live crabs, have your fishmonger kill 3 (5 1/4 to 6 lb. total), and clean and crack them. Marinate pieces (step 1), then lift out and add to hot oil (step 3), cover, and stir often for 5 minutes. Add marinade and 1 1/2 tablespoons pepper to pan and stir often until crab shells are bright red, about 5 minutes more.

Crab Dumplings - Slimmed

Servings: 8 | Prep: 45m | Cook: 10m | Ready In: 55m

Ingredients

- 1 tablespoon vegetable oil, like soy or corn
- 1/4 to 1/2 jalapeno chile (with seeds), minced
- 3 cloves garlic, minced
- 1 tablespoon sugar
- 1 cup grated carrots (about 2 medium carrots)
- 1 1/2 tablespoons chopped fresh coriander leaves (cilantro)
- 1/2 tablespoon freshly squeezed lime juice
- 1 teaspoon Southeast Asian fish sauce
- 1 scallion (white and green), chopped
- Dumplings:
- 1/2 pound lump crabmeat, picked over to remove bits of shell and cartilage
- 1/4 cup chopped water chestnuts
- 1 large egg white
- 1 tablespoon seasoned rice wine vinegar, plus more as needed
- 1 tablespoon chopped fresh coriander leaves (cilantro)
- Heaping 1/4 teaspoon kosher salt
- 24 wonton wrappers (3 1/2-inch square), thawed if frozen
- 2 romaine leaves
- Special equipment: 3 1/2-inch round biscuit cutter, bamboo steamer

Directions

Dumplings:

1. To make the salad: In a small non-stick skillet, stir together the oil, jalapeno, and garlic. Stir-fry over medium heat until fragrant, about 5 minutes. Remove the skillet from the heat and add the sugar. Transfer the mixture to a medium bowl, and cool slightly. Toss the carrot, coriander, lime juice, fish sauce, and scallion together with the jalapeno mixture. Set aside.
2. To make the dumplings: In a medium bowl, combine the crabmeat, water chestnuts, egg white, 1 tablespoon of vinegar, coriander, and salt.

3. Lay 6 to 8 wontons out on a work surface. Trim into rounds with the biscuit cutter. Lightly brush the surface of each wrapper with vinegar. Place a level tablespoon of the crab filling in the center of each wrapper. Gather the wrapper around the filling, in a loosely-pleated open dumpling. The dumpling should be flat on the bottom with about a 1/2-inch of the wrapper unfilled at the top in order to hold the salad after steaming. Repeat until the filling is used up.
4. Arrange the dumplings about 1/4-inch apart in 2 lettuce leaf-lined bamboo steamers. Fill a Wok or pan with enough water to come up to the bottom of the steamer rack, and bring the water to a boil over high heat. Stack the steamers in the pan, cover, and steam the dumplings until the filling is set, about 10 minutes.
5. Remove the steamer from the pan. Top each dumpling with 1/2 heaping teaspoon of the carrot salad. Serve immediately in the steamer pan.

Tips:

- Use this vegetable salad with other seafood and meat hors d'oeuvres instead of mayonnaise or cream based sauces
- Thai cuisine is often low in fat, just avoid dishes made with coconut milk

Crab vegetable stir fry

Servings: 2 | Cook: 10m

Ingredients

- 2 dash seasame oil
- 1 dash ground ginger
- 2 tsp soy sauce
- 1 clove garlic minced
- 3 stick crab meat chopped
- 1 1/4 cup mixed vegetables
- 1 pinch salt
- 1 pinch garlic pepper
- 1 cup cooked white rice

Directions

1. in a pan preheat sesame oil
2. brown the garlic. make sure not to burn it
3. add the crab meat making sure to stir so it wont stick
4. add the vegetables
5. Add the already cooked rice
6. if you notice it startsto sick add a little bit of water
7. add the soy sauce and seasonings
8. mix and serve

Spicy Crab Curry - Bangla Style

"A spicy crab curry cooked with hot Indian spices, sliced red onion, and sliced potatoes (what we Bengalis call Chocchori Aloo.) It's best eaten with hot rice."

Servings: 4 | **Prep**: 25m | **Cook**: 30m | **Ready In**: 55m

Ingredients

- 2 fresh Dungeness crabs, cleaned and with their shells cracked
- 2 teaspoons ground turmeric
- 1/2 teaspoon salt 1 tablespoon mustard seed
- 1 tablespoon hot water
- 1 tablespoon mustard oil
- 3 cups sliced red onion
- 3/4 cups boiling potatoes, peeled, halved lengthwise, and cut crosswise into 1/4-inch slices
- 2 whole cloves
- 1 (1 inch) piece cinnamon stick
- 2 pods green cardamom pods
- 5 whole black peppercorns
- 2 large tomatoes, coarsely chopped
- 4 Thai green chiles
- 1/2 teaspoons garlic paste
- 1/2 teaspoons ginger paste
- 1 teaspoon cayenne pepper
- salt to taste 1 teaspoon white sugar

Garnish:

- 1 wedge fresh lemon
- 1/2 cup chopped fresh cilantro

Directions

1. Rub the crabs with 1 teaspoon of the turmeric and 1/2 teaspoon salt; let them marinate for 1 hour. Combine the mustard seed and hot water in a small bowl and let stand for 10 minutes. Use a mortar and pestle to grind the seeds into a coarse paste.
2. Heat the oil in a Wok or kadhai over medium heat. Add the crabs and stir fry until they change color, about 4 minutes. Remove the crabs from the oil and set aside.
3. Add the sliced onions to the Wok and cook and stir over medium heat until the onions are translucent, about 5 minutes. Raise the heat to high, add the potatoes, and cook, stirring constantly, for about 2 minutes. Add the cloves, cinnamon stick, cardamom pods, and peppercorns, and stir for thirty seconds.
4. Stir in the tomatoes, ginger paste, and garlic paste. Halve three of the chiles and add them to the Wok. Cook and stir for an additional minute or two over high heat. Reduce the heat to medium; add the remaining 1 teaspoon turmeric, the cayenne pepper, and the mustard paste and stir to combine. Add the crabs to the Wok and pour in just enough water to cover the vegetables. Bring the water to a boil and stir in the sugar and salt to taste.
5. Cover the Wok, reduce the heat, and simmer until the potatoes are tender and the water is reduced by half, about 10 minutes. Remove the lid, stir, and simmer until the gravy is thickened, about 5 minutes more.
6. Squeeze the lemon wedge over the finished dish. Garnish with chopped cilantro and sliced green chile and serve hot, with rice.

Editor's Note

- Mustard oil and green cardamom pods are available in Indian groceries and specialty food stores. Black or white mustard seeds can be used to make the mustard paste.

Stir-Fried Crabmeat with Cellophane Noodles

Servings: 4 | Prep: 20m | Cook: 10m | Ready In: 30m

Ingredients

- 1 package (3 1/2 ounces) of cellophane noodles
- 2 tablespoons vegetable oil
- 2 tablespoons chopped shallots
- 1 cup thinly sliced snow peas
- 1 -ounce of dried tree ear mushrooms, reconstituted in water
- 2 teaspoons chopped garlic
- 1 cup bean sprouts (packed)
- Fish sauce (nuoc mam)
- Freshly ground black pepper
- 1/2 pound fresh crab meat, cartilage removed
- 1/4 cup chopped green onions

Directions

- Place the noodles in a large bowl. Cover with warm water and allow to sit for 20 minutes. Drain and pat dry. In a Wok, over medium heat, add the oil. When the oil is hot, add the shallots, peas, mushrooms, garlic and bean sprouts. Season with the fish sauce and black pepper. Stir-fry for 1 minute. Add the crabmeat. Season with the fish sauce and black pepper. Continue to stir-fry for 2 minutes. Add the noodles and green onions. Stir-fry for 1 minute. Remove and serve on a large platter.

Vietnamese-style Spicy Crab with Garlic Noodles

"Top homemade garlic noodles with spicy fried crab for a Vietnamese-inspired entrée that's sure to satisfy your cravings for Asian flavor."

Servings: 4-6 | Total time: 1h30m

Ingredients

- 1 cup flour
- 1 1/2 teaspoons plus 1 tbsp. salt

- 1 1/2 teaspoons freshly ground black pepper
- 1/2 teaspoon cayenne
- 2 Dungeness crabs, cooked, cleaned, quartered, and cracked
- Vegetable oil for frying, plus 3 tbsp.
- 10 cloves garlic, chopped
- 1/2 pound spaghettini (thin spaghetti)
- 3 tablespoons butter, at room temperature
- 6 small dried red chiles
- 2 tablespoons grated fresh ginger
- 4 green onions, chopped
- 4 serrano chiles, stemmed, seeded, and chopped
- 1/3 cup sake or other rice wine
- 1 cup basil leaves, chopped
- 1/2 cup mint leaves, chopped
- 1/2 cup cilantro leaves

Directions

1. Combine flour, 1 tsp. salt, 1 tsp. pepper, and the cayenne in a large bowl. Pat crab pieces dry with paper towels and toss (in batches) with flour mixture. Remove crab and shake off excess flour. Set aside.
2. In a Wok or large pot, heat 3 in. oil to 375°. Lay out paper towels for draining crab and garlic. Fry crab in batches (do not crowd Wok) until golden, about 5 minutes per batch. Drain on paper towels.
3. Using the same hot oil, fry garlic until golden brown, 2 to 3 minutes. Remove with a slotted spoon and drain on paper towels. Set garlic aside; cool and discard oil.
4. Bring a large pot of water to a boil. Add 1 tbsp. of the salt and the spaghettini. Cook until tender to the bite, 5 to 10 minutes. Drain, transfer to a serving bowl, and toss with butter and half of the fried garlic. Cover and put in a warm place.
5. Heat a Wok or pot large enough to hold all the crab over high heat. Add remaining 3 tbsp. oil, dried chiles, and ginger. Cook, stirring constantly, until fragrant, about 30 seconds. Add green onions, serrano chiles, and remaining 1/2 tsp. salt. Cook, stirring, until onions wilt, about 1 minute. Add sake and cook, stirring, until sake is reduced by about half. Stir in crab and cover. Cook until crab is heated through, about 3 minutes.
6. Remove lid and cook, stirring, until any liquid evaporates. Stir in basil, mint, cilantro, and remaining 1/2 tsp. pepper. Cook, stirring, until herbs have wilted. Stir in remaining fried garlic. Transfer crab to a warm platter and serve hot, with garlic noodles.

Wok-Fried Dungeness Crab

Servings: 6 | **Prep**: 20m | Cook: 10m | **Ready In**: 30m

Ingredients

- 1/2 cups fish stock
- 1/4 cup dark soy sauce
- 2 tablespoons lime juice
- 1/2 cup sherry
- 1 cup fermented black beans, rinsed
- 1/4 cup chopped cashews
- 1/2 cup chopped green onions
- 1/2 cup chopped cilantro leaves
- 1 pound cleaned Dungeness or jumbo lump crabmeat
- 1 tablespoon cornstarch mixed with 2 tablespoons water
- 1/4 cup peanut oil
- 5 garlic cloves, chopped
- 2 -inch piece fresh ginger, grated
- 1 Thai chile pepper, minced
- 4 Dungeness crabs, 1 1/2 pounds each, cleaned and broken into pieces
- 6 heads baby bok choy, halved and steamed

Directions

1. In a large skillet, combine fish stock, soy, lime juice, sherry, black beans, cashews, green onions, and cilantro. Simmer for 5 minutes or until sauce is starting to thicken. Add the cleaned crabmeat and cornstarch mixture and cook for 1 minute.
2. Meanwhile, in a large Wok over high heat, add the peanut oil. When oil is hot, add the garlic, ginger, chile, and crab pieces and stir-fry for 3 to 4 minutes.
3. Serve crab pieces with sauce over top and steamed bok choy on the side. Be careful to not to eat any pieces of shell!

Fish

***

Chinese Style Wok-Fried Whole Fish with Wokked Long Beans and Simple Stir Fried Rice

Servings: 4 | **Prep**: 30m | **Inactive**: 10m | **Cook**: 25m | **Ready In**: 1h5m

Ingredients

- Vegetable or peanut oil, for frying
- 1 (2-pound) whole fish, such as striped bass, scaled and gutted
- 1 1/2 cups rice flour
- 1 1/2 tablespoons Emeril's Original Essence, recipe follows
- 1 teaspoon salt
- 1 teaspoon freshly ground black pepper
- Wokked Long Beans, for serving
- Simple Stir Fried Rice, for serving

Emeril's ESSENCE Creole Seasoning (also referred to as Bayou Blast):

- 1/2 tablespoons paprika
- 2 tablespoons salt
- 2 tablespoons garlic powder
- 1 tablespoon black pepper
- 1 tablespoon onion powder
- 1 tablespoon cayenne pepper
- 1 tablespoon dried oregano
- 1 tablespoon dried thyme

Wokked long beans:

- 2 tablespoons soy sauce
- 1/4 teaspoon ground white pepper
- 8 ounces ground pork
- 1/4 cup peanut oil

- 3/4 pound long beans, washed, ends trimmed, cut into 4-inch lengths
- 3 tablespoons thinly sliced garlic
- 1/2 tablespoons hoisin sauce
- 2 tablespoons chili sauce with bean paste
- 1 tablespoon plus 1 teaspoon dark soy sauce
- 1/2 teaspoons sesame oil

Simple Fried Rice:

- 3 tablespoons peanut oil
- 1/2 teaspoons sesame oil
- 3/4 cup diced onion
- 1/2 cup diced carrot
- 1 teaspoon minced garlic
- 1 teaspoon minced ginger
- 1 teaspoon minced green onion bottoms
- 6 cups cooked white rice
- 1/2 cup frozen peas
- 3/4 cup soy sauce
- 2 teaspoons sugar
- 2 tablespoons chopped green onion tops

Directions

1. Preheat 1 1/2 to 2 inches of oil to 350 degrees F in a Wok large enough to hold the fish.
2. In a shallow bowl, combine the rice flour, Essence, salt, and pepper, and dredge the fish in the seasoned flour mixture until well coated on all sides. Shake to remove any excess flour.
3. When the oil is hot, add the fish carefully to the Wok; take care as it may splatter. Using a shallow ladle, ladle some of the hot oil over the top of the fish as it cooks in the Wok. Cook until golden brown and cooked completely through, 12 to 15 minutes. Transfer the fish to a wire rack set over paper towels to drain briefly before serving.
4. Cut the fish into portions and serve hot over the Stir Fried Rice and garnish with some of the Wokked Long Beans.

Emeril's ESSENCE Creole Seasoning (also referred to as Bayou Blast):

Combine all ingredients thoroughly.

Wokked long beans:

1. In a mixing bowl combine the soy sauce, white pepper and ground pork. Stir to combine well and set aside to marinate for 10 minutes.
2. Preheat a Wok over high heat until hot. Add the peanut oil and, when the oil is smoking, add the long beans and stir-fry until slightly wrinkled, about 3 minutes. Using a slotted spoon, transfer to a plate lined with paper towels and set aside.
3. Remove all but about 1 tablespoon of the oil from the Wok, then add the garlic and cook briefly until fragrant, about 10 seconds. Add the ground pork and stir fry until the pork is no longer pink, about 1 1/2 minutes. Add the hoisin sauce, chili sauce with bean paste, dark soy sauce and sesame oil to the Wok and stir to combine. Return the long beans to the Wok and stir to mix well. Serve as soon as everything is heated through.

Simple Fried Rice:

- Heat a Wok or 14-inch saute pan over high heat and, when hot, add the peanut oil and sesame oil and swirl to coat. Add the onion and carrots and cook, stirring, for 1 minute. Add the garlic, ginger and green onion bottoms and cook for 30 seconds. Add the rice, green peas, soy sauce, sugar, and green onion tops and cook, constantly stirring, until heated through and well blended, 3 to 4 minutes.

Chinese Whole Fish with Black Bean Sauce

Servings: 4 | Prep: 25m | Cook: 28m | Ready In: 53m

Ingredients

- Peanut oil or vegetable oil, for frying
- 2 (1 1/2 to 2-pound) Petrole soles, scaled and eviscerated, head off
- 2 tablespoons Chinese fermented black beans, rinsed well and drained
- 4 1/2 teaspoons minced garlic
- 1 tablespoon mirin
- 1 tablespoon sesame oil
- 2 teaspoons minced ginger
- 1 1/2 teaspoons sugar
- 1/4 teaspoon red pepper flakes
- 1/4 teaspoon salt
- 1/4 cup cornstarch

- 1/4 cup all-purpose flour
- Red Pepper Dipping Sauce, recipe follows, accompaniment
- Steamed white rice, accompaniment
- 1/4 cup green onions sliced on the bias, garnish

Red Pepper Dipping Sauce:

- 2 tablespoons soy sauce
- 1 tablespoon dark soy sauce
- 1 tablespoon dried red chile flakes
- 4 1/2 teaspoons peanut oil
- 2 tablespoons chopped green onions
- 2 teaspoons minced fresh ginger

Directions

1. In a large Wok or pot, heat the vegetable oil to 400 degrees F.
2. Make 2 or 3 slashes diagonally across the flesh of each side of the fish.
3. In a small bowl, mash the black beans and garlic. Add the rice wine, oil, ginger, sugar, pepper flakes, and salt, and whisk to combine. Rub the mixture over the outside of the fish, rubbing onto the slashes.
4. In a shallow bowl, combine the cornstarch and flour. Dredge the fish in the mixture and shake to remove any excess. Carefully slide the flour-coated fish into the hot oil. Fry until golden brown, about 5 to 8 minutes, turning as necessary with tongs. Remove and drain on paper towels.
5. To serve, arrange the fried fish on a platter with the red pepper sauce and rice. Garnish with the chopped green onions and serve immediately.

Red Pepper Dipping Sauce:

Combine all the ingredients in a decorative bowl and mix. Set aside at room temperature until ready to serve.

Stir Fry Greenbean-Meatball And Fried Cat Fish

"Marinate the fish for at least 30 minutes or put it in the frezzer and just take it out when needed"

Servings: 2 | **Ready In**: 20m

Ingredients

- 1 kg small cat fish
- 10 balls of meatball
- 200 gr green beans
- 1/4 cup dried anchovy
- 10 small red chili
- 3 cm ginger, grated
- 2 cloves garlic, grated
- 1 stalk spring onion
- oil to fry and saute
- salt and pepper
- ground cumin
- honey

Directions

1. Marinate the fish with salt, ground pepper, and ground cummin (for 1kg fish: @ 1 tbs) put it in the fridge for 30 minutes or overnight
2. Get the marinated fish from the fridge after 30 minutes and set it aside (make sure the fish at room temperature before frying)
3. Prepare stir fry inggredient while waiting the fish at room temperature
4. Chop meatballs, spring onion, chilli. Grate ginger and garlics.
5. Start heating Wok and add 1/2 cup oil to fry the fish (semi-deep fry). Coz it was for 2 serving mine just fry 2 fish but if you want to fry them all add more oil.
6. Cook the fish about 3-4 minutes on each side on medium high heat
7. While the fish cook. Start heating another Wok for stir fry on high heat. We gonna cook fast for this dish coz it on high heat we dont want to burn anything
8. Add ginger and garlic when the oil hot enough stir a little bit then add anchovy and meatball stir well
9. Add green beans when anchovy start to crips and continue to stir all around for 2 minutes
10. Turn off the heat and season with a pinch of salt (we dont want to much salt coz anchovy already salty) and add 1 tbs honey, spring onion and chilies and stir well
11. Its ready to serveeeeeee!!!

Shrimp

***

Asian Shrimp Rice Bowl

"Easy to prepare ahead of time and so much great flavor! Serve this on square, Asian-inspired dinnerware with chopsticks for a gorgeous presentation."

Servings: 4 | **Prep**: 15 m | **Cook**: 25 m | **Ready In**: 1 h 40 m

Ingredients

- 1/3 cup soy sauce
- 1/4 cup hoisin sauce
- 2 tablespoons honey
- tablespoon chile paste
- 2 tablespoons orange marmalade
- 1/2 pound cooked shrimp
- 2 cups uncooked jasmine rice
- 3 cups water
- 2 tablespoons olive oil
- 1 orange bell pepper, cut into 1/2-inch dice
- 1 red bell pepper, cut into 1/2-inch dice
- 2 cups sugar snap peas
- 1 sweet onion, cut into 1/2-inch dice
- 4 cloves garlic, minced
- 2 teaspoons minced fresh ginger root
- 1/4 teaspoon sesame oil
- 1/2 teaspoons sesame seeds

Directions

1. Whisk soy sauce, hoisin sauce, honey, chili paste, and orange marmalade together in a small bowl. Stir shrimp into the marinade; refrigerate for one hour.
2. Bring the rice and water to a boil in a saucepan over high heat. Reduce heat to medium-low, cover, and simmer until the rice is tender, and the liquid has been absorbed, 20 to 25 minutes.
3. Heat oil in a large skillet or Wok. Cook the orange pepper, red pepper, sugar snap peas, and onion in hot oil until they just begin to soften, 2 to 3 minutes. Toss the marinated shrimp, garlic, ginger, and sesame oil into the vegetables; continue to cook until shrimp is heated through, 2 to 3 minutes more.
4. Serve over hot jasmine rice, sprinkled with sesame seeds.

Chinese Take-Out Shrimp with Garlic

"There is a great garlic flavor to this with an underlying heat that is fabulous served over rice!"

Servings*: 4 |* ***Prep****: 15m |* ***Cook****: 10m |* ***Ready In****: 25m*

Ingredients

- 2 tablespoons canola oil
- 10 cloves garlic, chopped
- 1 teaspoon minced fresh ginger root
- 1 (8 ounce) can sliced water chestnuts, drained
- 1 cup snow peas
- 1 cup small white button mushrooms
- 1 teaspoon crushed red pepper flakes
- 1/2 teaspoon salt
- 1 teaspoon ground black pepper
- 1 pound peeled and deveined jumbo shrimp
- 1/2 cup chicken broth
- 1 tablespoon rice vinegar
- 2 tablespoons fish sauce
- 2 tablespoons dry sherry
- 1 tablespoon cornstarch
- 1 tablespoon water

Directions

1. Heat oil in Wok or large skillet until very hot. Cook and stir garlic and ginger in the hot oil until fragrant, about 30 seconds. Add the water chestnuts, snow peas, mushrooms, red pepper flakes, salt, pepper, and shrimp to the pan. Cook, stirring, until shrimp turns pink, 2 to 3 minutes.
2. Combine the chicken broth, rice vinegar, fish sauce, and dry sherry in a small bowl. Pour into the shrimp mixture; cook and stir briefly to combine. Combine the cornstarch and water and stir into the Wok. Stir until sauce has thickened, about 2 minutes.

Cook's Note:

- If you really like it spicy, add up to 1 teaspoon additional crushed red pepper flakes.

Coconut Shrimp and Rice

Servings: 6 | **Prep**: 5m | **Cook**: 22m | **Ready In**: 27m

Ingredients

- 1 1/2 cups basmati rice
- 1 tablespoon unsalted butter
- 1 clove garlic, finely chopped
- 1/4 teaspoon crushed red pepper
- 12 ounces medium shrimp, peeled and deveined
- 1 cup canned low-sodium chicken broth
- 1 cup canned coconut milk (shake before opening)
- 1/4 cup fresh lime juice (from about 3 limes)
- 1/2 teaspoon salt
- 1/4 cup finely chopped fresh cilantro

Directions

1. Rinse and drain rice several times in cold water to remove excess starch. Melt butter in a large saucepan over medium-high heat. Add garlic, crushed red pepper and shrimp and sauté until shrimp is cooked through, 3 to 4 minutes total. Transfer shrimp mixture to a plate and cover with foil to keep warm.
2. Add rice to saucepan and cook, stirring, until fragrant and lightly toasted, about 3 minutes. Stir in broth, coconut milk, lime juice and salt, and bring to a boil over high heat. Reduce heat to low, cover pan and cook until rice is tender, 15 minutes. Stir in cilantro, and serve topped with shrimp.

Crispy Shrimp Tempura

"Shrimp tempura, Japanese style. Serve this at dinner as an appetizer or to your party guests as finger food."

Servings: 6 | **Prep**: 20m | **Cook**: 15m | **Ready In**: 35

Ingredients

- 1 cup all-purpose flour
- 2 tablespoons cornstarch
- 1 pinch salt 1 cup water
- 1 egg yolk 2 egg whites, lightly beaten
- 1 pound medium shrimp, peeled and deveined, tails left on
- 2 cups vegetable oil for frying

Directions

1. Heat oil in a deep-fryer to 375 degrees F (190 degrees C).
2. Whisk flour, cornstarch, and salt in a large bowl. Make a depression in the center of the flour. Stir in the water and egg yolk. Mix just until moistened; batter will be lumpy. Stir in egg whites.
3. One at a time, dip shrimp into the batter to coat. Do not batter tails. Carefully place a few shrimp at a time into the hot oil. Fry until golden brown, about 1 1/2 minutes. Drain on paper towels.

Editor's Note

- We have determined the nutritional value of oil for frying based on a retention value of 10% after cooking. The exact amount will vary depending on cooking time and temperature, ingredient density, and the specific type of oil used.

Easy Shrimp Lo Mein

"Making a delicious Chinese dish is super easy. For better searing results, use a seasoned Wok."

Servings: 2| **Prep**: 10m | **Cook**: 25m | **Ready In**: 35m

Ingredients

- 1 (8 ounce) package spaghetti
- 2 tablespoons soy sauce
- 2 tablespoons oyster sauce
- 2 tablespoons brown sugar 2 teaspoons fish sauce
- 1/2 teaspoon garlic powder 1/2 teaspoon ground ginger
- 2 teaspoons vegetable oil
- 1 pound uncooked medium shrimp, peeled and deveined
- 1 cup chopped broccoli
- 1/4 yellow onion, thinly sliced
- 3 crimini mushrooms, sliced
- 2 cloves garlic, minced
- 2 large eggs

Directions

1. Bring a large pot of lightly salted water to a boil. Cook spaghetti in the boiling water until cooked through yet firm to the bite, about 12 minutes; drain.
2. Mix soy sauce, oyster sauce, brown sugar, fish sauce, garlic powder, and ground ginger in a bowl until the sugar dissolves.
3. Heat oil in a large skillet or Wok over medium heat; cook and stir shrimp in hot oil until they start to change color, 1 to 2 minutes. Add broccoli, onion, and mushrooms; cook until just beginning to soften, 3 to 5 minutes. Stir garlic through the vegetable mixture.

Push the vegetables to one side of the pan. Cook the eggs in the clear space in the pan, scrambling lightly, until no longer moist, 3 to 5 minutes. Stir the cooked egg with shrimp and vegetables. Add the cooked noodles and the sauce; cook and stir until hot and evenly mixed, about 2 minutes more. Serve immediately.

Footnotes

- Tip: Aluminum foil helps keep food moist, ensures it cooks evenly, keeps leftovers fresh, and makes clean-up easy.
- Stir cornstarch into honey until smooth, then add to vegetables, and simmer until thickened, about 2 minutes. Add shrimp, and cook until they turn pink, about 3 minutes. Season to taste with salt and pepper before serving.

Greek-Style Shrimp Linguine

*Servings: 4 | **Prep**: 5m | **Cook**: 15m*

Ingredients

- 8 ounces uncooked linguine
- 1 tablespoon olive oil
- 20 large shrimp, peeled and deveined (about 1 pound)
- 4 garlic cloves, minced
- 1 teaspoon dried oregano
- 1/4 teaspoon crushed red pepper
- 1 (14.5-ounce) can diced tomatoes, undrained
- 3/4 cup (3 ounces) crumbled feta cheese
- 2 tablespoons chopped fresh flatleaf parsley or basil

Directions

1. Cook linguine according to package directions.
2. Meanwhile, heat oil in a large nonstick skillet over medium-high heat. Add the shrimp, minced garlic, dried oregano, and red pepper; stir-fry 2 minutes. Add the tomatoes; reduce heat and simmer, uncovered, until shrimp is opaque, about 3 minutes.

3. Drain linguine; return to the same pot. Add shrimp mixture and cheese to the linguine; toss well, and transfer to 4 serving plates. Top with parsley or basil.

Honey-Ginger Shrimp and Vegetables

"I created this recipe for those who have a sweet tooth but also enjoy a bit of spice in their life! Substitute chicken for shrimp if desired."

Servings: 4 | *Prep*: 30m | **Cook**: 15m | **Ready In**: 45m

Ingredients

- 2 tablespoons olive oil
- 3 cloves garlic, minced
- 1/2 onion, chopped 1 1/2 teaspoons ground ginger
- 2 teaspoons red pepper flakes 1 red bell pepper, chopped
- 1/2 zucchini, halved lengthwise and sliced
- 3 cups fresh mushrooms, coarsely chopped
- 2 tablespoons cornstarch 1/2 cup honey
- 1 pound medium shrimp - peeled and deveined
- salt and pepper to taste

Directions

1. Heat olive oil in a Wok or large skillet over high heat until it begins to smoke. Stir in garlic, onion, ginger, and red pepper flakes. Quickly cook until the onion softens and just begins to brown. Stir in bell pepper, zucchini, and mushrooms; continue cooking until the zucchini softens, about 4 minutes.
2. Stir cornstarch into honey until smooth, then add to vegetables, and simmer until thickened, about 2 minutes. Add shrimp, and cook until they turn pink, about 3 minutes. Season to taste with salt and pepper before serving.

Kung Pao Shrimp

"For a spicier kick to the pungent Kung Pao glaze, leave the seeds in the chiles. Chinese black vinegar has a deep, almost smoky taste. Look for it in Asian markets, or substitute balsamic vinegar for a sweeter flavor to this shrimp dish."

Servings: 4

Ingredients

Shrimp:

- 1 tablespoon Shaoxing (Chinese rice wine), dry sherry, or sake
- 1 teaspoon cornstarch
- 1/2 teaspoon salt
- 1 pound peeled and deveined medium shrimp

Sauce:

- 1 tablespoon sugar
- 2 tablespoons water
- 1 tablespoon Chinese black vinegar or balsamic vinegar
- 1 tablespoon low-sodium soy sauce
- 3/4 teaspoon cornstarch
- 1/2 teaspoon dark sesame oil

Remaining Ingredients:

- 2 tablespoons canola oil
- 1 1/3 cups thinly sliced green bell pepper strips (about 1 large)
- 1 tablespoon minced garlic
- 1 tablespoon minced peeled fresh ginger
- 3 to 4 small dried hot red chiles, broken in half and seeded
- 1/4 cup chopped unsalted, dry-roasted peanuts
- 3 cups hot cooked short-grain rice

Directions

1. To prepare shrimp, combine first 4 ingredients; cover and chill 10 minutes.
2. To prepare sauce, combine sugar and next 5 ingredients (through sesame oil).
3. Heat a 14-inch Wok over high heat. Add canola oil to Wok, swirling to coat. Add bell pepper, garlic, ginger, and chiles to Wok; stir-fry 1

minute or just until chiles begin to lightly brown (do not burn). Add shrimp mixture to Wok; stir-fry 2 minutes or until shrimp are done. Stir sauce; add sauce to Wok. Stir-fry 30 seconds or until sauce thickens. Sprinkle with chopped peanuts. Serve over rice.

Lady Linda's Delightful Shrimp and Scallop Stir-Fry

"Tons of flavor with very little work! I spent the day looking for bay scallop recipes online and inspired I came up with this keeper! Serve over rice or noodles."

Servings: 4 | **Prep**: 45m | **Cook**: 15m | **Ready In**: 1h

Ingredients

- 1 pound bay scallops, tough muscle removed
- 1 tablespoon ground ginger
- 1 tablespoon crushed red pepper flakes
- 1 teaspoon seafood seasoning, such as Old Bay™
- 2 tablespoons fish sauce
- 1 tablespoon cornstarch
- 1/4 cup vegetable oil, divided
- 2 teaspoons minced garlic
- 1 tablespoon cornstarch
- 1/4 cup chicken broth
- 1 small onion, sliced
- 1 (8 ounce) package sliced fresh mushrooms
- 2 small zucchini, sliced
- 1 small yellow squash, sliced
- 1/4 cup julienned carrot
- 1 pound peeled and deveined cooked shrimp
- 1/2 green bell pepper, cut into
- 1/2-inch squares

Directions

1. Toss the scallops with the ginger, red pepper flakes, seafood seasoning, fish sauce, and 1 tablespoon of cornstarch in a bowl. Cover, and marinate 30 minutes.

2. Heat half of the oil in a Wok over high heat. Stir in the garlic, and cook until it begins to brown, about 30 seconds. Stir in the marinated scallops, and cook until they are no longer translucent in the center, about 3 minutes. Dissolve the remaining 1 tablespoon of cornstarch in the chicken broth. Pour into the Wok, and stir until thickened. Remove to a bowl.
3. Clean the Wok well, and heat the remaining oil over high heat; stir in the onion, mushrooms, zucchini, yellow squash, and carrot. Cook and stir until the vegetables are tender, about 5 minutes. Stir in the shrimp, green pepper, and scallop mixture. Stir until hot.

Lemongrass & Ginger Shrimp Stirfry

"We were super hungry today and wanted something quick. I put a few things together that I thought would work and .. YUMMMMMMMM-O so good and fresh! And it really only took 15 min (not including marinade time)"

Ingredients

- 1 zucchini, halved and sliced
- 1 Green pepper, sliced
- 1 Red pepper, sliced
- 1 lb Shrimp, deveined and peeled
- 1 1/2 tbsp thai yellow curry paste
- 1 can Coconut milk
- salt and pepper
- 1 tsp Coconut oil
- sesame seeds (optional) as a garnish
- Marinade
- 2 lemongrass stalks, minced (tough outer bit removed)
- 1/2 tbsp Fresh grated ginger

Directions

1. Mince the lemongrass the best you can, add ginger and marinade the shrimp for 30 min.
2. In a large pan heat coconut oil and add shrimp (not including marinade)

3. When shrimp just turns pink, add the yellow curry paste and 1/2 the can of coconut milk, mix to combine.
4. Add the veggies and cook for about 3 min.
5. After 3 min, add the rest of the coconut milk, mix and let cook for 5 min.
6. Serve with rice or noodles, it doesn't take very long, I like my veggies to be a little crisp but you're more than welcome to cook longer . ENJOY!!

Mike's Spicy Garlic Shrimp & Scallop Asian Stir Fry Over White Rice

"A dish stacked with massive, delicious, spicy, juicy seafood chunks, crispy vegetables and literally packed with fresh seafood flavor!

Do you love fresh, plump seafood? Love garlic? Love spicy & sweet too? Then you're going to love this easy layered Asian Stir Fry recipe! Serve this memorable dish alone, over rice or, over Asian noodles. Dealers choice!

By the way, 7 year old crazy little fingers not only made, but created, photographed and documented this dish all by themselves this evening! I kid you not! [sorry, excuse the pun]"

Servings: 4 | **Time**: 60m

Ingredients

- 2 Pounds Frozen Jumbo Raw Shrimp [husks on - reserve any de-thawed fluids]
- 1 Pound Frozen Jumbo Raw Scallops [reserve any de-thawed fluids]
- 2 tbsp Fine Minced Garlic [aromatic]
- 1 tsp Granulated Garlic [aromatic]
- 3 tbsp Garlic Olive Oil
- 1/2 tbsp Red Pepper Flakes [aromatic]
- 1/4 Cup Fried Fresh Garlic [optional - garnish]
- 1 tbsp Pickled Ginger [aromatic]
- to taste Fresh Cabbage [thick sliced]
- to taste Green Onions [added last]
- to taste Green Bell Peppers [thin Sliced]

- to taste Fresh Carrots [peeled slices]
- to taste Purple Onions [thin slices]
- as needed Water Chestnuts
- 1/4 Cup Fresh Parsley
- to taste Bamboo Shoots
- to taste Snap Peas [rinsed & blanched]
- to taste Fresh Broccoli [rinsed & blanched]
- 2 tbsp Soy Sauce [aromatic]
- 1 tbsp Oyster Sauce [aromatic]
- 1 tbsp Quality Fish Sauce [aromatic]
- 2 tbsp Hoisin Sauce [aromatic]
- 1/2 tsp Garlic Sea Salt + 1/2 tsp White Pepper [for your seafood stock]

Directions

1. Dethaw your raw jumbo shrimp with just enough water to cover them. About 3 to 4 cups. Reserve all fluids.
2. Dethaw your raw jumbo scallops with just enough water to cover them. About 2 cups. Reserve all fluids.
3. TO BRINE YOUR RAW SEAFOOD ● Pour enough water on your raw shrimp and scallops to cover them. Then, add 1 tbsp salt - 1 tbsp sugar - 1 tbsp granulated garlic powder and 1/2 tbsp granulated onion powder to your water. Add ice cubes as well. You'll want both at 35° to 42°. Cover, shake well and place in fridge for a half to 1 hour. Shake occasionally.
4. ● Peel shrimp and reserve all shells, tails, legs, veins and shrimp water. Place all leftovers back into shrimp water. ● Pour scallop water into shrimp water. Then, add 1 1/2 tsp garlic sea salt and 1/2 tsp white pepper and create your seafood stock. Bring to a boil and boil for 15 minutes. Be careful. She will boil over with the sea salt addition if you're not watching. Turn off heat.
5. Cut your jumbo raw scallops into halves or quarters depending upon their size.
6. After your shuck boil, strain your stock thru a very fine mesh strainer and place broth back in your pot. Discard shells and any residuals in your strainer.
7. Reheat your clear, clean seafood stock to a very steady boil. Man! Is she gonna smell and sample so deliciously tasty!
8. Place your rinsed snap peas and broccoli into your boiling seafood stock for 2 minutes. Watch these closely, remove them and set them to the side in ice water to arrest the cooking process. This method will kill any bacteria and slightly soften these very hard vegetables. Again, reserve your remaining seafood stock. I bring it

back up to a simmer and allow it to reduce even further for fullest flavor.
9. Blanched Broccoli.
10. Chop your fresh vegetables. Separate your hard vegetables, soft vegetables and blanched vegetables. Hard vegetables to be Wok'd first, blanched vegetables second and soft, last.
11. Fully drain your seafood from your brine water. Discard brine water and ice.
12. If opting for the crunchy garlic garnish: • Fry sliced garlic and red pepper flakes in garlic oil only until just slightly browned [before frying your hard vegetables] Anything darker will create a seriously bitter taste that will ruin your entire dish. So, watch it very closely. • Drain all on paper towels until dried and crispy. Reserve all residual oil. Fine chop your crispy fried garlic later. You'll be using this as a garnish.
13. If not, add 3 tablespoons garlic olive oil, your aromatics, your hard vegetables and 1 cup of your seafood stock to your Wok at a searing heat. Fry for 1 minute covered. No more.
14. Immediately add all blanched vegetables and Wok for 30 seconds longer. Then, add all fully drained seafood and soft vegetables for 2 to 3 minutes covered. 2 minutes if not fully chilled. Add additional seafood stock if needed for steaming seafood. Stir once. Covered.
15. Place your rice at the base of your bowl and pile on your seafood stir fry. Drizzle top with your residual seafood stock to hydrate and flavor your rice. Garnish with granulated garlic or crispy garlic and soy sauce. Serve with additional Soy Sauce.
16. Enjoy!

Monica's Japanese Garlic Dollop Shrimp

"This is a delightful Japanese-inspired shrimp recipe for garlic-lovers; served over rice or pasta or on it's own -- it's sure to make everyone scream, 'What's the recipe?!' I secured this sure-fire loads-o-goodness recipe while attempting to replicate something else entirely. Serve shrimps over freshly prepared rice or pasta with a salad, vegetable and/or hot bread and butter -- Happy Ending!"

*Servings: 4 | **Prep**: 20m | **Cook**: 20m | **Ready In**: 40m*

Ingredients

- 3/4 cup mayonnaise
- 2 tablespoons soy sauce
- 2 tablespoons mirin
- 2 cloves garlic, minced
- 2 tablespoons dried minced onion
- 1/4 teaspoon onion powder
- 1 teaspoon curry powder
- 1 teaspoon ground turmeric
- 1 teaspoon dried basil
- 1 tablespoon cayenne pepper
- 1/4 teaspoon salt
- 1/2 cup seasoned dry bread crumbs
- 16 peeled and deveined jumbo shrimp, tails still attached
- 2 tablespoons sesame oil 1/4 cup water

Directions

1. Stir together the mayonnaise, soy sauce, mirin, minced garlic, dried minced onion, onion powder, curry powder, turmeric, basil, cayenne pepper, and salt in a bowl. Fold in the bread crumbs until evenly moistened. Cover, and refrigerate at least an hour.
2. Cut each shrimp along the back and open the halves like a book. Place a hearty dollop of the mayonnaise mixture onto each shrimp, and spread over the top to completely cover. Heat the sesame oil in a large skillet over high heat until it begins to smoke. Place the shrimp in the pan, mayonnaise-side up, and add the water. Cover, and steam until the shrimp are no longer transparent, 2 1/2 to 3 minutes.

Orange Ginger Shrimp Stir-Fry

"A fresh alternative to an Asian classic dish, stir-fry. You can substitute the vegetables for your preference and seasons."

Servings: 4 | **Prep**: 20m | **Cook**: 10m | **Ready In**: 30m

Ingredients

- 1 pound peeled and deveined shrimp
- 2 tablespoons freshly squeezed orange juice
- 1 teaspoon minced garlic
- 1 teaspoon minced fresh ginger root
- salt and ground black pepper, to taste
- 1 tablespoon vegetable oil
- 1 tablespoon sesame oil
- 1 tablespoon vegetable oil
- 1 green bell pepper, diced
- 1 yellow summer squash, cut into
- 1/4-inch slices 1 cup chopped broccoli
- 1/2 cup diced onion
- 1/2 cup chopped carrot orange, zested
- 1/4 teaspoon cayenne pepper
- 1/2 cups cooked rice (optional)

Directions

1. Stir shrimp, orange juice, garlic, and ginger together in bowl; season with salt and pepper. Refrigerate 15 minutes.
2. Heat 1 tablespoon vegetable oil and sesame oil in a Wok or large skillet over medium-high heat. Remove shrimp from the marinade; cook and stir in the hot oil until opaque, about 2 minutes per side. Transfer shrimp to a plate.
3. Heat 1 tablespoon vegetable oil with the oil remaining in the Wok. Cook and stir bell pepper, squash, broccoli, onion, carrot, orange zest, and cayenne pepper in the hot oil until the vegetables are tender, about 5 minutes. Return shrimp to the skillet, stir into the vegetable mixture, and continue cooking 1 minute more.
4. Serve over cooked rice.

Paleo Spicy Shrimp Stir-Fry

"Paleo shrimp!"

Servings: 4 | **Prep**: 20m | **Cook**: 10m | **Ready In**: 30m

Ingredients

- 1/2 cup lemon juice
- 1 small onion, finely chopped
- 1/2 cup olive oil
- 3 cloves garlic, minced
- 1 tablespoon lemon zest
- 1 tablespoon grated ginger
- 1 teaspoon ground turmeric
- 24 large shrimp, peeled and deveined
- 1 tablespoon coconut oil, or as needed

Directions

1. Mix together lemon juice, onion, olive oil, garlic, lemon zest, ginger, and turmeric in a bowl. Place shrimp into marinade, cover, and refrigerate shrimp and marinade mixture overnight.
2. Remove shrimp, saving the marinade. Heat a Wok or skillet over medium-high heat; melt coconut oil in hot Wok. Stir-fry shrimp in coconut oil until shrimp are opaque and pink, 5 to 10 minutes. Add reserved marinade and bring to a boil, stirring constantly.

Editor's Note:

- The nutrition data for this recipe includes the full amount of the marinade ingredients. The actual amount of the marinade consumed will vary.

Quick Fried Brown Rice with Shrimp and Snap Peas

"Stir up your weeknight meal routine by serving up 20-minute Quick Fried Brown Rice with Shrimp and Snap Peas."

Servings: 4

Ingredients

- 1 1/2 (8.8-ounce) pouches precooked brown rice (such as Uncle Ben's)

- 2 tablespoons lower-sodium soy sauce
- 1 tablespoon sambal oelek (ground fresh chile paste)
- 1 tablespoon honey
- 2 tablespoons peanut oil, divided
- 10 ounce medium shrimp, peeled and deveined
- 3 large eggs, lightly beaten
- 1 1/2 cups sugar snap peas, diagonally sliced
- 1/3 cup unsalted, dry-roasted peanuts
- 1/8 teaspoon salt
- 3 garlic cloves, crushed

Directions

1. Heat rice according to package directions.
2. Combine soy sauce, sambal oelek, and honey in a large bowl. Combine 1 teaspoon peanut oil and shrimp in a medium bowl; toss to coat. Heat a Wok or large skillet over high heat. Add shrimp to pan, and stir-fry 2 minutes. Add shrimp to soy sauce mixture; toss to coat shrimp. Add 1 teaspoon peanut oil to pan; swirl to coat. Add eggs to pan; cook 45 seconds or until set. Remove eggs from pan; cut into bite-sized pieces.
3. Add 1 tablespoon oil to pan; swirl to coat. Add rice; stir-fry 4 minutes. Add rice to shrimp mixture. Add remaining 1 teaspoon oil to pan; swirl to coat. Add sugar snap peas, peanuts, salt, and garlic to pan; stir-fry for 2 minutes or until peanuts begin to brown. Add shrimp mixture and egg to pan, and cook for 2 minutes or until thoroughly heated.

Quick Shrimp Stir Fry

"Eating healthier can be quick and delicious!"

Servings: 3 | **Time**: 20m

Ingredients

- 1 pound shrimp
- 6 ounces sugar snap peas
- 1/2 cup onion, julienned

- 2 tablespoons oil
- 1 tablespoon fresh ginger, minced
- 1 teaspoon garlic & chili sauce
- 2 tablespoons soy sauce
- 2 tablespoons peanut sauce

Directions

1. Heat skillet or Wok over medium high heat with the oil, I use canola oil
2. Add the onion and ginger and sauté for a couple minutes, stirring constantly.
3. Add the sugar snap peas and sauces, stir and cook a couple minutes.
4. Finally add the shrimp, I use a cooked shrimp that I defrost in warm water, remove the tails then add to the pan and cook only a couple minutes more so shrimp doesn't overcook.
5. I served this over brown rice and sprinkled with a few peanuts for garnish and crunch.

Sake Marinated Shrimp with a Cucumber and Mango Salad

*Servings: 12-14 | **Prep**:1h15m | **Cook**: 10m | **Ready In**: 1h25m*

Ingredients

For the Marinade:

- 2 tablespoons peeled and grated fresh ginger root
- 1/4 cup chopped green onions, green part only
- 2 tablespoons chopped fresh cilantro
- 1 teaspoon minced garlic
- Salt
- Crushed red pepper
- 1/2 cup sake wine
- 3 tablespoons sesame oil
- 1 tablespoon rice wine vinegar
- 1 tablespoon soy sauce
- 1 teaspoon Worcestershire sauce

To Assemble:

- 2 pounds medium shrimp, peeled and deveined
- 1 cup julienne cucumbers, peels and seeds removed
- 1 cup julienne fresh mango
- Drizzle extra-virgin olive oil
- 2 teaspoons finely chopped fresh cilantro
- Salt
- Freshly ground white pepper

Directions

1. For the marinade: Combine all of the ingredients in a small bowl, stir well, and allow to sit at room temperature for about 30 minutes. Season the shrimp with salt and pepper. Toss the shrimp with the marinade, cover and refrigerate for 30 minutes. In a mixing bowl, combine the cucumbers and mango. Season with a drizzle of the oil, salt and white pepper. Mix well. Stir in the cilantro. Heat a medium Wok, over medium heat. Add the shrimp in batches, to the Wok and stir-fry for 2 to 3 minutes. Remove from the heat and cool. To serve, place a small amount on each serving plate. Spoon some of the salad on top. Gar

Salt and Pepper Shrimp

Servings: 6 | Prep: 20m | Cook: 12m | Ready In: 32m

Ingredients

- 2 quarts peanut oil
- Kosher salt and freshly ground black pepper
- 4 cups all-purpose flour, plus 2 cups for dredging
- 2 pounds large prawns, shelled and deveined, with tail attached
- 4 egg yolks
- 4 cups chilled soda water
- 2 tablespoons shaved garlic
- 2 tablespoons shredded ginger
- 1 bunch green onions, sliced on a bias angle
- 1 jalepeno pepper, sliced into rounds

- Serving suggestion: fresh lemon wedges

Directions

1. In a large Wok, heat the oil over medium-high to 370 degrees F.
2. Meanwhile, season 2 cups of the flour with salt and freshly ground black pepper. Dredge the shrimp in the seasoned flour.
3. In a large mixing bowl, whisk the remaining 4 cups of flour with the egg yolks and soda water. Hold the shrimp by their tails dip them into the batter.
4. Working in batches, fry the shrimp in the hot oil, turning them once, until they are golden brown, about 3 minutes per batch. Remove the shrimp from the oil and drain them on paper towels. While they are still hot, sprinkle the shrimp generously with salt and freshly ground black pepper. Transfer the shrimp to a serving tray.
5. When the shrimp are cooked, carefully pour off all but 1/2 cup of the oil. Add the garlic, ginger, green onions and jalapeno and fry until crispy. Spoon the seasoning over the shrimp and serve immediately accompanied by lemon wedges.

Salt-and-Pepper Shrimp

"This salt-and-pepper shrimp recipe is a lighter (stir-fried) version of the deep-fried Asian dish that's quick and keeps the intense flavor of the original."

Servings: 4-6 | **Total time**: 20m

Ingredients

- 1/2 teaspoon each black, green, red, and white peppercorns
- 2 pounds shrimp, shells on
- 2 teaspoons salt, divided
- 2 tablespoons vegetable or peanut oil
- 4 cloves garlic, chopped
- 1 cup cilantro leaves, roughly chopped

Directions

1. Put peppercorns in a mortar and crush roughly with a pestle. Or put peppercorns in a large resealable plastic bag, spread out on a hard, flat surface, and crush with the bottom of a heavy frying pan or rolling pin.
2. Put shrimp, half of the crushed peppercorns, and 1 tsp. salt in a large bowl and toss to coat shrimp evenly. Set aside.
3. Heat a Wok or large (not nonstick) pot over high heat. Add oil, garlic, remaining crushed peppercorns, and remaining 1 tsp. salt and cook, stirring constantly, until fragrant, about 1 minute. Add shrimp and cook, stirring constantly, until pink and cooked through, 3 to 4 minutes. Add cilantro, turn off heat, and toss to combine. Serve immediately.

Salt-Fried Shrimp

Servings: 4 | Prep: 15m | Cook: 10m | Ready In: 25m

Ingredients

- Kosher salt
- 1/2 cup oil, for frying
- 1/2 cup soy sauce
- 1/4 cup rice wine vinegar
- 1 teaspoon finely-minced ginger
- 1/2 teaspoon chili oil
- 2 tablespoons thinly-shaved scallions, plus extra for garnish
- 1 cup flour
- 2 tablespoons cornstarch
- 6 egg whites
- 1 cup kosher salt
- 1/2 cup coarsely cracked black pepper
- 1 pound large shrimp, shell-on, split down back and deveined

Directions

1. Slowly heat oil in a Wok or large skillet.
2. In a small bowl combine next 5 ingredients for sauce.

3. In 3 bowls, combine flour and cornstarch in first; beat egg whites with a fork until loose in second; mix salt and pepper in third. Dip shrimp first in flour mixture, shaking off excess; dip in egg whites, allowing excess to drip off. Lightly roll in salt mixture and add immediately to hot oil. Fry on all sides, remove and drain on paper towels.
4. Serve with sauce, garnished with extra scallions.

Sesame Shrimp Ramen

Servings: 4

Ingredients

- 5 individual packages ramen noodles (10 oz.) or 1 lb. spaghetti
- 2 tablespoons vegetable oil
- 1 bag fresh cut vegetables or coleslaw mix or frozen
- Asian-style stir-fry mix
- 1 cup bottled Thai peanut sauce
- 8 ounces small cooked shrimp (about 24)
- 2 scallions, finely chopped
- 2 tablespoons toasted sesame seeds

Directions

1. Bring a large pot of salted water to a boil. Cook ramen for 2 to 3 minutes. (If using spaghetti, cook until just al dente, about 8 minutes.) Drain and rinse under cold water.
2. In a large skillet, heat oil over high heat, add vegetables and stir-fry until just wilted, about 5 minutes.
3. In a large bowl, toss noodles with peanut sauce until well-coated. Add vegetables and shrimp and toss. Divide among 4 bowls and sprinkle each with scallions and sesame seeds. Serve at room temperature.

Shrimp and Broccoli Stir-Fry

"Just a touch of honey adds a slight sweetness that rounds out the flavor in this quick stir-fry. Pat the shrimp dry with paper towels before adding them to the Wok so they brown nicely. Serve with hot cooked brown rice."

Servings: 4 | Hands-on: 30m | Total time: 30m

Ingredients

- 1 pound medium shrimp, peeled and deveined
- 1 tablespoon cornstarch
- 2 1/2 tablespoons canola oil, divided
- 1/4 cup (1-inch) diagonally cut green onions
- 2 teaspoons minced peeled fresh ginger
- 3 garlic cloves, thinly sliced
- 2 cups broccoli florets
- 1/4 cup lower-sodium soy sauce
- 2 tablespoons rice vinegar
- 1 teaspoon honey
- 1/8 teaspoon crushed red pepper

Directions

1. Combine shrimp and cornstarch in a medium bowl, tossing to coat. Heat a large Wok or skillet over high heat. Add 1 tablespoon oil to pan; swirl to coat. Add shrimp; stir-fry 4 minutes. Remove shrimp from pan; place in a medium bowl. Add 1 1/2 teaspoons oil to pan; swirl to coat. Add green onions, ginger, and garlic to pan; stir-fry 45 seconds. Add onion mixture to shrimp.
2. Add 1 tablespoon oil to pan; swirl to coat. Add broccoli; stir-fry 1 1/2 minutes. Stir in shrimp mixture, soy sauce, and remaining ingredients; bring to a boil. Cook 1 minute or until shrimp are done and broccoli is crisp-tender.

Shrimp and Cabbage Stir-Fry

Servings: 4 | Prep: 20m | Cook: 10m | Ready In: 30m

Ingredients

- 1 large egg white
- 1 tablespoon plus 2 teaspoons cornstarch
- 1 tablespoon plus 1 teaspoon soy sauce
- 1 1/4 pounds medium shrimp, peeled and deveined
- 2 teaspoons hoisin sauce
- 1/2 teaspoons sherry vinegar or rice wine vinegar
- 1/2 cup low-sodium chicken broth or water
- 2 tablespoons vegetable oil
- 4 scallions, cut into 1/2-inch pieces, white and green parts separated
- 1 tablespoon finely grated peeled ginger
- 1 clove garlic, finely grated
- 1 pound Napa cabbage (1/2 head), cut into 1-inch pieces
- Cooked white rice, for serving (optional)

Directions

1. Whisk the egg white, 1 tablespoon cornstarch and 1 teaspoon soy sauce in a large bowl until frothy. Add the shrimp and toss to coat. Refrigerate 10 minutes. Meanwhile, whisk the hoisin sauce, vinegar and the remaining 1 tablespoon soy sauce and 2 teaspoons cornstarch in a small bowl, then whisk in the chicken broth. Set aside.
2. Drain the shrimp. Heat the vegetable oil in a Wok or large skillet over medium-high heat, then stir-fry the scallion whites, ginger and garlic, about 30 seconds. Add the shrimp and stir-fry until almost cooked through, about 3 minutes. Add the cabbage and stir-fry until wilted and the shrimp are just cooked through, about 2 more minutes.
3. Stir the hoisin sauce mixture, then add to the Wok and simmer, stirring occasionally, 2 minutes. Stir in the scallion greens. Serve with rice, if desired.

Shrimp and Egg Fried Rice with Napa Cabbage

Servings: 4 | Prep: 20m | Cook: 10m | Ready In: 30m

Ingredients

- 6 tablespoons peanut oil
- 2 shallots, thinly sliced
- 1 (2-inch) piece ginger, peeled and grated
- 1/2 small head napa cabbage, core removed and finely sliced
- Salt
- 2 cloves garlic, minced
- 1/2 pound medium shrimp, peeled and deveined
- 3 large eggs, lightly beaten
- 4 cups cooked long-grain white rice
- 1/2 cup frozen peas, thawed in warm water
- 3 tablespoons soy sauce
- 1/4 bunch scallions, sliced, for garnish
- 1/2 cup chopped peanuts, for garnish

Directions

1. Heat 2 tablespoons of the peanut oil in a Wok or a large nonstick skillet over medium-high flame. Give the oil a minute to heat up, then add the shallots, the ginger, and stir-fry for 1 minute until fragrant. Add the cabbage and stir-fry until the cabbage is wilted and soft, about 8 minutes; season with a nice pinch of salt. Remove the vegetables to a side platter and wipe out the Wok with dry paper towel.
2. Put the pan back on the heat and coat with 2 tablespoons of oil. Add the garlic and to the Wok and saute gently until fragrant. Add shrimp and cook for 2 to 3 minutes until pink. Set aside on platter with vegetables. Add remaining oil to the Wok and when hot, crack the eggs into the center. Scramble the egg lightly, then let it set without stirring so it stays in big pieces. Fold in the rice and toss with the egg until well combined, breaking up the rice clumps with the back of a spatula. Return the sauteed vegetables and shrimp to the pan along with the peas and season with salt and soy sauce. Toss everything together to heat through. Spoon the fried rice out onto a serving platter, and garnish with scallions and peanuts.

Shrimp and Ginger Siu Mai Dumplings

Servings: 4 | **Prep**:30m | **Cook**: 40m | **Ready In**: 1h10m

Ingredients

- 1 pound shrimp, shelled and deveined
- 1/2 pound ground pork
- 1 green onion, finely chopped
- 3 garlic cloves, minced
- 1 (2-inch) piece fresh ginger, grated
- 2 egg whites
- 2 teaspoons cornstarch
- 1/2 lemon, juiced
- 1 tablespoon low-sodium soy sauce, plus some for dipping
- 1 tablespoon sesame oil
- 1/4 teaspoon salt
- 1/4 teaspoon ground black pepper

For the Wrappers:

- 1 (10-ounce) package round wonton wrappers
- Canola oil, for brushing the steamer
- Savoy cabbage, for lining the steamer, optional
- Micro Arugula, for garnish

Directions

1. Special equipment: Wok, bamboo steamer
2. To make the shrimp filling: Pulse all the ingredients in a food processor until partly smooth but not completely pureed. It should have a little texture. Season with salt and pepper.
3. To assemble dumplings: Hold a wonton wrapper in your hand. Dip a spoon in cold water and then drop 1 tablespoon of the filling onto the center of a wrapper (dipping the spoon in cold water first will make the filling come off easier). Gather the edges of the wrapper up around the filling and squeeze the sides slightly with your fingers. The sides will naturally pleat, leaving the filling slightly exposed. Tap the dumpling on the table so the bottom is flat and it stands upright. Repeat with the remaining wrappers and filling. (You can freeze the leftover filling for 2 or 3 weeks.)
4. Lightly oil the bottom of a 10-inch bamboo steamer and line it with the whole cabbage leaves. Stand the dumplings in the steamer in a single layer and don't let them touch. You should be able to get 12 siu mai in the steamer at a time. Bring 1 to 2 inches of water to a boil in a pot. Set the bamboo steamer over the pot, then cover it

with the bamboo lid. Steam for 10 to 12 minutes or until the filling feels firm and is cooked through. Serve in the steamer basket and garnish with micro arugula and soy sauce.

Shrimp and Green Bean Stir Fry

"I love to make stir fry it easy and can include anything you have just hanging around"

Servings: 4 | **Time**: 30m

Ingredients

- 2 dozen shrimp
- 1 bunch green beans
- 1/2 small onion
- 1/2 medium bell pepper
- 1 cup rice
- 1 tbsp butter

Directions

1. First put the rice on to cook. (1 cup rice = 2 cups water)
2. Next: chop all the vegi's (you don't need anything specific! Just whatever you have around!)
3. Make sure that everything is uniform or at least are in manageable bite sizes.
4. Afterwards put the shrimp in a bowl of cold water(Cold water does not cook them it thaws them.)
5. Once thawed peel the shrimp (unless you bought pre-peeled)
6. The easiest way is to pull off the tail and then peel the sides
7. Next with the butter cook the vegis in a non-stick skillet.
8. Make sure that you know which veggies will cook faster.
9. Green beans* bell pepper* onion* is the order I cook them in.
10. I cook one vegi half way then add the next ingredient so that they are all even and cooked at the same time.
11. In a separate skillet (or wipe out the one you just used) put some oil or butter down.
12. Next season the shrimp with whatever you like and put them in the pan one side down.

13. Once they look white all they way to the middle (about 1-2 minutes) flip them over to cook (another 30-40 sec)
14. Then assemble your bowl or plate!

Shrimp and Tofu Stir-Fry

"This was delicious meal!!! Hope you enjoy it as much as we did!!"

Servings: 5 | **Time**: 30m

Ingredients

- 1 Large bag of medium shrimp, peeled and no tails
- 1 medium Sweet onion, diced
- 1 large Zucchini, diced
- 3 green onions, chopped
- 6 Baby portobella mushrooms, roughly chopped
- 1 tsp diced garlic
- 1 dash salt
- 2 tbsp Sesame seeds
- 2 tbsp olive oil, extra virgin for sauteing
- 1 can mini corns, drained and rinsed
- 1/2 can bean sprouts or 1/3 cup fresh bean sprouts
- 1 packages Super firm Tofu, cubed (bought mine cubed already)
- 1 Bottle of Orange Sauce, any brand will do
- 3 tbsp Teriyaki sauce
- 3 tbsp low sodium soy sauce
- 1 can water chestnuts, drained and rinsed
- 1 packages Broccoli slaw

Directions

1. In a large pot, over medium-high heat, add olive oil and let heat. Then add your onion, garlic, zucchini, and mushrooms. Saute until tender-crisp.
2. Add your broccoli slaw, Sesame seeds, soy sauce, Teriyaki sauce, water chestnuts, bean sprouts, and Tofu. Let the slaw become tender.

3. When the ingredients are nice and soft; add shrimp. Be sure to mix the shrimp together so it can cook evenly! Let cook until almost all the way pink. Then add the Orange sauce!
4. Let simmer for 10 minutes and remove from heat! Serve with your choice of side! We had ours with rice!
5. Enjoy!!

Shrimp and Vegetable Pad Thai

Servings: 4 | *Prep*: 35m | *Inactive*: 5m | *Cook*: 105m | *Ready In:* 50m

Ingredients

- 7 ounces medium rice stick noodles
- 1/4 cup fish sauce
- 1/4 cup rice wine vinegar
- 3 tablespoons palm sugar or dark brown sugar
- 1/2 teaspoon crushed red pepper
- 1/4 cup coconut milk
- 1 teaspoon tamarind concentrate, optional
- 1 tablespoon toasted sesame oil
- 3 tablespoons peanut oil
- 12 ounces medium shrimp, peeled and deveined
- 1 cup diced firm tofu
- 1 cup sliced shiitake mushroom caps
- 1 cup mung bean sprouts
- 2 large carrots, cut into matchstick-sized strips
- 1/2 cup matchstick-sized red bell pepper strips
- 2 tablespoons minced garlic
- 1/2 cup roasted, unsalted peanuts, roughly chopped
- 1/2 cup diagonally sliced green onions
- 2 tablespoons fresh lime juice
- 1/4 cup chopped cilantro leaves
- Sriracha (Thai hot sauce), for serving

Directions

1. Bring 4 cups of water to a boil. Place noodles in a large bowl and cover with the boiling water. Allow noodles to soak for 5 minutes,

drain, and rinse with cold, running water for 30 seconds. Drain well and set aside.
2. In a small bowl, combine the fish sauce, vinegar, sugar, red pepper, coconut milk, and if desired, the tamarind concentrate, stirring until the sugar is dissolved.
3. Heat the sesame and peanut oils in a Wok or large saucepan over medium-high heat. Just before the oil is smoking, add the shrimp and cook until pink, stirring constantly. Add the tofu, mushrooms, bean sprouts, carrots, red bell pepper, garlic, and reserved noodles, and cook until heated through, about 2 minutes.
4. Pour the sauce mixture into the Wok and toss until combined. Cook until the mixture is steaming and most of the liquid has evaporated. Add the peanuts and green onions and cook an additional 30 seconds.
5. Remove the Wok from the heat and season with the lime juice and cilantro. Serve hot with Sriracha, if desired.

Shrimp and Vegetable Stir-Fry

"Instead of take-out, make an easy shrimp stir-fry for dinner using steamed brown rice, forzen shrimp, and frozen stir-fry vegetables."

*Servings: 4 | **Prep**: 15m | **Cook**: 10m | **Ready In**: 25m*

Ingredients

- 3/4 cup chicken broth
- 1/4 cup fresh orange juice
- 2 tablespoons soy sauce
- 1 tablespoon cornstarch
- 1/2 teaspoon sugar
- 2 tablespoons peanut oil or vegetable oil
- 1 pound frozen deveined large shrimp, thawed and peeled
- 3 garlic cloves, minced
- 1 (1 lb.) bag frozen stir-fry vegetables, thawed and drained
- 4 cups steamed brown rice, for serving (cook about 2 cups dry)

Directions

1. In a small bowl, whisk together broth, orange juice, soy sauce, cornstarch and sugar; set aside.
2. Heat oil in Wok or large nonstick skillet over medium-high heat. Add shrimp and stir-fry for 2 minutes. Add half of garlic and stir-fry, about 2 more minutes. Transfer to plate.
3. Add vegetables and cook, stirring, until heated through, about 3 minutes. Stir sauce again and add to pan, stirring until thickened, about 2 minutes. Return shrimp to pan and toss to coat. Serve with rice.

Shrimp Coconut Soup

"Shrimp, coconut milk, ginger, and curry paste come together to make this easy and tasty soup."

Servings: 4 | **Prep**: 10m | **Cook**: 15m | **Ready In**: 25m

Ingredients

- 1 tablespoon sesame oil
- 1 pound medium fresh shrimp, peeled
- 1 tablespoon fresh grated ginger
- 2 garlic cloves, minced
- 1 red bell pepper, finely diced
- 2 teaspoons Thai green curry paste*
- 5 to 6 cups low-sodium chicken broth
- 1 (13.5-ounce) can coconut milk
- 3 tablespoons fish sauce (optional)
- 2 to 3 tablespoons fresh lime juice
- 1 tablespoon brown sugar
- Garnish: 2 green onions, cut into 1/2-inch pieces (about 1/4 cup)

Directions

1. Heat oil in a large pot over medium-high heat. Add shrimp; stir-fry 2 to 3 minutes or just until shrimp turn pink. Transfer shrimp to a plate. Add ginger, garlic, and bell pepper to pot, and sauté 1 to 2 minutes or until tender. Stir in curry paste, broth, coconut milk,

and, if desired, fish sauce. Add lime juice and brown sugar, and bring to a boil; reduce heat, and let simmer 5 minutes. Stir in shrimp. Garnish, if desired.

2. *Available in your grocer's ethnic foods section; red Asian chili sauce may be substituted.

Shrimp Fried Rice

*Servings: 1-2 | **Prep**: 45m | **Cook**: 15m | **Ready In**: 1h*

Ingredients

- Canola oil
- One 2-inch piece fresh ginger, peeled and grated
- 4 cloves garlic, smashed and minced
- 5 scallions, whites chopped and greens thinly sliced, separated
- 8 ounces large shrimp, peeled and deveined, cut into quarters
- 2 ounces thinly sliced Chinese sausage
- 1 cup thinly sliced Napa cabbage
- 1/4 to 1/2 cup edamame beans
- One 2-ounce can water chestnuts
- 1/4 cup soy sauce
- 1 1/2 tablespoons rice vinegar
- 1/2 teaspoon sambal
- 1/2 teaspoon XO sauce
- 1 cup mung bean sprouts
- 1 cup white rice, cooked and cooled
- 1 egg
- Fresh cilantro leaves, for garnish

Directions

1. To a Wok over medium-high heat, add a light coating of oil. Add half of the ginger, garlic and scallion whites to flavor the oil. Add the shrimp, sausage, cabbage, edamame and water chestnuts, tossing to heat through, 1 to 2 minutes. Add the soy sauce, rice wine vinegar, sambal, XO sauce and sprouts. Cook for 1 minute until the shrimp is pink. Move all to a bowl.
2. Add another light coating of oil to the Wok. Add the remaining half of the ginger, garlic and scallion whites to flavor the oil. Add the

rice and spread around the Wok to toast and get crispy. Add a little more oil to encourage golden-ness, and cook 4 to 5 minutes. Season with a splash of vinegar and soy. Add the sauteed shrimp and vegetables back into the Wok. Toss in your scallion greens and place onto a plate.

To the same Wok, turn the burner down, add the egg and cook, 1 to 2 minutes. Place the fried egg on top of the plate. Garnish with cilantro leaves.

Char Siu (Chinese BBQ Pork)

"This is pretty much like the shrimp lo mein you buy at an Asian takeout place. You can use chicken instead of shrimp, or even both for a delicious mix. To make it healthier, you can throw in some chopped veggies too."

Servings: 2 | ***Prep***: 10 m | ***Cook***: 20m | ***Ready In***: 30m

Ingredients

- 1 (8 ounce) package spaghetti
- 1/2 cup chicken broth
- 1 1/2 tablespoons white sugar
- 2 tablespoons hoisin sauce
- 2 tablespoons soy sauce 2 teaspoons cornstarch
- 2 tablespoons vegetable oil
- 1 1/2 cups uncooked medium shrimp, peeled and deveined
- 3 large cloves garlic, minced
- 1/4 cup green onions, chopped
- Add all ingredients to list

Directions

1. Bring a large pot of lightly salted water to a boil. Cook spaghetti in the boiling water until cooked through yet firm to the bite, about 12 minutes; drain.
2. Whisk chicken broth, sugar, hoisin sauce, soy sauce, and cornstarch in a bowl.
3. Heat oil in a large skillet or Wok over medium-high heat. Cook and stir shrimp and garlic in hot oil until shrimp are bright pink on the

outside and the meat is no longer transparent in the center, about 5 minutes. Reduce heat to medium-low. Add prepared sauce and chopped green onions to the shrimp mixture; cook until the sauce thickens, 2 to 3 minutes. Toss cooked spaghetti with the mixture to coat the noodles in sauce. Serve immediately.

Shrimp Pad Thai

Servings: 4 | Prep: 30m | Inactive: 10m | Cook: 10m | Ready In: 50m

Ingredients

- 8 ounces flat Thai rice noodles
- 1/4 cup fish sauce
- 1/4 cup raw or turbinado sugar
- 1 to 2 tablespoons hot Asian chili sauce (sambal oelek or sriracha)
- 2 tablespoons fresh lime juice, plus lime wedges for garnish
- 1/4 cup vegetable oil
- 1 pound large shrimp, butterflied with the shells on
- 4 large cloves garlic, chopped
- 1 12 -ounce package extra-firm tofu, cut into 1/2-inch cubes
- 6 radishes, cut into thin strips
- 4 scallions, halved lengthwise and cut into 1-inch pieces
- 1/2 cup roasted salted peanuts, coarsely chopped
- 2 cups bean sprouts
- 2 jalapeno peppers (red and green), seeded and thinly sliced into strips

Directions

1. Soak the noodles in a bowl of warm water until soft enough to separate, about 10 minutes. Mix the fish sauce, sugar, chili sauce and lime juice in a separate bowl. When the noodles are soft, drain and return to the bowl. Put the bowls and other ingredients next to the stove (this dish cooks quickly).
2. Heat a Wok or large skillet over high heat until very hot. Add the vegetable oil, then add the shrimp and stir-fry until pink, about 2 minutes. Transfer the shrimp to a bowl using a slotted spoon; leave the oil in the pan. Add the garlic and tofu to the pan; stir-fry until

just golden. Add the noodles and 1/4 cup fish-sauce mixture; stir-fry until the noodles absorb the sauce, about 3 minutes. Add up to 1/4 cup water if the noodles seem dry, but don't let them become mushy.
3. Add the radishes, scallions and 1/4 cup peanuts; toss to combine. Stir in the remaining fish-sauce mixture. Taste and adjust seasoning (you can add more water, lime juice or fish sauce).
4. Return the shrimp to the pan and heat through, about 2 minutes. Transfer the mixture to a platter; top with bean sprouts, jalapenos and the remaining 1/4 cup peanuts. Serve with lime wedges.

Shrimp Stir-fry I

"I actually learned how to make this in a high school food and nutrition class and loved it!"

Servings: 4 | **Prep**: 20m | **Cook**: 10m | **Ready In**: 30m

Ingredients

- 1 tablespoon sesame oil
- 1 tablespoon olive oil
- 1 pound tiger shrimp, peeled and deveined
- 1 cup chopped onion
- 1/2 cups sliced king mushrooms
- 1/2 cup chopped green bell pepper
- 3 cloves garlic, finely chopped
- 1 teaspoon minced fresh ginger
- 1/2 cup water
- 1 teaspoon oyster sauce, or to taste
- 1 pound fresh Chinese wheat noodles
- 2 cups bean sprouts

Directions

1. Heat sesame oil and olive oil in a large Wok or frying pan over medium heat; cook and stir shrimp and onion in the hot oil until coated. Mix mushrooms, green bell pepper, and garlic into shrimp mixture, stirring constantly. Add ginger and stir.

2. Pour water and oyster sauce into shrimp mixture; simmer until shrimp are bright pink on the outside and the meat is no longer transparent in the center, 5 minutes. Stir well.
3. Mix noodles and bean sprouts into shrimp mixture; toss to combine. Cook until noodles are heated through, 2 minutes. Toss again.

Shrimp Stir-Fry II

Ingredients

- 4 carrots thinly sliced
- 1 bell pepper cut in strips & halfed
- 1 C green onion (both green & white parts) cut to 2" strips
- 1-1/2 C green beans cut in half
- 1/4 C minced garlic
- 9 shrimp per person: marinated with (while prepping veggies) 1/2 t sesame oil, szechuan sauce drizzle to taste, & 1T soy sauce (drain extra sauce)
- Cooked rice
- Canola or peanut oil to coat bottom of cast iron skillet
- to taste salt
- to taste black pepper
- 1 T honey

Directions

1. Heat oil in large cast iron and wait until it shimmers, then add green beans & bell pepper: cook for 3 minutes
2. Add carrots & salt & pepper to taste: cook for 3 minutes
3. Add garlic: cook for one minute
4. Add shrimp cook for 3 minutes
5. Add green onion, 1/2 T sesame oil, 1/4 C soy sauce, honey: cook for one minute
6. Remove all from heat & let sauce thicken up, serve with rice

Shrimp Stuffed Crab Claws

Servings: 4 | Prep: 15m | Cook: 15m | Ready In: 30m

Ingredients

- 2 tablespoons olive oil
- 1/2 cup chopped onions
- 2 tablespoons brunoise red peppers
- 2 tablespoons brunoise yellow peppers
- Salt
- Cayenne
- 1/4 cup chopped green onions
- 1 tablespoon chopped garlic
- 2 tablespoons chopped fresh parsley
- 1 pound medium shrimp, peeled, deveined and finely chopped
- 1 large egg
- 1/2 cup bread crumbs
- 1/4 cup grated Parmigiano-Reggiano cheese
- 1 dozen cooked crab claws
- 1 cup all-purpose flour
- Creole seasoning, recipe follows
- Vegetable oil, for frying
- Chopped cilantro, for garnish

Emeril's ESSENCE Creole Seasoning (also referred to as Bayou Blast):

- 1/2 tablespoons paprika
- 2 tablespoons salt
- 2 tablespoons garlic powder
- 1 tablespoon black pepper
- 1 tablespoon onion powder
- 1 tablespoon cayenne pepper
- 1 tablespoon dried oregano
- 1 tablespoon dried thyme

Directions

1. In a medium saute pan, over medium heat, heat the olive oil. When the oil is hot, add the onions and peppers. Season the vegetables with salt and cayenne. Saute for 2 minutes. Add the green onions, garlic, and parsley. Saute for 30 seconds. Remove the mixture from the heat and turn into a mixing bowl. Cool the mixture for 2 minutes. Add the shrimp, egg, bread crumbs and cheese and mix

well. Season with salt and pepper. Form the mixture into 12 balls and with your hands, flatten each ball. Season the crab claws with Creole seasoning. Form the shrimp mixture around the meat of each crab claw. **If the filling is sticking to your hands, try wetting your hands and then form the filling around the claws. Place on a parchment lined baking sheet and refrigerate for 15 to 20 minutes, this will make the claws easier to handle. Season the flour with Creole seasoning. Preheat the Wok for frying. Holding the claw end, carefully dredge in the flour mixture. Fry in batches until golden brown, about 3 to 4 minutes, stirring occasionally for overall browning. Remove and drain on paper towels. Season with Creole seasoning. Place the stuffed claws on a servi

2. Emeril's ESSENCE Creole Seasoning (also referred to as Bayou Blast):
Combine all ingredients thoroughly

Shrimp Tempura with Soy Sake Dipping Sauce

Servings: 4 | *Prep*: 20m | *Cook*: 10m | *Ready In*: 30m

Ingredients

Dipping sauce:

- 1 cup soy sauce
- 1/4 cup sake
- 1 tablespoon hot chili sauce (recommended: Srirachi Hot Chili Sauce)
- 1 tablespoon chopped fresh ginger
- 2 tablespoons chopped fresh cilantro leaves

Tempura:

- 1 pound large shrimp, peeled and deveined
- 1 cup rice flour, plus 1 cup for dusting
- 1 cup cold seltzer water
- 1 egg yolk
- 1 tablespoon sesame oil, optional
- Vegetable oil, for frying
- Kosher salt

Directions

1. Make the dipping sauce: Combine all ingredients in a bowl. Set aside to allow the flavors to develop.
2. Butterfly the shrimp by cutting down the back, being careful not to cut all the way through. Open the shrimp like a book and rinse well with cold water.
3. Make the Tempura batter: Put 1 cup of rice flour in a bowl and pour in the seltzer. Stir with a whisk to get out all the lumps. Add the egg yolk and blend it in well. The batter should be the consistency of heavy cream. Flavor with sesame oil, if using.
4. Heat about 2 inches of vegetable oil to 375 degrees F in a Wok or deep fryer. Dry the shrimp well. Dust the shrimp in flour to soak up any remaining moisture, shake off excess. Dip the shrimp into the batter one by one. Drop 4 or 5 pieces at a time in the hot oil. Do not overcrowd the pan. Fry until golden brown, turning once, about 3 minutes. To keep the oil clean between batches, skim off the small bits of batter that float in the oil. Remove the fried shrimp from the oil and drain on paper towels; season them with salt. Serve with the dipping sauce.

Shrimp With Garlic in Olive Oil

"Serve this shrimp recipe with lemon wedges and crusty bread to sop up the delicious juices from the pan."

Servings: 6 | **Prep**: 5m | **Cook**: 2m

Ingredients

- 1/2 cup extra-virgin olive oil
- 6 garlic cloves, peeled and sliced
- 1 dried chile pepper, coarsely chopped, or 1 teaspoon crushed red pepper, or to taste
- 1 1/2 pounds peeled small shrimp, or large shrimp, peeled and chopped
- 1/2 teaspoon coarse salt, or to taste
- 2 teaspoons chopped fresh parsley for garnish
- 12 small pieces crusty bread (Italian-style)

- Lemon wedges for serving

Directions

1. Combine the olive oil, garlic, and chile pepper in a 10- to 12-inch skillet, preferably cast iron, and turn heat to medium. When the garlic begins to sizzle and turn golden, add the shrimp. Cook, stirring, until the shrimp just turn pink and opaque, 2-4 minutes.
2. Stir in salt, garnish with parsley, and serve immediately, directly from the pan, with lemon wedges and bread.

Shrimp-and-Black Bean Stir-Fry

"This tropical pairing of sweet and savory "

***Servings**: 4 | **Hands-on**: 30m | **Total time**: 30m*

Ingredients

- 1/2 medium-size red onion, sliced
- 1 medium-size red bell pepper, sliced
- 3 tablespoons olive oil, divided
- 1 cup fresh corn kernels (about 2 ears)
- 1 pound peeled and deveined large, raw shrimp
- 3 garlic cloves, sliced
- 1 cup chopped fresh mango or pineapple
- 1 (15-oz.) can black beans, drained and rinsed
- 1/2 cup teriyaki baste-and-glaze sauce
- 1/4 cup pineapple juice
- Hot cooked rice
- Garnish: cilantro leaves

Preparation

1. Stir-fry onion and bell pepper in 1 Tbsp. hot oil in a large cast-iron skillet over medium-high heat 2 to 3 minutes or until lightly browned. Remove from skillet.

2. Add corn and 1 Tbsp. oil to skillet; stir-fry 2 to 3 minutes. Remove from skillet.
3. Pat shrimp dry. Add shrimp, garlic, and remaining 1 Tbsp. oil to skillet; stir-fry 2 to 3 minutes or just until shrimp begin to turn pink. Add mango and black beans; stir-fry 2 to 3 minutes or until thoroughly heated. Add teriyaki sauce and pineapple juice, and cook 1 to 2 minutes or until mixture begins to bubble. Stir in corn-and-onion mixture. Serve over hot cooked rice.

Shrimp-Pineapple Fried Rice

"Stir-up Shrimp-Pineapple Fried Rice for dinner tonight. This one-Wok wonder is quick, easy, and full of flavor."

Servings: 4 | **Prep**: 15m | **Cook**: 8m

Ingredients

- 2 to 3 teaspoons sesame oil
- 1 pound peeled and deveined shrimp
- 1 tablespoon stir-fry oil or vegetable oil
- 3 garlic cloves, minced
- 1 tablespoon grated fresh ginger
- 2 cups chopped pineapple
- 3 to 4 cups cold, cooked long-grain rice
- 5 green onions, finely chopped
- 3 tablespoons soy sauce or tamari
- 1 to 2 teaspoons chili-garlic paste or sriracha
- 1 teaspoon sesame seeds

Directions

1. Heat Wok over high heat until a few drops of water evaporate immediately. Swirl sesame oil in pan to coat. (If using a nonstick skillet, heat oil over medium-high heat.) Add shrimp, and stir-fry 3 minutes or until done. Transfer to a large bowl; cover and keep warm.
2. Heat stir-fry oil in Wok over high heat (medium-high, if using a nonstick skillet). Add garlic and ginger; cook 30 seconds or until

fragrant. Stir in pineapple and rice, and stir-fry 1 to 3 minutes or until heated through. Stir in green onions and cooked shrimp.
3. Combine soy sauce and chili-garlic paste in a small bowl; stir into rice mixture. Sprinkle with sesame seeds, and serve immediately.

Skinny Protein Packed Shrimp Stir Fry

"Quick way to use up veggies and shrimp is protein packed :-)"

***Servings**: 5 | **Cook**: 35m*

Ingredients

- 1 lb Shrimp
- 3 tbsp Olive oil
- 1 cup Broccoli, chopped
- 1 cup Broccoli slaw
- 1 Green Pepper
- 1 Onion
- 1 tsp Agave Syrup
- 3 tbsp Low Sodium Soy Sauce
- 1 tbsp McCormick's Asian seasoning

Directions

1. Sauté shrimp in 1 tablespoon of Olive oil. Sprinkle with Asian seasoning. Remove from heat.
2. In a separate pan, heat 2 tablespoons of Olive oil over med-high heat. Sauté onions and zucchini but do not burn.
3. Sprinkle more Asian seasoning on the onions and broccoli. Lower heat to medium. Add the soy sauce and Cook for about 5 minutes
4. Add broccoli slaw, peppers and remaining Asian seasoning. Stir and flip ingredients throughly.
5. When peppers reach desired softness, add the shrimp. Stir and flip ingredients again. Lower heat and simmer for a few minutes, stirring occasionally.
6. Serve over Brown Rice (optional)

Slippery Shrimp

"After becoming mildly obsessed with Yang Chow in LA's China Town, I feel I've deciphered their dish as best as possible."

Servings: 4 | **Prep**: 15m | **Cook**: 05m | **Ready In**: 35m

Ingredients

- 2 cups peanut oil for frying
- 1 pound peeled and deveined large shrimp
- 1/4 cup cornstarch 2 large cloves garlic, minced
- 1/2 teaspoon minced fresh ginger
- 1/2 teaspoon cayenne pepper
- 1 tablespoon white wine 1 tablespoon white vinegar
- 1 tablespoon ketchup 5 teaspoons white sugar
- 1/2 teaspoon salt
- 1/4 cup water
- 2 teaspoons cornstarch
- 2 teaspoons water
- 5 green onions, sliced

Directions

1. Heat peanut oil in a Wok to 375 degrees F (190 degrees C).
2. Toss the shrimp with 1/4 cup of cornstarch to coat, then drop into the hot oil, and quickly fry until golden brown, about 45 seconds. When done, drain shrimp, and set aside.
3. Pour all but 1 tablespoon of oil from the Wok, then stir in the garlic, ginger, and cayenne pepper. Cook and stir until the garlic is fragrant and beginning to brown, about 30 seconds. Pour in the wine, vinegar, ketchup, sugar, salt, and 1/4 cup of water, and bring to a boil over high heat. Dissolve the cornstarch in 2 teaspoons of water, stir into the boiling sauce, and boil until thickened, about 1 minute. Stir the shrimp and green onions into the sauce until coated.

Spence's Secret Thai Red Shrimp Curry

"After traveling through Thailand for the first time over 10 years ago, I became enamored with the cuisine. This curry recipe is the result of many years of subtle refinements and fine tuning with an interesting Canadian twist! It's worth the effort to find fresh lemon grass and either fresh or freshly frozen kaffir lime leaves. Serve hot with basmati or jasmine rice."

Servings: 4 | **Prep**: 20m | **Cook**: 20m | **Ready In**: 40m

Ingredients

- 2 tablespoons sesame oil
- 1/2 tablespoons red curry paste, or more to taste
- 1 red onion, cut into 1/2-inch dice
- 2 large bell peppers, cut into 3/4-inch pieces
- 2 (14 ounce) cans coconut milk
- 1/2 cup chicken broth
- 1/2 tablespoons maple syrup
- 3 tablespoons fish sauce
- 3 stalks lemon grass, bruised and chopped
- 4 kaffir lime leaves, torn into quarters
- 1 pound medium shrimp, peeled and deveined
- 1/4 cup packed chopped fresh basil
- 2 tablespoons chopped fresh cilantro

Directions

1. Heat oil in a Wok over medium-high heat; stir in curry paste and cook until fragrant, about 1 minute. Stir onion into curry paste; cook until just tender, about 3 minutes. Stir in peppers; cook and stir for 3 more minutes.
2. Stir coconut milk, chicken broth, maple syrup, fish sauce, lemon grass, and lime leaves into vegetable mixture. Bring curry to a boil; reduce heat to low and simmer until vegetables are tender, about 8 minutes. Stir in shrimp; cook until shrimp is pink at the center, about 5 minutes.
3. Remove Wok from heat; stir basil and cilantro into curry. Serve hot.

Cook's Notes:

- Optional additional veggies such as chopped broccoli or zucchini can be added or substituted.
- Fresh lime leaves can be frozen in an airtight freezer bag for up to 6 months.
- If lemon grass is not very tender it can be tied into a bundle using cheesecloth before being added to the sauce (it saves picking out woody lemon grass pieces).

Spicy Shrimp and Pineapple Fried Rice

Servings: 6-8 | **Prep**: 55m | **Inactive**: 15m | **Cook**: 20m | **Ready In**: 1h30m

Ingredients

Shrimp:

- 1 pound medium (21/25 count) shrimp, shells and tails removed, deveined, halved lengthwise, then crosswise
- 2 tablespoons Ginger-Garlic Paste, recipe follows
- 2 teaspoons sambal oelek (Asian chile-garlic sauce)
- 1/2 cup soy sauce
- 1 teaspoon cornstarch
- Shredded Egg Crepes:
- 3 large eggs
- 1 teaspoon soy sauce
- Peanut oil

Fried Rice:

- 3 tablespoons peanut oil
- 1/2 medium yellow onion, diced
- 1/4 cup finely diced celery
- 1 tablespoon Ginger-Garlic Paste, recipe follows
- 2 tablespoons toasted sesame oil
- 4 cups cold cooked white rice
- 1/2 cup frozen peas, thawed
- 1/2 cup frozen shelled edamame, thawed
- 1 cup diced fresh pineapple
- 1 cup bean sprouts

- 1/4 cup soy sauce
- 2 tablespoons sambal oelek (Asian chile-garlic sauce)
- 3 scallions, chopped
- Ginger-Garlic Paste::
- 1/2 cup garlic cloves, peeled
- 1/2 cup fresh ginger, broken into broken pieces
- 2 tablespoons canola oil

Directions

Fried Rice:

1. For the shrimp: In a large bowl, combine the shrimp with the soy sauce, Ginger-Garlic Paste, sambal and cornstarch. Mix well to coat the shrimp. Cover and refrigerate for 15 minutes.
2. For the egg crepes: In a bowl, whisk together the eggs, soy sauce and 1/4 teaspoon water. Set a medium nonstick skillet over medium-low heat and coat it lightly with peanut oil. Pour in half the egg mixture and swirl the pan so the egg coats the bottom. Cook over low heat until firm, then carefully turn with a spatula and finish cooking on the other side, about 45 seconds per side. Transfer the egg crepe to a plate to cool. Repeat with remaining egg mixture. When the crepes are cool enough to handle, stack, roll and slice them into thin julienne strips. Set aside until ready to use.
3. For the fried rice: Set a large Wok or large nonstick skillet over high heat and swirl in 1 tablespoon of the peanut oil. Add the marinated shrimp and stir fry until slightly pink, about 2 minutes. Transfer the shrimp to a plate and set aside. Reduce the heat to medium and add the remaining 2 tablespoons peanut oil. Add the onions, celery and Ginger-Garlic Paste and stir fry until softened and fragrant, about 3 minutes. Add the sesame oil and the rice and stir fry until hot and a little crispy, about 2 minutes, breaking up the rice with a wooden spoon as you go. Fold in the peas, edamame, pineapple and bean sprouts and continue to stir fry until the vegetables heated through, about 2 minutes more. Stir in the soy sauce and sambal. Fold in the cooked shrimp and the sliced egg crepe. Transfer to a serving platter and garnish with chopped scallions.
4. Ginger-Garlic Paste:
   Pulse the garlic and ginger in a food processor. With the processor running, stream in the canola oil and process to a paste. (You'll need 3 tablespoons of the paste for the above recipe. Refrigerate remaining paste for up to a week.)

Spicy Shrimp Spring Rolls

Servings: 4-6

Ingredients

- Peanut oil for frying
- 2 tablespoons vegetable oil
- 1/2 pound Chinese sausage, finely chopped
- Freshly ground black pepper
- 1/2 cup minced yellow onions
- 1 tablespoon chopped garlic
- 1/4 pound Bok Choy, shredded
- 1/2 pound medium shrimp, peeled, deveined and chopped
- Nuoc Cham sauce, recipe follows
- Freshly ground black pepper
- 1 tablespoon chopped green onions
- 16 rice papers or spring roll wrappers
- 1 cup bean sprouts
- 1 cup match-stick carrot strips
- 1 cup packed cilantro leaves
- 1 cup packed fresh mint leaves

NUOC CHAM

- Recipe courtesy of Emeril Lagasse, 1999
- 1 small fresh chile pepper
- 1 teaspoon chopped garlic
- 3 teaspoons sugar
- 1 fresh lime
- 2 tablespoons fish sauce (nuoc mam)
- 3 tablespoons water

Directions

1. Preheat a Wok of peanut oil for frying. In a separate Wok, heat the vegetable oil. When the oil is hot, add the sausage. Stir-fry for 3 minutes. Add the onions and garlic. Cook for 2 minutes. Add the cabbage and the shrimp. Season with nuoc cham and black pepper. Stir-fry for 1 minute. Remove from the heat and cool completely. Stir in the green onions. Bring 2 cups of water to a boil in a 10-inch

saute pan and remove from the heat. Submerge each spring roll wrapper, one at a time, in the hot water. Move the wrappers around in the water until they become soft and pliable, about 10 to 15 seconds. Remove from the water and lay on parchment paper. Spread 1 tablespoon of the shrimp mixture evenly over each spring roll wrapper. On top of the shrimp mixture, sprinkle 1 tablespoon of the sprouts. Top the sprouts with 1 tablespoon of the carrots, 1 tablespoon of the cilantro, and 1 tablespoon of the mint. Fold two sides of the wrapper toward the center and then roll like a jelly roll, pressing the edges together to seal. Repeat until all 8 rolls are done. Fry until crispy, about 2 to 3 minutes. Remove and drain on paper towels. Serve with Nuoc Cham sauce.
2. NUOC CHAM
Stem the chile. Split the chile in half, remove and discard the seeds and membrane. Finely chop the chile. Combine the chopped chile, garlic and sugar in a mortar. Pound the mixture into a paste. Remove the zest and pith from the lime, and discard. Add the lime to the chile mixture. Mash well. Add the fish sauce and the water. Mix well. Serve as a seasoning agent instead of salt and pepper. Yield: about 1/3 cup

Spicy Wok Seared Shrimp

Ingredients

- 1/3 cup reduced-sodium chicken broth
- 1 teaspoon reduced-sodium soy sauce
- 1/4 teaspoon salt
- 1/4 teaspoon crushed red pepper
- 2 teaspoons vegetable oil
- 1 tablespoon minced fresh ginger
- 1 teaspoon minced garlic clove
- 1 pound (about 20 to 25) large shrimp, peeled and deveined
- 1/3 cup minced green onion

Directions

1. Combine broth, soy sauce, salt, and crushed red pepper in a small bowl.
2. Heat oil in a large Wok or heavy skillet over high heat until hot but not smoking; add ginger and garlic and cook 30 seconds or until

fragrant. Add shrimp and stir-fry 2 minutes until shrimp is almost completely pink. Stir broth mixture and swirl it into Wok and stir-fry about 1 minute until shrimp are just cooked. Remove from heat and stir in green onion. (Serving size: about 5 to 6 shrimp)

Stir Fry Round Cabbage with dried shrimps (炒高丽菜)

Ingredients

- 1/2 Round Cabbage (not Napa Cabbage)
- 1 tbsp dried shrimps
- 3 slices ginger (sliced to thin strips)
- 4 cloves garlic (minced)
- 4 shiitake mushrooms (sliced)
- 1/2 carrot (thinly shredded)
- 2 stalks spring unions (green part only) sliced to 2 inches

Sauce

- dried shrimp's soaking water
- 1/2 tsp soya sauce
- 1/2 tsp sesame oil
- 2 dashes white pepper powder

Directions

1. Rinse dried shrimps and soak them with 1/3 cup hot water in a small bowl until softened. Drain the dried shrimps, setting aside the soaking water. Pat dry the shrimp with kitchen towel.
2. In a pot, add oil over medium heat.
3. In with ginger and dried shrimp and cook for 2 mins.
4. Add garlic and mushroom in.
5. Add cabbage in and sauce to coat everything.
6. Cover the pot with lid and simmer until soften.
7. Add carrots, spring unions.
8. Serve with steamed rice.

Stir Fry With Shrimp

"Couldn't find exactly what I was looking for so.... After reading through several recipes, I shot from the hip and here is what I came up with, and it was awesome!"

Servings: 4 | **Time**: 30m

Ingredients

- 12 medium shrimp
- 1/4 cup soy sauce
- 1/4 teaspoon corn starch
- 1 tablespoon chopped garlic
- to taste Crushed red pepper flakes
- 1 tablespoon chopped parsley
- 1 tablespoon sesame seeds
- 1 tablespoon olive oil
- 2 eggs
- 1 small bag stir fry veggies (not frozen)
- 1 small bag spinach (not frozen)
- to taste Chopped green onion
- to taste Chopped celery
- to taste More parsley
- 2 cups cooked rice
- to taste More sesame seeds
- to taste More soy sauce

Directions

1. Cook rice. You can do this ahead have time, but have it warm when you add it.
2. Do all your chopping and put all the veggies aside
3. Thaw shrimp in cold water.
4. Whisk together soy sauce, corn starch, garlic, parsley, crushed red pepper flakes, and sesame seeds.
5. Place shrimp in shallow backing dish and marinade in sauce from step 2.
6. Set oven to low broil.
7. Heat olive oil and scramble the eggs in Wok or large fry pan.

8. Place shrimp in the shallow baking dish in oven to broil for 5 minutes, turning them over half way through.
9. Add all the veggies to the Wok or large fry pan and cook until the spinach starts to reduce.
10. Add your cooked rice and stir into the veggies
11. Add sesame seeds and soy sauce to taste.
12. Plate up and put shrimp on top. Drizzle with the sauce left in the baking dish.

Stir-Fried Ginger Shrimp

"The peppery flavor of ginger in this shrimp stir-fry complements the spiciness of the chile paste and sweetness of the rice wine. Serve with jasmine rice and melon slices."

Servings: 4

Ingredients

- 1 pound medium shrimp, peeled and deveined
- 1 teaspoon chopped peeled fresh ginger
- 1/2 teaspoon salt
- Dash of white pepper
- 1/2 cup water
- 1 tablespoon mirin (sweet rice wine)
- 2 teaspoons low-sodium soy sauce
- 1 1/2 teaspoons cornstarch
- 1 teaspoon sugar
- 1 teaspoon dark sesame oil
- 1/2 teaspoon chile paste with garlic (such as sambal oelek)
- 1 tablespoon canola oil, divided
- 1 cup thinly vertically sliced onion
- 4 garlic cloves, minced
- 1 cup diagonally cut celery

Directions

1. Place shrimp in a medium bowl. Sprinkle with ginger, salt, and pepper; toss well. Let stand 5 minutes.

2. Combine 1/2 cup water and next 6 ingredients (through chile paste) in a small bowl, stirring with a whisk.
3. Heat 1 teaspoon canola oil in a large nonstick skillet over medium-high heat. Add shrimp mixture to pan; stir-fry 2 minutes. Remove shrimp mixture from pan; set aside. Wipe pan dry with a paper towel. Heat remaining 2 teaspoons canola oil in pan over medium-high heat. Add onion and garlic; stir-fry 1 minute. Add celery; stir-fry 1 minute. Return shrimp mixture to pan; stir-fry 1 minute or until shrimp are done.
4. Add water mixture to pan. Bring to a boil; cook 1 minute or until thick, stirring constantly with a whisk. Serve immediately.

Stir-Fried Noodles with Shrimp and Peas

Servings: 4 | **Prep**: 5m | **Cook**: 15m | **Ready In**: 20m

Ingredients

- Salt
- 8 ounces spaghetti, broken in half
- 1 tablespoon sesame oil
- 2 tablespoons vegetable oil
- 1 pound shrimp, peeled and deveined
- 6 scallions, white and light green parts, chopped
- 2 cups frozen peas, defrosted
- 6 tablespoons teriyaki sauce

Directions

1. Bring a large pot of salted water to boil and cook spaghetti until just tender, about 8 minutes. Drain and toss with sesame oil.
2. Warm vegetable oil in large skillet over medium-high heat. Add shrimp and scallions and cook, stirring, until shrimp are pink and cooked through and scallions have softened, 3 to 5 minutes.
3. Add spaghetti, peas and teriyaki sauce and cook, tossing to coat and heat through, about 2 minutes.

Stir-Fried Shrimp and Bok Choy

"For a simple weeknight meal, toss together Stir-Fried Shrimp and Bok Choy. All you need for a balanced meal is tossed together in this one-dish dinner."

Servings: 4 | **Prep**: 20m | **Cook**: 20m

Ingredients

- 3 cups instant brown rice
- 1/4 teaspoon salt
- 1/2 cup low-sodium chicken broth
- 2 tablespoons low-sodium soy sauce
- 2 tablespoons rice wine or cooking sherry
- 1 teaspoon toasted sesame oil
- 1 tablespoon cornstarch
- 3 tablespoons vegetable oil
- 12 ounces shrimp, peeled and deveined (thawed if frozen)
- 1 tablespoon finely chopped fresh ginger
- 2 cloves garlic, finely chopped
- 3 scallions, white and light green parts, finely chopped
- 4 cups thinly sliced bok choy stalks (about 1 medium head)

Directions

1. Bring 2 1/2 cups water to boil in a large pot. Stir in rice and salt, cover, reduce heat to low and let cook until water has been absorbed, 5 to 10 minutes. Remove from heat, stir, cover, and let stand 5 minutes. Fluff with a fork; cover again.
2. Whisk broth, soy sauce, rice wine, sesame oil and cornstarch in a medium bowl.
3. Warm 1 Tbsp. vegetable oil in a large skillet or Wok over high heat. Add shrimp and cook, stirring, until just pink, about 2 minutes. Transfer to a bowl. Add remaining 2 Tbsp. vegetable oil to skillet along with ginger, garlic and scallions. Cook, stirring, until fragrant, about 30 seconds. Add bok choy and cook, stirring, until tender, 3 to 5 minutes.
4. Return shrimp to skillet and pour in soy sauce mixture. Cook, stirring, until sauce has thickened slightly, about 2 minutes. Serve immediately, over rice.

Stir-Fried Shrimp with Garlic and Chile Sauce

"A platter of succulent stir-fried orange-pink shrimp symbolizes gold coins (wealth) and good fortune for the coming year. Order fresh shrimp from the fishmonger; have it peeled and deveined while you shop for the rest of the menu."

Servings: 4 | **Total time**: 17m

Ingredients

- 1/2 cup fat-free, lower-sodium chicken broth
- 2 teaspoons cornstarch
- 1 teaspoon sugar
- 2 teaspoons Shaoxing (Chinese rice wine) or dry sherry
- 2 teaspoons lower-sodium soy sauce
- 1/4 teaspoon white pepper
- 1 tablespoon canola oil
- 1 1/2 pounds large shrimp, peeled and deveined
- 2 tablespoons minced garlic
- 1 1/2 teaspoons minced peeled fresh ginger
- 1 jalapeño pepper, seeded and finely chopped
- 1/2 cup (1-inch) slices green onions
- 1/2 teaspoon dark sesame oil
- Cilantro sprigs (optional)

Directions

1. Combine first 6 ingredients in a small bowl, stirring with a whisk.
2. Heat a Wok or large skillet over high heat. Add canola oil to pan. Add shrimp to pan; stir-fry 1 minute or until shrimp begin to turn pink. Add garlic, ginger, and jalapeño; stir-fry 1 minute. Stir in broth mixture; cook 1 minute or until shrimp are done and sauce is thickened, stirring constantly. Remove from heat; stir in onions and sesame oil. Garnish with cilantro sprigs, if desired.

Stirfry Shrimp and Broccoli

"super easy and yummy lunch served with jasmine steamed rice :hungry"

Servings: 5 | **Cook**: 15m

Ingredients

- 1 bunch broccoli
- 250 grams shrimp
- 1 clove garlic, slice thin
- 1 onion slice thin
- 4 tbsp oyster sauce
- 3 tbsp soy sauce
- 1 tbsp brown sugar
- 1 salt
- 1 black pepper
- 2 tbsp salted butter

Directions

1. Mix in together soy, oyster, brown sugar, black pepper
2. Medium heat the pan, melt 1 tbs butter and saute onion and garlic until fragrant
3. Add 1 tbs butter, Put in the shrimp into the pan, cook until change colour
4. Pour in the mixing sauce, stirfry
5. Put in the brocolly until bright colour. Salt it, and done :D

Summer Special Shrimp and Fruit Fried Rice

"This light and easy recipe is ideal for a weeknight meal, or anytime you have leftover rice. Serve hot with a chilled cucumber and tomato salad."

Servings: 2 | **Prep**: 40m | **Cook**: 20m | **Ready In**: 1h

Ingredients

- 1 tablespoon vegetable oil, divided
- 2 eggs, beaten
- 1/2 pound peeled and deveined medium shrimp
- 1 (1 inch) piece fresh ginger root, minced
- 2 red onions, sliced
- 3 green chile peppers, chopped
- 2/3 cup fresh pineapple, diced
- 1/2 cup orange segments 6 walnuts, chopped
- 2 cups cold, cooked white rice
- 1 tablespoon soy sauce
- 2 tablespoons chopped fresh cilantro
- salt and pepper to taste

Directions

1. Heat 1 teaspoon of the vegetable oil in a Wok over medium-high heat. Pour in the onions, and cook until just set; set aside. Increase the heat to high, and pour another 1 teaspoon of oil to the Wok. Stir in the shrimp, and cook until the shrimp turn pink, and are no longer translucent in the center, about 3 minutes; set aside.
2. Wipe out the Wok, and heat the remaining teaspoon of oil over high heat. Stir in the ginger, and cook quickly for a few seconds until the ginger begins to turn golden brown. Stir in the onion and chile peppers; cook for a minute or two until the onions begin to soften and turn brown around the edges. Add the pineapple and oranges, and gently cook until the pineapple is hot.
3. Stir in the rice, walnuts, and soy sauce. Stir for a few minutes until the rice is hot. Fold in the egg, shrimp, and cilantro. Season to taste with salt and pepper, and cook to reheat.

Footnotes

- Tip: Aluminum foil helps keep food moist, ensures it cooks evenly, keeps leftovers fresh, and makes clean-up easy.

Sweet and Sour Shrimp

***Servings**: 4 | **Prep**: 20m | **Cook**: 5m | **Ready In**: 25m*

Ingredients

- 6 tablespoons chicken stock or water
- 3 tablespoons ketchup
- 3 tablespoons sugar
- 3 tablespoons pineapple or orange juice
- 2 tablespoons vinegar
- 2 teaspoons soy sauce
- 3/4 teaspoon crushed red pepper flakes
- 2 teaspoons cornstarch
- 1 pound shrimp
- 2 teaspoons minced ginger
- 2 teaspoons minced garlic
- 2 tablespoons peanut or vegetable oil
- 1 cup thinly sliced onions
- 1 cup 1-inch chunks green bell peppers
- 1 cup pineapple chunks
- 12 maraschino cherries
- 6 tablespoons thinly sliced green onions
- Hot white rice, accompaniment

Directions

1. To make the sauce, in a bowl, combine 1/4 cup of stock, the ketchup, sugar, juice, vinegar, soy, and 1/2 teaspoon of the pepper flakes. Set aside.
2. In a small bowl, combine the cornstarch with the remaining 2 tablespoons of stock and stir to dissolve. Set aside.
3. In a bowl, toss the shrimp with the ginger, garlic, and remaining 1/4 teaspoon pepper flakes. Set aside for 10 to 20 minutes.
4. Heat a large Wok over high heat. Add the oil, swirling to coat the sides and bottom of the pan. Add the shrimp, garlic, and ginger and stir-fry until pink, about 2 minutes. Remove from the pan. Add the onions and peppers and stir-fry until crisp-tender, about 2 minutes. Add the sauce and cook, stirring, until the sugar dissolves. Add the cornstarch mixture and bring to a boil. Return the shrimp to the pan and add the pineapples, cherries, and green onions. Cook until the sauce is thick, about 1 minute.
5. Remove from the heat and serve over rice.

Sweet and Spicy Shrimp with Rice Noodles

Servings: 4 | *Hands-on*: 30m | *Total time*: 1h

Ingredients

- 1 tablespoon rice vinegar
- 2 1/2 teaspoons honey
- 1 tablespoon sambal oelek (ground fresh chile paste, such as Huy Fong)
- 1 tablespoon lower-sodium soy sauce
- 12 ounces peeled and deveined medium shrimp
- 4 ounces uncooked flat rice noodles (pad thai noodles)
- 1 tablespoon peanut oil
- 2 tablespoons chopped unsalted cashews
- 1 tablespoon thinly sliced garlic
- 2 teaspoons chopped peeled fresh ginger
- 1 green Thai chile, halved
- 12 sweet mini peppers, halved
- 3/4 cup matchstick-cut carrot
- 1/4 teaspoon salt
- 3/4 cup snow peas, trimmed
- 3/4 cup fresh bean sprouts

Directions

1. Combine first 4 ingredients in a medium bowl, stirring well with a whisk. Add shrimp to vinegar mixture; toss to coat. Cover and refrigerate 30 minutes.
2. Cook noodles according to package directions, omitting salt and fat; drain. Rinse with cold water; drain.
3. Heat a large skillet or Wok over medium-high heat. Add oil to pan; swirl to coat. Add cashews, garlic, ginger, and chile to pan; stir-fry 1 minute or until garlic begins to brown. Remove cashew mixture from pan with a slotted spoon, and set aside.
4. Increase heat to high. Add sweet peppers, carrot, and salt to pan; stir-fry 2 minutes. Add shrimp mixture (do not drain); stir-fry 2 minutes. Stir in noodles and peas; cook 1 minute, tossing to coat. Return cashew mixture to pan. Add bean sprouts; cook 1 minute or until thoroughly heated, tossing frequently.

Thai Shrimp Curry

Servings: 4 | **Prep**: 40m | ***Inactive***: 30m | **Cook**: 18m | ***Ready In:*** 1h28mm

Ingredients

- 2 tablespoons peanut oil
- 1/2 cup chopped shallots
- 1 large red bell pepper, cut into strips
- 2 medium carrots, trimmed and shredded
- 2 teaspoons minced garlic
- 3 tablespoons Thai Red Curry Paste, recipe follows
- 2 tablespoons fish sauce
- 2 teaspoons palm sugar or light brown sugar
- 1 (14-ounce) can coconut milk
- 1 pound medium shrimp, peeled and deveined
- 3 tablespoons chopped Thai basil leaves
- 3 tablespoons chopped fresh cilantro leaves
- Cooked jasmine rice, accompaniment
- Sprigs fresh cilantro, garnish

Directions

1. In a large Wok or saute pan, heat the oil over medium-high heat. Add the shallots, bell peppers, carrots, and garlic, and stir-fry until soft, 2 to 3 minutes. Add the curry paste and cook, stirring, until fragrant, 30 seconds to 1 minute. Stirring, add the fish sauce and sugar, then the coconut milk and bring to a boil. Simmer until thickened slightly, about 2 minutes. Add the shrimp and cook, stirring, until pink and just cooked through, about 2 minutes.
2. Remove from the heat and stir in the basil and cilantro.
3. Serve over jasmine rice, garnished with cilantro sprigs.

Thai Red Curry Paste:

- 12 dry Thai chili peppers or other small red peppers, seeded and soaked in warm water 30 minutes
- 1 tablespoon coriander seeds
- 1/2 teaspoon black peppercorns

- 1/2 cup chopped shallots
- 1/4 cup chopped garlic
- 3 stalks lemon grass, tough outer leaves and tops removed, tender stalks minced
- 3 tablespoons peeled and chopped fresh ginger root, or galanga
- 2 tablespoons chopped cilantro stems
- 2 teaspoons chopped lime zest, preferably Kaffir lime
- 1 teaspoon shrimp paste
- In a skillet, dry roast the coriander and peppercorns over low heat until fragrant, about 3 minutes. Remove and let cool. Grind in a spice grinder or mortar and pestle.
- Return the pan to medium heat. Add the shallots and garlic and cook, stirring, until starting to brown, about 3 minutes. Remove from the heat and let cool.
- Drain the chiles, reserving the liquid, and roughly chop.
- In a blender or food processor, combine all the ingredients with about 1/4 cup of the reserved soaking liquid. Process to make a smooth paste, scraping down the sides several times and adding more liquid through the top 1 tablespoon at a time with the motor running.
- Transfer to an airtight container and keep refrigerated until ready to use. Paste will keep refrigerated for up to 1 month.

Thai Shrimp Stir-fry with Tomatoes and Basil - Slimmed

Servings: 4 | Prep: 20m | Cook: 10m | Ready In: 30m

Ingredients

- 2 tablespoons soy sauce
- 1 tablespoon water
- 2 teaspoons Southeast Asian fish sauce
- 4 teaspoons light brown sugar
- 3 tablespoons peanut oil
- 3 cloves garlic, chopped
- 1 tablespoon grated, peeled, fresh ginger
- 1/2 to 1 teaspoon red chile flakes
- 1 pound large shrimp, peeled and deveined
- 1/2 medium red onion, cut in 1-inch dice
- 1 medium yellow pepper, seeded, cut in 1-inch dice

- 1 jalapeno chile, thinly sliced into rounds
- 2 cups cherry tomatoes, halved
- 3/4 cup torn fresh basil leaves
- 1/4 cup torn fresh mint leaves
- 2 tablespoons freshly squeezed lime juice
- Serving suggestion: Jasmine rice

Directions

- In a small bowl, combine the soy sauce, water, fish sauce, and sugar; set aside. Heat the oil in a large non-stick skillet over medium-high heat. Add the garlic, ginger, and chile flakes, and cook until fragrant, about 30 seconds. Add the shrimp and stir-fry until pink but still translucent in the middle, about 2 minutes. Transfer the shrimp to a medium bowl with a slotted spoon. Add the onion, pepper, and chile to the skillet, and stir-fry until lightly browned, about 2 minutes. Return the shrimp to the pan along with the soy sauce mixture. Bring to a boil, and stir-fry until the sauce glazes the shrimp, about 1 minute more. Add the tomatoes and stir until coated with sauce, about 15 seconds. Remove pan from the heat, stir in the basil, mint, and lime juice. Transfer to a serving dish, serve immediately.

Chapter 7: Italian Recipes

***

Awesome Stir Fry Semi-Italian

"Go to semperfryllc.com to watch our video recipes, and get the Hot Sauces and spicy oils used in our dishes"

Servings: 5 | **Time**: 25m

Ingredients

- 2 bunch Three Large Crowns of Broccoli
- 1 One large Scallion
- 1 One very large red onion
- 1 A sh*t Ton of mushrooms
- 1 Optional (Mild peppers) I didn't use any this time
- 4 tbsp Butter
- 1 Spicy Extra Virgin Olive oil. I'll teach you how to make this next
- 2/3 cup Generic Italian Seasoned Bread crumbs
- 1 Your choice of meat. Here we used shrimp
- 7 clove large peeled garlic
- 2 pinch Dried sweet basil
- 1 Pink Himilayan salt

Directions

1. Chop, slice, & dice ingredients however way you like the most. Set aside
2. In a large skillet, melt butter and add your spicy extra virgin olive oil. Then put your chopped veggies into the skillet and turn up the heat
3. Cover with a glass skillet top and cook the crisp raw vegetable texture out of them
4. Periodically remove cover and stir contents. Recover.
5. When vegetables begin to soften, add your cooked shrimp and sweet basil
6. Once vegetables are cooked to your liking, you may add the bread crumbs, and stir in evenly. This measure rids the Stir Fry of excess moisture while adding flavor and texture
7. Leave cover off and let stir fry cook on heat an additional 2 minutes.

8. You're done! Top rice, Italian pasta, etc with your Italian style stir fry.
9. Or, if you're us, you'll use this stir fry to compliment a skillet grilled Porterhouse steak!

Italian Pasta Stir-fry

"Great way to use tise fresh garden veggies"

Servings*: 20 | **Cook**: 4m*

Ingredients

- 8 oz package of linguini
- 1 tbsp olive oil
- 2 clove garlic, minced
- 1 zucchini, sliced
- 1 onion, chopped
- 2 tomatoes, chopped
- 1/4 cup fresh parsley, chopped
- 1 tsp basil
- 1 tsp oregano
- 1 pinch salt
- 1 pinch black pepper
- 1/4 cup grated parmesan cheese

Directions

1. Cook pasta, drain and keep warm
2. Heat oil in Wok or pan
3. Add garlic...15 seconds
4. Add zucchini and onion...2 minutes
5. Add tomatoes, parsley, and spices...1-2 minutes
6. Remove from heat and toss into pasta. Sprinkle with cheese and serve

Italian Sausage Stir Fry

Servings: 2 | Time: 30m

Ingredients

- 3 Italian Sausages
- 1 Green Pepper
- 1/2 Yellow Onion
- 1 Cup Baby Spinach
- 1 Tomato
- 2 Whole White Mushrooms
- Salt & Pepper
- Feta
- 1 Avocado

Directions

1. Cut casings from mild italian sausage.
2. Chop sausage into small pieces.
3. Chop green pepper, onion, mushrooms, and spinach.
4. Cook italian sausage on the stove until done.
5. Place cooked sausage in a bowl.
6. Cook vegetables in the same pan as the sausage was cooked in.
7. Once the vegetables are tender, chop and add the tomato to the pan.
8. Then add the italian sausage back to the pan and let simmer for a few minutes.
9. Top with salt, pepper, feta, and avocado.

Italian Stir Fry

"Seen many versions of this dish over the years but this is the one I came up w to marry my fav...pasta w my moms fav...Italian gyros! Its delicious, very easy & pretty quick!!"

Cook: 35m

Ingredients

- 1 packages Italian sausages (mild, hot or sweet) cooked & browned on both sides
- 1 small or medium green pepper sliced in thin strips & then cut strips in half
- 1 small red, yellow or white onion sliced into strips
- 1 1/2 tbsp garlic, finely minced or 1/2 teaspoon garlic powder
- 1 tbsp dried Italian seasoning or 1 tbsp dried oregano
- 1/2 tsp dried parsley or bout 1 tbsp minced fresh parsley
- 1 can diced tomatoes (do not drain)
- 1/2 lb or whats needed of ur favorite pasta cooked & drained (i use spaghetti or rotini but used elbow mac this time)
- 1 1/2 cup to 2 cups of ur favorite pasta sauce or even marinara or pizza sauce

Directions

1. Fry ur sausages in oil in large skillet, take out when done, set aside & let rest 10 minutes
2. While ur sausages r resting saute or "stir fry" ur peppers & onions in same skillet till mostly done, add minced garlic & herbs, stir through, drain oil
3. Slice sausages diagonally about 1/4 inch thick, add peppers, onions & sliced sausages back to skillet
4. Add tomatoes & sauce to the skillet with the sausages, stir through & simmer on medium-low for bout 15 minutes or a little longer if u want thicker sauce
5. After it has cooked then taste the sauce...if it needs salt add a little. If its to tangy or sour u can add a little white sugar or I use 1 tbsp of grape jelly to balance the flavor & the slight hint of grape gives it a nice flavor...almost like red wine! Don't use any other flavor jelly, jam or preserves because u don't want chunks of fruit or seeds in ur sauce!
6. Spoon this over ur cooked pasta! Also just to let u know if u don't have or don't use pasta this is also delicious over white or brown rice! Yumminess!! Hope u all love this dish as much as we do!!
7. Just a little note so u know... This usually feeds bout 3-5 people depending on how big of an appetite they may have... U can usually get more or less servings by adjusting the amount of pasta or rice u cook but if u have a big family or big eaters then I'd suggest doubling the recipe! :)

Chapter 8: Noodles Recipes

***

Asian Zucchini Noodles Stir Fry

Servings: 2 | **Time**: 15 m

Ingredients

- 2 zucchini.. made into noodles
- 1 yellow bell pepper
- 1 cup zucchini
- 1/2 cup snow peas
- 3 tbsp garlic chopped
- 2 tbsp ginger chopped
- 3 tbsp red chilli flakes
- 2 tbsp peanut oil
- 3 tbsp soy sauce
- 2 tbsp sugar
- 1 salt

Directions

1. Heat peanut oil in a pan.. add ginger garlic and fry for a min. Add all the veggies and fry for till cripsy
2. Add soy sauce and sugar and mix well. Cook for 2 mins
3. Add zucchini noodles and cook for another 2-3mins.
4. Add salt according to taste

Authentic Pad Thai Noodles

"This is an authentic Thai recipe, with the proper ingredients (no ketchup or peanut butter). It is easy, quick, and absolutely delicious."

Servings: 4 | **Prep**: 30m | **Cook**: 20m | **Ready In**: 2h

Ingredients

- 2/3 cup dried rice vermicelli
- 1/4 cup peanut oil
- 2/3 cup thinly sliced firm tofu
- 1 large egg, beaten
- 4 cloves garlic, finely chopped
- 1/4 cup vegetable broth
- 2 tablespoons fresh lime juice
- 2 tablespoons soy sauce
- 1 tablespoon white sugar
- 1 teaspoon salt
- 1/2 teaspoon dried red chili flakes
- 3 tablespoons chopped peanuts
- 1 pound bean sprouts, divided
- 3 green onions, whites cut thinly across and greens sliced into thin lengths - divided
- 3 tablespoons chopped peanuts
- 2 limes, cut into wedges for garnish

Directions

1. Soak rice vermicelli noodles in a bowl filled with hot water until softened, 30 minutes to 1 hour. Drain and set aside.
2. Heat peanut oil over medium heat in a large Wok.
3. Cook and stir tofu in the Wok, turning the pieces until they are golden on all sides.
4. Remove tofu with a slotted spoon and drain on plate lined with paper towels.
5. Pour all but 1 tablespoon of used oil from the Wok into a small bowl; it will be used again in a later step.
6. Heat the remaining 1 tablespoon of oil in the Wok over medium heat until it starts to sizzle.
7. Pour in beaten egg and lightly toss in the hot oil to scramble the egg.
8. Remove egg from the Wok and set aside.
9. Pour reserved peanut oil in the small bowl back into the Wok.
10. Toss garlic and drained noodles in Wok until they are coated with oil.
11. Stir in vegetable broth, lime juice, soy sauce, and sugar. Toss and gently push noodles around the pan to coat with sauce.
12. Gently mix in tofu, scrambled egg, salt, chili flakes, and 3 tablespoons peanuts; toss to mix all ingredients.

13. Mix in bean sprouts and green onions, reserving about 1 tablespoon of each for garnish. Cook and stir until bean sprouts have softened slightly, 1 to 2 minutes.
14. Arrange noodles on a warm serving platter and garnish with 3 tablespoons peanuts and reserved bean sprouts and green onions. Place lime wedges around the edges of the platter.

Ebi's Stir Fry Noodles

"Delicious!!!"

Servings: *4 |* **Time:** *25m*

Ingredients

- 300 grams chinese soup noodles
- 2 carrots, sliced to 1cm thick
- 10 baby corns, rinse in cold running water
- 100 grams cabbage, sliced
- 300 grams steak beef, slice and dry with kitchen paper
- 150 grams sugar peas, cut the ends
- 2 tsp soy sauce
- 1 tomato, sliced
- 1 onion, sliced
- Salt
- Powdered (mild) chili pepper
- 1 cube maggi
- 80 ml olive oil
- 100 grams butter
- 2 litres boiling water

Directions

1. Bleach cabbage and sugar peas with a litre of boiling water for 10 minutes and drain.
2. Soak noodles in a bowl with a litre of boiling water.
3. Season meat with salt, and pepper. Heat up oil in a frying pan and fry meat till a bit brown. Add onions, cook for 3 minutes then add tomatoes, cooking for another 2 minutes.

4. Add carrots, cabbage, sugar peas, soy sauce, Maggi cube, chilli pepper, salt and cook slowly for another 10 minutes.
5. Pour in noodles, stir thoroughly, add butter and cook for another 10 minutes. Serve hot.

Indonesian Stir-Fried Noodles (Bakmi Goreng)

"This easy Indonesian Stir-Fried Noodles (Bakmi Goreng) is a street-food noodle classic. For this noodle bowl's success, it depends on two things: serving it piping hot, right out of a very hot Wok, and finding some kecap manis, a molasses-thick sweet soy sauce."

Servings: 4 | Hands-on: 28m | Total time: 35m

Ingredients

- 3 tablespoons peanut oil, divided
- 2 large eggs, lightly beaten
- 6 ounces dried Chinese egg noodles or spaghetti
- 6 ounces skinless, boneless chicken breast, thinly sliced
- 4 ounces boneless pork loin chop, sliced
- 2 garlic cloves, minced
- 2 cups thinly sliced napa cabbage
- 3/4 cup sliced green onions
- 1 celery stalk, thinly sliced
- 3 tablespoons fat-free, lower-sodium chicken broth
- 1 tablespoon kecap manis (sweet soy sauce)
- 1 tablespoon lower-sodium soy sauce
- 1/2 cup packaged fried onions

Directions

1. Heat 1 tablespoon oil in a large nonstick skillet over medium-high heat. Pour eggs into pan; swirl to form a thin omelet. Cook 1 minute or until cooked on bottom. Carefully turn omelet over; cook 30 seconds. Remove from pan. Roll up omelet; cut roll crosswise into thin strips. Keep warm.
2. Cook noodles according to package directions. Drain and rinse with cold water; drain and set aside.

3. Heat a Wok over high heat. Add 2 tablespoons oil; swirl. Add chicken, pork, and garlic; stir-fry 1 1/2 minutes. Add cabbage, green onions, and celery; stir-fry 1 minute. Stir in broth, kecap manis, and soy sauce. Add noodles; stir-fry 3 minutes or until thoroughly heated and noodles begin to lightly brown. Add egg; toss gently. Top with fried onions. Serve immediately.

Long Life Noodles

"Any type of noodle—thin chow mein noodles to broad rice noodles to the thicker Shanghai wheat noodles—is a must at Chinese New Year's. However, long noodles represent a long unbroken life (so cutting them into shorter strands would symbolically shorten your life). Pull out your largest skillet or Wok because this Asian recipe creates a full pan."

Servings: 8

Ingredients

- 1 pound fresh Asian-style wheat noodles
- 1 1/2 tablespoons Shaoxing (Chinese rice wine) or dry sherry
- 1 1/2 teaspoons hoisin sauce
- 1/2 teaspoon cornstarch
- 6 ounces boneless pork tenderloin cut into 2 x 1/4–inch julienne strips
- 3 tablespoons dark soy sauce
- 2 tablespoons oyster sauce
- 1 tablespoon low-sodium soy sauce
- 1/2 teaspoon sugar
- 2 tablespoons canola oil, divided
- 3 cups chopped napa (Chinese) cabbage
- 1/2 teaspoon minced garlic
- 1 1/4 cups (1-inch) slices green onions

Directions

1. Cook noodles according to package directions, omitting fat and salt. Drain and rinse with cold water; drain. Set aside.

2. Combine wine, hoisin sauce, and cornstarch in a small bowl, stirring with a whisk. Add pork; stir to coat. Cover and let stand 10 minutes.
3. Combine dark soy sauce, oyster sauce, low-sodium soy sauce, and sugar in a small bowl, stirring with a whisk; set mixture aside.
4. Heat 1 teaspoon oil in a Wok or large skillet over high heat. Add cabbage to pan; stir-fry 2 minutes. Transfer cabbage to a bowl.
5. Heat 2 teaspoons oil in pan. Add garlic; stir-fry 10 seconds or until fragrant. Add pork mixture; stir-fry 3 minutes or until done. Add pork mixture to bowl with cabbage.
6. Wipe pan clean with paper towels; return to heat. Heat remaining 1 tablespoon oil. Add reserved noodles; stir-fry 1 minute. Add onions and soy sauce mixture to pan; stir-fry 1 minute. Add pork mixture; stir to combine. Cook 1 minute or until hot.

Simple Stir-fry Noodles

Ingredients

- 1/4 packages Rice Noodles
- slice red bell pepper and yellow bell pepper
- 100 grams Chicken
- pinch chili peppers
- slice fresh ginger
- 1/2 An apple peeled and diced

Directions

1. Cook rice noodles according to package and slice and dice the veg and chicken.
2. In a Wok or frying pan add the chillies and ginger and the chicken. After 3 minutes add a dash of soy sauce.
3. Add the bell peppers and apple and stir. Leave for 5 mins.
4. Drain the noodles and add to Wok. Stir in the ingredients. Serve.

Singapore Noodles

"This is a recipe I came across from my friend's dad. When I tasted it and it

tasted a lot like a hot pot dish I had at one of my Chinese friend's house. So I made some changes to it to make it my own."

Servings: 6 | **Prep**: 25m | **Cook**: 10 | **Ready In**: 45m

Ingredients

- 6 dry Chinese egg noodle nests
- 1/4 cup peanut oil
- 6 cloves garlic, minced
- 2 tablespoons slivered fresh ginger
- 2 teaspoons crushed red pepper flakes
- 1 pound skinless, boneless chicken breast halves
- 1/3 cup green onions, chopped
- 2/3 cup julienned carrot
- 1 (8 ounce) can sliced water chestnuts, drained
- 2 (15 ounce) cans whole straw mushrooms, drained
- 1/4 cup peanut butter
- 1/4 cup oyster sauce
- 3 tablespoons curry powder
- 2 teaspoons soy sauce

Directions

1. Bring a large pot of lightly-salted water to a rolling boil; add the egg noodle nests and return to a boil. Turn off the heat and let stand for 5 minutes; drain and set aside.
2. Heat the peanut oil in a Wok over high heat. Stir in the garlic, ginger, and red pepper flakes; cook a few seconds until the garlic begins to turn golden. Add the chicken, green onions, and carrots. Cook and stir until the chicken is no longer pink, about 5 minutes. Stir in the water chestnuts, mushrooms, peanut butter, oyster sauce, curry powder, and soy sauce until the peanut butter has dissolved into the sauce.
3. Stir the noodles into the chicken mixture; cover and reduce heat to warm or very low. Let stand 10 to 15 minutes for the noodles to absorb some of the sauce.

Soba Noodle Stir Fry

Ingredients

- 4 oz soba noodles
- 1 clove garlic, minced
- 1 fresh ginger, minced
- 2 spring onions, chopped
- 1 carrot, sliced
- 3 mushrooms, chopped
- bunch long green beans, halved
- 1/4 cup soy sauce
- 2 tbsp hot sauce
- 1 tsp sesame seeds
- 1 tsp chili flakes

Directions

1. In a pot boil water and cook soba noodles until tender, not fully cooked.
2. In a Wok or skillet heat a tablespoon of olive oil. Add the spring onions. Cook until tender, add the garlic. Stir for 2 minutes.
3. Add the sliced carrots and chopped green beans. Season with salt and pepper and stir.
4. Add the chopped mushrooms. Add a little bit of the soy sauce and 1 tbsp of hot sauce. Stir, cover and lower the heat. Leave for 15 mins, stirring occasionally.
5. Add the soba noodles and stir. Add the remaining soy sauce and more if necessary. Cook for a further 10 mins.
6. Serve and top with sesame seeds and chili flakes.

Somen Noodle Stir Fry with Mackerel and Miso

"This is a healthy somen recipe with minced mackerel. The miso gives it a touch of sweetness. Kids will love it!"

Servings: 2 | **Time**: 15m

Ingredients

- 1 fillet mackerel
- 1 small chunk ginger

- 1/2 Onion, finely chopped
- 1 Egg
- 2 to 3 servings somen noodles
- 1 Tbsp sesame oil
- 1 pinch salt and pepper
- 1 Tbsp each sake, mirin, miso, sugar
- 2 Tbsp soy sauce

Directions

1. Remove the bones from the mackerel and chop it along with the ginger until it's finely minced. Season with salt.
2. Heat sesame oil in a frying pan and cook the onion and minced mackerel. When everything is cooked through, add the sake, mirin, miso, sugar and soy sauce, and simmer until the liquid is nearly gone.
3. While the fish is cooking, boil the somen noodles. Rinse with water and drain well.
4. Add the somen into the pan along with some more sesame oil. Stir fry on high but do not over mix or the somen will get too soft and sticky. Season a beaten egg with salt & pepper and pour over the noodles. Turn off heat and let the egg slowly cook as the pan cools down.
5. Once the egg is cooked through, mix lightly. Season with shichimi pepper if you like.

Spicy Szechuan Noodles Dan Dan Mian

Servings: *4* | **Prep**: *15m* | **Cook**: *18m* | **Ready In**: *33m*

Ingredients

- 1 pound ground pork
- 4 tablespoons soy sauce
- 1/2 cup peanut oil
- 2 tablespoons minced garlic
- 2 tablespoons finely chopped ginger
- 2/3 cup finely chopped green onions (scallions)
- 1 tablespoon Chinese sesame paste

- 3 tablespoons chili oil
- 1 cup chicken stock
- 1 tablespoon dried Szechuan peppercorns (roasted and ground) or 3 tablespoons Szechuan chile paste
- 3/4 pound Chinese thin egg noodles
- 1 cup matchstick-cut radish, for garnish

Directions

1. In a large saucepan heat 2 quarts of lightly salted water to a boil.
2. While waiting for the water to come to a boil, combine the pork and 2 tablespoons of the soy sauce in a small bowl and mix well. Add the oil to a Wok or saute pan and heat over medium high heat until very hot. Add the pork and stir-fry, stirring with a spatula to break it into small pieces. When the pork is crispy and dry, about 5 minutes, remove it with a slotted spoon and transfer to a paper-lined plate to drain. Pour off most of the oil, leaving 2 tablespoons in the Wok. Reheat the Wok, add the garlic, ginger, and scallions, and stir-fry for 30 seconds. Add the sesame paste, remaining 2 tablespoons of soy sauce, chili oil, chicken stock, and ground peppercorns or chile paste and simmer for 4 minutes.
3. When the water has come to a boil, cook the noodles until al dente, for 2 minutes if they are fresh or 5 minutes if they are dried. Drain the noodles and add to the reduced sauce in the Wok, along with the reserved pork, and toss until thoroughly combined and coated with the sauce.
4. Top with the matchstick radishes and serve immediately.

Stir Fry Noodle In Dark Sauce Hokkien Mee

*Servings: 4 | **Cook**: 20m*

Ingredients

- 300 grams fresh yellow egg noodle
- 2 cup choy sam vegetable
- 1/2 cup spring onion
- 10 medium cooked fish ball cut in half
- 10 medium shrimp / prawn

- 1 tbsp oil
- 2 small red cili

Sauce

- 3 tbsp soy sauce
- 1 tbsp dark sauce
- 2 tbsp oyster sauce
- 2 cup stock / water
- 2 tbsp fine dice garlic and shallot

Directions

1. in pan with oil saute dice garlic and shallot then add in prawn and fish ball with green vegetable then add water / stock bring it to a boil
2. add yellow noodle and mix well till sauce start to dry and starchy off heat add scallion and serve hot

Stir Fry Noodles

Servings: 3 | Time: 30m

Ingredients

- 1 bout half small broccoli
- 1 packages chinese noodles
- 1 some cabbage and carrots
- 1 bell pepper red and green
- 1 soy sauce
- 1 chicken breast or any other meat and shrimp
- 1 salt and blck pepper to taste.
- 1 vegetable oil for stir fry

Directions

1. Fry onions and garlic till it done.add the chicken cut.then stir fry for few mins more.

2. Add some water enough to cook the chicken season with soy sauce and add the vegetables.cover and cook for 10min.
3. Add the noodles and stir occasionally don't let it dry.cook till the noodles done.serve

Thai Pad Thai Noodles

"Pad Thai is our most classic common dish. It goes great with a nice tall glass of Thai iced tea."

Servings: 4 | **Prep**: 10m | **Cook**: 25m | **Ready In**: 35m

Ingredients

- 3 cups water
- 1 (8 ounce) package wide rice noodles
- 1/2 tablespoons vegetable oil
- 2 cloves garlic, smashed
- 1 (4 ounce) boneless pork chop, cut into small pieces
- 1 cup bean sprouts 3 tablespoons dried small shrimp
- 1/2 tablespoons palm sugar
- 2 tablespoons fish sauce
- 1 tablespoon soy sauce
- 1 tablespoon lime juice
- 2 tablespoons chopped salted radish (optional)
- 1/4 cup unsalted roasted peanuts, chopped
- 1/4 cup chopped fresh cilantro for garnish

Directions

1. Bring water to a boil in a pot.
2. Place rice noodles in a large bowl. Pour boiling water over noodles and allow to soak until softened, about 20 minutes. Drain.
3. Heat vegetable oil in a Wok over medium heat.
4. Cook and stir garlic and pork in hot oil until pork is no longer pink in the center, about 5 minutes.
5. Stir in soaked rice noodles, bean sprouts, dried shrimp, palm sugar, fish sauce, soy sauce, and lime juice, stirring until palm sugar has dissolved. Cook until noodles are heated through, 3 to 4 minutes.

6. Stir in salted radish until combined.
7. Lightly toss peanuts and noodle mixture together until combined Transfer to a platter. Garnish with cilantro.

Veggie Noodle Stir-Fry

"A great way to make sure you're getting the vitamins and minerals your body needs is to eat the rainbow. Eating a mixture of different coloured vegetables, like in this stir-fry, will help you do that. This dish will give you two of your 5-a-day. Of course, feel free to use whatever vegetables you have in the fridge – this is a great dish for using up leftovers too!"

Servings: 4

Ingredients

- 200 g (8 oz) thick flat rice noodles or chow mein-style egg noodles
- 1 red onion
- 2 cloves garlic
- 5 cm (2 inch) piece of ginger
- 1/4-1/2 bunch fresh coriander/cilantro
- 1 small head of broccoli
- 1 red or yellow pepper
- 350 g (12 oz) firm tofu
- 1 carrot
- 1/2 fresh red chilli (Optional)
- 100 g (3/4 cup) raw, unsalted cashew nuts
- Vegetable oil
- 100 g (4 oz) snow peas or mangetout
- 100 g (4 oz) baby spinach
- 2 limes
- Sesame oil
- Low-salt soy sauce

Directions

1. Cook the noodles according to the packet instructions.
2. Then drain and refresh in cold water (this stops them from over-cooking) and place to one side.

3. On a chopping board, peel and finely slice the onion.
4. Then peel and finely chop the garlic.
5. Peel the ginger using a teaspoon...
6. Then chop into matchsticks.
7. Pick the coriander leaves...
8. And finely chop the stalks.
9. Cut the broccoli florets off the stalk...
10. Halve any larger florets...
11. Then thinly slice the stalk.
12. Halve the pepper, scoop out the seeds and pith with a teaspoon.
13. Then slice into strips.
14. Cut the tofu into rough 2cm (3/4 inch) cubes.
15. Using a vegetable peeler/speed-peeler, peel the carrot lengthways into long ribbons.
16. Trim and halve the chilli lengthways (if using)...
17. Then run a teaspoon down the cut side to scoop out the seeds and white pith.
18. Finely slice at an angle, then wash your hands thoroughly.
19. Place a Wok or large non-stick frying pan on a medium heat, add the cashew nuts, and toast until golden, stirring regularly.
20. Tip into a small bowl.
21. Place the pan back on a high heat and drizzle in 1 tablespoon of vegetable oil.
22. Add the red onion, garlic, ginger and coriander stalks...
23. Then fry for 2 minutes, or until lightly golden, stirring regularly.
24. Throw in the broccoli, pepper, tofu and snow peas or mangetouts...
25. And fry for 2 minutes, stirring regularly.
26. Stir in the spinach and allow it to wilt.
27. Then add the noodles and carrot ribbons.
28. Toss well for a minute to heat through.
29. Squeeze over the juice from half the lime.
30. Add 1 teaspoon of sesame oil and 2 tablespoons of soy sauce...
31. Then toss to coat.
32. Sprinkle over the sliced chilli (if using), toasted nuts...
33. And the reserved coriander leaves.
34. Then serve with lime wedges for squeezing.

Zucchini Noodles Pad Thai

"A healthier adaptation of a Pad Thai recipe. Serve with extra lime wedges."

Servings: 4 | **Prep**: 45m | **Cook**: 12m | **Ready In**: 57m

Ingredients

- 3 large zucchini
- 1/4 cup chicken stock
- 1/2 tablespoons tamarind paste
- 2 tablespoons low-sodium soy sauce
- 2 tablespoons oyster sauce
- 1/2 tablespoons Asian chile pepper sauce
- 1 tablespoon Worcestershire sauce
- 1 tablespoon fresh lime juice
- 1 tablespoon white sugar
- 2 tablespoons sesame oil
- 1 tablespoon chopped garlic
- 12 ounces skinless, boneless chicken breasts, cut into 1-inch cubes
- 8 ounces peeled and deveined shrimp
- 2 eggs, beaten
- 2 tablespoons water, or as needed (optional)
- 3 cups bean sprouts, divided
- 6 green onions, chopped into 1-inch pieces
- 2 tablespoons chopped unsalted dry-roasted peanuts
- 1/4 cup chopped fresh basil

Directions

1. Make zucchini noodles using a spiralizer.
2. Whisk chicken stock, tamarind paste, soy sauce, oyster sauce, chile pepper sauce, Worcestershire sauce, lime juice, and sugar together in a small bowl to make a smooth sauce.
3. Heat sesame oil in a Wok or large skillet over high heat. Add garlic and stir until fragrant, about 10 seconds. Add chicken and shrimp; cook and stir until chicken is no longer pink in the center and the juices run clear, 5 to 7 minutes.

4. Push chicken and shrimp to the sides of the Wok to make a space in the center. Pour eggs and scramble until firm, 2 to 3 minutes. Add zucchini noodles and sauce; cook and stir, adding water if needed, about 3 minutes. Add 2 cups bean sprouts and green onions; cook and stir until combined, 1 to 2 minutes.
5. Remove Wok from heat and sprinkle peanuts over noodles. Serve garnished with remaining 1 cup bean sprouts and fresh basil.

Chapter 9: Pork and Lamp Recipes

***

Baja Pork Stir-Fry

Servings: 4 | *Hands-on:* 26 m | *Total time:* 26 m

Ingredients

- 1/4 cup fat-free, lower-sodium chicken broth
- 1 1/2 teaspoons cornstarch
- 1/2 teaspoon ground cumin
- 2 garlic cloves, minced
- 1 (1-pound) pork tenderloin, cut into 1-inch pieces
- 3/4 teaspoon salt, divided
- 1/2 teaspoon black pepper, divided
- 2 tablespoons canola oil, divided
- 1/2 red onion, cut into wedges
- 1/2 cup julienne-cut yellow bell pepper
- 1/2 cup julienne-cut green bell pepper
- 1/2 cup julienne-cut red bell pepper
- 1/2 jalapeño pepper, minced
- 10 cherry tomatoes, halved
- 1/4 cup fresh cilantro leaves

Directions

1. Combine first 4 ingredients.
2. Sprinkle pork with 1/4 teaspoon salt and 1/4 teaspoon black pepper; toss. Heat a large skillet over medium-high heat. Add 1 tablespoon canola oil; swirl. Add pork, and cook for 3 minutes, browning on all sides. Remove pork from pan; keep warm.
3. Heat pan over high heat, and add remaining 1 tablespoon canola oil, and swirl to coat. Add onion, and stir-fry for 1 minute. Add the bell peppers and jalapeño; stir-fry for 1 minute. Return pork to pan, and stir-fry for 1 minute. Stir in broth mixture, the remaining 1/2 teaspoon salt, and remaining 1/4 teaspoon black pepper, and bring to a boil. Remove from heat, and stir in tomatoes. Sprinkle with cilantro.

Cajun Spiced Pork Stir Fry with Mushrooms

"A yummy Chinese style meal that's quick, and easy! This can be served with Rice for an oriental meal for 2. If you don't like Pork then change for Lamb or Beef. Feeling inventive? Combine all 3 together!"

Servings: 2

Ingredients

- 400 g Pork
- 2 Red Onions
- 2 Flat Mushrooms
- 2 tbsp tomato puree
- 1-2 tbsp Paprika
- 2-3 tbsp Cajun
- 200 ml Chicken Stock
- 2 Tbsp Olive Oil
- Pinch Salt and Pepper
- 2 Cloves Garlic

Directions

1. Cook up the Pork in the Oven. I used a Pork Fillet. Cover it in foil for around 30 minutes on a preheated oven of around 190c. To save time you can also pre-cook your mushrooms.
2. Once cooked, leave to cool and then slice in strips.
3. Over a heated oil and pan, slice your onions and mushrooms and crush your garlic and brown them off. Once browned throw in your Pork.
4. Add the tomato puree and mix together. Put in the Paprika and mix and then Cajun and mix. Add/Reduce to your liking.
5. Once all combined, add in your chicken stock. Bring to boil and then let it simmer on a low to med heat for a further 20 minutes.
6. Once simmered and the stock has reduced a good amount, add your seasoning. You are ready to serve with Rice.

Caramelized Pork Belly (Thit Kho)

"This dish is very popular in Vietnamese households for everyday eating but is also traditionally served during Tet, the Vietnamese Lunar New Year. The longer you cook the pork belly, the more tender it becomes. If you make this dish ahead, the fat will congeal on the surface, making it easier to remove, and a little healthier! This also allows the flavors to meld a little more. Serve with rice."

Servings: 6 | ***Prep***: 20m | ***Cook***: 1h | ***Ready In***: 1h20m

Ingredients

- 2 pounds pork belly, trimmed
- 2 tablespoons white sugar
- 5 shallots, sliced
- 3 cloves garlic, chopped
- 3 tablespoons fish sauce ground black pepper to taste
- 13 fluid ounces coconut water
- 6 hard-boiled eggs, peeled

Directions

1. Slice pork belly into 1-inch pieces layered with skin, fat, and meat.
2. Heat sugar in a large Wok or pot over medium heat until it melts and caramelizes into a light brown syrup, about 5 minutes. Add pork and increase heat to high. Cook and stir to render some of the pork fat, 3 to 5 minutes.
3. Stir shallots and garlic into the Wok. Add fish sauce and black pepper; stir to evenly coat pork. Pour in coconut water and bring to a boil. Add eggs, reduce heat to low, and simmer, covered, until pork is tender, about 1 hour.
4. Remove Wok from the heat and let stand, about 10 minutes. Skim the fat from the surface of the dish.

Cook's Note:

- Check occasionally while the pork is simmering that the liquid doesn't evaporate too much. Add water a little at a time if sauce seems to be drying out.

Crispy Pork Stir-Fry with Baby Bok Choy

"Hot! Hot! Hot! That is exactly how your Wok should be before the food goes in so that you get the crispy, browned edges you want. Get the thinnest slices of meat by using a serrated knife to cut it or by freezing it for 30 minutes."

Servings: 4 | **Hands-on:** 30m | **Total time**: 30m

Ingredients

- 10 ounce very thinly sliced pork shoulder
- 1 1/2 teaspoons dark sesame oil
- 1/2 teaspoon kosher salt
- 1/4 teaspoon white pepper
- 1 tablespoon canola oil
- 2 heads baby bok choy, quartered lengthwise
- 1 1/2 cups (2-inch) pieces haricots verts (French green beans)
- 1 tablespoon finely chopped peeled fresh ginger
- 3 large garlic cloves, thinly sliced
- 1 red bell pepper, cut into thin strips
- 2 tablespoons rice vinegar
- 1 tablespoon lower-sodium soy sauce
- 2 teaspoons brown sugar
- 1/4 cup sliced green onions
- 2 cups hot cooked long-grain brown rice

Directions

1. Heat a large Wok over high heat until very hot. Toss pork with sesame oil, salt, and pepper. Add pork to pan; let stand 2 minutes, without stirring, so that pork gets crispy and browned. Stir-fry pork for 2 minutes or until well browned on all sides. Let stand 1 minute without stirring. Spoon pork into a bowl; set aside.
2. Reheat pan over high heat until very hot. Add canola oil; swirl to coat. Add bok choy; stir-fry 2 minutes. Add green beans, ginger, garlic, and bell pepper; stir-fry 3 minutes or until crisp-tender. Combine vinegar, soy sauce, and brown sugar, stirring until sugar dissolves. Remove pan from heat; stir in vinegar mixture, tossing to coat. Stir in pork. Sprinkle with green onions. Serve over rice.

Garlic-Pork Stir-Fry

"Garlic-Pork Stir-Fry is a one-Wok wonder that will satisfy the appetites of your hungry crew and meet your desire for a simple, fast dinner."

Servings: 4 | **Prep**: 15m | **Marinate**: 15m | **Cook**: 10m

Ingredients

- 1/2 cup chicken or vegetable broth
- 1/3 cup hoisin sauce
- 1/4 cup soy sauce
- 1 tablespoon cornstarch
- 1/2 to 1 teaspoon chili-garlic paste or sriracha
- 12 ounces pork tenderloin, cut into strips
- 3 baby bok choy or 1 medium bok choy
- 5 teaspoons stir-fry oil or vegetable oil, divided
- 6 garlic cloves, sliced
- 1 tablespoon minced fresh ginger
- 2 shallots, halved and sliced
- 1 red bell pepper, thinly sliced
- 8 ounces cremini mushrooms, sliced
- Hot cooked soba noodles or rice noodles

Directions

1. Combine first 5 ingredients in a small bowl. Toss pork with 1/4 cup sauce mixture in a medium bowl, reserving remaining sauce mixture. Marinate 15 to 30 minutes.
2. Meanwhile, trim root end of bok choy. Slice white stems; tear or cut large leaves in half.
3. Heat Wok over high heat until a few drops of water evaporate immediately. Swirl 2 teaspoons oil in pan to coat. (If using a nonstick skillet, heat oil over medium-high heat.) Add pork; stir-fry 3 minutes or until browned. Transfer to a plate, and wipe Wok clean.
4. Heat remaining 3 teaspoons oil in Wok over high heat (medium-high, if using a nonstick skillet). Add garlic, ginger, and shallots; stir-fry 30 seconds or until fragrant. Stir in bok choy stems, bell pepper, and mushrooms, and cook 5 minutes or until tender.

5. Stir in reserved sauce mixture. Bring to a boil, reduce heat, and simmer 1 minute or until thickened. Stir in bok choy leaves and pork, and cook until heated through. Serve with hot cooked noodles.

Ginger-Orange Pork Stir-fry

"Found a recipe in Good Housekeeping Mag and added a few ingredients to change it up a bit. This is a great recipe for a quick meal."

Servings: 4

Ingredients

- 1 pork tenderloin thinly sliced (about 12 ounces)
- 2 tbsp ground ginger
- 1 cup chicken broth
- 2 tbsp teriyaki sauce
- 3 tsp cornstarch
- 2 tbsp brown sugar
- 2 tsp canola oil
- 8 oz snow peas (strings removed)
- 1 cup sliced sweet red peppers (I used a mixture of red, yellow and orange)
- 3 green onion sliced thin
- 2 tbsp orange marmalade

Directions

1. In a bowl mix ginger, chicken broth, teriyaki sauce, cornstarch and brown sugar. Set aside.
2. Salt and pepper tenderloin slices. Set aside.
3. In a large skillet heat 1tsp oil over medium-high heat until hot. Add snow peas and peppers, cook while stirring for 1 minute. Add green onion slices and cook for another minute. Veggies should be crisp. ** (Be sure and slice green onions lengthwise like shown in first pic)**
4. Remove veggies and set aside.
5. In same skillet, heat remaining teaspoon of oil then add pork slices. Cook until pork just loses its pink (2-3 min) then remove pork from

pan and set aside. (Pork will cook fast because of how thin it is sliced, don't overcook)
6. Now pour your sauce mixture in skillet. Cook and stir constantly until bubbly. Continue to cook and stir until sauce slightly thickens, about 1 minute.
7. Stir in marmalade. Taste your sauce, add more marmalade if you prefer a sweeter sauce.
8. Return pork and veggies to sauce. Stir and coat with sauce. Heat through.
9. Serve immediately.

Green Bean Pork Stir Fry

"Delicious"

Servings: 6

Ingredients

- 2 lb pork loin
- 2 lb fresh or frozen whole green beans
- 1/2 large chopped onion
- 1/2 tsp salt
- 2 tbsp olive oil, extra virgin
- 3 clove sliced garlic cloves
- 1 cup mixed coloured sweet/ bell peppers
- 1/4 tsp ground ginger
- 6 large egg

Directions

1. Beat eggs and fry in a pan very quickly. Leave no colouration on eggs if possible. Set aside.
2. Slice the pork thinly. Add in a pan with hot oil stir fry. When pork is done remove and set aside.
3. Add the green beans, garlic, onions, ginger, salt, and peppers. Stir fry till the green beans are desired doneness. Add back the pork stir fry till mixed well.
4. Remove from heat stir in the eggs serve hope you enjoy!

Hawaiian Pork Stir Fry

"Wanted something different to cook for dinner for my hubby and children. Came up with this and they LOVED it. For all the working parents, it's a quick go to if you're running behind and wanna get a hot meal on the table. Plus it gets in a serving each of fruit and vegetables."

***Servings**: 4 | **Time**: 30m*

Ingredients

- 1 packages Pork Strips (used for stir fry)
- 1/4 cup Low Sodium Soy Sauce
- 1/4 cup Light Brown Sugar
- 2 cup 100% Pineapple Juice
- 1 can Cubed/Crushed Pineapple
- 1/3 cup Maraschino Cherries (optional)
- 1/2 cup Slivered Sweet Orange Peppers
- 1/2 cup Slivered Sweet Red Peppers
- 2 cup Cooked Jasmine Rice (According to Package)

Directions

1. Marinate Pork strips with the first three ingredients (Sugar, Soy sauce and Pineapple Juice) overnight in refrigerator . If you're not able to marinate overnight, give the meat at least 4 hours to sit in juices.
2. Cut up your peppers in slivers. Add a little olive oil to saute pan. Just enough to cook off peppers. Saute on low for about 7 minutes.
3. Add pineapples. IF YOU'RE USING CRUSHED PINEAPPLES, SAVE THIS STEP FOR LAST. Cook the pineapples with peppers for another 4 minutes. Remove from pan and set aside.
4. At this time start preparing your Jasmine rice according to the package.
5. Add meat to your pan. Cook until fully cooked. Add veggies, pineapples and maraschino cherries to pan. Just reheat until all ingredients are hot and steamy.
6. Cup out Jasmine Rice and place stir fry atop rice.
7. Enjoy...!!

Honey Ginger Sriracha Pork Stir-fry

Servings: 2 | **Time**: 30m

Ingredients

- 1/2 lb pork tenderloin
- 1 cup raw broccoli florets
- 1/2 cup raw baby carrots, julienned
- 1/2 cup baby corn, sliced lengthwise
- 1 sesame oil
- 1 tsp garlic, minced or chopped
- 1 tbsp cornstarch
- 2 tbsp cool water
- 1 ground black pepper (to taste)
- Marinade
- 1 tbsp honey
- 1 tbsp sriracha sauce
- 2 tbsp dry white wine
- 2 tbsp soy sauce
- 1/2 tsp ground ginger

Directions

1. Trim pork tenderloin removing fat and sinew, slice thinly across the grain (1/4" thickness), place in a bowl.
2. Add marinade ingredients (soy sauce, white wine, sriracha sauce, honey and ginger), mix to distribute sauce evenly and set aside. Chop veggies.
3. Heat Wok on high heat for a few minutes, add sesame oil, when oil just starts to smoke, add pork slices, turning frequently. Stir-fry until pork is mostly cooked and opaque, about 5 - 8 minutes.
4. Remove pork from Wok into a clean bowl/plate, set aside. In the juices left in the Wok, stir in chopped garlic, then add broccoli & carrots. Stir-fry for 2-3 minutes, adding more sesame oil if desired. Add baby corn and stir-fry for another 1-2 minutes.
5. Return pork to Wok and stir into veggies, add more soy sauce, sriracha, and honey if needed to create a liquid gravy of about 1/2

cup in volume. Push food to the outer edges so liquid is settled in the bottom of Wok.
6. In a seperate bowl combine cool water & corn starch. Add mixture to liquid gravy in the Wok and stir until thickened. Mix everything together and voila!
7. Serve immediately with cooked rice. (Basmati/wild blend cooked in chicken stock and nutmeg is nice!)

Mhu Pad Prik Waan Or Pork Stir Fry In Sweet Peppers And Thai Chillies

Servings: 2 | *Time*: 30m

Ingredients

- 1 For the 200 g of slice
- 1 half of slices onion,
- 1 s pork, 1 tb spoon of whisky any kind, 2tb spoon of oyster sauce 2ts spoon of sugar, 1 ts of fish sauce, 1tb spoon of chopped garlic 1tb spoon of chopped thai chillies, 1 ts of soy sauce.
- 3 stripes of green onion cut in about 2inc long, half thin slices of carrot, half red sweet paprika and half sweet yellow paprika slices and a hand full of holy basil.

Directions

- In the heating fry pan add oil in the garlic fry till golden brown, add pork fry till cook add carrots and onion fry for 2 minutes add sweet paprika and thai chillies right away add flavours by adding whisky oyster sauce, light soy sauce, sugar and end with fish sauce, add green onion and holy basil.

Mongolion Lamb Hot Pot

Servings: 4 | **Prep**: 25m | **Inactive**: 10m | **Cook**: 40m | **Ready In**: 1h15m

Ingredients

- 8 cups rich lamb or chicken stock*
- 1 tablespoon ginger, minced
- 1 tablespoon garlic, minced
- 6 green onions, finely chopped
- 4 ounces dried bean thread noodles, soaked and cut into bite-size pieces
- 1 pound leafy greens, such as spinach, bok choy, or Napa cabbage, chopped into bite-size pieces
- 3/4 pound boneless lamb, sliced paper thin (this is easier to do if lamb is partially frozen)
- Sesame Chile Sauce, recipe follows
- Star Anise Black Vinegar Reduction, recipe follows

Sesame Chile Sauce:

- 3 dried chiles, seeded and minced
- 3 cloves garlic, minced
- 1 tablespoon sugar
- 1 teaspoon sesame paste
- 1 teaspoon sesame oil
- 1/2 cup soy sauce
- 2 tablespoons black vinegar

Star Anise Black Vinegar Reduction:

- 1 cup black vinegar
- 2 whole pods star anise

Directions

- Place the stock, ginger, garlic and green onions in a large pot; bring to a boil. Reduce the heat, cover, and simmer for 30 minutes. Soak the noodles in warm water until softened; drain. Cut into bite-size lengths. Cut the greens into bite-size pieces. Cut the lamb into paper-thin, bite-size slices. Arrange the noodles, lamb and vegetables on a large platter. Cover and chill until ready to cook. Reheat the broth to simmering. Set a Mongolian hot pot or electric Wok in the center of a table. Pour the broth into the pot and adjust the heat so that the broth simmers gently. The guests use chopsticks or Chinese wire strainers to cook the lamb and vegetable slices in the simmering broth, and then dip into the sauce of their choice. After the meat and vegetables are consumed, guests add the noodles and any remaining greens to the broth to make the soup.

*Note: the success of this dish depends on starting with a full-flavored stock or broth.

Sesame Chile Sauce:

- Mince chiles and garlic finely and place in a mortar. Mash with the heel of a cleaver or pestle. Add sugar and stir until it dissolves. Add sesame paste, sesame oil, soy sauce, and black vinegar stirring between each addition.

Star Anise Black Vinegar Reduction:

- Place vinegar and star anise in a small saucepot and simmer over medium-low heat until reduced by 1/2 about 7 minutes. Remove star anise before serving.

Pad Thai with Pork

Servings: 4 | **Prep**: 40m | **Cook**: 8m | **Ready In**: 48m

Ingredients

- 6 ounces medium, dry rice stick noodles
- 1 tablespoon dark sesame oil
- 1 tablespoon cornstarch
- 1 pound pork loin, thinly sliced strips
- 1/4 cup Thai fish sauce
- 1/4 cup fresh lemon juice
- 3 tablespoons sugar
- 1/4 cup peanut oil, divided
- 4 garlic cloves, minced
- 1/2 tablespoon crushed red pepper flakes, or to taste
- 3/4 tablespoon green onions, thinly sliced
- 3 eggs, beaten
- 1 cup fresh bean sprouts
- 1/2 cup roasted peanuts, finely chopped
- 1 lime, cut into wedges
- 1/4 cup fresh cilantro leaves

Directions

1. In a bowl of hot water, soak the dry rice noodles until softened, about 30 to 45 minutes. Drain and set aside.
2. In a medium mixing bowl, whisk the sesame oil and cornstarch. Add the pork and toss well.
3. In a small mixing bowl, whisk the fish sauce, lemon juice and sugar. Set aside.
4. Preheat a Wok or large skillet over high heat. Pour in half the peanut oil and heat (but do not bring oil to smoking point). Add pork and cook until cooked through, about 2 minutes. Remove pork and set aside.
5. Reheat Wok or skillet and pour in the remaining peanut oil. Add the garlic, crushed red pepper flakes and green onions. Cook until soft and fragrant, about 1 minute. Slowly add the eggs, stirring constantly. Once cooked, add the drained noodles, fish sauce mixture and cooked pork. Toss until combined.
6. Transfer the Pad Thai to a serving platter and top with bean sprouts, peanuts, lime wedges and cilantro leaves. Serve immediately.

Pork and Bamboo Shoots

"Bamboo shoots pepped up with pork and spices."

Servings: 2 | **Prep**: 15m | **Cook**: 15 | **Ready In**: 30m

Ingredients

- 1 tablespoon peanut oil
- 1 (14 ounce) can thinly sliced bamboo shoots
- 2 tablespoons peanut oil
- 2 cloves garlic, minced
- 1 fresh red chile pepper, seeded and minced
- 1/2 teaspoon crushed red pepper flakes
- 3 ounces ground pork
- 1 teaspoon Shaoxing rice wine salt to taste
- 2 teaspoons rice vinegar
- 2 teaspoons soy sauce

- 3 tablespoons chicken broth
- 3 green onions, thinly sliced
- 1 teaspoon sesame oil

Directions

1. Heat one tablespoon peanut oil in a Wok set over medium heat. Add the bamboo shoots to the pan; stir-fry until dry and fragrant, about 3 minutes. Remove from Wok and reserve.
2. Increase temperature to high, and pour in the remaining peanut oil. Quickly fry the garlic, red chile, and red pepper flakes in the hot oil until fragrant. Stir in the pork, and continue to stir-fry until it is cooked through. Pour in the wine; season with salt to taste.
3. Return the bamboo shoots to the Wok, and heat until sizzly. Stir in the rice vinegar, soy sauce, chicken broth, and additional salt to taste. Cook and stir for 1 to 2 minutes to allow the flavor to penetrate the bamboo shoots. At the end of cooking, stir in green onions. Remove Wok from heat; stir in sesame oil before serving.

Cook's Notes:

- Dry sherry can be substituted for the Shaoxing rice wine, if desired.
- Water can be substituted for the chicken stock, if desired.

Pork and Pepper Stir-fry

"Sweeten the pot with roasted red peppers. No time to shop? Open a jar of roasted red peppers and try one of these delicious dinners."

Servings: 4 | **Prep**: 10m | **Cook**: 15m | **Ready In**: 25m

Ingredients

- 1 tablespoon vegetable oil
- 1 pound ground pork
- 1 onion, thinly sliced
- 1 large garlic clove, smashed
- 1 cup jarred roasted red peppers, drained and sliced
- 1 1/4 cups chicken broth

- 2 tablespoons soy sauce
- 2 teaspoons cornstarch
- 1 tablespoon oyster sauce
- 8 ounces sliced water chestnuts

Directions

1. Heat oil in a large nonstick skillet. Add pork and cook over medium-high heat until it's no longer pink. Transfer to plate.
2. Stir-fry onion and garlic for 1 minute. Add peppers; stir-fry until onions are tender. In a cup, mix broth, soy sauce and cornstarch. Add to vegetables and stir-fry until thickened, 2 to 3 minutes. Stir in oyster sauce and water chestnuts and cook until heated through, 1 to 2 minutes.

Pork and Stir-Fried Vegetables with Spicy Asian Sauce

"Use your favorite sliced vegetables in place of the zucchini and bell pepper; mushrooms and water chestnuts would also be good. To round out the meal, serve with quick-cooking rice stick noodles."

Servings: 4

Ingredients

- 1 teaspoon canola oil
- 1/4 cup hoisin sauce
- 1/4 cup ketchup
- 1 teaspoon low-sodium soy sauce
- 1/2 teaspoon bottled minced garlic
- 1/8 to 1/4 teaspoon ground red pepper
- 1 (1-pound) pork tenderloin, trimmed, cut into 1/2-inch pieces
- 1 teaspoon black pepper
- 1/4 teaspoon salt
- 2 teaspoons dark sesame oil
- 1 cup presliced zucchini
- 1 cup presliced red bell pepper
- 1 teaspoon bottled ground fresh ginger (such as Spice World)
- 1/2 cup chopped green onions

- 1 teaspoon toasted sesame seeds

Directions

- Heat canola oil in a large nonstick skillet over medium-high heat. Combine hoisin sauce and next 4 ingredients (through ground red pepper), stirring until blended; set side. Add pork to pan; sprinkle with black pepper and salt. Cook 3 minutes on each side or until done. Remove from pan. Add sesame oil to pan. Add zucchini, bell pepper, and ginger; stir-fry 4 minutes or until bell pepper is tender. Stir in onions and pork. Add hoisin mixture to pan; toss to coat. Sprinkle with sesame seeds.

Pork and Vegetable Stir-Fry with Cashew Rice

"For a satisfying, lower-calorie dinner, serve this stir-fry loaded with tender pork and crisp veggies with a side of homemade cashew rice."

Servings: 4

Ingredients

- 3/4 cup uncooked long-grain rice
- 1/3 cup chopped green onions
- 1/4 cup dry-roasted cashews, salted and coarsely chopped
- 1/2 teaspoon salt
- 2/3 cup fat-free, less-sodium chicken broth
- 2 tablespoons cornstarch, divided
- 3 tablespoons low-sodium soy sauce, divided
- 2 tablespoons honey
- 1 (1-pound) pork tenderloin, trimmed and cut into 1/2-inch cubes
- 1 tablespoon canola oil, divided
- 2 cups sliced mushrooms (about 4 ounces)
- 1 cup chopped onion
- 1 tablespoon grated peeled fresh ginger
- 2 garlic cloves, minced
- 2 cups sugar snap peas, trimmed (about 6 ounces)
- 1 cup chopped red bell pepper (about 1)

Directions

1. Cook the rice according to package directions, omitting salt and fat. Stir in 1/3 cup chopped green onions, chopped dry-roasted cashews, and salt; set aside, and keep warm.
2. Combine 2/3 cup chicken broth, 1 tablespoon cornstarch, 2 tablespoons low-sodium soy sauce, and honey in a small bowl, and set aside.
3. Combine pork, remaining 1 tablespoon cornstarch, and the remaining 1 tablespoon soy sauce in a bowl, tossing well to coat. Heat 2 teaspoons oil in a large nonstick skillet over medium-high heat. Add pork; sauté 4 minutes or until browned. Remove from pan.
4. Add remaining 1 teaspoon oil to pan. Add mushrooms and 1 cup onion; sauté 2 minutes. Stir in ginger and garlic; sauté 30 seconds. Add peas and bell pepper to pan; sauté 1 minute. Stir in pork; sauté 1 minute. Add reserved broth mixture to pan. Bring to a boil; cook 1 minute or until thick, stirring constantly. Serve over cashew rice.

Pork Chop Suey

"This chop suey recipe is a quick and easy stir-fry that can be on the table in no time. You can substitute your favorite choice of meat for the pork or add different vegetables if you want to make it your own."

Servings: 4

Ingredients

- 1 (1-pound) pork tenderloin
- 1/4 cup all-purpose flour
- 2 tablespoons vegetable oil, divided
- 2 cups thinly sliced bok choy
- 1 cup sliced celery
- 1 cup red bell pepper strips
- 1 cup sliced mushrooms
- 1 (8-ounce) can sliced water chestnuts, drained
- 2 garlic cloves, minced
- 1/4 cup fat-free, less-sodium chicken broth
- 1/4 cup low-sodium soy sauce
- 1 tablespoon cornstarch

- 1 tablespoon dry sherry
- 1/2 teaspoon ground ginger
- 2 cups hot cooked long-grain rice
- 1/4 cup sliced green onions

Directions

1. Trim fat from pork; cut into 1-inch pieces. Lightly spoon flour into a dry measuring cup; level with a knife. Combine flour and pork in a zip-top plastic bag; seal and shake well.
2. Heat 1 tablespoon oil in a large nonstick skillet over medium-high heat. Add pork; cook 3 minutes or until browned. Remove from pan; keep warm.
3. Add 1 tablespoon oil to pan. Add bok choy and next 5 ingredients (bok choy through garlic); stir-fry 3 minutes. Combine broth, soy sauce, cornstarch, sherry, and ginger; stir well with a whisk. Add pork and broth mixture to pan; cook 1 minute or until thick. Serve over rice; sprinkle with green onions.

Pork Egg Rolls with Sweet and Sour Sauce

Servings: 5 | Prep: 50m | Inactive: 30m | Cook: 25m | Ready In: 1h45m

Ingredients

- 2 tablespoons vegetable oil
- 1 pound ground pork
- 1/2 cup minced yellow onions
- 1 tablespoon chopped garlic
- 1 pound bok choy, shredded
- 1/2 pound medium shrimp, peeled, deveined and chopped
- 1 tablespoon dark sesame oil
- Soy sauce, to taste
- 1/4 cup sake
- 1 tablespoon sugar
- 1 pound fresh bean sprouts, washed and patted dry
- 1/4 cup green onions, green part only
- 20 (6-inch) egg roll wrappers
- 1 egg, beaten, for egg wash

- Oil, for frying
- Essence, recipe follows
- 1/4 cups Sweet and Sour Sauce, recipe follows

Directions

1. Preheat the fryer.
2. In a Wok, heat the oil. When the oil is hot, add the pork. Season with salt and pepper. Stir fry for 3 minutes. Add the onions and garlic, continue to cook for 2 minutes. Add the bok choy and shrimp. Season with salt and pepper. Stir-fry for 1 minute. Season with the sesame oil, soy sauce, sake and sugar. Add the sprouts and green onions and mix thoroughly. Remove from the heat and cool completely.
3. To assemble, spoon about 1/4 cup of the filling in a rectangular shape on the center of each wrapper. Fold in the ends toward the center about 1/4-inch. Then, beginning at the bottom, roll up the wrapper, like a jelly roll, using a little of the egg wash to seal the end tightly. Repeat until all of the egg rolls are done.
4. Fry the egg rolls in batches until golden brown, stirring occasionally for overall browning, about 2 to 3 minutes. Remove from the oil and drain on paper towels. Season the egg rolls with Essence. Serve warm with the Sweet and Sour Sauce.

Emeril's ESSENCE Creole Seasoning (also referred to as Bayou Blast):

- 1/2 tablespoons paprika
- 2 tablespoons salt
- 2 tablespoons garlic powder
- 1 tablespoon black pepper
- 1 tablespoon onion powder
- 1 tablespoon cayenne pepper
- 1 tablespoon dried oregano
- 1 tablespoon dried thyme
- Combine all ingredients thoroughly.

Sweet and Sour Sauce:

- 1 tablespoon vegetable oil
- 1/2 medium onion, chopped
- 1/2 teaspoon grated ginger
- 1/4 cup finely diced pineapple
- 1/3 cup rice vinegar
- 1/4 cup ketchup

- 2 tablespoons chili garlic sauce (recommended: Sriracha)
- 1/4 cup sugar
- 1/4 cup chicken broth
- 2 teaspoons cornstarch

1. Heat the oil in a small saucepan over medium-high heat. When hot, add the onions and cook, stirring, until softened, about 2 minutes. Add the ginger and cook, stirring constantly, for 30 seconds. Stir in the pineapple, vinegar, ketchup, chili garlic sauce, and the sugar. Bring the sauce to a simmer and cook, stirring, for 3 minutes. In a small bowl, whisk together the chicken broth and cornstarch until smooth. Add to the sauce mixture and bring to a boil. Cook for 1 minute, remove from the heat, and cool slightly.
2. Pour the sauce into a small food processor or blender and pulse several times, if desired. Alternatively, leave the dipping sauce chunky. Serve warm.

Pork Slices in Hoisin Sauce

*Servings: 4-6 | **Prep**: 15m | **Cook**: 10m | **Ready In**: 25m*

Ingredients

- 1/2 pounds pork tenderloin (2 whole tenderloins)

For the marinade:

- 2 tablespoons dark soy sauce
- 2 tablespoons dry Sherry
- 1 tablespoon cornstarch
- 2 tablespoons vegetable oil
- 4 scallions (green and white parts) minced
- 1 tablespoon minced peeled fresh ginger
- 1 medium green bell pepper, seeded and diced
- 1 medium red bell pepper, seeded and diced
- 1/4 cup hoisin sauce
- 1/4 cup dry Sherry
- Pinch salt
- 2 teaspoons freshly ground black pepper
- 1 tablespoon Asian sesame oil

Directions

1. Slice the pork tenderloin into 1/4-inch-thick pieces. In a bowl, combine the marinade ingredients: the dark soy sauce, sherry, and cornstarch. Add the pork and mix; let stand for at least 10 minutes.
2. In a carbon-steel Wok, heat the vegetable oil over high heat until just smoking. Add the scallions and ginger, and stir-fry until aromatic, about 30 seconds. Add the pork, reserving any remaining marinade, and stir-fry for about 5 minutes, until the pork is just done.
3. Add the green and red peppers, and stir-fry for another minute. Add the hoisin sauce, sherry, salt, and black pepper, and combine. Add 2 tablespoons of water to the marinade remaining in the bowl and add to the Wok. Toss to blend well.
4. Remove from the heat, drizzle with the sesame oil, and serve immediately.

Pork Stir Fry

Servings*: 4 | **Time***: 30m

Ingredients

- 1/2 cup Julienne Carrots
- 1/2 cup Sliced Mushrooms
- 1/2 cup Julienne Red and Green Bell Pepper
- 1 lb Pork (Sliced Thin)
- 1/2 cup Soy Sauce
- 2 tbsp Honey
- 1/2 cup Oyster Sauce
- 1 cup Chicken Broth
- 2 clove Garlic (Sliced Thin)
- 1/2 cup Broccoli (Chopped)
- 1 tbsp Cornstarch

Directions

1. Slice pork into thin strips, and marinate with 1/2 cup of Soy Sauce. For best flavor, I would recommend marinating pork for at least 1-4 hours. Overnight taste amazing.

2. Julienne and chop all veggies. You want to make sure they are bite size, and around the same size to have equal cook time.
3. After all your prep is done, place oil in a skillet and turn burner to med-high and let the oil get hot. If you have a Wok, I highly recommend using it for this dish. After oil gets hot, place pork in slowly. Be careful, and try not to burn yourself.
4. After pork cooks for couple minutes, you want to place in your veggies. You can use any kind of veggies for this dish. A helpfulp tip, whatever veggies you use, make sure harder veggies go in first since they will taken longer to cook. I did mine in this order; carrots, peppers, mushrooms, and broccoli. You want your veggies to still have a little crunch.
5. In a bowl mix in chicken broth, oyster sauce, honey, and corn starch. Mix very well and pour into your hot skillet or Wok.
6. Cook until the sauce has slightly thickened. Remove from heat. Cook rice according to directions.
7. Plate and serve. Remember, you can add any kind of twist to it. Try different meats and veggies.

Pork Thai Stir-Fry

"Definitely need rice or cauliflower mixed in with this. Use less fish sauce and it won't be as salty."

Servings: 4

Ingredients

- 1 T coconut oil
- 2 cloves garlic, minced
- 4-5 scallions, chopped
- 1 lb boneless pork or ham, cubed or thinly sliced
- 1 T fresh ginger, grated
- 1 large head broccoli, cut into florets
- 4 oz mushrooms, sliced
- 1/2 c coconut milk
- 1 tsp curry
- 1/2 c fish sauce

Directions

1. In large skillet, heat oil. Cook garlic and scallions. Add meat and ginger. Cook, stirring occasionally until meat is no loner pink.
2. Add broccoli, mushrooms, coconut milk, curry and fish sauce. Cover and cook until broccoli is tender.
3. Serve with 1 cup cooked riced cauliflower.

Pork Tofu with Watercress and Bean Sprouts

"Tofu and watercress are a great, flavorful combination, and a wholesome one, too! My teenage boys who don't like greens actually love this dish. Red chile garlic paste can be substituted for the ground black pepper."

Servings: 8 | **Prep**: 20m | **Cook**: 1h | **Ready In**: 1h20m

Ingredients

- 1 (2 pound) boneless pork loin, cut into
- 1/2 inch strips
- 1 cup soy sauce
- 3/4 cup water
- 1 teaspoon minced fresh ginger root
- 1 tablespoon coarsely ground black pepper
- 2 bunches watercress - rinsed, dried, cut into
- 1/2 inch lengths, thick stems discarded
- 8 ounces bean sprouts
- 1 (16 ounce) package firm tofu, drained and cubed

Directions

1. Place pork in a Wok or skillet over medium heat. Cook and stir until pork is browned on all sides, about 5 minutes. Stir in the soy sauce, water, ginger, and black pepper; bring to a boil over medium-high heat. Reduce heat to medium, cover, and simmer until meat is tender, about 40 minutes.
2. Stir in the watercress and bean sprouts, and continue to simmer until tender yet still crisp, about 10 minutes more. Mix in the tofu, cover, and simmer 5 minutes more.

Rice Noodle Salad with Pork and Snow Peas

"On a busy weeknight, Rice Noodle Salad with Pork and Snow Peas is a family-pleasing meal that's sure to satisfy."

Servings: 6 | **Prep**: 15m | **Cook**: 15m

Ingredients

- 1/4 cup fresh lime juice
- 1/4 cup rice vinegar
- 3 tablespoons sugar
- 1 tablespoon fish sauce
- 1 clove garlic, minced
- Salt
- 1 16-oz. package rice noodles
- 1 1/2 cups snow peas, ends trimmed
- 1 tablespoon vegetable oil
- 2 boneless pork chops (about 1 lb. total), trimmed and thinly sliced
- 1/4 cup finely chopped fresh mint

Directions

1. Bring a large pot of water to a boil. In a small bowl, whisk together lime juice, rice vinegar, sugar, fish sauce, garlic and 1/4 tsp. salt.
2. Add noodles to pot with boiling water, stir and cook until noodles are tender, 5 to 8 minutes or as package label directs. During last minute of cooking time, add snow peas to pot. Drain, rinse noodles and peas under cold water, drain again, and transfer to a large bowl.
3. Warm vegetable oil in a large skillet over medium-high heat. Sprinkle pork with salt. Stir-fry until meat loses its pink color, 3 to 5 minutes. Transfer meat to bowl with noodles and peas.
4. Drizzle reserved dressing over noodle mixture, sprinkle with mint and toss to coat. Serve immediately.

Rice Noodles with Pork, Spinach, and Peanuts

"Notes: Look for Asian rice noodles (also called rice sticks) or bean threads in well-stocked supermarkets or Asian grocery stores. If you don't have a Wok, substitute either a 5- to 6-quart pan or 12-inch frying pan with sides at least 2 inches tall; if the pan is too shallow, the noodles may fly out. This stir-fry is also good with beef."

Servings: 3

Ingredients

- 8 ounces dried thin rice noodles (up to 1/4 in. wide; see notes) or dried bean threads
- 1 onion (6 oz.)
- 10 ounce baby spinach leaves (3 qt.)
- 4 ounces bean sprouts
- About 3/4 cup fat-skimmed chicken broth
- 1/4 cup rice vinegar
- About 3 tablespoons reduced-sodium soy sauce
- 1 teaspoon coarse-ground pepper
- 1 tablespoon vegetable oil
- 8 ounces ground lean pork
- 1 tablespoon minced fresh ginger
- 2 cloves garlic, peeled and pressed
- 1/3 cup chopped roasted unsalted peanuts

Directions

1. Pour 2 1/2 to 3 quarts boiling water into a large bowl. Add noodles and let stand until soft and pliable, 5 to 15 minutes.
2. Meanwhile, peel and chop onion. Rinse and drain spinach and bean sprouts. In a small bowl, mix 3/4 cup broth, vinegar, 3 tablespoons soy sauce, and pepper.
3. Pour noodles into a colander and drain. If desired, cut noodles into shorter lengths with scissors. Set a 14-inch Wok or 12-inch frying pan with 2-inch-tall sides (see notes) over high heat. When hot, add oil and swirl to coat bottom. Crumble pork into pan and stir until lightly browned, 1 to 2 minutes. Add onion, ginger, and garlic; stir often until onion begins to brown, 1 to 2 minutes.
4. Add spinach, noodles, and broth mixture. Mix until noodles are tender to bite and hot, about 3 minutes. If more liquid is desired, stir in 2 to 4 more tablespoons broth. Add bean sprouts and peanuts; mix and add more soy sauce to taste. Pour into a wide serving bowl.

Shiitake Mushroom & Pork Stir-fry

"Shittake mushroom & Pork stir-fry in Garlic Soy sauce"

***Servings**: 2 | **Time**: 15m*

Ingredients

- 250 g Pork
- 10-12 Shiitake Mushrooms
- Green onions
- 1 tbsp Garlic
- 1.5 tbsp Soy sauce
- 2 tsp Sesame oil
- Pinch White ground pepper

Directions

2. Slice pork, shiitake mushrooms & finely chop the green onions
3. Marinate sliced pork in 1 tsp of sesame Oil and ground pepper
4. Mix light soy sauce and garlic in a bowl
5. Heat remaining sesame oil in a pan and stir fry the marinated sliced pork
6. Add in sliced shiitake mushrooms onced the sliced pork are around 70% cooked
7. Stir fry for 2 minutes on medium heat and add in the garlic soy sauce mixture
8. Add in finely chopped green onions, stir fry for another 3 minutes and serve

Shrimp, Scallop and Pork Shumai

***Servings**: 40shumai | **Cook**: 10m | **Ready In**: 10m*

Ingredients

- 1/2 pound medium shrimp, shelled and deveined
- 1/2 pound bay scallops
- 1/2 pound ground pork
- 2 tablespoons minced fresh ginger
- 2 tablespoons minced fresh cilantro leaves
- 2 tablespoons minced shallots
- 2 teaspoons rice wine vinegar
- 1 tablespoon sesame oil
- 2 egg white, whipped
- Sea salt and freshly ground black pepper
- 2 teaspoons cornstarch
- 1/2 lemon, juiced
- 1 (10-ounce) package round wonton wrappers (about 40 to 50 wrappers per package)
- 1 cup frozen peas
- Canola oil, for brushing the steamer
- Savoy cabbage, for lining the steamer, optional
- Minced green onions, for garnish
- Serving suggestion: soy sauce or dipping sauces of your choice

Directions

1. To make the filling: Combine the shrimp, scallops, pork, ginger, cilantro, shallots, vinegar, sesame oil and egg whites in a food processor. Season with salt and pepper, add the corn starch and lemon juice and pulse to combine-- I like my fillings to have a little texture. (Alternatively chop the shrimp and scallops finely then add the pork, ginger, cilantro and vinegar and chop together. Transfer the mixture to a bowl and rapidly mix in the vinegar, sesame oil, egg whites, seasoning, corn starch and lemon juice.)
2. To make the shumai: Hold a wonton wrapper in your hand. Spoon 1 tablespoon of the filling into the center of the wrapper (rinse the spoon in cold water so the filling doesn't stick). Gather the edges of the wrapper up around the filling and squeeze the sides together with your fingers forming a little pleated cup. (The sides will naturally pleat, leaving the filling slightly exposed.) Tap the dumpling on the table so the bottom is flat and it stands upright then set aside on a baking sheet. Repeat with the remaining wrappers and filling. Top each shumai with a pea. (You can freeze any leftover filling.)
3. Lightly oil the bottom of a bamboo steamer then line it with the cabbage leaves. Stand the dumplings in the steamer in a single

layer taking care that they don't touch one another. (A 10-inch steamer will accommodate 12 shumai). Bring about 2 inches of water to a boil in a Wok. Set the bamboo steamer in the Wok, cover it with the bamboo lid and steam until the shumai feel firm, 10 to 12 minutes. Serve the shumai immediately garnished with green onions and accompanied by soy sauce or dipping sauces of your choice.

Smoky Pork Stir-Fry

"Smoked paprika and dark sesame oil add depth to this stir-fry. Serve over precooked brown rice or soba noodles."

Servings: 4

Ingredients

- 2 teaspoons canola oil
- 10 ounce pork tenderloin, trimmed and cut into bite-sized pieces
- 1/2 teaspoon smoked paprika
- 1/4 teaspoon kosher salt
- 2 teaspoons dark sesame oil
- 1 1/2 cups thinly sliced orange bell pepper (1 medium)
- 1 cup snow peas
- 1 tablespoon minced peeled fresh ginger
- 1 garlic clove, minced
- 3 tablespoons rice vinegar
- 1 tablespoon lower-sodium soy sauce
- 2 teaspoons sugar
- 1 teaspoon chili garlic sauce
- 3 cups tricolor coleslaw
- 3 green onions, thinly sliced

Directions

1. Heat a large skillet over high heat. Add canola oil; swirl to coat. Sprinkle pork with paprika and salt. Add pork to pan; sauté 3 minutes or until browned. Remove pork from pan.

2. Return pan to medium-high heat. Add sesame oil; swirl to coat. Add bell pepper, peas, ginger, and garlic; stir-fry 3 minutes or until vegetables are crisp-tender, stirring frequently. Combine vinegar, soy sauce, sugar, and chili garlic sauce in a bowl, stirring with a whisk. Add pork and soy sauce mixture to pan; cook 1 minute. Stir in coleslaw; cook 1 minute or until slightly wilted. Remove pan from heat; sprinkle with green onions.

Snow Pea-and-Pork Fried Rice

"This easy pork stir-fry recipe is filled with lean pork, fresh vegetables and rice and makes a great one-dish meal for busy weeknights. If you don't want to use the sherry, just leave it out and use 1 tablespoons of water."

Servings: 5

Ingredients

Shrimp:

- 2 (4-ounce) boned center-cut loin pork chops
- 1 tablespoon low-sodium soy sauce
- 1 tablespoon dry sherry
- 2 large egg whites
- 1 large egg
- Cooking spray
- 2 teaspoons dark sesame oil, divided
- 2 cups vertically sliced onion
- 2 cups snow peas
- 2 cups sliced mushrooms
- 1 tablespoon minced peeled fresh ginger
- 2 garlic cloves, minced
- 4 cups cooked long-grain rice, chilled
- 1/4 teaspoon salt
- 1/3 cup chopped green onions

Directions

1. Trim fat from pork chops; cut pork into 2- x 1/4-inch strips. Combine pork, soy sauce, and sherry; cover and marinate in refrigerator 30 minutes. Drain; discard sherry mixture.
2. Combine egg whites and egg in a medium bowl; stir well with a whisk. Place a large nonstick skillet or Wok coated with cooking spray over medium-high heat until hot. Add egg mixture; cook 2 minutes or until egg is done. Remove egg mixture from skillet.
3. Add 1/2 teaspoon oil to skillet. Add pork; stir-fry 2 minutes or until done. Remove pork from skillet; keep warm. Add 1/2 teaspoon oil to skillet. Add sliced onion and snow peas; stir-fry 2 minutes. Add mushrooms, ginger, and garlic; stir-fry 1 minute. Remove onion mixture from skillet, and keep warm.
4. Add 1 teaspoon oil to skillet; add rice, and cook 1 minute without stirring. Stir in egg mixture, pork, onion mixture, and salt, and stir-fry 1 minute or until thoroughly heated. Sprinkle each serving with about 1 tablespoon green onions.

Spicy Eggplant, Pork, and Tofu Stir-fry

"In this stir-fry pork recipe, a garlicky sauce adds spicy flavor to tofu and eggplant. Serve with rice to complete the meal."

Servings: 4

Ingredients

- 1 pound eggplant
- 1 tablespoon vegetable oil
- 1 tablespoon Asian sesame oil
- 1 tablespoon minced ginger
- 1 tablespoon minced garlic
- 8 ounces ground pork
- 1/4 cup soy sauce
- 1 tablespoon sugar
- 1 tablespoon rice or white wine vinegar
- 1/2 teaspoons Asian red chili paste
- 2 teaspoons cornstarch
- 8 ounces extra-firm tofu, drained and cut into 1-inch cubes
- 1/4 cup thinly sliced green onions

Directions

1. Rinse eggplant and cut crosswise into 1-inch thick rounds. Cut rounds into 1-inch-wide strips.
2. Pour vegetable and sesame oils into a 12-inch nonstick frying pan or a 14-inch Wok over medium-high heat. When hot, add eggplant and stir frequently until soft when pierced and lightly browned, about 8 minutes. Transfer eggplant to paper towels to drain.
3. Add ginger and garlic to pan and stir frequently until fragrant, about 1 minute. Add pork and stir until crumbled and brown, about 5 minutes.
4. In a bowl, mix soy sauce, sugar, vinegar, chili paste, cornstarch, and 1/4 cup water. Pour into pan and stir until mixture is simmering and thickened, about 1 minute.
5. Gently stir in tofu, eggplant, and green onions until heated through.

Spicy Green Beans and Pork, Asian Style

"My favorite side dish to order in Chinese restaurants. A chef gave me the ingredients and the tip of blistering the green beans. After some trial and error, I came up with this. My family and friends now demand that it be on the menu for gatherings - even if it doesn't go with the course! Can be made in advance. The amount of heat is determined by the amount of chili garlic sauce used."

Servings: 4 | **Prep**: 20m | **Cook**: 15m | **Ready In**: 35m

Ingredients

- 2 cups vegetable oil for frying
- 1 pound fresh green beans, trimmed and dried well with paper towels

Pork Sauce:

- 1 tablespoon vegetable oil
- 3 cloves garlic, minced
- 2 teaspoons minced fresh ginger root
- 2 green onions, minced
- 1/2 pound ground pork

- 2 tablespoons Asian chili garlic sauce
- 1/4 cup chicken broth
- 2 teaspoons soy sauce
- 2 teaspoons cornstarch
- 2 tablespoons cold water

Directions

1. Heat 2 cups of vegetable oil in a large Wok or deep sided skillet to 375 degrees F (190 degrees C). Carefully add the beans to the hot oil, and fry, stirring occasionally, until the beans are blistered, 3 to 5 minutes. Dip the beans out of the oil with a strainer, and quickly rinse them in cold water.
2. Remove the oil from the Wok, but do not wipe the pan. Heat 1 tablespoon of vegetable oil in the Wok over medium heat, and stir in the garlic, ginger, and green onion. Cook and stir until fragrant, about 30 seconds, and stir in the ground pork. Cook and stir the pork, breaking it up as it cooks, until no longer pink, about 4 minutes. Stir in the chili garlic sauce, chicken broth, and soy sauce, and bring to a boil.
3. Mix the cornstarch with the water in a small bowl, stir into the pork mixture, and let simmer until the sauce thickens, 1 to 2 minutes. Gently stir the green beans into the pork sauce, heat through, and serve.

Cook's Note

- It is important to use an Asian/Chinese Style chili garlic sauce in this recipe (found in almost all Chinese/International sections of stores, or buy from web sites). Fresh garlic, ginger and onions are also key to an authentic taste.

Editor's Note

- We have determined the nutritional value of oil for frying based on a retention value of 10% after cooking. The exact amount will vary depending on cooking time and temperature, ingredient density, and the specific type of oil used.

Spicy Pork Stir-Fry with Coconut Scallion Rice

Servings: 4 | **Prep**: 20m | **Cook**: 10m | **Ready In**: 30m

Ingredients

- 1 teaspoon cornstarch
- 1 tablespoon plus 1 teaspoon soy sauce
- 12 ounces lean pork loin, cut into thin strips
- 3 tablespoons plus 1 teaspoon black bean chili sauce
- 1/2 cup chicken stock
- 1 teaspoon sugar
- 3 tablespoons peanut oil/palm kernel oil
- 2 Japanese eggplant, cut in 1/2 and sliced diagonally into 1/2-inch sections
- 1 medium red onion, thinly sliced
- 1 red bell pepper, thinly sliced
- 2 cloves garlic, minced
- 2 red jalapenos, thinly sliced
- 2 green jalapenos, thinly sliced
- Coconut Scallion Rice, recipe follows, for serving
- Coconut Scallion Rice:
- 2 cups jasmine rice
- 1/2 cups coconut milk
- 1/2 cups chicken stock
- 1/2 teaspoon salt
- 1/2 teaspoon pepper
- 3 to 4 bunches scallions, sliced thinly on a bias

Directions

1. Stir together the cornstarch and soy sauce and pour over the pork strips. Stir to combine and set aside.
2. Stir together the black bean chili sauce, chicken stock and sugar. Set aside until ready to use.
3. Preheat the Wok over medium-high to high heat and add 2 tablespoons of the oil. Swirl quickly to coat the sides of the pan with the oil. Add the eggplant and cook until tender, stirring frequently, 3 to 4 minutes. Remove with a slotted spoon and set aside on a plate lined with paper towels. Add the remaining tablespoon of oil and swirl again to coat all sides. Cook the onions,

stirring, until slightly tender, 1 to 2 minutes. Add the bell peppers and cook until tender, 1 to 2 minutes. Add the garlic and cook for 5 to 10 seconds. Add the red and green jalapenos and cook for 30 seconds. Return the eggplant to the Wok and add the pork. Cook, stirring, until pork is no longer pink, 2 to 3 minutes. Add the black bean mixture and bring to a boil. Cook, stirring, until everything is well coated with the sauce and heated through. Serve hot with the Coconut Scallion Rice.

Coconut Scallion Rice:

- In a medium saucepan combine the jasmine rice with the coconut milk, chicken stock, salt and pepper. Bring to a boil, reduce heat to a simmer, cover, and cook for 20 minutes. Remove from the heat and let sit, undisturbed for 5 minutes. Add the scallions and fluff the rice with a fork. Serve immediately.

Stir Fry Noodle With Pork And Spicy Shrimp Hokkien Mee

"Hokkien mee top favourite noodle stir fry"

***Servings**: 4 |**Time**: 20m*

Ingredients

- 1 tbsp each of dice garlic and shallot
- 1 cup slice up cooked roasted pork
- 1 cup slice up chinese bbq pork / char siew
- 3 cup choy sum vegetable / any green vegetable
- 500 ml any stock
- 350 grams fresh yellow noodles

Oyster sauce mixture

- 3 tbsp oyster sauce
- 1 1/2 tbsp dark soy sauce
- 2 tbsp light soy sauce

Deep fried pork lard

- 1/2 cup small cube pork lard
- 1 tbsp oil

Directions

1. Deep Fried Pork Lard Deep Fried Pork Lard
2. With oil saute dice garlic and shallot with cooked roasted pork and chinese bbq pork / char siew till its,fragrance and make sure garlic are not burn
3. Add the green vegetables with stock and bring it to a simmer then add in fresh yellow noodle together with the (oyster sauce mixture) and stir fry to mix well and let it comes to a simmer and gravy starts to thicken up
4. Add in the crispy deep fried lard
5. Serve as it is or optional add on (drunken spicy garlic shrimp)

Stir Fry Pork Heart

***Servings*: 6 | *Cook*: 15m**

Ingredients

Vegetable

- 1 carrot
- 1 onion
- 3 clove garlic
- 1 chinese sausage or ham optional
- 1 tbsp olive oil
- 6 small cherry tomato

Pork heart

- 2 tbsp butter
- 2 pork heart

Seasoning

- 1 tsp salt and pepper
- 1 dash Worcestershire sauce

Directions

Stir fry vegetable

1. In pan with olive oil saute onion with carrot and sausage in low heat till carrot cook then add tomato and garlic stir fry for 1 minute
2. Off heat set aside

Stir fry pork heart

1. In pan with butter till melted then add pork heart for 3 minute in medium heat till no longer pink
2. Add seasoning and mix well
3. Add cooked vegetables and stir fry for 1 minute then serve immediately

Stir Fry Somen With Lamb In Spicy Dark Sauce

"Only Had 1 Lamb Shoulder ,

Made Easy And Quick Asian Style Stir Fry (Hokkien Char) For 2"

Ingredients

- 1 lamb shoulder
- Dash salt
- 3 tbsp oil
- 2 bundle Somen noodle
- 600 ml water
- 1 cup scallion
- For Pounded Paste
- 2 inches ginger
- 4 clove garlic
- 5 small or shallot
- Spicy Dark Sauce
- 3 tbsp dark soy sauce
- 2 tbsp peri peri Chili sauce
- 3 tbsp light soy sauce

Directions

1. With little oil pan fry the lamb on both side for about 7 minutes then set aside then cut into small chunk
2. With little oil Pan fry the pounded paste in light flame, do not burn it then add in the cooked lamb,add water and bring it to a boil then add in the spicy dark soy and Somen Noodle
3. Stir Somen Noodle with Chopstick to (prevent Noodle sticking together) then add in scallion and gently stir with a chopstick till its sauce evaporate then off heat and serve immediately

Stir-fried Pork and Long Beans

"This recipe is loosely based on a Szechuan dish that incorporates long beans. (It also works with regular green beans, of course.)"

Servings: 4 | Total time: 15m

Ingredients

- 2 tablespoons vegetable oil, divided
- 1 pound long beans, trimmed and cut into 3-in. lengths
- 1/2 pound ground pork
- 1 tablespoon dry sherry
- 1 tablespoon soy sauce
- 2 teaspoons Asian chili garlic sauce

Directions

1. Heat a Wok or large frying pan over medium-high heat. Add 1 tbsp. oil, swirling to coat pan. Add beans; stir-fry until blistered and mostly tender, about 6 minutes. Transfer beans to a bowl.
2. Heat remaining 1 tbsp. oil in Wok. Add pork and cook, stirring frequently to break up big pieces, about 2 minutes. Stir in sherry, soy sauce, and chili garlic sauce and cook until pork is no longer pink, about 3 minutes. Return beans to Wok and stir-fry until hot.

Sweet and Sour Pork

Servings: 4 | **Prep**: 15m | **Cook**: 10m | **Ready In**: 25m

Ingredients

1. 1 pound pork tenderloin, cut into 1/2-inch pieces
2. 1/2 tablespoons balsamic vinegar
3. Kosher salt
4. 2 teaspoons low-sodium soy sauce
5. 1 tablespoon cornstarch
6. 3 tablespoons ketchup
7. 3 tablespoons sugar, plus a pinch
8. 3 tablespoons peanut or vegetable oil
9. 3 cloves garlic, minced
10. 2 carrots, thinly sliced
11. 3 scallions, cut into 1/2-inch pieces
12. 3 cups snow peas, cut in half

Directions

1. Toss the pork with 1/2 tablespoon vinegar and a pinch of salt in a bowl. Mix the remaining 2 tablespoons vinegar, the soy sauce, cornstarch, ketchup, 3 tablespoons sugar, 1/3 cup water and 1/2 teaspoon salt in another bowl.
2. Heat 2 tablespoons peanut oil in a large skillet or Wok over high heat. Add the pork and slowly stir until it turns mostly opaque, about 2 minutes. Remove the pork with a slotted spoon and transfer to a plate. Discard the oil and wipe out the skillet.
3. Heat the remaining 1 tablespoon peanut oil in the skillet, then stir-fry the garlic with a pinch each of salt and sugar, 15 seconds. Add the carrots and scallions and stir-fry until crisp-tender, 2 minutes. (Add a little water if the garlic starts to stick to the skillet.) Add the pork, snow peas and soy sauce mixture; stir until the pork is cooked through and the sauce is thickened, about 3 minutes.

Sweet and Spicy Pork with Pineapple

***Servings**: 4 | **Prep**: 15m | **Cook**: 10m*

Ingredients

- 2 cloves garlic, minced
- 1 tablespoon fresh ginger, peeled and chopped
- 4 scallions, white parts only, thinly sliced (reserve greens)
- 1 teaspoon crushed red pepper
- 1/3 cup rice vinegar
- 1 8-oz. can pineapple chunks, drained, juice reserved
- 2 tablespoons sugar
- 2 teaspoons cornstarch
- 1 pound pork tenderloin, sliced
- Salt
- 2 tablespoons vegetable oil
- 1 red bell pepper, seeded, cut into thin strips
- 1 1/2 cups snow peas, trimmed
- 1 8-oz. can sliced water chestnuts, drained
- 3 cups cooked white rice
- 1/4 cup chopped roasted unsalted peanuts

Directions

1. In a bowl, whisk together garlic, ginger, scallions, crushed red pepper, rice vinegar, 1/3 cup pineapple juice (from can), sugar, cornstarch and 1/4 cup water.
2. Sprinkle pork with salt. Warm a large skillet over medium-high heat. Pour in vegetable oil, and when very hot add pork and stir-fry until no longer pink, 3 to 4 minutes. Add bell pepper, snow peas and water chestnuts; sauté for 3 minutes. Stir in pineapple.
3. Add reserved sauce to skillet and cook, stirring, until thickened, about 3 minutes. Divide rice among 4 plates and spoon pork mixture on top. Sprinkle with peanuts and scallion greens and serve immediately.

Vietnamese Caramel Pork

"Instead of making caramel from scratch, we use brown sugar, which is much quicker."

Servings: 4 | **Total time**: 20m

Ingredients

- 1 tablespoon dark sesame oil
- 1 (1-pound) pork tenderloin, trimmed and cut into 1-inch pieces
- 1 cup chopped onion
- 1 cup chopped carrot
- 1 tablespoon minced peeled fresh ginger
- 5 garlic cloves, thinly sliced
- 1 cup unsalted chicken stock (such as Swanson)
- 3 tablespoons dark brown sugar
- 1 tablespoon fish sauce
- 1 tablespoon lower-sodium soy sauce
- 2 teaspoons cornstarch
- 2 teaspoons rice vinegar
- 1/2 teaspoon crushed red pepper
- 1 (8.8-ounce) package precooked white rice
- 1 cup thinly sliced napa (Chinese) cabbage
- 1/4 cup chopped unsalted roasted peanuts
- 1/4 cup cilantro leaves
- 4 lime wedges

Directions

1. Heat a Wok or large skillet over high heat. Add oil to pan; swirl to coat. Add pork; stir-fry 6 minutes, browning on all sides. Remove pork from pan. Add onion, carrot, ginger, and garlic to pan; stir-fry 2 minutes. Combine stock and next 6 ingredients (through red pepper) in a bowl, stirring with a whisk. Add stock mixture to pan; bring to a boil. Reduce heat; simmer 4 minutes or until sauce is thick and bubbly. Return pork to pan; cook 1 minute, stirring to coat.
2. Spoon 1/2 cup rice onto each of 4 plates; top each serving with 3/4 cup pork mixture and 1/4 cup cabbage. Sprinkle each serving with 1 tablespoon peanuts and 1 tablespoon cilantro. Serve with lime wedges.

Chapter 10: Rice Dishes

***

Anything Stir Fry And Spiced Rice

"I never measure ingredients when cooking or baking so when someone asks for the recipe I can't help my daughter told me to start writing down what I put in stuff so I did hope you enjoy"

Servings: 4 | ***Time***: 20m

Ingredients

- 1 packages chicken, stew beef, or ground pork
- 5 tbsp garlic powder
- 4 tbsp smoked paprika
- 1/4 tbsp sea salt
- 2/3 tbsp ground ginger
- dash sage
- 3 peppers chopped(I prefer yellow and red)
- 1 onion, chopped
- 1/2 a head of broccoli
- 1/4 cup brown sugar
- 1/8 cup of soy sauce
- 1/2 cup basmati rice
- 3 1/4 cup water
- 1 cup water
- 1 cup mixed frozen veggies

Directions

1. Put rice, water and half the garlic paprika and sage on to boil cook approx. 15 min
2. Brown the beef in a skillet
3. Add half of the garlic paprika and sage
4. Add veggies, brown sugar and soy sauce
5. Slowly add remaining water into meat mixture let simmer till rice is done
6. Remove from heat 2 min then serve over spiced rice

Asian Meatballs with Mushrooms and Rice Noodles

"So much Asian food is prepared by stir-frying in a Wok that we tend to forget how many other dishes are powered by steam. Here's a twist on turkey-and-mushroom meatballs taken on a trip along the old spice route."

Servings: 2

Ingredients

- 1 regular-size foil oven bag
- Cooking spray
- 1/2 pound ground turkey breast
- 1/4 cup finely diced mushrooms
- 2 tablespoons thinly sliced green onions
- 1 tablespoon cornstarch, divided
- 1 tablespoon low-sodium soy sauce, divided
- 1 teaspoon dark sesame oil
- 4 cups hot water
- 4 ounces uncooked rice sticks (rice-flour noodles) or cooked vermicelli
- 1/4 cup fat-free, less-sodium chicken broth
- 2 tablespoons dry sherry
- 1 tablespoon fresh lime juice
- 1 1/2 cups sliced mushrooms
- 2 teaspoons minced peeled fresh ginger
- 1 1/4 teaspoons curry powder
- 1 garlic clove, minced
- 2 teaspoons minced fresh cilantro

Directions

1. Preheat oven to 450°.
2. Coat the inside of the oven bag with cooking spray. Place bag on a large shallow baking pan.
3. Combine ground turkey, diced mushrooms, green onions, 2 teaspoons cornstarch, 1 teaspoon soy sauce, and sesame oil in a bowl, and shape into 16 (1-inch) meatballs. Place meatballs on a single layer of wax paper.
4. Combine hot water and rice sticks in a bowl, and let stand 15 minutes. Drain well, and snip with scissors twice. Combine 1

teaspoon cornstarch and broth in a large bowl. Add 2 teaspoons soy sauce, sherry, and lime juice. Add rice sticks, sliced mushrooms, ginger, curry, and garlic, and toss well.
5. Place the noodle mixture in the prepared oven bag. Place the meatballs on noodle mixture, and fold edges of bag over to seal. Bake at 450° for 20 minutes or until the meatballs are done. Place the oven bag on platter, cut open with a sharp knife, and peel back foil. Sprinkle with minced cilantro.

Asparagus Fried Rice

"The trick to perfect fried rice is to use cold cooked rice (like leftover takeout) and stir-fry it long enough so that each grain dries out and puffs up. As with any stir-fry, make sure all your ingredients are ready to go before you fire up the pan."

Servings: 4-6

Ingredients

- 4 cups cold cooked long-grain white rice
- 2 tablespoons plus 2 tsp. vegetable oil
- 1 small onion, chopped
- 1 tablespoon chopped ginger
- 1 teaspoon chopped garlic
- 2 Chinese sausages (lop chong)*, diced, or 4 slices thick-cut bacon, chopped
- 7 ounces asparagus, cut into 1-in. pieces
- 3 large eggs, beaten
- 1 teaspoon kosher salt
- 1/2 teaspoon white pepper
- 1 tablespoon toasted sesame oil
- 1 green onion, sliced
- Soy sauce (optional)

Directions

1. Break up large clumps of rice with a fork. Heat 2 tbsp. vegetable oil in a Wok or large frying pan (not nonstick) over medium-high heat. Add onion, ginger, garlic, and sausages and cook, stirring

constantly, until fragrant, about 30 seconds. Add rice and cook, stirring often, until each grain of rice is dry and fluffy, 2 to 3 minutes. Add asparagus and cook until bright green, about 1 minute.
2. Push rice to outsides of Wok to create a well in the center. Add remaining 2 tsp. vegetable oil. Pour eggs into well and cook, stirring occasionally, until large curds form and eggs are fully cooked, about 2 minutes.
3. Add salt, white pepper, and sesame oil and toss rice until all ingredients are well combined. Sprinkle with green onion and serve with soy sauce if you like.

*Find Chinese sausages at East Asian markets.

Bacon Fried Rice

Servings: 4-6 | **Prep**: 30m | **Inactive**: 2h10m | **Cook**: 40m | **Ready In**: 3h20m

Ingredients

- 2 cups jasmine rice
- 8 ounces bacon, cut into 1-inch pieces
- 1 teaspoon sesame oil
- 1 large yellow onion, small dice
- 6 cloves garlic, minced
- 2 inches fresh ginger, peeled and grated
- 1 1/2 teaspoons kosher salt
- 3/4 teaspoon freshly ground black pepper
- 2 medium carrots, shredded
- 1 cup diced fresh pineapple
- 3 tablespoons sake (Japanese rice wine)
- 3 tablespoons light soy sauce
- 3 tablespoons rice wine vinegar
- 1 scallion, sliced
- 10 to 12 fresh cilantro leaves
- 4 to 6 sunny-side up eggs

Directions

1. Add the rice to a medium saucepan and cover with water. Swish the rice with your fingers and then strain through a fine-mesh strainer. Repeat the process 2 more times. Place the washed rice back into the saucepan and add 1 1/2 cups water. Cover the saucepan with a tight-fitting lid and cook over medium-low heat until all the water has been absorbed and the rice is cooked through, 20 to 25 minutes. Remove from the heat and keep covered for an additional 10 to 15 minutes. (If using a rice cooker, follow the manufacturers' instructions.) Fluff the rice with a fork, transfer to a tray and allow to cool in the refrigerator until the rice is no longer sticky, about 2 hours.
2. In a large skillet or Wok, cook the bacon over high heat until crispy, about 10 minutes. Remove the cooked bacon and reserve about 2 tablespoons bacon fat in the skillet. Reserve the remaining bacon fat for another use.
3. Return the skillet to high heat and add the sesame oil. Add the onions, garlic and ginger. Add 3/4 teaspoon salt and 3/8 teaspoon pepper and stir until the onions are translucent, 5 to 7 minutes. Add the carrots, pineapple and remaining 3/4 teaspoon salt and 3/8 teaspoon pepper. Continue stirring until the pineapple and carrots are cooked through, 5 to 7 minutes. Add the sake, soy sauce and rice wine vinegar and continue stirring. Add the cooled rice and reserved bacon and continue stirring. If necessary, add a touch more bacon fat or oil to the pan to avoid sticking. Adjust seasoning with salt and pepper.
4. Transfer the fried rice to serving bowls and garnish with the scallions, cilantro and a sunny-side up egg on top.

Breakfast Fried Brown Rice

"This quick and easy, one-pot recipe will make your next breakfast feng shui by shifting variety and flavor into overdrive for your morning meal."

Servings: 4 | **Prep**: 5m | **Cook**: 10m | **Ready In**: 15m

Ingredients

- 3 tablespoons peanut oil, divided, or more as needed
- 1/2 onion, chopped 2 large eggs
- 1 cup diced fully cooked

- 2 tablespoons butter
- 3 cups cooked brown rice kosher
- salt and freshly ground black pepper to taste
- 1/2 cup shredded Cheddar cheese

Directions

1. Preheat a Wok or skillet on high heat for 1 minute.
2. Coat Wok thoroughly with 2 tablespoons peanut oil; reduce heat to medium. Cook and stir onion until beginning to soften, about 3 minutes.
3. Crack eggs directly into the Wok. Stir quickly to scramble until eggs begin to set but are still fluid, about 1 1/2 minutes.
4. Stir ham into the Wok and cook just until warmed through, about 1 minute.
5. Stir butter and remaining 1 tablespoon of peanut oil into the Wok; let warm for 10 seconds. Add rice and stir constantly for 3 to 4 minutes, adding more oil if rice begins to stick.
6. Season fried rice with salt and pepper; top with Cheddar cheese.

Cook's Notes:

- Ensure your stir-fry is properly worked over the "hot spot" in your Wok. Do this by flipping and stirring repeatedly, moving the bottom of the mixture to the top. If rice sticks to the Wok, add a light amount of oil to help keep it moving.
- Its important not to add to the serving size too much because of the limited amount of "hot spot" in your Wok.
- For more flavor, add a tablespoon of oyster sauce and a tablespoon of soy sauce. To clean out the fridge, substitute ham with yesterday's meat leftovers. To be more traditional, add frozen peas with the meat.

Creole Fried Rice

"Cold rice works best in this recipe. If possible, make the rice a day ahead, and store it in the fridge. If you're in a hurry, follow Step 1 to cool it on a baking sheet."

Servings: 6 | **Prep**: 20m | **Cook**: 36m | **Cool**: 30m

Ingredients

- 1 cup uncooked long-grain rice
- 2 cups chicken broth
- 1 pound skinned and boned chicken thighs
- 1 1/2 teaspoons Creole seasoning, divided
- 2 tablespoons vegetable oil
- 1/2 pound andouille or smoked sausage, sliced
- 1/2 small onion, chopped
- 1/2 small green bell pepper, chopped
- 2 garlic cloves, chopped
- 1 cup frozen sliced okra, thawed
- 3 plum tomatoes, chopped
- 2 green onions, sliced (green part only)

Directions

1. Cook rice according to package directions, substituting chicken broth for water. Spread cooked rice in a thin layer on a baking sheet. Let cool 30 minutes or until completely cool.
2. Cut chicken thighs into 1-inch pieces, and toss with 1 tsp. Creole seasoning.
3. Cook chicken in hot oil in a large skillet over medium heat 3 minutes; add sausage, and cook 3 to 4 minutes or until lightly browned. Add onion, bell pepper, and garlic, and cook 5 minutes or until onion is tender. Stir in okra and remaining 1/2 tsp. Creole seasoning. Increase heat to high; add rice, and cook, stirring constantly, 4 minutes or until thoroughly heated. Stir in tomatoes. Sprinkle with sliced green onions, and serve immediately.

Duck Fried Rice

"This is how I like to use up leftovers from our favorite take-out meal of Chinese roast duck and barbequed pork. Ingredient amounts may vary depending on what's left from your meal. But fried rice dishes are very forgiving."

Servings: 4 | **Prep**: 15m | **Cook**: 25m | **Ready In**: 40m

Ingredients

- 1 cup chopped Chinese roast duck meat, skin and fat separated and set aside
- 1/2 cup thinly sliced Chinese barbecued pork
- 6 green onions, thinly sliced
- 2 tablespoons soy sauce
- 2 eggs, beaten
- 3 cups cooked long-grain rice
- salt and pepper to taste

Directions

1. Cook the duck skin and fat in a Wok or large skillet over medium heat until the skin is crispy, and the fat has rendered, about 10 minutes. Increase heat to medium-high, and stir in the duck meat, pork, half of the green onions, and the soy sauce. Cook and stir until the meats are heated through, about 5 minutes.
2. Add rice and toss together until rice is hot and sizzling, about 5 minutes. Make a wide well in the middle of the rice, exposing the bottom of the pan. Pour in the beaten eggs and stir until the eggs have scrambled. Then stir the scrambled eggs into the rice along with the rest of the green onions. Toss and stir until the rice is very hot, about 5 minutes. Season to taste with salt and pepper before serving.

Tip

- Aluminum foil helps keep food moist, ensures it cooks evenly, keeps leftovers fresh, and makes clean-up easy.

Fried Rice with Broccoli and Eggs

"Stir-frying rice is a great way to turn leftover rice into a quick and easy meal. It's important that the rice is cold so it won't become sticky while cooking; the oil coats the chilled grains and prevents clumping."

Servings: 6

Ingredients

- 3 cups small broccoli florets
- 4 large eggs
- 2 tablespoons water
- 1 tablespoon vegetable oil, divided
- 1 tablespoon minced peeled fresh ginger
- 2 garlic cloves, minced
- 4 cups cooked long-grain rice, chilled
- 1/2 cup shredded carrot
- 1/4 cup fat-free, less-sodium chicken broth
- 2 tablespoons low-sodium soy sauce
- 2 teaspoons dark sesame oil
- 1/4 teaspoon salt
- 1/4 cup thinly sliced green onions

Directions

1. Steam broccoli, covered, 2 minutes or until crisp-tender; rinse with cold water. Drain; cool.
2. Combine eggs and 2 tablespoons water. Heat 1 teaspoon vegetable oil in a large nonstick skillet or Wok over medium-high heat. Add egg mixture; stir-fry 30 seconds or until soft-scrambled, stirring constantly. Remove egg mixture from pan.
3. Add 2 teaspoons vegetable oil to pan. Add ginger and garlic; stir-fry 30 seconds. Add rice; stir-fry 3 minutes. Add broccoli, carrot, and broth; cook 1 minute. Add cooked eggs, soy sauce, sesame oil, and salt; stir-fry 1 minute or until thoroughly heated. Sprinkle with green onions.

Fried Rice with Chinese Sausage

*Servings: 4 | **Prep**: 10m | **Cook**: 12m | **Ready In**: 22m*

Ingredients

- 4 cup canola oil, divided
- 2 eggs, lightly beaten
- 1 tablespoon chopped ginger
- 1 tablespoon chopped garlic

- 1 carrot, finely diced
- 2 stalks celery, finely diced
- 3 links Chinese sausage, sliced
- 1 small bunch scallions, sliced, divided
- 4 cups cooked white rice
- 1/4 cup low-sodium soy sauce

Directions

- Heat 2 tablespoons of canola oil in a Wok over high heat. Add the beaten eggs and fry until they are fully cooked. Transfer them to plate. Add the remaining oil, ginger, garlic, carrot, and celery, and stir-fry for 2 minutes. Add the sausage and half of the scallions and cook for 1 minute. Add the cooked rice, soy sauce and rice wine vinegar. Stir-fry until the rice is hot, about 2 minutes. Stir in the reserved eggs and transfer to a serving dish. Garnish with the remaining scallions and serve.

Fried Rice with Lychees (Koa Pad Lin Gee)

"This is a sweeter rice dish, with lychees and raisins adding a pleasant and refreshing sweetness, balanced with salty cashew nuts. Maggi sauce is a German savory sauce popular in Thailand."

Servings: 4 | **Prep**: 15m | **Cook**: 30m | **Ready In**: 45m

Ingredients

- 1 cup uncooked jasmine rice
- 1/2 cup water
- 3 tablespoons vegetable oil
- 2 cloves garlic, minced
- 2 tablespoons chopped carrot
- 1 tablespoon chopped onion
- 3 tablespoons soy-based liquid seasoning (such as Maggi®)
- 1/4 cup reduced-sodium soy sauce
- 2 tablespoons chopped green onion
- 1 tablespoon chopped cashews
- 1 teaspoon raisins

- 1/4 teaspoon white sugar
- 1/4 teaspoon white pepper
- 5 canned lychees, drained and quartered

Directions

1. Bring the rice and water to a boil in a saucepan over high heat. Reduce heat to medium-low, cover, and simmer until the rice is tender, and the liquid has been absorbed, 20 to 25 minutes. Once cooked, spread the rice into a shallow dish, and refrigerate until cold, or use 1 1/2 cups leftover cooked rice.
2. Heat the oil in a Wok or large skillet over medium-high heat. Stir in the garlic and cook a few seconds until fragrant, then stir in the carrots and onion, and continue cooking until the onion begins to soften. Add the cold rice, and cook and stir until hot. Pour in the soy sauce, soy seasoning, green onions, cashews, raisins, salt, and white pepper. Cook and stir until hot, then stir in the quartered lychees to serve.

Fried Rice with Scallions, Edamame and Tofu

*Servings: 6 | **Prep**: 10m | **Cook**: 10m | **Ready In**: 20m*

Ingredients

- 1 tablespoon plus 1 teaspoon canola oil, divided
- 2 large cloves garlic, minced
- 4 scallions, greens included, rinsed, trimmed and thinly sliced
- 1 tablespoon minced ginger
- 4 cups leftover cooked brown rice
- 3/4 cup finely diced red pepper
- 3/4 cup cooked, shelled edamame
- 1/2 cup fresh or frozen, thawed, corn
- 6 ounces firm tofu, cut into 1/4-inch cubes
- 2 eggs, beaten
- 3 tablespoons low-sodium soy sauce

Directions

- Heat 1 tablespoon of oil in a Wok or large skillet until very hot. Add the garlic, scallions and ginger and cook, stirring, until softened and aromatic, about 2 to 3 minutes. Add the rice, red pepper, edamame, corn and tofu and cook, stirring, until heated through, about 5 minutes. Make a 3-inch well in the center of the rice mixture. Add 1 teaspoon of canola oil, then add the eggs and cook until nearly fully scrambled. Stir the eggs into the rice mixture, then add soy sauce and incorporate thoroughly. Serve hot.

Fried Rice

*Servings: 4-6 | **Prep**: 20m | **Cook**: 30m | **Ready In**: 50m*

Ingredients

- 8 dried shiitake mushrooms
- 3 tablespoons peanut oil
- 2 large eggs, lightly beaten with a pinch of kosher salt
- 4 scallions (white and green), thinly sliced
- 1/4 cup minced carrot
- 1 large clove garlic, minced
- Pinch red chile flakes
- 1 teaspoon minced peeled fresh ginger
- 2 tablespoons soy sauce
- 1 teaspoon toasted sesame oil
- 3 cups cooked long-grain rice
- 1 cup cooked meat cut in 1/2-inch cubes, such as pork, ham, beef, or chicken
- 1/2 cup frozen peas, defrosted in a strainer at room temperature

Directions

1. Put the mushrooms in a small bowl and cover with boiling water and soak until re-hydrated, about 20 minutes. Drain, squeeze dry, and cut mushrooms in quarters. Set aside.
2. Heat 1 tablespoon of the peanut oil in a well-seasoned Wok or large non-stick skillet over medium-high heat. Swirl to coat the pan. Pour in the eggs, swirl the pan so the egg forms a large thin pancake.

(Lift the edge of the egg to allow any uncooked egg to run to the center.) As soon as the egg has set, turn it out of the pan onto a cutting board. Cool, cut into 1 inch pieces.
3. Wipe out the pan with a paper towel and heat the remaining peanut oil over high heat. Add the scallions and carrots and stir-fry for 1 1/2 minutes. Add the mushrooms, garlic, chile, and ginger, stir-fry for 1 minute more. Add the soy sauce, sesame oil and rice and stir-fry for 2 to 3 minutes. Add the meat, peas, and reserved egg, cook, stirring until heated through, about 2 to 3 minutes. Serve immediately.

Grapes and Rice Stir Fry

"This is a simple rice stir fry that is easily made vegetarian."

Servings: 4 | **Prep**: 15m | **Cook**: 10m | **Ready In**: 25m

Ingredients

- 1 tablespoon vegetable oil
- 1 cup sliced red grapes
- 1 cup cubed cooked chicken
- 2 cups cooked rice
- 1/4 cup chicken broth

Directions

- Heat the vegetable oil in a Wok or large skillet over medium high heat. Stir in the grapes and chicken; cook and stir until the chicken is hot, and the grapes are tender, about 3 minutes. Add the rice and chicken broth; continue cooking until the rice is hot, about 2 minutes more.

Cook's Note

- Make this vegetarian by substituting marinated tofu for the chicken, and vegetable broth for the chicken broth.

Tip

- Aluminum foil helps keep food moist, ensures it cooks evenly, keeps leftovers fresh, and makes clean-up easy.

Ham and Veggie Fried Rice

"Tossing in frozen green peas at the end of cooking keeps them bright and lively."

Servings: 4

Ingredients

- 2 (8.5-ounce) pouches precooked brown rice (such as Uncle Ben's)
- 2 teaspoons lower-sodium soy sauce
- 2 teaspoons chili garlic sauce
- 1 teaspoon toasted sesame oil
- 2 tablespoons canola oil, divided
- 1 cup cubed reduced-sodium ham
- 1 large egg, lightly beaten
- 1 cup sliced cremini mushrooms
- 1/2 cup chopped red bell pepper
- 1/2 cup bean sprouts
- 1/3 cup sliced green onions
- 2 large garlic cloves, peeled and sliced
- 1 (1/2-inch) piece fresh ginger, peeled and thinly sliced
- 1/2 cup frozen green peas

Directions

1. Prepare rice according to package directions; set aside.
2. Combine soy sauce, chili garlic sauce, and sesame oil in a bowl. Heat a Wok over high heat. Add 1 tablespoon canola oil. Add ham; cook 2 minutes, stirring frequently. Transfer ham to soy sauce mixture.
3. Add egg to pan; cook 30 seconds. Remove from pan; chop.
4. Add remaining 1 tablespoon oil to pan. Add mushrooms and next 5 ingredients (through ginger); stir-fry 2 minutes. Add rice; stir-fry 2 minutes. Add ham mixture and peas; cook 2 minutes. Stir in egg.

Indonesian Fried Rice (Nasi Goreng)

"Nasi Goreng, Indonesian fried rice. This dish can be enjoyed by itself or as the basis of a larger meal, for example with a rijsttafel. It is very easy to make and won't take more than 20 minutes to prepare."

Servings: 4 | **Prep**: 20m | **Cook**: 40m | **Ready In**: 1h

Ingredients

- 1 cup uncooked white rice
- 2 cups water cooking spray
- 3 eggs, beaten 1 tablespoon vegetable oil
- 1 onion, chopped 1 leek, chopped
- 1 clove garlic, minced
- 2 green chile peppers, chopped
- 1/2 pound skinless, boneless chicken breasts, cut into thin strips
- 1/2 pound peeled and deveined prawns
- 1 teaspoon ground coriander
- 1 teaspoon ground cumin
- 3 tablespoons sweet soy sauce (Indonesian kecap manis)

Directions

1. Bring the rice and water to a boil in a saucepan over high heat. Reduce heat to medium-low, cover, and simmer until the rice is tender, and the liquid has been absorbed, 20 to 25 minutes. Spread onto a baking sheet, and refrigerate 2 hours until cold.
2. Heat a large nonstick skillet over medium heat. Spray with nonstick cooking spray. Pour eggs into hot skillet. Cook until the eggs begin to set, lifting up the edges of the set eggs to allow the uncooked egg to contact the hot pan, about 1 minute. Flip omelet in one piece and cook until fully set, about 30 seconds. Slice omelet into 1/2 inch strips.
3. Heat the vegetable oil in a Wok or large frying pan over high heat. Stir in the onion, leek, garlic, and chile peppers. Cook, stirring, until onion is soft, 3 to 5 minutes. Stir in the chicken, prawns, coriander, and cumin, mixing well. Cook and stir for approximately 5 minutes.

4. Mix in the cold rice, sweet soy sauce, and omelet strips; cook until shrimp are bright pink and chicken is no longer pink in the center, 3 to 5 minutes.

Tip

- Aluminum foil helps keep food moist, ensures it cooks evenly, keeps leftovers fresh, and makes clean-up easy.

Makato's Bacon Fried Rice

"A simple fried rice recipe chock-full of bacony goodness. It's very versatile - you can add chicken, eggs, or whatever you wish prior to adding the rice!"

Servings: 4 | **Prep**: 15m | **Cook**: 10m | **Ready In**: 25m

Ingredients

- 1/2 pound bacon, sliced into small pieces
- 2 tablespoons soy sauce
- 2 green onions, chopped
- 1/4 teaspoon sea salt
- 2 cups steamed white rice

Directions

- Place bacon in a Wok or large skillet and cook over medium heat, stirring occasionally, until starting to brown, about 5 minutes. Pour in soy sauce and scrape up any brown bits from the bottom of the Wok. Add green onions and salt; cook until wilted, 30 seconds to 1 minute. Add rice; cook, stirring frequently, until heated through, 3 to 4 minutes.

Mixed Stir Fry Rice

Servings: 6 | **Time**: 45m

Ingredients

- 3 each Italian Sauage Sliced
- 4 large Chicken Thighs
- 2 cup Cooked White Rice
- 1 packages Mixed Vegetables
- 2 packages Stir Fry Sauce

Directions

1. Fry Sliced Sausage. While sausage is frying, season chicken with your favorite season or basic Season All
2. Place cooked white rice on stove to steam along with vegetables
3. After sausage is done frying, remove sausage and add chicken to frying pan.
4. Once chicken is done frying, shred chicken. Add chicken and sausage to pot with rice & vegetables. Stir until mixed well together
5. Add both stir fry sauces to pot and mix well until you see no more white colored rice. Let simmer for about 5mins
6. Foods Ready !! Enjoy !

Rice Stir Fry

Servings: 4 | **Cook**: 30m

Ingredients

- 1 lb Chicken
- 1 box White rice
- 1 packages Frozen bag of veggies
- 2 cup Shredded carrots
- 2 cup Bean sprouts
- 1 cup Water chestnuts
- 1 cup Teriyaki sauce

Directions

1. Cook rice to the directions on the box
2. While the rice is cooking, cut up the chicken into 2 inch square pieces
3. Cook the chicken in a medium sauce pan, adding about half a cup of teriyaki
4. When chicken is almost done cooking add in the water chestnuts, carrots, the rest of the teriyaki sauce and frozen mixed vegetables
5. Let cook until your liking
6. When the rice is done cooking, put into a bowl then put your stir fry mixture on top, add teriyaki sauce to your liking
7. And enjoy.

Special Fried Rice

*Servings: 4 | **Prep**: 10m | **Cook**: 25m | **Ready In**: 35m*

Ingredients

- 3/4 cups water
- 1 1/2 cups white rice
- 3 tablespoons vegetable or Wok oil, 3 turns of the pan
- 2 eggs, beaten
- 2 cloves garlic, chopped
- 2 inches fresh ginger, minced or grated
- 1/2 cup shredded carrots, available in pouches in produce section, a couple of handfuls
- 1 small red bell pepper, diced
- 4 scallions, thinly sliced on an angle
- 1/2 cup frozen peas
- 1/3 cup Tamari, dark aged soy sauce

Directions

1. Bring water to a boil. Add rice, reduce heat, cover and cook over medium low heat until tender, 15 to 18 minutes. Spread rice out on a cookie sheet to quick cool it.
2. Heat a Wok, Wok shaped skillet or large nonstick skillet over high heat. Add oil to the pan. Add egg to hot oil and break into small bits

as it scrambles. When eggs are scrambled, add garlic and ginger to the pan. Add carrots, pepper, scallions to the pan and quick stir-fry veggies 2 minutes. Add rice to the pan and combine with veggies. Fry rice with veggies 2 or 3 minutes. Add peas and soy sauce to the rice and stir fry 1 minute more, then serve.

Tofu Stir-Fry with Fried Rice

Servings: 4-6 | Prep: 10m | Cook: 20m | Ready In: 30m

Ingredients

- 3 tablespoons sesame oil, divided
- 1 package firm tofu, cut into 1-inch cubes, marinated, recipe follows
- 1/2 cup quartered white button mushrooms
- 1 medium carrot, julienned
- 1 baby bok choy, quartered
- 1/2 yellow pepper, sliced
- 3 scallions, sliced
- 2 tablespoons soy sauce
- 3 teaspoons oyster sauce
- 2 eggs, lightly beaten
- 2 cups short-grain rice, recipe follows

For rice:

- 2 cups water
- 1/2 teaspoon salt
- 1 cup short-grain white rice

Directions

- Place Wok over medium heat. Add 2 tablespoons sesame oil once hot add marinated tofu and cook for 2 minutes, then add mushrooms, carrots, bok choy, yellow pepper and scallions. Stir-fry vegetables quickly then add the soy sauce and oyster sauce. Stir well. Within 5 minutes stir-fry should be cooked. Once satisfied with texture place mixture on a serving plate. In the same Wok add the remaining tablespoon of oil and add the lightly beaten eggs.

Scramble the eggs then add the cooked rice. Stir and fry. Serve with tofu vegetable mixture.

For tofu marinade:

- In a medium bowl add tofu, red chili flakes, soy sauce and rice wine vinegar. Stir making sure tofu is covered. Let tofu sit for 10 minutes.

For rice:

- In medium saucepan add 2 cups water and salt, bring to a boil add rice and cover. Lower heat and cook for about 20 minutes.

Traditional Mandarin Fried Rice

Servings: 4 | **Prep**: 5m | **Cook**: 12m | **Ready In**: 17m

Ingredients

- Canola oil
- 3 eggs
- 2 tablespoons minced garlic
- 2 tablespoons minced ginger
- 1 bunch chopped scallions, green and white separated
- 1 lapchang, diced (Chinese sausage), can substitute with 4 strips of cooked bacon
- 8 cups cooked, day-old long grain rice
- 3 tablespoons thin soy sauce
- 1/2 teaspoon white pepper
- Salt to taste

Directions

- In a Wok, add 2 tablespoons of oil and quickly soft-scramble the eggs. Remove the eggs. In the same Wok, coat with oil and stir-fry garlic and ginger. Add white scallions and lapchang. Add rice and mix thoroughly. Add soy sauce, white pepper and scrambled eggs. Check for seasoning. Serve immediately.

Tsao Mi Fun (Taiwanese Fried Rice Noodles)

"My mom's been making me tsao mi fun, in Mandarin, or tsa bi whun, in Taiwanese, since I was a little girl. Tsa bi whun literally translates to 'fried rice noodles'. You'll most likely find all the ingredients at your local supermarket except for the five spice powder, dried Chinese black mushrooms and rice vermicelli which can be found at your local Asian food mart. All the measurements here are pretty much to taste, some people like more pork, some less, some more soy sauce, some less, etc."

Servings: 4 | **Prep**: 35m | **Cook**: 15m | **Ready In**: 1h10m

Ingredients

- 1/2 pound thinly sliced pork loin
- 1/4 cup soy sauce
- 1/4 cup rice wine
- 1 teaspoon white pepper
- 1 teaspoon Chinese five-spice powder
- 1 teaspoon cornstarch
- 4 dried Chinese black mushrooms
- 1 (8 ounce) package dried rice vermicelli
- 1/4 cup vegetable oil, divided
- 2 eggs, beaten
- 1/4 clove garlic, minced
- 1 tablespoon dried small shrimp
- 3 carrots, cut into matchstick strips
- 1/2 onion, chopped
- 3 cups bean sprouts
- 4 leaves napa cabbage, thinly sliced
- salt to taste
- 3 sprigs fresh cilantro for garnish

Directions

1. Place the pork into a mixing bowl and pour in the soy sauce and rice wine. Sprinkle with the white pepper, five-spice powder, and cornstarch. Mix well, then set aside to marinate. Soak the mushrooms in a bowl of cold water for 20 minutes, then pour off the water, cut off and discard the stems of the mushrooms. Slice the mushrooms thinly and reserve. Soak the rice vermicelli in a

separate bowl of cold water for 10 minutes, then pour off the water and set the noodles aside.
2. Heat 1 tablespoon of the vegetable oil in a Wok or large skillet over medium heat. Pour in the eggs, and cook until firm, flipping once, to make a pancake. Remove the egg pancake, and allow to cool, then thinly slice and place into a large bowl. Heat 2 more tablespoons of the vegetable oil in the Wok over high heat. Stir in the garlic and dried shrimp, and cook until the shrimp become aromatic, about 20 seconds. Next, add the pork along with the marinade, and cook until the pork is no longer pink, about 4 minutes. Stir in the carrots and onion, and cook until the carrots begin to soften, about 3 minutes. Finally, add the bean sprouts, napa cabbage, and sliced mushrooms; cook and stir until the vegetables are tender, about 3 minutes more. Scrape the pork mixture into the bowl along with the eggs, then wipe out the Wok and return it to the stove over medium-high heat.
3. Heat the remaining vegetable oil in the Wok, then stir in the drained rice vermicelli noodles. Cook and stir for a few minutes until the noodles soften, then stir in the reserved pork mixture. Scrape the mixture in to a serving bowl and garnish with cilantro to serve.

Chapter 11: Soups

***

Creamy Wok Soup

"Soup inspired by asian cuisine"

Servings: 5 | **Ready In:** 45m

Ingredients

- 3/4 tbsp Wok oil
- 2 carrots
- 1 cup shiitake mushrooms
- 1 cm ginger root, peeled
- 2 cup hokkaido squash, peeled and diced
- 200 grams peas, thawed
- 2 cup water (approximately)
- 3/4 tbsp soy sauce
- 3/4 tbsp sesame oil
- 1/2 tsp (or to taste) sambal oelek (spicy chili sauce)
- 1 squeeze of lime juice
- 2 tsp curry
- 150 grams rice noodles
- garnish (all optional)
- 1 scallion, finely chopped
- 1 fresh chili, finely chopped
- 1 coconut milk

Directions

1. Heat Wok oil in a Wok over high heat
2. Add finely chopped carrots, finely chopped ginger and roughly chopped mushrooms. Fry until nicely browned
3. Add squash and thawed peas to Wok. Fry for about a minute or until softened
4. Add water and cover loosely with a lid. Simmer for about 20 minutes or until the squash softens and some of the water evaporates. Soup should be creamy
5. Add soya sauce, sesame oil, sambal oelek (it's very spicy so add a little at a time), lime juice and curry

6. Add the rice noodles to the boiling soup, take immediately off heat and cover tightly with a lid
7. Serve with chopped chili and scallion. Pour some coconut milk if desired

Hot and Sour Soup

***Servings**: 6 | **Prep**: 30m | **Inactive**: 30m | **Cook**: 1h20m | **Ready In**: 2h20m*

Ingredients

- 4 dried Chinese fungi (about 1 ounce), such as wood ears or cloud ears
- 2 tablespoons canola oil
- 1 -inch piece fresh ginger, peeled and grated
- 1 tablespoon red chile paste, such as sambal oelek
- 1/2 cup canned bamboo shoots, sliced
- 1/4 pound barbecued pork, shredded
- 1/4 cup soy sauce
- 1/4 cup rice vinegar
- 1 teaspoon salt
- 1 teaspoon ground white pepper
- Pinch sugar
- 2 quarts Chinese Chicken Stock, recipe follows
- 1 square firm tofu, drained and sliced in 1/4-inch strips
- 3 tablespoons cornstarch mixed with 1/4 cup water
- 1 large egg, lightly beaten
- Chopped green onions and cilantro leaves, for garnish

Chinese Chicken Stock:

- 1 (4-pound) whole chicken
- 1 bunch green onions, halved
- 4 garlic cloves, smashed
- 3 -inch piece fresh ginger, whacked open with the flat side of a knife
- 1 onion, halved
- 1 teaspoon whole white peppercorns
- About 3 quarts cold water

Directions

1. Put the wood ears in a small bowl and cover with boiling water. Let stand for 30 minutes to reconstitute. Drain and rinse the wood ears; discard any hard clusters in the centers.
2. Heat the oil in a Wok or large pot over medium-high flame. Add the ginger, chili paste, wood ears, bamboo shoots, and pork; cook and stir for 1 minute to infuse the flavor. Combine the soy sauce, vinegar, salt, pepper, and sugar in a small bowl, pour it into the Wok and toss everything together - it should smell really fragrant. Pour in the Chinese Chicken Stock, bring the soup to a boil, and simmer for 10 minutes. Add the tofu and cook for 3 minutes.
3. Dissolve the cornstarch in the water and stir until smooth. Mix the slurry into the soup and continue to simmer until the soup thickens. Remove the soup from the heat and stir in 1 direction to get a current going, then stop stirring. Slowly pour in the beaten eggs in a steady stream and watch it spin around and feather in the broth (it should be cooked almost immediately.) Garnish the hot and sour soup with chopped green onions and cilantro before serving.

Chinese Chicken Stock:

1. Put the chicken in a large stockpot and place over medium heat. Toss in the green onions, garlic, ginger, onion, and peppercorns. Pour about 3 quarts of cold water into the pot to cover the chicken by 1-inch. Simmer gently for 1 hour, uncovered, skimming off the foam on the surface periodically.
2. Carefully remove the chicken from the pot and pass the stock through a strainer lined with cheesecloth to remove the solids and excess fat. Cool the chicken stock to room temperature before storing in the refrigerator, or chill it down over ice first.

Seared Scallops and Hot and Sour Soup

Servings: 4-6 | **Prep**: 15m | **Inactive**: 30m | **Cook**: 30m | **Ready In**: 1h5m

Ingredients

- 2 ounces dried wooden ear mushrooms
- 1 cup warm water
- 2 tablespoons vegetable oil

- 1/2 pound lean pork, julienned
- Salt and freshly ground black pepper
- 4 ounces straw mushrooms, washed, trimmed and sliced
- 4 ounces bamboo shoots
- 6 ounces bean curd, shredded
- 2 quarts chicken stock
- 1/3 cup cornstarch
- 1/2 cup water
- 1/4 cup soy sauce
- 1/4 cup rice wine vinegar
- 4 eggs, beaten
- 1/2 cup chopped green onions, green part only
- 2 tablespoons canola oil
- 2 dozen sea scallops
- 1 tablespoon sesame oil
- Sriracha
- Chili oil, to taste

Directions

1. Soak the mushrooms in the warm water for 30 minutes. Drain and julienne the mushrooms. In a Wok, over medium heat, add the oil. Season the pork with salt and pepper. When the oil is hot, add the pork and stir-fry for 2 minutes. Add the straw mushrooms, bamboo shoots, bean curd, and wood ear mushrooms. Season with salt and pepper. Saute for 2 minutes. Add the stock and bring to a boil. Reduce to a simmer and cook for 5 minutes. Dissolve the cornstarch in the water. Stir the cornstarch mixture into simmering liquid. Bring the liquid back to a boil and cook for 2 to 3 minutes. Reduce the heat to a simmer and add the soy sauce and rice wine vinegar. Stir in the beaten eggs, making wide circles in Wok. Stir gently until the eggs are cooked. Re-season with salt and pepper. Stir in the green onions.
2. In a large saute pan over high heat, add canola oil. When the oil is hot but not smoking, add scallops. Turn after 30 seconds, and continue to cook on other side until rare. Place scallops into bowls, sprinkle with sesame oil and drizzle with sriracha. Ladle soup directly over scallops. Pass the chili oil at the table.

Stir-fry Noodle Soup

"In the style of Shandong, and taken with liberties from Martin Yan, this soup has a seriously savory body that invites you to eat everything broth and all. It starts with a stir fry of pork, mushrooms, and veggies, followed by an Asian stock, which poaches eggs. The soup is labeled over noodles. Surprisingly hearty yet light."

Servings: 6 | **Ready In**: 30m

Ingredients

- 1 handful dried wood ear mushrooms
- 4 dried shitakii mushrooms
- 1 lb pork chops, sliced in thin strips
- 2 Tbsp corn starch
- 2 tsp soy sauce
- 2 tsp sesame oil
- 1 tsp shitakii powder (optional)
- oil
- 2 cloves garlic, minced
- 1/2 head Napa cabbage, sliced in 1/2 strips
- 8 oz bamboo shoots, sliced
- 8 oz oyster mushrooms, sliced in chunks
- 4 green onions, sliced
- 3 cups chicken or pork stock
- 3 Tbsp soy sauce
- 1 Tbsp black vinegar
- 1 lb fresh noodles
- 6 eggs

Directions

1. Rehydrate the mushrooms by covering in boiling water and allowing to sit for several hours. Thinly slice the shitakii and roughly tear the wood ear (also called black fungus in some Asian markets). Keep the mushrooms separate after cutting.
2. Combine the pork, shitakii, corn starch, 2 tsp soy sauce, shitakii powder, and sesame oil in a bowl and set aside.
3. Combine the cabbage, wood ear, oyster mushrooms, green onion, and bamboo shoots in a large bowl and set aside.
4. Gather all your ingredients mise en place. The soup will come together very quickly.

5. Prepare the soup base by combining the the stock, soy sauce, and black vinegar and setting over low heat.
6. Set a pot of water, for the noodles, to boil. Add a Tbsp of salt and a tsp of baking soda to the water. The soda will increase the pH and give you noodles more spring, like Asian style noodles.
7. Boil the noodles for 3 min or until al dente
8. Drain and rinse the noodles to stop the cooking
9. Place the noodles in handfuls into a bowl. Extra noodles should be stored in small zip lock bags as single servings.
10. Add the oil to a Wok over high heat and add the garlic stirring for 30 seconds until fragrant.
11. Add the pork and shitakii and continue to stir fry until browning
12. Remove the cooked pork and set aside.
13. Stir fry the veggies/mushrooms until starting to brown.
14. Add the soup base and set heat to simmer
15. Make a well in the simmering soup to poach the eggs. One egg per person.
16. Poach the eggs. Labeling soup broth over the eggs after 3-4 minutes.
17. Place a poached egg in each bowl
18. Add soup to the noodles and egg and serve

Chapter 12: Thai Recipes

***

Butternut Squash Zoodles Stir Fry In Spicy Thai Sauce, Cherry Tomatoes, Broccolini, Feta

"Friday night, I walk out of the office with the prospects of more work waiting for me once I get home: I need something healthy and quick to cook but I have been binging on salads all week and I can't get myself to make another one... Then the epiphany: zoodles!"

Servings: 2 | **Time**: 15m

Ingredients

- 1 pack butternut squash zoodles
- 1 bag M&S' southern thai stir fry sauce (or any spicy coconut creamy sauce)
- 100 g cherry tomatoes
- 100 g tenderstem broccoli
- 50 g feta cheese (I used the reduced fat one)
- 1 handful almond flakes (optional)
- 1 garlic clove
- Oregano
- Dried chilli (optional)
- Salt
- Pepper

Directions

1. Preheat the over at 220C. Place the broccoli on a over tray on a sheet of baking paper. Rub with a splash of olive oil, add salt and peper to taste and roast in the oven for 10 min or until brown and crispy.
2. Warm up a Wok or large pan with a dash of olive oil, over medium heat. Add the garlic and let it fry until it starts to turn brown - then remove. Cut the tomatoes in half, sprinkle with oregano and chilli and let cook for 3-5 mins.
3. In the meantime, pierce the zoodles bag and steam in the microwave for 2min 30sec.

4. Add the sauce to the pan and stir well. Let it warm up for about 1 min, then add the zoodles and the broccoli. Mix well for 1-2 min, then place on a plate(s).
5. Add cubes of feta on top and sprinkle with almond flakes. Serve straight away!

Classic Pad Thai

"This recipe is a perfect example of Thai cooking for beginners. Once mastered, you'll forget stopping for take-out and make this easy stir-fry a weeknight staple."

Servings: 4 | ***Prep***: 15m | ***Cook***: 15m | ***Ready In***: 30m

Ingredients

- 8 ounces medium width rice vermicelli noodles
- 3 tablespoons vegetable oil
- 1/4 pound ground chicken
- 1 teaspoon hot pepper sauce
- 1 red pepper, thinly sliced
- 1/2 pound peeled, deveined raw shrimp
- 3 cloves garlic, minced
- 2 teaspoons freshly grated gingerroot
- 1/2 cup vegetable or chicken broth
- 1/2 cup Heinz Tomato Ketchup
- 1/4 cup lime juice
- 3 tablespoons granulated sugar
- 3 tablespoons fish sauce
- 1/2 cups bean
- 3 green onions, thinly sliced
- 1/4 cup fresh coriander or parsley leaves chopped peanuts

Directions

1. Cover noodles with boiling water and let stand for 5 minutes; drain well and reserve.

2. Heat half the oil in a Wok or deep skillet set over high heat. Crumble in chicken and add hot sauce; stir-fry for 3 to 5 minutes or until browned. Reserve on a platter.
3. Add remaining oil and peppers to pan; stir-fry for 3 minutes. Add shrimp and stir-fry for 2 minutes. Stir in garlic, ginger, broth, ketchup, lime juice, sugar and fish sauce. Bring to a boil. Add noodles and reserved meat; toss mixture to combine. Heat through.
4. Add sprouts and toss gently. Sprinkle with onions, coriander and peanuts.

Twists:

- Twist 1: For a pork variation, try ground pork instead of ground chicken.
- Twist 2: For a meatless version, substitute chopped, firm tofu for the chicken and a chopped 3-egg omelet for the shrimp.
- Twist 3: Simplify this recipe by omitting hot pepper sauce and replacing ketchup with Heinz Hot & Spicy Ketchup.

Goong Tod Kratiem Prik Thai (Prawns Fried with Garlic and White Pepper)

"This dish uses a classic Thai preparation method of protein. It might not sound like much, but it's a very satisfying dish, especially made with shrimp that's shell-on. We eat the shrimp shell and all, as to not miss out on any flavor. It's also a very kid-friendly dinner dish. Serve with lots of rice."

*Servings: 4 | **Prep**: 5m | **Cook**: 4m | **Ready In**: 9m*

Ingredients

- 8 cloves garlic, chopped, or more to taste
- 2 tablespoons tapioca flour
- 2 tablespoons fish sauce
- 2 tablespoons light soy sauce
- 1 tablespoon white sugar
- 1/2 teaspoon ground white pepper
- 1/4 cup vegetable oil, divided, or as needed
- 1 pound whole unpeeled prawns, divided

Directions

1. Combine garlic, tapioca flour, fish sauce, soy sauce, sugar, and white pepper in a bowl; add prawns and toss to coat.
2. Heat 2 tablespoons oil in a heavy skillet over high heat. Add 1/2 of the prawns in single layer; fry until golden brown and crispy, 1 to 2 minutes per side. Repeat with remaining oil and remaining prawns.

Cook's Notes:

- Use Wok instead of skillet, if desired.
- Prawns can be fried in 3 batches or more, if needed, depending on the size of your skillet or Wok.

Nicola's Pad Thai

"The result of loving pad Thai and endless tweaks to the ingredients lead me to this amazing dish."

Servings: 4 | **Prep**: 15m | **Cook**: 15m | **Ready In**: 30m

Ingredients

- 2 cups pad Thai rice noodles, soaked in water overnight and drained
- 1/2 cup vegetable broth
- 2 tablespoons vegetable oil
- 1 tablespoon brown sugar
- 1 tablespoon soy sauce
- 1 tablespoon rice wine vinegar
- 1/2 teaspoons peanut butter
- 1 teaspoon chopped fresh cilantro
- 1 teaspoon onion powder
- 1 teaspoon tamarind paste
- 1 teaspoon hot chile paste
- 3/4 teaspoon garlic powder
- 1/2 teaspoon sesame oil
- 1/2 teaspoon crushed red pepper flakes

- 1/4 teaspoon ground coriander
- 1/4 teaspoon ground ginger salt and ground black pepper to taste
- 3 tablespoons vegetable oil
- 1/3 cup chopped broccoli
- 1/3 cup chopped carrots
- 1/3 cup snow peas, trimmed
- 1/3 cup sliced water chestnuts, drained
- 1/3 cup baby corn, drained
- 1/3 cup sliced fresh mushrooms
- 1/3 cup sliced zucchini
- 1 tablespoon vegetable oil
- 1 tablespoon chopped peanuts for topping
- 1 tablespoon chopped cilantro
- 1 pinch paprika for garnish

Directions

1. Soak uncooked noodles in 8 cups of water until soft, 8 hours or overnight.
2. Drain rice noodles and set aside.
3. Whisk together vegetable broth, 2 tablespoons vegetable oil, brown sugar, soy sauce, rice wine vinegar, peanut butter, 1 teaspoon fresh cilantro, onion powder, tamarind paste, hot chile paste, garlic powder, sesame oil, red pepper flakes, ground coriander, ground ginger, salt, and ground black pepper in a saucepan.
4. Heat sauce over medium heat until it bubbles; reduce heat to low, and simmer sauce while you prepare the remaining ingredients.
5. Heat 3 tablespoons of vegetable oil in a large Wok over medium heat.
6. Cook and stir broccoli, carrots, snow peas, water chestnuts, baby corn, mushrooms, and zucchini in the Wok until tender, 8 to 10 minutes.
7. Add the drained noodles and 1 tablespoon vegetable oil to vegetables. Cook and stir until noodles are heated through, 2 to 3 minutes.
8. Remove the Wok from heat and pour the sauce over vegetables and rice noodles.
9. Toss to fully coat the vegetables and rice noodles with sauce.
10. Garnish with peanuts, 2 tablespoons chopped cilantro, and paprika.

Cook's Note:

- Everyone has a different idea of what pad Thai should taste like, this is as close (vegan) as I have come to my favorite restaurant's take on this wonderful dish. I hope you enjoy.

Okinawan-Style Pad Thai

"This is a famous dish popularized in Thailand. Although the recipe varies from cook to cook and region to region, this is a good attempt at recreating what I ate from Thai-owned hole-in-the-wall restaurants in Okinawa, Japan. Key to the flavor are the sugar levels, unsalted peanuts, peanut oil, and either oyster or fish sauce."

Servings: 8 | **Prep**: 10m | **Cook**: 20m | **Ready In**: 30m

Ingredients

- 1/2 cup rice wine vinegar
- 1/2 cup white sugar
- 1/4 cup oyster sauce
- 2 tablespoons tamarind pulp
- 1 (12 ounce) package dried rice noodles cold water, as needed
- 1/2 cup peanut oil
- 4 eggs
- 1/2 teaspoons minced garlic
- 12 ounces chicken breast, cut into 1/2-inch strips
- 1/2 tablespoons white sugar, or more to taste
- 1/2 teaspoons salt 1
- 1/2 cups dry-roasted, unsalted peanuts
- 1/2 teaspoons dried ground Asian radish
- 1 teaspoon chili powder, or more to taste
- 1/2 cup chopped fresh chives
- 2 cups fresh bean sprouts
- 1 lime, cut into wedges

Directions

1. Whisk together rice wine vinegar, 1/2 cup sugar, oyster sauce, and tamarind pulp in a saucepan over medium heat until sugar dissolves, about 5 minutes; remove from heat and set aside.
2. Place rice noodles in a large bowl and pour enough cold water to cover noodles. Allow to soften, about 10 minutes. Drain.
3. Heat peanut oil in a Wok or large skillet over medium heat. Cook and stir eggs and garlic in hot oil until eggs are softly cooked, 2 to 3 minutes.
4. Stir chicken and noodles into eggs and cook until chicken is no longer pink in the center and juices run clear, about 5 minutes.
5. Pour rice wine vinegar sauce, 1 1/2 tablespoons sugar, and 1 1/2 teaspoons salt into the noodle mixture.
6. Stir peanuts, ground radish, and chili powder into noodle mixture; cook until peanuts soften slightly, about 5 minutes. Add more sugar or chili powder if desired.
7. Remove from heat and toss chives with noodle mixture. Top with bean sprouts and garnish with lime wedges.

Opal's Thai Stir-Fry

Servings: 2 | **Prep**: 10m | **Cook**: 5m | **Ready In**: 15m

Ingredients

- 1 teaspoon vegetable oil
- 1 teaspoon minced garlic
- 2 Thai chiles, chopped
- 6 ounces chicken, pork, shrimp or tofu
- 1/2 cup chopped white onion
- Fistful of flat wide rice noodles, cooked
- 1 tablespoon dark soy sauce
- 1/2 tablespoon fish sauce
- 1/2 teaspoon sugar
- 1/2 cup chopped green bell pepper
- 1/2 cup chopped red bell pepper
- 1 large tomato, chopped
- 1 tablespoon chopped fresh basil

Directions

1. Preheat a medium Wok over high heat. Add the oil, garlic and chilies. Add your protein selection and brown the outside. Add the onions, noodles, dark soy sauce, fish sauce and sugar. Cook for about 2 minutes. Throw in the peppers, tomato and basil and cook for 1 minute.
2. This recipe was provided by a chef, restaurant or culinary professional and may have been scaled down from a bulk recipe. The Food Network Kitchens chefs have not tested this recipe, in the proportions indicated, and therefore, we cannot make any representation as to the results.

Pad Thai Quinoa Bowl

"This recipe uses quinoa which is gluten-free, high in protein and fiber, and has a nice nutty flavor. But you can always substitute for either rice or noodles. Take out the chicken and add extra edamame and you have a great vegetarian meal instead. Or add shrimp if you like. A seriously good, versatile recipe!"

Servings: 8 | **Prep**: 30m | **Cook**: 30m | **Ready In**: 1h

Ingredients

- 4 cups low-sodium chicken broth
- 2 cups quinoa, rinsed and drained
- 1 tablespoon coconut oil, divided
- 1 large boneless, skinless chicken breast, cut into thin strips
- 3/4 cup shredded cabbage
- 1/2 cup edamame
- 1/4 cup diced broccoli stems
- 2 carrots, cut into matchsticks
- 2 green onions, chopped
- 3 eggs
- 1 teaspoon sesame oil

Thai peanut sauce:

- 1/4 cup natural peanut butter
- 1/4 cup reduced-sodium soy sauce

- 3 tablespoons rice vinegar
- 2 tablespoons chili garlic sauce
- 2 tablespoons chopped fresh ginger
- 3 cloves garlic, minced
- 1 teaspoon sesame oil
- 1/2 cup salted peanuts, chopped
- 3 tablespoons chopped fresh cilantro

Directions

1. Bring chicken broth and quinoa to a boil in a saucepan. Reduce heat to medium-low, cover, and simmer until quinoa is tender, 15 to 20 minutes. Set aside.
2. Heat 1 1/2 teaspoons coconut oil in a Wok or large skillet over medium-high heat. Add chicken; stir until cooked through; about 5 minutes. Remove chicken from Wok. Heat remaining 1 1/2 teaspoons coconut oil. Add cabbage, edamame, broccoli, carrot, and green onions and saute until vegetables soften slightly, 2 to 3 minutes.
3. Whisk eggs with sesame oil in a small bowl. Push vegetables to the sides of the Wok to make a well in the center; pour eggs in and stir to scramble, about 3 minutes.
4. Combine peanut butter, soy sauce, rice vinegar, chili garlic sauce, ginger, garlic, and sesame oil together in a small bowl. Pour Thai peanut sauce over vegetable and egg mixture in the Wok.
5. Return chicken to the Wok and add quinoa; mix well to combine. Stir in chopped peanuts and cilantro and serve.

Cook's Note:

- You can tell when quinoa is cooked because it will increase in size and seem more transparent with a ribbon around the edges. Make sure all the liquid is cooked off.

Tip

- Parchment can be used for easier cleanup/removal from the pan.

Pad Thai

Servings: 2 | **Prep**: 40m | **Inactive**: 12h | **Cook**: 5m | **Ready In**: 12h45m

Ingredients

- 1 -ounce tamarind paste
- 3/4 cup boiling water
- 2 tablespoons fish sauce
- 2 tablespoons palm sugar
- 1 tablespoon rice wine vinegar
- 4 ounces rice stick noodles
- 6 ounces Marinated Tofu, recipe follows
- 1 to 2 tablespoons peanut oil
- 1 cup chopped scallions, divided
- 2 teaspoons minced garlic
- 2 whole eggs, beaten
- 2 teaspoons salted cabbage
- 1 tablespoon dried shrimp
- 3 ounces bean sprouts, divided
- 1/2 cup roasted salted peanuts, chopped, divided
- Freshly ground dried red chile peppers, to taste
- 1 lime, cut into wedges

Marinated Tofu:

- 6 ounces extra-firm tofu, not silken
- 1/2 cups soy sauce
- 1 teaspoon Chinese five-spice powder

Directions

1. Place the tamarind paste in the boiling water and set aside while preparing the other ingredients.
2. Combine the fish sauce, palm sugar, and rice wine vinegar in a small bowl and set aside.
3. Place the rice stick noodles in a mixing bowl and cover with hot water. Set aside while you prepare the remaining ingredients. Once the other ingredients are measured out into separate bowls, drain the water from the noodles and set them aside. Cut the tofu into 1/2-inch wide strips, similar to French fries.
4. Press the tamarind paste through a fine mesh strainer and add to the sauce. Stir to combine.
5. Place a Wok over high heat. Once hot, add 1 tablespoon of the peanut oil. Heat until it shimmers, then add the tofu. Cook the tofu

until golden brown, moving constantly, for no longer than 1 minute. Remove the tofu from the pan to a small bowl and set aside.
6. If necessary, add some more peanut oil to the pan and heat until shimmering. Add 2/3 of the scallions and then the garlic, cook for 10 to 15 seconds. Add the eggs to the pan; once the eggs begin to set up, about 15 to 20 seconds, stir to scramble. Add the remaining ingredients in the following order and toss after each addition: noodles, sauce, cabbage, shrimp, and 2/3 of the bean sprouts and peanuts. Toss everything until heated through, but no longer than 1 to 2 minutes total. Transfer to a serving dish. Garnish with the remaining scallions, bean sprouts, and peanuts. Serve immediately with the ground chile peppers and lime wedges.

Marinated Tofu:

1. Wrap the tofu firmly in a tea towel. Place the wrapped tofu into an 8-inch cake pan. Top with another cake pan and weigh down with a 5-pound weight. (Bags of dried beans or grains work well.) Place in refrigerator and press for 12 to 15 hours.
2. Place pressed tofu in a 2-cup container. Combine soy sauce and five-spice powder and pour over tofu. Cover and refrigerate for 30 minutes, turning once. Remove the tofu from the marinade and use immediately or store in the refrigerator for up to 2 to 3 days.

Stir Fry Sweet Chili Glazed Tofu With Peppers & Onions And Thai Baisil

"Great fresh recipe as a main dish or just as a side dish"

Servings: 5 | **Time**: 40m

Ingredients

- 2 packages extra firm or firm tofu
- 2 each green bell pepper, red bell pepper sliced into strips
- 1 Yellow onion cut into strips
- 1 bunch Thai basil
- 1 box of corn starch
- 1 bottle sweet chili sauce
- oil to fry tofu

Directions

1. Take tofu out of package and place on paper towel and then another on top and place some kind of weight on it to help drain excess water out of it. Cut the tofu in 1 inch square pieces after you feel that it is done draining usually about 30min
2. As the tofu is draining. Slice the onions and bell peppers and chop up the Thai basil and heat up oil to fry tofu.
3. After you finished slicing the pepper and onions and dicing the tofu. ..take the corn starch and place in a bowl and now take tofu and a few pieces at a time and cover it with the cornstarch then fry them till golden brown
4. After you have fried up all the pieces take your Wok or fry pan heat up the pan with oil as needed and saute the peppers and onions for about 2 to 3 min then add the tofu and finish off with the chili sauce make sure it glazes over all the tofu
5. Now plate it up add the Thai basil and enjoy

Thai Fried Bananas

Servings: 3-4 | Prep: 5m | Cook: 10m | Ready In: 15m

Ingredients

- 2 tablespoons butter
- 4 fresh, firm bananas, peeled and cut into 1 to 2-inch pieces
- 1/4 cup brown sugar
- 1 teaspoon black sesame seeds
- 1 lime, juiced

Directions

- Heat a Wok over high heat and add 2 tablespoons of butter. Once melted, toss in bananas and add the 1/4 cup of sugar. Cook down sugar and add the sesame seeds and the lime juice. Stir together and serve.

Vegan Thai Peanut Tofu Stir Fry

"This is a recipe I came up with last summer which I thought was pretty good. I found my old profile on Allthecooks, so i redid the recipe here"

Servings: 4 | **Time**: 30m

Ingredients

- 2 tbsp virgin coconut oil
- 2 green onions, sliced thin
- 4 cloves garlic, minced
- 2 mushrooms, sliced
- 4 sundried tomatoes, chopped
- 1 cup fresh basil, chopped
- 1/4 cup coconut flakes
- 1/4 cup cashews
- 1 package firm tofu, cubed
- Mr Spice Organic Thai Peanut Sauce
- 2 tbsp red or yellow curry
- water

Directions

1. Heat coconut oil in a large pan, and sautée the green onion, garlic, mushroom, and sundried tomatoes.
2. After a few minutes, add basil, coconut flakes and cashews
3. Add tofu cubes, sauce, curry, add a bit of water. Let simmer until flavours are fully absorbed by the tofu

Chapter 13: Vegetarian Recipes

***

Asian Vegetable Stir-Fry

"This vegetarian stir-fry recipe is particularly low in calories. To make it a more substantial main dish, add tofu or chicken."

Servings: 6

Ingredients

- 2 tablespoons tomato paste
- 1 tablespoon rice vinegar
- 1 tablespoon low-sodium soy sauce
- 1 teaspoon curry powder
- 1/2 teaspoon salt
- 1/8 teaspoon black pepper
- 2 tablespoons oil
- 1 Vidalia or other sweet onion, cut into 8 wedges
- 1 medium zucchini, quartered lengthwise and cut into 1-inch-thick slices (about 2 cups)
- 1 medium yellow squash, quartered lengthwise and cut into 1-inch-thick slices (about 2 cups)
- 1 cup chopped celery
- 2 cups (1/4-inch-thick) sliced green bell pepper
- 1/2 cup water
- 1/4 cup drained, sliced water chestnuts
- 2 cups thinly sliced napa (Chinese) cabbage
- 1 tablespoon pine nuts

Directions

1. Combine first 6 ingredients in a small bowl; set aside.
2. Heat oil in a stir-fry pan or Wok over medium heat. Add onion; stir-fry 1 minute. Increase heat to medium-high. Add zucchini, yellow squash, and celery; stir-fry 5 minutes. Add bell pepper, water, and water chestnuts; stir-fry 3 minutes.
3. Add tomato paste mixture; bring to a boil, and cook 1 minute. Stir in cabbage and pine nuts.

Bibimbop (Rice and Vegetable Medley)

"Bibimbop is a popular Korean one-dish lunch of piping hot rice, an assortment of vegetables, often a small bit of meat, and always an egg on top. Koreans like this spicy, so they usually add at least 2 tablespoons chile paste per serving after cooking. It's customary to stir everything together before eating; omit that step to taste each element independently."

Servings: 4

Ingredients

- 2 teaspoons low-sodium soy sauce
- 1/2 teaspoon minced peeled fresh ginger
- 1 garlic clove, minced
- 4 ounces eye of round or top round steak, thinly sliced
- Cooking spray
- 1 cup (2-inch) julienne-cut carrot
- 1 cup (2-inch) julienne-cut English cucumber
- 1/2 teaspoon sesame seeds, toasted
- 1/2 teaspoon rice vinegar
- 1/8 teaspoon kosher salt
- 1/8 teaspoon dark sesame oil
- 1 garlic clove, minced
- 4 large eggs, divided
- 1/4 teaspoon kosher salt
- 3 cups hot cooked short-grain rice
- 1 cup thinly sliced shiitake mushroom caps
- 1 cup Seasoned Spinach
- 4 teaspoons sambal oelek or Thai chile paste

Preparation

1. Combine first 4 ingredients in a zip-top plastic bag. Seal and marinate in refrigerator 30 minutes. Heat a small nonstick skillet coated with cooking spray over medium-high heat. Add beef mixture; stir-fry 3 minutes or until done. Remove from pan. Cover and keep warm.
2. Cook carrot in boiling water 1 minute or until crisp-tender. Drain. Rinse with cold water; drain and set aside.

3. Combine cucumber and next 5 ingredients (cucumber through 1 garlic clove); set aside.
4. Heat skillet coated with cooking spray over medium-high heat. Break 1 egg into hot skillet. Cook egg 1 minute; carefully turn over. Sprinkle with dash of salt. Cook an additional minute or until desired degree of doneness. Remove from pan. Cover and keep warm. Repeat procedure with remaining eggs and salt.
5. Spoon 3/4 cup rice into each of 4 bowls. Arrange 1/4 cup each of beef, carrot, cucumber mixture, mushrooms, and Seasoned Spinach over each serving. Top each serving with 1 egg and 1 teaspoon sambal oelek.

Ginger Vegetable Stir-fry

Servings: 4

Ingredients

- 1 tbsp cornstarch
- 3 cloves garlic, minced
- 2 tsp fresh ginger, grated, divided
- 3 tsp olive oil, divided
- 1 head broccoli, chopped
- 1 cup snow peas, trimmed
- 1 cup carrot chips
- 1 cup bell peppers, diced
- 2 tbsp soy sauce
- 1/2 tbsp water
- 1/2 sweet onion, chopped
- 1 tsp salt

Directions

1. Mix cornstarch, garlic, 1 tsp ginger, and 2 tsp oil until well dissolved
2. Mix with broccoli, snow peas, carrots, and bell peppers until evenly coated.
3. Heat remaining tsp oil in large skillet Add onions and cook until tender.

4. Add remaining veggies, cook for 2 minutes stirring constantly.
5. Stir is soy sauce, water, salt and remaining ginger. Cook until vegetables are your desired tenderness.

Nikki's BAE Vegetarian Udon Noodle Stir-Fry

"My youngest daughter is vegetarian and was complaining last night that there "wasn't anything in the house for me to eat" - Challenge Accepted, found all of these ingredients and promptly whipped up this dish for her. The fact that she said it was BAE (before Anything / Anyone Else) was THE best compliment she could have given me. Thought I'd share"

Servings: 4 | **Time**: 20m

Ingredients

- 1 tbsp coconut oil
- 1/4 cup water
- 1 head broccoli
- 8 oz cauliflower
- 8 oz asparagus
- 1 red bell pepper
- 1 can black beans (rinsed and drained)
- 2 packages Udon noodles
- 1/4 cup soy sauce
- 1 avocado-puree

Directions

1. In a large sauté pan or Wok, heat oil and water to simmering point then add vegetables. Begin to stir-fry vegetables for five minutes
2. Continue to stir-fry for another minute, then add Udon noodles, soy sauce and avocado-puree (I make an avocado-lime puree that I keep on hand in a squeeze bottle in the refrigerator) . Combine all of the ingredients together for 3 to 4 minutes to allow the noodles to absorb some of the sauce.
3. Enjoy

Ramen Vegetable Stir Fry

"Quick, cheap, healthy ish, and tasty. When you don't feel like cooking, this is super easy and brainless."

Servings: 4 | **Time**: 20m

Ingredients

- 2 frozen vegetable stir fry bags
- 2 top ramen packets
- 12 oz chicken breast, chopped
- 1 sweet n sour mix
- 1 tbsp vegetable oil

Directions

1. Boil water for the top ramen. Discard the flavor packets. Cook while you prep and get other pan ready.
2. Get pan hot (Wok works best), and add oil. Add chicken. Cook until no longer pink. About 3 minutes.
3. Add frozen veggies. Stir and cook for about 5 minutes. Add noodles and mix in.
4. Add sauce. I used sweet n sour. You can also use teriyaki or any other sauce you like. Mix and cook another couple of minutes, about 5.

Simple Vegetable Stir Fry

"Great as a side dish and easy to prepare."

Servings: 4 | **Cook**: 15m

Ingredients

- 1 yellow pepper (sliced)
- 6 medium mushrooms (sliced)

- 6 baby sweetcorn (sliced in half)
- 2 small Tat soi (leaves whole with stalks chopped)
- 50 grams Snow pea (cut in half)
- 2 tbsp ground nut oil
- 1/4 tsp seasoned Salt

Directions

1. Prepare all your vegetables before cooking.
2. In a Wok heat the oil on a medium heat.
3. Add the corn and thicker stalks in first as they take slightly longer to cook. Cook for around 2 minutes.
4. Add all the other vegetables other than the mushrooms and leaves. Cook for a further 3-4 minutes. Stir occasionally.
5. Add the salt.
6. Add the mushrooms and leaves and cook for a further 2-3 minutes. Stirring regularly.
7. And serve when done.

Slivered Vegetable and Tofu Stir-Fry

"One of the most important things for a stir-fry is to have everything cut uniformly, so it cooks evenly," says Chef Martin Yan. Once you've done that, this fresh, lightly crunchy dish cooks in about 5 minutes. It's great with noodles or rice."

Servings: 4 | **Total time:** 45m

Ingredients

- 2 tablespoons vegetable oil
- 1 teaspoon mashed or minced fresh ginger
- 1 teaspoon mashed or minced garlic
- 1/2 cup julienned jicama
- 1 small carrot, thinly sliced on a diagonal and julienned
- 1/4 red onion, thinly sliced lengthwise and separated into slivers to make 1/2 cup
- 4 asparagus spears, sliced on a long diagonal 1/4 in. thick
- 1 1/2 cups (about 6 oz.) julienned baked tofu*, such as teriyaki flavor

- 5 medium mushrooms, thinly sliced
- 1/2 red bell pepper, parallel cut and julienned
- 2 tablespoons prepared oyster sauce; or use hoisin for a vegetarian dish
- 1 tablespoon soy sauce
- 1 teaspoon toasted sesame oil
- Sriracha chili sauce (optional)

Directions

1. Heat a Wok or large frying pan over high heat until hot. Add vegetable oil, swirling to coat sides. Add ginger and garlic; cook, stirring until fragrant, 10 to 15 seconds. "I put in the things that take longest to cook first: jicama, carrot, onion, and asparagus," says Yan. Add them and the tofu with about 2 tbsp. water; stir-fry until asparagus turns bright green, 1 to 2 minutes.
2. Add mushrooms and bell pepper with 1 more tbsp. water; stir-fry until vegetables are tender-crisp, about 1 minute.
3. Quickly combine oyster and soy sauces with sesame oil and add to Wok. "Always put sesame oil in toward the end," Yan says. If it goes in too early, "it loses its aroma." Add a little Sriracha if you like.

*Find baked tofu (sometimes called pressed tofu) at well-stocked grocery stores.

Stir-Fried Egg Noodles with Vegetables

"Stir-Fried Egg Noodles with Vegetables makes a great side dish to chicken, beef, pork or fish. Or consider adding protein to these Stir-Fried Egg Noodles for a one-skillet-meal."

Servings: 6 | **Prep**: 20m | **Cook**: 10m

Ingredients

- Salt
- 8 ounces wide egg noodles
- 1 tablespoon vegetable oil
- 2 cloves garlic, minced
- 1 tablespoon minced fresh ginger

- 1/2 cup chopped scallions (about 4)
- 1 small red bell pepper, seeded and thinly sliced
- 3 small carrots, sliced 1/4-inch thick (about 1 cup)
- 1 1/2 cups snow peas, trimmed, halved
- 3/4 cup low-sodium chicken broth
- 4 tablespoons reduced-sodium soy sauce
- 1/4 teaspoon crushed red pepper
- 1 tablespoon sesame oil, optional

Directions

1. Bring a large pot of salted water to a boil. Cook egg noodles according to package label directions until tender, about 9 minutes. Drain well.
2. Warm oil in a skillet over medium-high heat. Stir-fry garlic, ginger and scallions for 30 seconds. Add bell pepper and carrots; stir-fry for 3 minutes. Add snow peas and stir-fry for 30 seconds.
3. Stir in broth, soy sauce and red pepper. Bring to a boil and cook, stirring constantly, until slightly thickened, 3 to 4 minutes. Add noodles; stir until thoroughly heated, about 1 minute. Drizzle with sesame oil before serving, if desired.

Sunshine's Steak And Vegetable Stir Fry

"oh this is goood"

Servings: 4

Ingredients

- 1 lb sirloin steak
- 1/4 cup soy sauce
- 1 tbsp minced garlic
- 1/2 tsp ground ginger
- 1/4 cup vegetable oil
- 1 cup sliced green onions (1 inch slices)
- 1/2 cup green peppers cut into 1 inch squares
- 1/2 cup red peppers cut into 1 inch squares
- 2 stalks celery chopped

- 1 tbsp cornstarch
- 1 salt and.pepper to taste
- 1/2 cup chopped white onions
- 1/2 cup water divided

Directions

1. Cut sirloin into strips, combines the next 3 ingredients, in a shallow container mix well add steak, let set in refrigerator for 30 minutes
2. In a heated skillet with the vegetable oil, put in the steak and soy sauce mixture, brown meat for 3 minutes,
3. Now add ur onion,green onion, bell peppers and celery, cook for 8 minutes, stirring constantly,until vegetables are cooked and tender. Remove the meat and vegetables into a bowl set aside
4. Combine your cornstarch and 1 cup water , mix well pour into liquid in skillet , mix well.cook and stir, until smooth and thick, add meat and veggies, add 1/2 cup water more to mixture, let it come to a boil then trun down heat to a low simer, cook for another 5 minutes.add salt and pepper to taste. Done let set 10 minutes before serving...... Serve over hot white rice...enjoy!!!!

Tempura Vegetables with Soy Sauce

Servings: 6 | *Prep*: 10m | *Cook*: 10m | *Ready In*: 20m

Ingredients

- 1 cup all-purpose flour
- 1/4 cup cornstarch
- 1 teaspoon salt
- 1 cup club soda, chilled
- Vegetable oil
- 1 red pepper, cut into large chunks
- Large handful green beans, trimmed
- 1 medium zucchini, sliced on a bias
- 1/2 cup soy sauce, for dipping

Directions

- Sift first 3 ingredients over a large mixing bowl. Add 1/2 cup of chilled club soda and mix with chop sticks or fork. Add the rest of the club soda and mix. Be careful not to over mix. The lumps give the tempura batter its unique texture. Over moderately high heat fill a deep pan or Wok with about 3 inches of vegetable oil. Add vegetables sparingly to the batter making sure they are covered. Place vegetables 1 at a time in the oil and fry until batter has turned golden brown about 1 minute. Repeat until all vegetables have been cooked. Serve with soy sauce for dipping.

Tofu Vegetables Stir Fry I

"What to do with leftover fried tofu?"

Servings: 4 | **Time**: 20m

Ingredients

- 1 zucchini sliced diagonally
- 1 carrot sliced diagonally
- 2 c. long beans cut in half
- 1 c. leftover fried tofu
- 2 tbs vegetarian oyster sauce
- 1 tsp soy sauce
- pinch ground pepper
- 1 c. walnuts

Directions

1. In frying pan, add little oil and beans first, fry medium heat 5 min. Then add sliced carrots and zucchini, fried tofu, and walnuts, fry another 5 min.
2. Add veg. Oyster sauce, soy sauce, ground pepper and stir to coat for another minute.

Tofu-Vegetable Stir-Fry II

Servings: 4 | **Prep**: 15m | **Cook**: 10m | **Ready In**: 25m

Ingredients

- 1 cup white or jasmine rice
- 3 tablespoons low-sodium soy sauce
- 3 tablespoons hoisin sauce
- 2 tablespoons balsamic vinegar
- 1 tablespoon Asian chile sauce (such as Sriracha)
- 2 teaspoons cornstarch
- 2 tablespoons sesame oil
- 4 scallions, sliced (white and green parts separated)
- 2 cloves garlic, minced
- 1 -inch piece ginger, peeled and finely chopped
- 4 ounces shiitake mushrooms, stemmed and chopped
- 4 ounces snow peas
- 14 -ounce package soft tofu, drained and cut into 1-inch cubes

Directions

1. Cook the rice as the label directs. Meanwhile, whisk the soy sauce, hoisin sauce, vinegar, chile sauce, cornstarch and 1 cup water in a small bowl until smooth; set aside.
2. Heat the sesame oil in a Wok or large skillet over medium-high heat. Add the scallion whites, garlic and ginger and stir-fry 30 seconds. Add the mushrooms and stir-fry until golden brown and tender, about 3 minutes. Add the snow peas and stir-fry 30 more seconds.
3. Whisk the reserved soy sauce mixture and add it to the Wok. Bring to a simmer, then add the tofu. Cook, stirring occasionally, until the sauce is thick, about 2 minutes. Sprinkle with the scallion greens.
4. Fluff the rice with a fork and divide among bowls. Top with the stir-fry and sauce.

Vegetable Fried Rice with Bacon

Servings: 4 | *Prep*: 20m | *Cook*: 5m | *Ready In*: 25m

Ingredients

- 1 tablespoon vegetable oil
- 1/4 pound thick-cut bacon, cut into 1/4-inch pieces
- 3/4 teaspoon sugar
- 2 1/4 teaspoons soy sauce
- 3 cloves garlic, thinly sliced
- 1 2-inch piece ginger, peeled and minced
- 1/4 to 1/2 teaspoon red pepper flakes
- 1/2 head broccoli, florets and stalks cut into 1/4-inch pieces
- 5 cups cooked long-grain white rice
- 1/4 cup low-sodium chicken broth
- 4 large eggs
- 1 bunch watercress, stems removed
- Spicy mustard or chili sauce, for serving (optional)

Directions

1. Place a Wok or large skillet over high heat. Add the vegetable oil and bacon and stir-fry until golden and crisp, about 2 minutes. Sprinkle the sugar over the bacon and toss. Add 1/4 teaspoon soy sauce (watch out-the oil will bubble up) and continue to stir-fry until the bacon is glazed, about 30 seconds. Transfer the bacon to a bowl with a slotted spoon. Add the garlic, ginger and red pepper flakes to the drippings in the pan and stir-fry until fragrant, about 30 seconds. Add the broccoli and cook until crisp, 2 to 3 minutes. Add the rice, the remaining 2 teaspoons soy sauce, the broth and glazed bacon. Toss to heat through.
2. Push the fried rice to one side of the pan, crack the eggs into the other side and scramble until set, about 1 minute. Mix the eggs into the rice and stir in the watercress. Divide among bowls and serve with mustard or chili sauce, if desired.

Vegetable Fried Rice

"When you're making instant brown rice for this recipe, add extra flavor by cooking the rice in vegetable broth (a 14-ounce can) instead of 1 3/4 cups

water."

Servings: 4 | **Prep**: 5m | **Cook**: 7m | Ready In: 12m

Ingredients

- 2 teaspoons dark sesame oil
- 3/4 cup sliced shiitake mushrooms
- 1/2 cup matchstick-cut carrots
- 1/2 cup sliced green onions
- 2 teaspoons bottled minced garlic
- 1/4 teaspoon pepper
- 4 cups chilled cooked brown rice
- 1 large egg, lightly beaten
- 2 tablespoons low-sodium soy sauce
- 1 tablespoon water
- 3 tablespoons dry white wine
- 1/3 cup frozen green peas

Directions

- Heat sesame oil in a large nonstick skillet over high heat. Add mushrooms and next 4 ingredients; stir-fry until tender. Add cooked rice; stir-fry 2 minutes. Push rice mixture to sides of pan, forming a well in center. Add egg to center of pan, and let cook 30 seconds; toss with rice, and stir-fry until egg is cooked. Stir in soy sauce and remaining ingredients; cook until thoroughly heated.

Thai Fried BananasVegetable Pad Thai

Servings: 4-6 | **Prep**: 40m | **Inactive**: 15m | **Cook**: 10m | **Ready In**: 1h5m

Ingredients

- 1 (12-ounce) pack dried rice stick noodles (sen lek)
- 6 eggs
- 1/4 cup vegetable oil
- 2 tablespoons smashed garlic

- 2 tablespoons finely chopped onion
- 1/2 cup red bell peppers, julienned
- 1/2 cup green bell peppers, julienned
- 1/2 cup ground peanut
- 1/2 cup fish sauce
- 1/2 cup soy sauce
- 1/4 cup sugar
- 2 teaspoons Thai pepper powder
- 1 cup fresh bean sprouts, for garnish
- 1/4 cup shelled peanuts, for garnish
- 2 tablespoons chopped fresh cilantro leaves, for garnish

Directions

1. Soak the rice stick noodles in tepid water for about 15 minutes. Remove them to a cutting board and cut into 4-inch pieces then place in a strainer to let all water drain off, and set aside.
2. Coat the bottom of an omelette pan with a small amount of oil and pour off excess. Beat the eggs together and add to pan forming a thin layer, and cook as you would a thin omelette. Remove from heat and chop cooked egg roughly and set aside, keeping warm until ready to serve.
3. Heat the oil over medium-high heat in a Wok or large skillet and add garlic, onion, and red and green peppers, and cook for 2 minutes. One at a time, add the ground peanut, fish sauce, soy sauce, sugar and pepper powder, stirring the mixture the entire time. (Note: chicken, shrimp, or tofu can be added to this dish at the saute stage.) Add the noodles and be sure to stir! The noodles tend to burn if not continuously stirred. Check to see if the taste of the dish is suitable to you, if not, then add in either fish sauce or soy sauce (both salty), or sugar (sweet). (Here is where a matter of preference comes into play.) To serve, place the noodle mixture on a plate, top with cooked egg and garnish with bean sprouts, peanuts and cilantro.

Vegetable Udon Wok

Servings: 2 | Ready In: 40m

Ingredients

- 100 g udon noodles
- sesame seeds

Veggies:

- 1 onion
- 1 carrot
- 150 g broccoli
- 1/3 red bell pepper
- 100 g soja shoots
- 75 g corn

The sauce:

- 150 ml water
- 1 tbsp soja sauce
- 1 tbsp oyster sauce
- 1 tbsp apple cider vinegar
- 1 tbsp sugar
- 1 clove garlic
- 1.5 cm fresh ginger

Directions

2. Chop onions, carrots and the bell pepper to long strips and broccoli to small florets.
3. Fry all veggies adding them to the pan in the same order as listed. Fry until nice and aromatic and starting to brown, preferably with a little butter.
4. Prepare the sauce. Grate the garlic and ginger and add the rest of the ingredients.
5. Boil noodles according to instructions on the packet.
6. And finally mix everything together on the pan.
7. Serve and garnish with some sesame seeds. Enjoy !

Vegetables and Chickpeas Wok

"Very delicious. The chickpeas are a good variation for pasta or rice :hungry"

Servings: 3

Ingredients

- 3 medium Carrots
- 2 clove Garlic
- 1 Onion (I used red onion)
- 2 Leek Stalks
- 3 Fresh Tomatos
- 1 Chicken Cube
- 1 Pepper and basil to taste
- 1 Parsley to taste
- 1 can Chickpeas (about 400grams)

Directions

1. Peel and dice carrots, onion, garlic, tomatos and leek
2. Heat oil in a Wok
3. Add onions and fry till glazed
4. Add carrots and fry till softened
5. Add leek and mix well
6. Add chicken cube
7. Add tomatos and mix well
8. Season with pepper and basil
9. Add chickpeas
10. Let sit for a moment and finish with some parsley
11. It is important to stir a lot to mix everything well but you also have to let it rest every once in a while to really cook through

Chapter 14: More Wok Recipes

***

Amazing! Boneless BBQ Rib Stir Fry!!

"I wanted to use up leftover boneless BBQ rib meat and I sure found a way and this is a new fave of mine!! the interesting flavors that come together is so delicious!"

Servings: 4 | **Cook**: 25m

Ingredients

- 1 packages boneless bbq rib meat (use about 4 strips or 3 even depends on how many guests you may have) i bought mine from costco fyi
- 1 cup julienned carrots
- 2 cup sliced cabbage (the greenish colored one, not red)
- 1 cup sliced onion
- 2 clove garlic minced
- 3 tbsp soy sauce
- 2 dash sriracha or red pepper flakes
- 2 cup steamed long grain white rice or if you prefer brown that's cool too.
- 1 salt and pepper to your liking
- 4 tbsp olive oil

Directions

1. Cook your white rice according to packaging directions
2. Cook your bbq rib meat accordingly as well then chop and dice into small pieces
3. In a Wok or a pan add your onion carrots garlic in medium heat with 2 tablespoons of olive oil saute for 2 minutes or so
4. Now go ahead and add your garlic and cabbage. Mix together then add chopped rib meat and soy sauce and sriracha or red pepper flakes and fold into your total mixture.
5. Serve your veggie & rib mixture over steamed rice add soy sauce if you wish
6. Eat hot & enjoy!!

Aninikad / Sea Snail Garlic Butter Stirfry

"Ah! This is one of those shellfish that makes my weekend. I don't mind waking up at 5am just to visit the seafoods market and hope to grab these beauties.

We end up eating almost all 3 servings when I realized I haven't taken a photo of the finish product... so the actual photo of the dish (what's left of it) can be found in step 7.

bemski bemski"

Servings: 3 | **Ready In**: 20-30m

Ingredients

- 1/2 kilo aninikad or sea snail
- 4 tomatoes chopped
- 1/4 cup butter (salted/ unsalted)
- 2 inches sliced ginger approx
- 1 large onion chopped
- 8 cloves garlic chopped
- 2 tbsp parmesan cheese
- to taste salt and pepper
- green onions for garnish
- 2 tbsp cooking oil

Directions

1. Clean the shells throughly by scrubbing using a wire brush. Be sure to remove moss and sand. The picture below shows what a sea snail looks like before cleaning.
2. The sea snail shells will look pretty, shiny and its pattern are more clear when cleaned. Aren't they pretty? 🙂
3. Boil the cleaned sea snails in a pot with onions, 2 cloves garlic, ginger, tomatoes, salt and pepper. Cook until a portion of the meat or 'feet' comes out. The 'feet' is the small shell like thing that's attached at the tip of the meat.
4. Once cooked, drain the sea snails and set aside.
5. In another pan, heat up oil and add remaining onions, garlic, tomatoes and ginger.
6. When onions become transparent, add in the cooked sea snails, butter and parmesan.

7. Add salt and pepper to taste. Optional: papprika and oregano.
8. You will need a sterilizes safety pin to remove the meat from the shell.

Ants in a Tree

Servings: 4-6 | **Prep**: *15m* | **Cook**: *25m* | **Ready In**: *40m*

Ingredients

- Kosher salt
- 1/2 pound cellophane noodles (bean threads) or angel hair pasta
- 1 pound ground pork
- 1/4 cup soy sauce
- 1 tablespoon Asian (toasted) sesame oil
- 2 teaspoons cornstarch
- 6 scallions, white and green parts, thinly sliced
- 3 tablespoons vegetable oil
- 1 (2-inch) piece fresh ginger, peeled and finely grated
- 4 garlic cloves, minced
- 1 tablespoon Asian chile paste
- 2 cups shredded Napa cabbage
- 2/3 cup chicken stock, preferably homemade
- Freshly ground black pepper

Directions

1. Bring a large pot of salted water to a boil over high heat. Add the noodles and bring back to a boil. Boil for 1 minute for cellophane noodles and 2 to 3 minutes for angel hair pasta. Drain in a colander and rinse under running water. Set aside.
2. Stir the pork with 2 tablespoons of the soy sauce, the sesame oil, the cornstarch, and 1/2 of the scallions in a small bowl.
3. Heat the vegetable oil in a Wok or large skillet over high heat until almost smoking. Add the ginger, garlic, and chile paste. Cook, stirring constantly, until fragrant, about 30 seconds. Add the pork mixture and cook for 1 minute longer. Stir in the cabbage and the remaining 2 tablespoons soy sauce. Cook, stirring, until the cabbage is almost wilted, 1 to 2 minutes. Add the cooked noodles and cook,

cutting them slightly with the side of the spatula, until the pork is no longer pink, about 1 minute. Pour in the chicken stock and add the remaining scallions. Season with salt and pepper and reduce the heat to medium-low. Cover loosely with foil and simmer until the noodles have absorbed some of the stock, about 3 minutes

Asian Rubbed Baby Back Ribs with Hoisin BBQ Sauce and Lotus Root Stir Fry

Servings: 4-6 | *Prep*: 15 m | *Cook*: 3 h 25 m | *Ready In*: 3 h 40 m

Ingredients

- 3 pounds baby back ribs
- 1/2 cup canola oil
- Asian Essence (Chinese five-spice powder, clove, salt and pepper)
- Stock or sake, for steaming
- 3 tablespoons chopped garlic
- 1 tablespoon minced fresh ginger
- 12 cups chicken stock
- 2/3 cup hoisin sauce
- 2 tablespoons miso
- 1 tablespoon sake
- 1 tablespoon soy sauce
- 2 teaspoons honey
- 2 teaspoons chili paste with garlic
- 1 small bunch fresh cilantro, leaves chopped
- 1/2 bunch fresh parsley, leaves chopped

For Lotus Root Stir-fry:

- 1 tablespoon roughly chopped garlic
- 3 cups thinly sliced lotus root
- 1 cup chicken stock
- 1 cup blanched soy beans

Directions

1. Preheat oven to 300 degrees F. Place ribs in a large baking dish and rub with blend of spices. Place dish into oven for 3 hours, occasionally adding stock or sake into the pan to help steam the ribs.
2. In a medium saucepan over medium heat, add garlic and ginger and saute until fragrant. Add additional ingredients and whisk to combine.
3. Serve ribs directly from oven with Hoisin BBQ sauce and Lotus Root Stir-Fry.
4. For Lotus Root Stir-fry:
   In a large saute pan or Wok over high heat, add garlic and saute until fragrant. Add lotus root and cook for 2 minutes. Add stock and cook an additional minute. Turn off heat, mix in soy beans and serve.

Asian Snap Pea Salad with Sesame-Orange Dressing

"Vitamin C from the orange juice, bell pepper, and peas helps your body absorb iron in this asian snap pea salad. And with only 89 calories, who could resist? Serve with stir-fried chicken breast and brown rice or buckwheat noodles to complement the nutrient-rich package."

Servings: 6

Ingredients

Dressing:

- 1 large orange
- 1 tablespoon rice vinegar
- 2 teaspoons low-sodium soy sauce
- 1 1/2 teaspoons dark sesame oil
- 1 teaspoon brown sugar
- 1 teaspoon hot chile sauce (such as Sriracha)

Salad:

- 2 teaspoons canola oil
- 1 1/2 cups thinly sliced red bell pepper
- 3/4 cup thinly sliced carrot

- 12 ounces sugar snap peas, trimmed
- 1/2 teaspoon kosher salt
- 1/2 cup diagonally cut green onions
- 1 (6-ounce) package fresh baby spinach
- 1 teaspoon sesame seeds, toasted

Directions

1. To prepare dressing, grate 1 teaspoon rind; squeeze 1/3 cup juice from orange over a bowl. Set rind aside. Combine juice, vinegar, and next 4 ingredients (through chile sauce) in a small bowl; stir with a whisk.
2. To prepare salad, heat 2 teaspoons canola oil in a large nonstick skillet over medium-high heat. Add bell pepper and carrot to pan; sauté 1 minute, stirring occasionally. Add reserved orange rind, sugar snap peas, and salt to pan; sauté 2 minutes, stirring occasionally. Transfer pea mixture to a large bowl; cool 5 minutes. Stir in green onions and spinach. Pour dressing over salad; toss gently to coat. Sprinkle with sesame seeds. Serve immediately.

Bacon and Tofu stir-fry in Japanese Style gravy

"Japanese style stir-fry with gravy (It's called "An-kake, pronounced "kakay"). Made with whatever I found in the fridge. You can use any vegetable or meat for this dish. I used home-made bacon to add flavor, but you can omit it if you are vegetarian. I would have added mushrooms if I had them. The gravy (An) is usually made with potato starch as a thickener, but you can use corn starch (or corn flour) if you don't have it. By the way, "kake" means to "pour over" so un-kake is a dish with gravy on it."

Servings: 6 | Ready In: 15m

Ingredients

- 3-4 slices bacon
- 3-4 green onions or half an onion
- 50 g carrot
- 1 block firm tofu (350g)
- 200 ml Chicken Broth
- 1/4 tsp salt

- 1-2 tsp soy sauce
- 1/2 Tbsp vegetable oil
- 2 tsp potato starch (or corn starch)

Directions

1. Cut the Tofu in half length wise and then cut it 2 cm wide. Place it in a pan and cover with water. Turn the heat on high and bring to boil. Reduce heat and simmer for 2 minutes and drain. This will prevent the tofu from falling apart when cooking.
2. Cut the bacon 1 cm wide. Slice the green onions diagonally 2 cm wide. Thinly slice the carrots into quarters.
3. Heat the vegetable oil in the skillet over medium heat and add the bacon, green onions and carrots.
4. Mix salt and soy sauce with the chicken broth and pour over the vegetables. Add the tofu and bring to boil. Turn down the heat to medium low and cook for 1 minute.
5. Mix potato starch with the same amount of water and pour over the tofu. Gently mix it until it thickens. Let it cook for 1 minute.
6. Remove from heat and serve immediately. The sauce will liquefy once it is cool. To thicken the sauce, reheat it until hot.

Balsamic Vinegar and Ginger Bok Choy

"This is a great vegetable to serve hot. Even those who turn up their noses at trying new things clean their plate!"

Servings: 4 | **Prep**: 15 m | **Cook**: 15 m | **Ready In**: 30 m

Ingredients

- 4 heads baby bok choy
- 3 tablespoons olive oil
- 1/4 cup water 2 tablespoons capers
- 1 1/2 teaspoons minced garlic
- 1 1/2 teaspoons minced fresh ginger root
- 2 tablespoons balsamic vinegar
- 1 dash fresh lemon juice, or to taste

Directions

1. Separate the leaves from the stems of the bok choy. Cut the stems into bite-sized chunks and shred the leaves.
2. Heat the olive oil in large skillet over medium heat.
3. Cook the bok choy stems in the oil until slightly tender, about 3 minutes; add the water and leaves and cook until the water evaporates, about 10 minutes more. Stir in the capers, garlic, and ginger; cook and stir 1 minute more. Sprinkle the vinegar and lemon juice over the bok choy and remove from heat; serve immediately.

Footnotes

- Tip: Aluminum foil helps keep food moist, ensures it cooks evenly, keeps leftovers fresh, and makes clean-up easy.

Basil Mushroom Stirfry - quick & easy side dish

"Serve as side to meat dishes."

Servings: 3 | **Time**: 20m

Ingredients

- 1 can button mushrooms, washed and drained
- 3 cloves garlic
- 1/4 bar butter or margarine
- 1 bunch fresh basil or 1 tsp dried
- to taste Salt & pepper

Directions

1. Melt butter in pan. Sauté garlic then drop in quarter sliced button mushrooms.
2. Season with salt and pepper. Sauté mushrooms until cooked (15m).
3. Drop in basil. (In photo: used dried) Mix in well. Turn off heat and transfer to serving plate.

Bekki's Mexican Egg Rolls

"This amazingly tasty recipe was given to me by my aunt about 10 years ago. My family has continued to make it often, and it always is a smashing success! It's adaptable for both for meat-eaters and vegetarians, and is great out of the oven and reheats well. It's a terrific dish for football parties and whenever you're attacked by the munchies. A vegetarian version of ground beef can also be used for the filling. "

Servings: 10 | **Prep**: 20m | **Cook**: 30m | **Ready In**: 50m

Ingredients

- 2 tablespoons vegetable oil
- 1 pound ground beef
- 1 large onion, chopped
- 5 cloves garlic, minced
- 1 red bell pepper, chopped
- 1 (1 ounce) package taco seasoning
- 1 (8 ounce) jar taco sauce
- 4 (16 ounce) packages egg roll wrappers
- 1 (1 pound) loaf processed cheese food (i.e. Velveeta®), cut into 1/4 inch thick slices
- 2 egg whites, lightly beaten
- 2 quarts canola oil

Directions

1. Place the vegetable oil and ground beef into a large skillet; cook over medium-high heat until the meat is evenly browned and no longer pink. Reduce the heat to medium. Mix in the onion, garlic, and bell pepper; cook until the vegetables are softened, about 5 minutes. Stir in the taco seasoning and taco sauce. Continue to cook and stir the mixture until the sauce begins to bubble, about 5 minutes more.
2. Working on a clean, flat surface, place 1 egg roll wrapper with a corner facing you. Place 1 tablespoon of the meat mixture in the center of the wrapper and top with a slice of cheese. Fold the corner closest to you over the meat mixture and roll the wrapper over the mixture 1-1/2 times. Fold in the two opposite side corners and continue rolling the wrapper so it covers these corners, tucking

them in. Dip two fingers in the egg whites and brush the remaining corner, pressing it to seal. Repeat these steps with a second egg roll wrapper. Let the egg roll rest briefly so the egg white dries and holds the last corner in place.
3. If the egg rolls will not be served right away, preheat oven to 325 degrees F (165 degrees C). Line a heat-proof dish with paper towels.
4. Pour the canola oil into a large Wok set over medium-high heat. When the oil begins to shimmer, carefully slip two to three egg rolls into the Wok. Cook until the wrappers turn golden brown and bubble slightly, 30 seconds to 1 minute. Use a slotted spoon or strainer to remove from the Wok. Place the egg rolls in the prepared dish and put the dish in the heated oven, making sure to remove it after 15 minute or lower the temperature. Continue cooking the remaining egg rolls.

Footnotes

- It is very important to use TWO egg roll wrappers and wrap them twice around the filling, tucking in the corners each time. If the egg roll is not double-wrapped and sealed, its contents will leak out when cooked.

Besan Ladoo

"Ladoos are an Indian and Pakistani sweet. I added a twist to mine and included coconut...my family loves these. They can be enjoyed at any holiday, as a treat during tea time, etc. And they're easy to make, in my opinion."

Servings: 10 | **Prep**: 25m | **Cook**: 20m | **Ready In**: 45m

Ingredients

- 3/4 cup ghee (clarified butter)
- 2 cups chickpea flour (besan)
- 1/2 cup shredded sweetened coconut (optional)
- 3 tablespoons ground almonds
- 1/2 cup superfine (castor) sugar
- 1/2 teaspoon ground cardamom

Directions

1. Heat the ghee in a Wok over low heat. Stir in the chickpea flour and cook over low heat until the chickpea flour is toasted and the mixture smells fragrant, about 10 minutes. The mixture should be pasty, not powdery.
2. Remove the mixture from the heat and cool slightly until it is warm, not hot. Grind the coconut, if using, in a coffee grinder until fine. Add the ground almonds, superfine sugar, ground coconut, and ground cardamom to the Wok and mix thoroughly.
3. While the mixture is warm, shape it into round balls that are about 1- to 1 1/4 inches in diameter. Store the ladoos in an airtight container and let them sit for 2 to 3 hours to cool completely. They can be eaten immediately, but taste better after several hours.

Cook's Note

- I use a coffee grinder to grind the nuts (I recommend a combination of cashews, pistachios, almonds, and pecans). I also grind granulated sugar, coconut, and cardamom in the coffee grinder until fine.

Best Bok Choy

Servings: 4 | **Prep**: 15m | **Cook**: 8m | **Ready In:** 23m

Ingredients

- 2 tablespoons grapeseed oil
- 1 medium red onion, thinly sliced
- 1 red bell pepper, julienned
- 1/2 cups green beans, ends trimmed, cut into 2 to 3-inch pieces
- 2 cups cremini mushrooms, wiped clean, halved and sliced
- 3 baby bok choy, sliced into 1/2-inch pieces
- 3 cloves garlic, thinly sliced
- 1 tablespoon soy sauce
- 2 teaspoons fish sauce
- Freshly cracked black pepper

Directions

1. In a Wok or large saute pan, add the grapeseed oil and when almost smoking, add the onions and bell peppers. Saute, stirring constantly, for 2 minutes. Add the green beans and mushrooms and cook for 2 minutes more.
2. Add the bok choy, garlic, soy sauce, and fish sauce and saute until just wilted. Add pepper, to taste, and serve immediately.
3. Recipe courtesy of Guy Fieri

Breakfast Veggie Stir Fry on Toast

"This recipe basically came from me needing to use up leftover veggies and wanting to make something a little different for breakfast."

Ingredients

- 1/4 cup red onion, chopped
- 1 red bell pepper, chopped
- 1 cup asparagus, chopped
- 6 portobello mushrooms, sliced
- 2 tbsp soy sauce
- 1 tbsp oyster sauce
- 1 tbsp teriyaki sauce
- 1 tbsp dijon mustard
- 1/2 tsp prepared horseradish
- 1/2 tsp black pepper
- 1 slice multigrain bread
- 1 small sprinkle of shredded mozerella cheese
- 1 hard-boiled egg

Directions

1. In a medium saucepan add veggies, soy sauce, oyster sauce, teriyaki sauce, dijon mustard, horseradish and black pepper. Saute until veggies are tender.

2. Toast bread slice and spoon sautéed veggies over top. Sprinkle with shredded mozerella cheese to melt. (can pop it in the microwave for 10 to 15 seconds as well)
3. Top the veggies and cheese with a sliced hard-boiled egg. Season egg with salt & pepper or whichever seasonings you prefer.

Broccoli and Tofu Stir Fry

"I like to serve this broccoli and tofu stir fry over white rice. If you don't have cashews, pecans or almonds will work as well."

***Servings**: 4 | **Prep**: 5m | **Cook**: 25m | **Ready In**: 30m*

Ingredients

- 1 tablespoon peanut oil
- 4 cloves garlic, minced
- 1 red bell pepper, seeded and sliced into strips
- 2 crowns broccoli, cut into florets
- 1/3 cup chicken broth
- 3 tablespoons soy sauce
- 1 tablespoon dry sherry
- 2 teaspoons cornstarch
- 8 ounces extra firm tofu, diced
- 2 tablespoons cashew pieces

Directions

1. Heat peanut oil in a Wok or large skillet over high heat. Stir in garlic and cook for a few seconds until it begins to brown. Add the bell pepper and broccoli; cook until the pepper begins to brown and soften, about 5 minutes.
2. Stir together the chicken broth, soy sauce, sherry, and cornstarch until dissolved. Pour the sauce into the Wok and bring to a boil. Stir in the tofu, and cook until hot, about 1 minute. Garnish with cashew pieces to serve.

Brussels Sprouts with Mushrooms and Ginger

*Servings: 4 | **Prep**: 10m | **Cook**: 15m | **Ready In**: 25m*

Ingredients

- 8 ounces shiitake mushrooms, stems removed
- 3 tablespoons vegetable oil
- Kosher salt and freshly ground black pepper
- 1 pound Brussels sprouts, stem ends trimmed, quartered
- 1 tablespoon peeled and grated fresh ginger
- 1 cup chicken broth (not low sodium)

Directions

1. Cut the shiitake caps into bite-size pieces (quartered or halved, depending on the size).
2. Heat 2 tablespoons of the vegetable oil over high heat in a Wok or large skillet. When almost smoking, add the mushrooms, season with salt and pepper and cook until browned and slightly crispy, 3 to 4 minutes, stirring once halfway through. Resist the urge to move them too much unless they are burning. Remove to a plate. Lower the heat to medium-high and add the remaining tablespoon oil and the Brussels sprouts. Season with salt and pepper and cook until browned or charred on one side, about 3 minutes. Stir in the ginger and cook until aromatic and slightly browned, stirring constantly, about 15 seconds. Reduce the heat to medium. Add the chicken broth (the sprouts should be just submerged in the liquid) and cook at a rapid simmer until the sprouts are tender when pierced with a knife and the liquid has boiled away, 6 to 8 minutes more.
3. Return the mushrooms to the Wok, fold to combine and season. Serve on a platter.

Buddha's Delight with Tofu, Broccoli, and Water Chestnuts

"This simple version of Buddha's Delight, a popular Chinese takeout dish, will work with just about any combination of vegetables."

Servings: 6

Ingredients

- 3 tablespoons low-sodium soy sauce
- 1 tablespoon dark sesame oil
- 1 tablespoon rice vinegar
- 1 teaspoon sugar
- 1 (14-ounce) package water-packed extra-firm tofu, drained and cut into 1-inch cubes
- 5 cups small broccoli florets
- 1 1/2 cups (1/4-inch) diagonally sliced carrot
- 1/2 cup peeled, chopped broccoli stems
- 2 tablespoons canola oil
- 1 1/2 cups sliced green onions
- 1 tablespoon grated peeled fresh ginger
- 2 garlic cloves, minced
- 1 cup snow peas, trimmed
- 1 (14-ounce) can whole baby corn, drained
- 1 (8-ounce) can sliced water chestnuts, drained
- 1/2 cup vegetable broth
- 1 tablespoon cornstarch
- 1/2 teaspoon salt
- 4 cups hot cooked short-grain rice

Directions

1. Combine first 5 ingredients, tossing to coat; cover and marinate in refrigerator 1 hour. Drain in a colander over a bowl, reserving marinade.
2. Cook broccoli florets, carrot, and broccoli stems in boiling water 1 1/2 minutes; drain. Plunge into ice water. Drain.
3. Heat canola oil in a Wok or large nonstick skillet over medium-high heat. Add tofu; stir-fry 5 minutes or until lightly browned on all sides. Stir in onions, ginger, and garlic; stir-fry 30 seconds. Stir in broccoli mixture, snow peas, corn, and water chestnuts; stir-fry 1 minute. Combine broth and cornstarch, stirring with a whisk. Add cornstarch mixture, reserved marinade, and salt to pan; bring to a boil. Cook 2 1/2 minutes or until slightly thick, stirring constantly. Serve over rice.

Cabbage Coconut Stir Fry

"This is a South Indian dish. It is called "Thoran". You can replace cabbage with other vegetables like beans, carrot, beetroot etc or add them along with the cabbage. Change the amount of coconut used according to your wish. Add more or less. You can use any oil, but coconut oil adds more flavour. Slit the chillies,if you don't want spicy stir fry."

***Servings**: 2 | **Time**: 15m*

Ingredients

- 2 cup Cabbage
- 1/2 cup Grated Coconut
- 1 clove Garlic
- 1 medium Onion
- 1/4 tsp Turmeric Powder
- 2 Green Chillies
- 1 stick Curry Leaves
- 1/4 tsp Mustard Seeds
- 1 tbsp Coconut Oil
- Salt
- Method

Directions

1. Heat a pan & add the coconut oil. Put the mustard seeds into it. After one minute, chop the garlic & add it.
2. When the garlic starts to turn brown, chop the onion & add it. After a few minutes, add the chillies & curry leaves.
3. When the onion turns mushy, add the chopped cabbage into it. Mix the coconut & turmeric powder.
4. When the cabbage is half cooked, add the coconut. Add salt to taste. Mix & cook well.

Caribbean Jerk Stir-Fry

"This combination of Asian stir-fry and fiery Caribbean seasoning makes

sweet and spicy dish. Serve over hot cooked white rice."

Servings: 2 | ***Prep***: 15m | ***Cook***: 20m | ***Ready In***: 35m

Ingredients

- 1 tablespoon vegetable oil
- 1 green bell pepper, seeded and cubed
- 1 red bell pepper, seeded and cubed
- 1/4 cup sliced sweet onions
- 3/4 pound skinless, boneless chicken breast, cut into strips
- 2 1/2 teaspoons Caribbean jerk seasoning
- 1/2 cup plum sauce 1 tablespoon soy sauce
- 1/4 cup chopped roasted peanuts

Directions

- Heat the oil in a large skillet over medium-high heat. Cook and stir the bell pepper and onion in the oil until slightly tender, 5 to 7 minutes. Remove pepper and onion from the skillet and set aside. Add the chicken to the skillet; season with jerk seasoning; cook and stir chicken until no longer pink inside. Pour the plum sauce in with the chicken; add the bell peppers and onions; toss to combine. Cook until the peppers and onions are heated completely, 3 to 5 minutes. Sprinkle with soy sauce and chopped peanuts to serve.

Cauliflower and Tomato Stir-Fry

Ingredients

- 2 medium tomatoes
- 1 cauliflower
- 1 scallion
- 2 tablespoons oil
- 1 tablespoon ketchup
- 1 tablespoon sugar
- 1 teaspoon salt

Directions

1. Chop 1 scallion into 1 inch pieces. 2 medium tomatoes (about half pound), each cut into 6 wedges. And use your clean hands to separate 1 cauliflower into small pieces.
2. Heat 2 tablespoon oil in a pan over medium-high heat until hot. Add scallions and stir-fry until just softened, about 30 seconds.
3. Add tomatoes and cook, stirring and turning occasionally, until juices are released, around 4 to 6 minutes.
4. While the tomatoes turn soft, add 1 tablespoon of ketchup and 1 tablespoon of sugar, keep stirring.
5. Add cauliflowers and 1 cup of water, cook 10 to 12 minutes. Turning occasionally. In the end, add 1 teaspoon of salt and stir around thoroughly.
6. Serve it using a big plate!!

Celery & Carrot Kimpira Stir-fry

"Usually kimpira is made with gobo (burdock root and carrot), but I tried celery! It tastes so good! This will go great with rice or for your lunch (bento!!). If you like spicy stir fries, try adding a red chili or chili flakes. Leave it out if you don't or if making for kids ^^"

Servings: 3 | **Time**: 15m

Ingredients

- 2 stalks celery with leaves
- 1 carrot
- 1 dried red chili (if you want spicy flavor)
- 1 Tbsp sesame oil (or veg. oil)
- 1 tsp sugar
- 2 tsp mirin/sweet cooking sake
- 1 Tbsp soy sauce
- 1 pinch salt
- 1 handful katsuobushi/bonito flakes for dashi (Okay to leave out)

Directions

1. Slice the celery stalks into 1 cm diagonal pieces. Mince the leaves and set aside. Cut the carrot into thin matchsticks.
2. Heat oil in a frying pan. Add the celery stalks and carrots. Stir fry for a few minutes on medium until the celery and carrots are starting to get a little softer.
3. Add the sugar, mirin, soy sauce and salt. Keep stir frying until almost all of the liquid evaporates.
4. Add the chopped up celery leaves and stir fry for another 1 - 2 minutes.
5. Lastly put in a handful of katsuobushi (if you have it), mix and it's done ~♪
6. Enjoy! Sometimes I like to put some sesame seeds on top too ^^

Chef Kiran's Okra Stir Fry

"Okra, sweet and delish. Stir-fry turns okra golden brown and tender. I served as a side dish with grilled lamb or pork chops. Add rice and you have a complete quick meal."

Servings: 4 | **Prep**: 15m | **Cook**: 15m | **Ready In**: 30m

Ingredients

- 2 tablespoons vegetable oil
- 1 pound small okra
- 1/2 teaspoon ground turmeric
- 1 clove garlic, chopped
- 1/2 teaspoon chopped fresh ginger
- 2 onions, cut into quarters
- 2 roma (plum) tomatoes, cut into quarters
- 1 tablespoon chopped fresh cilantro

Directions

1. Heat vegetable oil in a Wok or large skillet over medium-high heat; cook and stir okra until tender and golden brown, about 3 minutes. Transfer okra to a plate.

2. Sprinkle turmeric into hot oil; heat until turmeric becomes aromatic, 1 to 2 minutes. Add garlic, ginger, onions, and tomatoes; cook and stir until onions are tender, about 10 minutes. Stir okra into onion mixture. Garnish with cilantro.

Chile-Lemongrass Prawns

Servings: 6 | Prep: 25m | Cook: 8m | Ready In: 33m

Ingredients

- 1 tablespoon vegetable oil
- 1 tablespoon peeled, chopped fresh ginger
- 3 cloves garlic, chopped
- 2 shallots, chopped
- 36 prawns (16 to 20 count), peeled and deveined, heads on, if desired
- 1/2 cup mirin
- 2 tablespoons very finely minced lemongrass
- 1/2 cup chicken stock
- 1/4 cup sweet hot chile sauce or mae ploy
- Soy sauce

Directions

1. Heat the vegetable oil in a Wok or very large saute pan over very high heat until very hot. Add the ginger, garlic, and shallots, and saute for 1 minute. Add the prawns and cook just until they start to turn pink, 2 to 3 minutes.
2. Add the mirin and lemongrass, and cook, stirring often, 2 to 3 minutes longer. Add the stock and chile sauce, and cook until the prawns are just cooked through. Season, to taste, with soy sauce. Serve warm.

Chop Suey

Servings: 4 | Prep: 20m | Cook: 16m | Ready In: 36m

Ingredients

- 8 (3 by 3-inch) packaged Chinese wonton skins, separated
- 1 tablespoon plus 2 teaspoons canola oil
- 1/4 teaspoon salt
- 2 scallions, greens included, trimmed and thinly sliced (about 1/4 cup)
- 3 cloves garlic, sliced
- 4 cups sliced napa cabbage
- 3/4 cup celery, thinly sliced (about 4 celery hearts or 2 long stalks)
- 1 (8-ounce) can bamboo shoots, drained and julienned
- 2 cups shiitake mushrooms, cleaned, trimmed and thinly sliced (about 6 ounces)
- 3/4 teaspoon sugar
- 1 cup low-sodium chicken broth
- 1/2 tablespoons low-sodium soy sauce
- 2 tablespoons toasted sesame oil
- 1 1/2 teaspoons cornstarch dissolved in 1 tablespoon cooking sherry
- 2 cups cubed or shredded cooked turkey or chicken
- 2 cups cooked brown rice
- 1 tablespoon toasted sesame seeds

Directions

1. Preheat the oven to 375 degrees F.
2. Brush a baking sheet and the wonton skins lightly on both sides with 2 teaspoons of oil. Season with salt and bake for 10 to 12 minutes, or until browned and crisp. Transfer to a cooling rack and reserve.
3. In a large heavy skillet or Wok, heat the remaining 1 tablespoon of canola oil over medium-high heat. Add the scallion, garlic, cabbage, celery, bamboo shoots, and mushrooms and stir-fry until cabbage is soft and wilted, about 3 to 4 minutes. Add the sugar, 3/4 cup of the chicken broth, soy sauce, and sesame oil and cook for 3 minutes. Add the sherry-cornstarch mixture and, if the mixture is a little dry, the additional 1/4 cup chicken stock. Add the turkey or chicken and heat through. Serve the chop suey over the cooked brown rice and top with sesame seeds and reserved crushed wonton skins.

Chopsuey

"Chopsuey (chop or "tsap" means 10; and sui means vegetables) in Chinese Amoy dialect literally means "ten vegetables". It is basically a mix of sorts of vegetables easily available in the market with meat. while some say that it is a mix of leftover food. Either way, chopsuey is a stir fry of vegetables and meat. A few vegetables will do for this dish but I like keeping my Chopsuey true to its meaning: 10 different kinds of vegetables in one. The more the merrier (delicious and nutritious), right? :D

Hubby told me that the "old" chinese kitchen actually use innards instead of seafood or meat cuts when cooking chopsuey. Nah, it's not my type of plate.

And.... my photo is not the best - again- because we end up eating the served dish before I got to take a proper picture. (T-T)"

Servings: 4 | **Ready In**: 30m

Ingredients

- Vegetable/cooking oil
- 1/4 kg pork cutlets - chopped to smaller pieces
- 1/4 kg shrimp - remove whiskers/ or better yet remove shell
- 8 pcs fish balls
- 4 clove garlic- crushed
- 1 pc small onions- chopped
- 2 pcs small tomatoes - chopped
- 1 bunch Pechay/Napa Cabbage - remove hard stalks and chop
- 1/4 kg Green Cabbage - remove hard stalks and chop
- 1 small bunch of broccoli - remove hard stem and separate
- 1 small bunch of cauliflower - remove hard stem and separate
- 1 small carrot - cut to circles
- 1/2 part of small chayote -chopped
- 1/8 kg flat beans - fiber removed
- 1 handful bean sprouts - cleaned
- 1 stalk celery - chopped

Chopsuey Sauce:

- 2 tbsp oyster sauce
- 2 tbsp soy sauce

- 1 cup chicken broth
- 1 tbsp cornstarch
- 1 tsp sesame oil
- 1 tsp grounded black pepper

Pork Marinade:

- 2 tbsp oyster sauce
- 2 tbsp soy sauce
- 1 tsp black grounded pepper
- 1 tsp chopped ginger

Directions

1. Mix the pork marinade and let it for at least 20 min
2. Heat vegetable/cooking oil in a Wok on medium heat. Cook the marinated pork.
3. Add the shrimp and cook until shrimp is pink.
4. Drop in onions, garlic and tomatoes. Stir fry on high heat.
5. Pour the sauce. Drop in the vegetables and fish balls when sauce starts boiling. Mix well
6. Cook until sauce is reduced and vegetables are cooked.

Combination Stir-Fry with Cashew Nuts

"Great flavour. Really nice dish!"

Servings: 8| **Ready In:** 60m

Ingredients

- 300 g rump steak, strips
- 300 g chicken breast filler, strips
- 600 g peeled prawns
- 1 large brown onion, wedges
- 1 bunch broccolini, 4cm pieces
- 1 large carrot, julienne
- 1 red capsicum, strips
- 3 stems celery, sliced
- 3 stems green onion, sliced

- 1 bunch pak choy, chopped
- 1 large red chilli, sliced
- 2 tsp minced garlic
- 2 tsp minced ginger
- 2 tsp minced lemon grass
- 1 tsp Chinese 5 spice
- 1/2 cup oyster sauce
- 3/4 cup chicken stock
- 2 cup raw cashews
- Canola oil
- Sesame oil

Directions

1. Prep all your meat and veggies- keep brown onion separate. Also hard veggies in a container together and soft veggies in another container.
2. In a large Wok, throw some canola in with a few drops of sesame oil (for flavour)- on high heat, fry you meat in small batches and set aside.
3. Clean Wok if need be and stir fry brown onion and set aside.
4. Now stir fry your hard veggies- (carrots, celery, pak choy stems, broccolini stems). Set aside.
5. Now throw in the soft veggies (broccolini tips, capsicum, pak choy leaves, chilli, green onion)- cook to soften slightly and set aside with the rest.
6. Clean Wok- toast your cashews and set aside.
7. Now to put it all together- throw your 5 spice, ginger, garlic, lemongrass into Wok- fry to release flavours. Add your oyster sauce and stock- bring to the boil before returning meat and veggies.
8. Return everything to the Wok and stir well to coat in sauce. Serve with rice or egg noodles! Yum! Enjoy!!

Crawfish Dumpling with a Ginger Soy Dipping Sauce

Servings: 4 | Prep: 25m | Cook: 15m | Ready In: 40m

Ingredients

- 1 pound Louisiana crawfish tails
- 1 large egg white
- 2 tablespoons chopped yellow onions
- 1 tablespoon chopped fresh cilantro leaves
- 1/4 teaspoon salt
- 1/8 teaspoon cayenne
- 1 teaspoon sesame oil
- 2 dozen round wrappers
- 1 recipe Ginger Orange Sauce, recipe follows
- 1 tablespoon chopped chives

Directions

- Put the crawfish, egg white, onions, cilantro, salt, cayenne, and sesame oil in a food processor and pulse two or three times to finely chop. Do not puree. Working 1 dumpling at a time, place 1 tablespoon of the filling the center of each wrapper. Lightly wet the edges of the wrappers with water. Fold in half, forming a semicircle and crimp the edges. Place the finished dumplings on a parchment-lined baking sheet and cover with a damp cloth. Fill half of the Wok with water. Place over medium-high heat and bring to a boil. Line the bottom of a medium bamboo steamer with the squares of parchment paper or Romaine lettuce leaves. Lay the dumplings on top of the parchment paper and cover with the lid. Place the steamer in the Wok and steam for 6 minutes. Carefully remove the steamer and remove the dumplings. Place the dumplings on a large platter and serve with the dipping sa

Curry flavored stir-fry with okra & onion

"I harvest okra from my garden everyday. I normally eat okra, just boil and make salad, but today I made stir-fry dish with curry flavor."

Servings: 2 | **Time**: 15m

Ingredients

- 6 okra
- 1 onion

- 1 teaspoon, curry powder
- 1/2 teaspoon, soy sauce
- 1 little, salt & pepper
- 1 teaspoon, coconut oil

Directions

1. Boil okra 30 seconds
2. Cut onion and okra
3. Heat a large skillet. When hot, add coconut oil and cook okras and onions over medium-low heat for about few minutes.
4. Add ingredients, curry powder, salt & pepper, soy sauce and stir several times.

Delicious Turkey Flakes Stir fry

"I was looking for something to cook but I don't have any more meat in the fridge. I looked in the cupboard and I found the can of turkey so I decided to make a stir fry with it.

This recipe is simple, easy, fast, and delicious!

Let me know what you think :)"

Servings: 2 | **Cook**: 20m

Ingredients

- 1 can Maple Leaf Flakes of Turkey
- 1/2 medium Onion - sliced
- 1 cup Sliced carrots
- 2 stick Celery - slanted slice
- 1 cup Baby spouts - cut in halves
- 2 clove Smashed garlic
- 2 tbsp Cooking oil
- 1/4 large Bell pepper - long & thinly sliced

Directions

1. Heat oil in a Wok or pan
2. Add garlic and wait til golden, then add the onions and stir til sautéed
3. Add in your flakes of turkey, mix and let cook for 2 mins
4. Add all the veges and cook for about 7-10mins depending on how you like your veges cooked.
5. Serve hot over rice and add green onions on top (optional) and enjoy! :)

Dol Sot Bi Bim Bap

"Dol Sot Bi Bim Bap is Korean for Hot Stone Bowl with Mixed Rice - oh, and vegetables, and meat, and egg. My 'go to' favorite Korean dish, next to haemul pajeon and Bulgogi. I'm a big carnivore so my version has about 25% more meat than the traditional version. Mmmmmm, cow! "

Servings: 6 | ***Prep***: 1h | ***Cook***: 1h | ***Ready In***: 2h

Ingredients

- 1/2 cup soy sauce
- 1/2 cup white sugar
- 1/2 cup brown sugar
- 1/4 cup minced garlic
- 1/3 cup chopped green onion
- 4 tablespoons toasted sesame seeds
- 20 ounces rib-eye steak, sliced thin
- salt and pepper to taste
- 3 cups uncooked glutinous (sticky) white rice, rinsed
- 1/2 cups water
- 4 dried shiitake mushrooms
- 1 pound fresh spinach, washed and chopped
- 12 ounces cucumber, julienned
- 12 ounces carrots, julienned sesame oil
- 8 ounces fresh bean sprouts
- 6 eggs
- 6 sheets nori, crumbled
- 6 tablespoons sesame oil
- 1/4 cup chili bean paste (Kochujang)

Directions

1. Make the marinade for the beef. Combine the soy sauce, sugars, garlic, green onions, sesame seeds in a large bowl; add the sliced beef strips to the marinade, and season with salt and pepper. Cover, and refrigerate for at least 2 hours.
2. Bring the rice and water to a boil in a saucepan over high heat. Reduce heat to medium-low and cover; simmer until the rice is tender and the liquid has been absorbed, 20 to 25 minutes.
3. Preheat an oven to 425 degrees F (220 degrees C), and place 6 Korean stone bowls in oven. Combine shiitake mushrooms and 1/2 cup hot water in a small bowl, and soak for about 10 minutes, until pliable. Trim off and discard the stems. Thinly slice the caps. Set aside.
4. Bring a saucepan of water to a boil. Add spinach to the water just long enough to wilt the leaves, and then drain and pat dry. Set aside. Combine cucumber and carrots in a bowl, and season with salt and pepper. Set aside.
5. Preheat Wok over medium-high heat. Cook carrots and cucumbers in a small amount of sesame oil to soften, stirring frequently. Remove from pan, and set aside. Add a small amount of sesame oil to the pan, and cook spinach in sesame oil for a minute or two. Remove spinach from pan, and set aside. Add the meat strips and marinade to the Wok; cook, stirring frequently, until the liquid reduces in volume, about 4 to 5 minutes.
6. Transfer the stone bowls from the oven to suitable heat resistant surface. Brush each bowl with sesame oil to coat. Divide the rice into the bowls, and gently pack to the bottom (the rice should sizzle as you arrange). Arrange the cucumbers and carrots, bean sprouts, greens, shiitake mushrooms, and beef mixture over each potion of rice. Immediately before serving , add one raw egg yolk to each bowl, drizzle with about a tablespoon of sesame oil, and top with the nori. Serve Kochujang sauce as a condiment.

Footnotes

- You can substitute zucchini for the cucumber.
- For Dol Sot Bi Bim Bap, you can either fry the egg and place on top, or just add the raw egg yolk on top immediately before serving to allow the person eating to mix it in.

Down South Stir Fry Sauce

"A BBQ inspired Asian stir fry sauce, I came up with this sauce to compliment left over kabobs (chicken, shrimp, beef) and seared asparagus (bacon-wrapped).

I really think the combination of bacon and brown sugar with the seared taste from the grill create a southern BBQ taste that pairs perfectly with the citrus Asian flair. Try it and let me know what you think!"

Servings: 2 | **Time**: 25m

Ingredients

- 1/2 lb. cooked grilled chicken, steak, or shrimp
- 8 seared bacon-wrapped asparagus (cut into 1 in. pieces)
- 2 Tbsp dark sweet soy sauce
- 1 Tbsp apple cider vinegar
- 1 Tbsp Stubbs Citrus & Onion Marinade
- 2 1/2 Tbsp brown sugar
- 1 tsp. course black pepper
- 1 tsp. fresh minced ginger
- 1 tsp. fresh minced garlic
- 1/2 tsp. cornstarch

Directions

1. First pre-heat a pan to medium heat and cube the left over meat and cut the bacon-wrapped asparagus into 1 inch pieces
2. Add all the meat and bacon-wrapped asparagus to the hot pan and let warm through
3. While the meat and vegetables are warming, in a separate container, combine all remaining ingredients, stirring thoroughly, to create the sauce.
4. Pour the sauce mixture over the meat and vegetables. Let simmer until the sauce thickens and begins to glaze the meat.
5. Serve with rice or make extra to enjoy over egg noodles. Try it and enjoy! My significant other even enjoyed it (she doesn't even like Asian food)

Easy & Spicy Stir Fry

"I always love to make dish which is healthy and yummy AND quick. Stir fry is my go-to meal whenever I want something easy, nutritious, and delicious!"

Servings: 3 | **Time**: 15m

Ingredients

- 1/2 medium onion, chopped
- 2 clove garlic, minced
- 250 grams shrimp
- 1 cup button mushroom, sliced into 2
- 3 medium red chillies, sliced
- 450 grams broccoli florets
- 3 tbsp oyster sauce
- 1 tbsp olive oil
- 1 tbsp fish sauce
- 1 salt, pepper, and red pepper flakes to taste

Directions

1. Blanch broccoli florets in boiling water and a dash of salt while peel the shrimp.
2. Marinate shrimp with a pinch of salt, pepper, and red pepper flakes.
3. After broccoli is tender, put in ice cold water and set aside.
4. Preheat non-stick pan in small heat with olive oil.
5. Cook onion, garlic, and chillies until just tender.
6. Add mushroom and shrimp, toss them together with the onion and garlic.
7. Add oyster sauce and fish sauce, turn to medium heat.
8. Add broccoli florets and stir fry for 2-3 minutes. You can add a bit of water if you want.
9. Add salt, pepper, and red pepper flakes to your liking.
10. Turn the heat off and put the dish into the plate. Serve with rice.

Easy Black Bean & Left-over Veg Stir-fry

"Easy and quick vegan, low-fat meal using leftover ingredients :)"

***Servings**: 2 | **Time**: 30m*

Ingredients

- 1 Black beans - small tin
- 1 Garlic glove
- 1 Onion
- Any left over veggies. This recipe:
- 1/4 Red cabbage
- 1/4 Mushrooms - tray
- 1/4 Grilled pineapple with cinnamon
- 1/4 Courgette
- 1/4 Cauliflower
- Ground cumin powder
- Soy sauce
- 1 bunch Baby spinach

Directions

1. Saute onions and garlic in a little water
2. Add other left-over chopped veggies, squirt over as much soy sauce as desired and a little more water if needed
3. As veggies start to soften, sprinkle over cumin and and other herbs if desired
4. Add washed black beans. Stir through til hot
5. Serve with potato/rice/salad/stuff in pepper to roast etc. Served in pic with roasted new potatoes (roasted in oven after washing with no fat and rosemary sprinkled on top)

Easy Greens Stir-Fry

"Something easy and tasty. And quick! I am a lazy mom and I do not feel like cooking for hours. This one is tasty and you can choose many kinds of green vegetables, like bok choy, kai-lan, and the like. You can also add slices or meat or chicken or tofu, if you like."

***Servings**: 4 | **Time**: 15m*

Ingredients

- 2 cups sliced green vegetables (immerse them first in water + a pinch of salt or apple cider for five minutes, then pat dry, slice accordingly)
- 1 onion, thinly sliced
- 1 garlic, smashed, thinly sliced
- 1 tsp shoyu
- 1/2 tsp salt
- 1 pinch sugar
- 1 pinch dashi
- 1 tsp oil
- 2 tsp sesame seeds

Directions

1. Heat oil in a pan (low). Add garlic, then onion, mix until fragrant.
2. Add green vegetables and the rest of the condiments save for sesame seeds. Mix evenly. Cover for 3 minutes.
3. Uncover the pan, sprinkle the sesame seeds.

Easy Japanese-Style Vegan Collard Greens

"I made this impromptu for my family, and everyone freaked out. It contains no meat, so it's perfect for vegetarians or those who are trying to cut down on meat. It's amazingly simple to make...no more than 15 minutes, start to finish."

Servings: 6 | **Prep**: 10m | **Cook**: 5m | **Ready In**: 15m

Ingredients

- 2 tablespoons Asian (toasted) sesame oil
- 1 bunch collard greens, thinly sliced
- 3 tablespoons gomasio (such as Eden Organic Foods®)
- 1 tablespoon mirin (Japanese sweet wine)
- 2 cloves garlic, minced, or more to taste
- Sea salt to taste (optional)

Directions

1. Heat sesame oil in a large skillet or Wok until sizzling; add collard greens, gomasio, and mirin. Cook until collard greens are tender, 3 to 5 minutes.
2. Stir garlic into collard green mixture and cook just until garlic is fragrant, about 30 seconds; remove from heat. Season with additional sea salt if desired.

Cook's Notes:

- If you cannot find gomasio, simply buy sesame seeds and toast them lightly in a dry skillet. Then transfer seeds to a spice grinder or mortar and pestle and coarsely grind with a ratio of 1/4 cup sesame seeds to 1 teaspoon sea salt.
- I prefer to cook the collard greens at a medium-high temp for a short period of time, thereby preserving the pungent flavor of the greens.
- Onion can be added to this dish if fried for five minutes before adding the collards, but I enjoy the character of this dish without them.

Easy Ramen Stir Fry

"heres the photo:) easy simple and yummy"

Servings: 24 | **Cook**: 15m

Ingredients

- 1 Ramen Noodle (any)
- 1 tbsp Oyester Sauce
- 2 each carrots
- 1 tbsp oil
- 1/4 slice onion
- 1 tbsp soy sauce

Directions

1. Get a bowl of hot water, really hot water, and soak noodles. (Do not boil because boiling will make noodle to soft. Soaking leaves it tender for frying later)
2. Slice your onions and carrots
3. Pour oil of your choice in a skillet on medium heat.
4. Brown onions in oil. Add a tbs of soy sauce to give it a richer brown.
5. When onions are browned, throw the carrots in. Cover skillet so carrots until carrots are tender.
6. When carrots are tender enough, drain the noodles and add to skillet.
7. Add oyster sauce + soy sauce + flavoring package
8. Stir until noodles are coated evenly.
9. Enjoy. (:

Easy-Peezy Caramel Granola

"This is super easy to make and goes great with yogurt, ice cream, or just by itself! It's much sweeter than the classic honey granola."

Servings: 8 | ***Prep***: 10m | ***Cook***: 20m | ***Ready In***: 30m

Ingredients

- 2 cups quick cooking oats
- 1 cup brown sugar
- 2 tablespoons ground cinnamon
- 1/2 cup butter, melted
- 5 tablespoons caramel sauce
- 2 tablespoons white sugar

Directions

- Stir together the oats, brown sugar, and cinnamon in a Wok or large skillet over high heat, cook 5 to 10 minutes; remove from heat and add the butter and caramel sauce; stir until evenly coated. Spread the mixture onto a flat platter or baking sheet in a thin layer. Sprinkle the white sugar over the granola. Allow to cool completely before serving.

Egg Rolls

Servings: 4 | *Prep*: 25m | *Inactive*: 15m | *Cook*: 15m | *Ready In*: 55m

Ingredients

- 4 tablespoons vegetable oil
- 1-inch grated fresh ginger
- 2 cloves garlic, finely chopped
- 2 scallions, sliced thinly
- 1 carrot, cut into 1-inch julienne strips
- 1 small red pepper, cut into 1-inch julienne strips
- 1 cup Napa cabbage, shredded
- 1/4 cup chicken broth
- 2 tablespoons reduced-sodium soy sauce
- 1 tablespoon sugar
- 1 to 2 tablespoons sesame oil
- 20 wonton wrappers covered loosely with a damp paper towel to prevent drying
- 10 shrimps, cooked and minced
- Dipping Sauce:
- 1/3 cup lite soy sauce
- 1/3 cup rice vinegar
- 1 tablespoon honey
- 1 to 2 teaspoons sesame oil
- Pinch of red pepper flakes

Directions

1. In a Wok or skillet, stir-fry the ginger and garlic in 2 tablespoons of oil until fragrant, about 30 seconds. Add scallions, carrots, and red pepper and stir-fry over high heat for 2 minutes.
2. In a bowl, combine the chicken broth, soy sauce, and sugar. Add the Napa cabbage and broth mixture. Bring to a boil and simmer 5 minutes, stirring occasionally, until the vegetables are soft. Add sesame oil, cool for at least 15 minutes, and strain. Fold in the minced shrimp.
3. Fill and roll the egg roll wrappers, using 1 tablespoon of filling for each roll. Working with 1 wonton wrapper at a time, place the

wrapper with one corner of the diamond closest to you. Place 1 teaspoon of the filling in the center of the wrapper. Roll the corner closest to you over the filling. Brush the top corner with water. Fold in the sides of the wonton and continue rolling the egg roll up until it is closed. Press to seal, set aside, and continue with the remaining ingredients.
4. In a skillet set over moderately high heat, heat the remaining oil and saute the egg rolls until golden brown on all sides, using tongs to turn them. Serve when cool enough to eat, with dipping sauce.
5. Dipping Sauce:
6. Combine all ingredients in a bowl.

Eggplant and Green Beans in Spicy Garlic Sauce

Servings: 5 | *Prep*: 15m | *Cook*: 30m | *Ready In*: 45m

Ingredients

- 6 ounces ground pork
- 1 1/2 tablespoons soy sauce
- 1/2 cup cooking oil
- 1/2 pound frozen blanched cut green beans, defrosted
- 1 pound Asian eggplants, ends trimmed, cut on the diagonal into 3/4-inch slices or roll cut
- 8 garlic cloves, thinly sliced
- 1/2 cup basil leaves, torn
- 2/3 cup chicken stock
- 4 1/2 tablespoons hoisin sauce
- 1/4 cup dark soy
- 2 tablespoons black vinegar
- 2 tablespoons chili garlic sauce
- 1 teaspoon sesame oil
- 3/4 teaspoon cornstarch dissolved in 1 teaspoon water

Directions

1. Combine the pork with the soy sauce and allow to stand while you prepare the green beans and eggplant.

2. Heat a large nonstick skillet or Wok over high heat and, when hot, add 1/4 cup of the vegetable oil. When the oil is hot, add the green beans (careful - this will splatter!) and stir-fry until the green beans are slightly wrinkled, 5 to 6 minutes. Using a slotted spoon, remove the green beans and transfer to paper-lined plate to drain. Add the remaining oil to the pan and add the eggplants and cook, stirring occasionally, until eggplants are lightly browned on all sides, 4 to 5 minutes. Remove the eggplant to a shallow bowl and set aside.
3. Add the garlic and basil to the skillet and cook for 10 to 15 seconds. Add the pork and cook, stirring, until it changes color, 1 to 2 minutes. Return the eggplants to the skillet and add the chicken stock, hoisin, dark soy, black vinegar, chili garlic sauce and sesame oil and stir to mix well. Reduce the heat to medium, cover, and cook until the eggplants are tender, 8 to 10 minutes. Return the green beans to the pan along with the cornstarch mixture and bring mixture up to a boil. When the sauce has thickened, serve immediately.

Eggplant and Summer Veggie Sweet and Sour Stir-fry

"My friend in Japan taught me this recipe. The vinegar and soy sauce make it refreshing for a summertime lunch and perfect to go with Asian noodles! You can substitute other veggies on hand if you like."

Servings: 2 | **Time**: 15m

Ingredients

- 1 Japanese eggplant
- 1 cucumber (or another eggplant)
- 6 shishito peppers (or 1 green bell pepper)
- 1 tbsp vegetable oil
- 1 tbsp sesame seeds, lightly ground
- 20 ml vinegar (I used brown rice vinegar)
- 40 ml soy sauce
- 2 tsp sugar
- 2 servings somen, soba or other Asian noodles (optional)

Directions

1. Chop the eggplant into larger bite-size pieces. Cut shishito peppers in half and cucumber into smaller bite-size pieces.
2. Heat the vegetable oil in a frying pan and add the sesame seeds. Fry for about 1-2 minutes.
3. Add the eggplant and stir fry for 2-3 minutes until coated in oil. Add the rest of the vegetables and stir fry for another 2 minutes or so.
4. Pour in the soy sauce, vinegar and sugar. Briefly mix.
5. Cover with lid and cook for 2-3 minutes until eggplants are soft.
6. Remove lid and stir-fry until eggplants are brown and soft.
7. Enjoy as-is or serve over chilled somen noodles, soba noodles or other Asian noodles.

Five-Spice Tofu Stir-Fry

"from Canadian Living: The Vegetarian Collection"

Servings: 4 | **Cook**: 30m

Ingredients

- 1/2 cup vegetable broth
- 2 tbsp vegetarian oyster sauce
- 1 tbsp cornstarch
- 1 tbsp sodium-reduced soy sauce
- 1 tsp packed brown sugar
- 1 packages medium-firm tofu, drained
- 1/2 tsp Five-Spice powder
- 2 tbsp vegetable oil
- 3 clove garlic, thinly sliced
- 1/4 tsp hot pepper flakes
- 1 head bok choy, chopped
- 8 oz shiitake mushrooms, stemmed and halved

Directions

1. whisk together broth, oyster sauce, cornstarch, soy sauce, sugar, and 1/2 cup water.

2. cut tofu into 1-inch cubes; gently toss with five-spice powder. In Wok or skillet, heat half of the oil over medium-high heat; stir-fry tofu until golden, about four minutes. Transfer to paper towel-lined plate.
3. heat remaining oil over medium-high heat; stir-fry garlic and hot pepper flakes for about 30 seconds. add bok choy and mushrooms; stir-fry for 3 minutes.
4. stir in tofu and broth mixture; bring to boil. reduce heat and simmer, covered, until sauce is thickened and vegetables are softened, about 3 minutes.

Garlic Prawn Stir-Fry with Spinach & Peppers, Gluten, Dairy, Egg, Soy & Nut-Free

"A really quick recipe that takes 5 minutes to prepare and cook"

Servings: 4 | ***Time***: 5m

Ingredients

- Spray oil
- 1 red bell pepper, sliced
- 1 yellow bell pepper, sliced
- 600 g raw, peeled king prawns
- 3 tsp fish sauce
- 4 cloves garlic, thinly sliced
- 200 g baby spinach
- 1/2 tsp chilli flakes or to taste

Directions

1. Spray a frying pan lightly with oil and set over a medium high heat
2. Fry the pepper for 1 minute
3. Add the raw prawns and fry 1 more minute
4. Add the garlic and fish sauce and fry another minute
5. Throw in the spinach and wilt for 1 final minute. Stir through the chilli flakes
6. Serve immediately

Garlicky Asparagus and Mushroom Stirfry

"This is a deliciously simple recipe, with amazing bang (flavor) for buck(time). Ready in minutes, the flavors are sure to tickle your taste buds, and leave you yearning for more :)

Serve as an appetizer, or a very fulfilling main course portion. Enjoy!"

Servings: 2 | **Time**: 10m

Ingredients

- 1 bunch Asparagus stalks
- 10 Baby bella mushrooms, quartered
- 8 clove garlic, finely minced
- 1 tsp red chilli flakes
- 1/4 tsp salt, or to taste
- 1/4 tsp freshly ground black pepper
- 1/2 tsp lime juice
- 1 tsp chopped parsley
- 2 tsp olive oil, extra virgin
- Garnish
- 1 small parsley leaf
- 1 small green onion, sliced lengthwise

Directions

1. In a wide, heavy bottom pan, take the olive oil, and place on high heat. Once hot, the oil slightly thins, and spreads on the pan.
2. Add the minced garlic, and lower the heat to medium. Fry the garlic for about a minute until the aroma changes. The garlic shouldn't go brown.
3. In the meantime, prep the asparagus. Break the hard "woody" portion of the stock by naturally bending the stalks. Then, chop the remaining portion of the stalks diagonally, to get the beautiful slices shown in the picture. Do not discard the "spear tip" of the asparagus, that is also usable in the dish. The woody part of the stalk is inedible, and can be discarded, unless you are planning to

make a soup of some kind - the stalks are a great ingredient for the stock, in that case.
4. Add the chopped asparagus into the garlic flavored oil. Sauté the asparagus stems for about 2 minutes. Add the seasoning (salt and pepper)
5. Once the asparagus is about half done (2 minutes), add the mushrooms.
6. Sauté for another 2-3 minutes. Then add the lime juice and the chilli flakes.
7. Stir fry for another 2 minutes. Asparagus should still be green, tender, and yet have a crunch. Add the parsley. Plate it onto the serving dish.
8. Garnish with the parsley leaf and the green onions.
9. Serve warm - right off the pan, if you can :) Enjoy!

Goya Chanpuru, Okinawan Cuisine

"Goya chanpuru is a cuisine of Okinawa, southern Japan and often eaten in summer season in Japan. Goya is a bitter melon with rich vitamin B and C. I somehow believe its bitterness helps me beat the heat in the summer. You can find goya in Asian or Latin market in the United States. If you cannot eat pork, try with chicken. It goes well, too."

Servings: 3 | ***Time***: 40m

Ingredients

- 15 g sake (cooking alcohol or Japanese sake)
- 25 g soy sauce
- 1 Tablespoon Bonito stock (dashi)
- 1 pinch salt
- 15 g mirin
- 15 g sesame oil
- 1 Goya
- 150 g bacon
- 2 eggs
- 1 extra firm tofu
- Katuobushi, as needed

Directions

1. First, prepare the sauce for goya chanpuru. Mix sake, soy sauce, mirin, salt, bonito stock all together.
2. Hull the goya and cut it in the half lengthwise and take all seeds with a spoon or your fingers and discard them.
3. Slice goya thin like the shape of letter C. Goya is a bitter melon. (If you do not like this bitterness, put the sliced goya in a water with salt and soak it for 10 minutes. I don't do this because I like this bitter taste)
4. Wrap the extra firm tofu with 4 kitchen papers and microwave it for 1 minutes. This is for removing some of the water from the tofu so it makes a good crispy tofu.
5. Prepare the bacon while microwaving the tofu. Cut the bacon in 5 cm length.
6. Sprinkle salt and black paper on the sliced bacon
7. Take the tofu out from the microwave and cut it into large cubes.
8. Heat the large frying pan, add the olive oil, and cook the tofu till they brown.
9. Remove the browned tofu from the pan.
10. Put the sesame oil to the heated pan and add the bacon.
11. Add the goya to the pan after the bacon is almost cooked. Mix well and continue stirring until the goya becomes wilted.
12. Add the tofu and mix gently. Be careful not to scramble the tofu.
13. Beat the eggs.
14. Add the beaten egg and pour the sauce from step 1. When the egg is cooked, goya chanpuru is ready to be served!
15. Add katsuobushi if you'd like! I always add one pack of katsuobushi to the goya chanpuru. This is available in an Asian market.
16. Place the chanpuru on the plate and itadakimasu!

Grill Roasted New Potatoes with Onions, Mushrooms & Cambazola Cheese

Servings: 4-6 | Cook: 40m | Ready In: 40m

Ingredients

- 1 large pot
- 1 grill basket or grill Wok basket
- 2 lbs. mini potatoes

- 1 tbsp. salt
- 2 cups Cremini mushrooms, halved
- 1 medium sweet onion, sliced ½ inch thick rings
- 2 tbsp. Olive Oil
- 1 tbsp. Balsamic Vinegar
- 4 cloves garlic, minced
- Pinch red chili flakes
- ½ cup cubed cambazola cheese
- 1 tbsp. chopped fresh parsley
- 1 tsp. chopped fresh thyme
- Tony Roma's BBQ Baby Back Ribs

Directions

1. Place potatoes in a large pot. Add enough cold water to cover potatoes completely.
2. Cook over high heat until water comes to a boil.
3. Add salt to the water and continue to cook until potatoes are just tender but still firm in the center, about 20-30 minutes. Drain well and transfer to a large bowl. Set aside allowing to cool slightly.
4. Preheat grill to medium heat, about 400-500° F. Add mushrooms and onions to the cooked potatoes.
5. Toss potato/mushroom/onion mixture with olive oil, balsamic vinegar, minced garlic and red chili flake and season to taste with salt and freshly ground black pepper.
6. Pour potato mixture into a grill basket.
7. Grill potatoes/onion/mushroom mixture for 8-10 minutes per side until lightly charred, tender and heated through. Carefully remove vegetables from grill basket and transfer to a large bowl.
8. Add cambazola cheese, parsley and thyme and season to taste with a little salt and freshly ground black pepper. Toss until the cheese starts to melt and get gooey. Serve immediately. Serve with Tony Roma's BBQ Baby Back Ribs.

Ground Bison and Asian Greens Stir-fry

"I got some ground bison from a local rancher in Ohio (Owl Creek Bison) and wanted to really enjoy its flavor so I kept the recipe & spices simple! I learned from the rancher that bison has almost no fat so it's super healthy, but you have to be careful not to cook it too long or it will dry out. You can use basically any leafy greens like kale or Asian greens like tatsoi, komatsuna,

etc."

Servings: 4 | **Time**: 25m

Ingredients

- 1 lb ground bison (sub. lean beef)
- 1/2 tsp kosher salt
- 1/2 tsp ground coriander
- 1/2 tsp ground cumin
- 1/4 tsp white pepper (sub. black pepper)
- 1 bunch tatsoi, kale or any Asian greens
- 1/2 onion, minced
- 2 cloves garlic, minced
- 2 Tbsp olive oil

Directions

1. In a medium bowl, mix the bison with the salt, pepper, coriander and cumin.
2. Chop the greens into smaller pieces, separating the stems from the leaves of the greens.
3. Mince onions and garlic. In a large frying pan, sauté in the olive oil in medium heat until soft and translucent.
4. Add the stems from the greens and stir fry about 5 minutes until bright green.
5. Add the ground bison, briefly mix into the onions and stems.
6. Add the leaves, a splash of water or white wine, a sprinkle of salt and cover with lid. Steam for about 3 minutes until leaves start to wilt.
7. Remove lid and stir until bison is just browned and the leaves are completely wilted. Bison is very lean so you don't want to cook a long time or it will dry out.
8. Adjust seasoning to taste and serve as filling for lettuce wraps, tortillas or with rice.

Indian Sabji Recipe

"This is the traditional way to prepare most vegetables in the part of India my husband is from. You can substitute other vegetables into this recipe as well:

eggplant and potato, or cauliflower and potato, or peas and carrots. Serve with flat bread, dal, and jeera rice."

Servings: 4 | **Prep**: 10m | **Cook**: 50m | **Ready In**: 1h

Ingredients

- 2 tablespoons canola oil
- 1 teaspoon cumin seeds
- 1 teaspoon mustard seed
- 1 tablespoon ground coriander
- 1/2 teaspoon ground turmeric
- 1/2 teaspoon red chile powder
- 1/2 head cabbage, sliced
- 2 potatoes, chopped
- 1 tablespoon ginger-garlic paste
- 1 teaspoon salt
- 1/2 cup water, or as needed
- 1/4 cup chopped fresh cilantro, or to taste

Directions

1. Heat canola oil in a Wok over medium heat. Cook and stir cumin and mustard seeds in the hot oil until they begin to dance, 1 to 2 minutes. Add coriander, turmeric, and cayenne pepper; cook about 1 minute.
2. Stir cabbage, potatoes, ginger-garlic paste, and salt into spice mixture; stir to coat. Pour enough water into Wok to steam vegetables; cover and cook, stirring occasionally and adding more water as needed, until potatoes and cabbage are very tender, about 45 minutes. Remove from heat; sprinkle vegetables with cilantro.

Cook's Notes:

- Cayenne pepper can be substituted for the red chile powder. If you don't have ginger-garlic paste, just use equal parts fresh ginger and garlic and mash it up.
- To make jeera rice, heat about 1 tablespoon oil in a pan. When hot, add 1/2 teaspoon cumin seeds, fry for a minute. Add 1 cup of basmati rice. Stir to coat and let it fry for a minute or 2. Add 2 cups of water and 1/2 teaspoon salt. When the water boils, cut it down to low and cook, covered for 15 to 20 minutes.

Tip

- Aluminum foil helps keep food moist, ensures it cooks evenly, keeps leftovers fresh, and makes clean-up easy.

Jumbo King Prawn Stir-fry with Soy Sauce

Servings: 2 | **Time**: 10m

Ingredients

- 6 jumbo king prawns
- 1/2 tsp corn oil
- 1-2 Tbsp light soy sauce

Directions

1. Clean and snip off the sharp points.
2. Dry the prawns with a paper towel.
3. Place a fry pan on the hob and heat until it is hot, then turn the heat to low, add the jumbo king prawns and cook for 3-4 minutes. Turn to the other side cook for 3-4 minutes as well.
4. Add the corn oil and fry both sides about 30 seconds, then put in the light soy sauce in it and mix well. Serve at once.

Ken Shoe Green Beans

"A great way to make string beans..like the way they do in Chinese restaurants...only better! Also good with asparagus or broccoli. "

Servings: 4 | **Prep**: 15m | **Cook**: 5m | **Ready In**: 20p

Ingredients

- 1/2 cup peanut oil for frying
- 1 pound fresh green beans, trimmed and cut into 2-inch pieces
- 1 tablespoon minced fresh ginger root
- 1 tablespoon minced garlic
- 1/2 teaspoons dark soy sauce 1/2 teaspoon white sugar
- 1 pinch black pepper

Directions

- Heat the peanut oil in a Wok or skillet with high sides over medium-high heat until almost smoking; add the green beans. Quickly cook and stir the beans in the hot oil until they are bright green and starting to show brown spots, about 2 minutes. Remove the beans to a bowl. Drain all but 2 tablespoons of oil from the pan and return to heat. Cook and stir the ginger and garlic in the oil until they have started to brown, about 2 minutes. Return the green beans to the Wok; add the dark soy sauce, sugar, and black pepper. Cook until hot; about 30 more seconds.

Editor's Note

- We have determined the nutritional value of oil for frying based on a retention value of 10% after cooking. The exact amount will vary depending on cooking time and temperature, ingredient density, and the specific type of oil used.

Kinpira Gobo (Spicy Burdock Root and Carrot Stir-fry)

"A simple and classic Japanese dish usually made in autumn when gobo root is in season. The red chili gives it a nice kick! Goes great with over white or brown rice."

Servings: 3 | **Time**: 15m

Ingredients

- 1 large gobo/burdock root or a few small

- 1 carrot
- 1/2 to 1 whole dried red chili, seeds removed
- 1 Tbsp sugar
- 1 Tbsp mirin/sweet cooking sake
- 1 1/2 Tbsp soy sauce
- 1/2 Tbsp sesame seeds (optional)

Directions

1. Scrub or peel the burdock root, cut into matchsticks and soak in water. Rinse until water runs clear. Cut carrots into matchsticks as well.
2. Measure out the sugar, mirin and soy sauce.
3. Heat sesame oil in a pan and saute burdock, carrot and red chili on medium heat until carrot is soft. Burdock root will remain a bit harder, but make sure it's not too tough!
4. Add in sugar and mirin first. Mix well for a minute or two, then add in soy sauce. Stir fry until soy sauce begins to caramelize and gives off a nice smell.
5. Stop heat and sprinkle on sesame seeds. Serve and enjoy! Goes good with rice and keeps well for leftovers and lunches!

Kristy's Le Tofu Orange

"Spice up weeknight dinner with this flavorful dish made with tofu and bell peppers cooked in orange liquor and served with riced cauliflower. This recipe appears on an episode of the Dinner Spinner TV Show on The CW!"

Servings: 4 | **Prep**: 30m | **Cook**: 20m | **Ready In**: 50m

Ingredients

- 1 (14 ounce) package baked firm tofu, cut into 1-inch cubes
- 2 tablespoons olive oil, or as needed, divided
- 12 ounces riced cauliflower (such as Trader Joe's®)
- 2 onions, chopped
- 3 scallions, chopped
- 2 cloves garlic, minced
- 2 green bell peppers, chopped

- 2 tablespoons water
- 1 tablespoon orange liqueur (such as Grand Marnier®)
- 1 tablespoon soy sauce
- 2 red chile peppers, shredded
- 1 pinch salt

Directions

1. Wrap tofu in a paper towel and cover with plate; rest until moisture is removed, about 10 minutes.
2. Heat 1 tablespoon olive oil in a skillet over medium heat. Add cauliflower; cook and stir until tender, about 5 minutes.
3. Preheat oven to 425 degrees F (220 degrees C). (If using a countertop convection oven, preheat to 400 degrees F (200 degrees C)). Place baking sheet inside to warm.
4. Remove paper towel from tofu; discard. Place tofu onto heated baking sheet using heatproof gloves.
5. Bake in the preheated oven, flipping once, until tofu is heated through, about 3 minutes per side in the conventional oven and 2 minutes per side in the countertop induction oven.
6. Heat remaining 1 tablespoon olive oil in a Wok on medium heat. Add onions and scallions; cook and stir until onions are slightly softened, about 5 minutes. Stir in garlic. Turn Wok to high heat; stir in green peppers.
7. Combine water and orange liqueur in a bowl. Pour 1 tablespoon liqueur mixture into Wok; toss with 2 wooden spoons until mixed. Repeat with remaining liqueur mixture; cook and stir until evaporated, 3 to 5 minutes.
8. Sprinkle soy sauce into the Wok. Fold in tofu until coated.
9. Place cauliflower in serving bowls and top with tofu mixture. Garnish with red chile peppers; season with salt.

Lazy Stir Fry

Servings: *3* | **Time**: *30m*

Ingredients

- 1 lb Ground beef, sliced chicken, or sliced steak (I prefer steak strips)

- 1 tsp Minced garlic
- 1 dash Onion powder
- Salt and pepper
- 1 Worchestershire sauce
- 1 Low sodium soy sauce
- 3 packages Ramen noodles, any flavor (we won't be using the season packet)
- 1 packages Mixed frozen vegetables of your choice (steamable bag is easiest here)

Directions

1. Cook your choice of meat in a large skillet or Wok. If using chicken or steak, add a little olive oil to pan first. Add the garlic, onion powder, salt, pepper, and a bit of worchestershire and soy sauce.
2. You can also use packaged pre-cooked strips of chicken or steak to make this even easier.
3. Meanwhile, pop your bag of frozen veggies in the microwave. (If it is a steamable bag! If not, cook accordingly.)
4. Prepare a pot of boiling water while finishing up the meats.
5. Break the blocks of ramen noodles into four pieces and toss the season packet (or keep it for something later). You only need to boil the noodles for about 3 minutes, just until they separate. Drain noodles.
6. Add cooked veggies to meat in pan with a dash more soy sauce and mix well.
7. Add noodles, more soy sauce to flavor noodles, (to your taste or maybe try another seasoning) and toss well.
8. You can definitely make this recipe your own. It's an easy way to throw something together on a week day after work! :)

Leah's Napa Cabbage Stir Fry

"Very tasty! I've also used regular shredded cabbage. I order this at a local restaurant, after several tries, i think I've gotten it down. May be even better! ;-)"

Servings: 4 | **Time**: 30m

Ingredients

- 1 tbsp olive oil, extra virgin
- 2 clove garlic, minced
- 1 tbsp minced and peeled fresh ginger
- 1 cup shredded carrots
- 1/2 cup chopped onion
- 1 medium head of napa cabbage, rinsed and sliced thin
- 2 tbsp soy sauce
- 1 tsp sesame oil
- 1 tsp Sambal Oelek (chili paste)
- 1/4 cup minced fresh cilantro

Directions

1. Heat a Wok or large skillet over high heat. Add the olive oil and stir fry the garlic, ginger. Do not allow garlic to brown.
2. Add and stir fry the carrots and onion. About 3 minutes.
3. Add the cabbage and stir fry until tender. About another 3 minutes.
4. Add and mix well the soy sauce, sesame oil, sambal oelek.
5. serve immediately sprinkled with the cilantro.
6. Delicious!

Lg Stir Fry Calamari Squid (Asian Style Cooking)

"My version

Lightly spicy and garlicky flavour calamari

Loving it"

Servings: 2 | **Cook**: 5m

Ingredients

- 1 tbsp pounded garlic
- 3 small bird eye red chili
- 1 1/2 tbsp oil
- 2 medium calamari/squid
- 1/2 cup spring onion

Garnish

- 1 tbsp fresh lemon juice

Seasoning

- 1 dash salt and pepper

Directions

1. In pan with oil fry calamari for 2 minute then add garlic and seasoning fry for 1 minute then add chili and spring onion
2. Stir fry for another 1 minute then off heat and serve immediately top lemon juice

Ma Po Tofu

"This recipe for ma po tofu, a Chinese stir-fry, is simple to make and good for you, too. Add a side of chilled melon and a cold glass of dry riesling for a satisfying supper."

Servings: 4

Ingredients

- 1 (1-pound) package reduced-fat firm tofu, cut into 6 slices
- 1/2 cup fat-free, less-sodium chicken broth
- 1 tablespoon cornstarch
- 2 tablespoons low-sodium soy sauce
- 1 tablespoon oyster sauce
- 1 to 2 teaspoons chili garlic sauce (such as Lee Kum Kee)
- 4 ounces lean ground pork
- 1 tablespoon grated peeled fresh ginger
- 3 garlic cloves, minced
- 2 cups hot cooked long-grain brown rice
- 1/3 cup chopped green onions

Directions

1. Place tofu slices on several layers of paper towels; cover with additional paper towels. Place a dinner plate on top of covered tofu; let stand 30 minutes. Remove plate; discard paper towels. Cut tofu slices into 1/2-inch cubes.
2. Combine broth, cornstarch, soy sauce, oyster sauce, and chili garlic sauce, stirring with a whisk.
3. Heat a large nonstick skillet over medium-high heat. Add pork; cook 4 minutes or until done, stirring to crumble. Add ginger and garlic; cook 1 minute, stirring constantly. Add tofu; cook 4 minutes or until golden, stirring frequently. Add broth mixture to pan. Bring to a boil; cook 1 minute or until mixture thickens. Remove from heat.
4. Serve tofu mixture over rice. Sprinkle with onions.

Macadamia Nut Crusted Opah with Cabbage Stir Fry

Servings: 4 | *Prep*: 5m | *Cook*: 10m | *Ready In*: 15m

Ingredients

- 1 cup macadamia nuts, ground in a food processor
- 1 cup all-purpose flour
- 2 cups panko bread crumbs
- 2 cups buttermilk
- 2 teaspoons Thai garlic-chile paste (recommended: Sriracha)
- 6 (6-ounce) opah (moonfish) fillets
- Salt
- Freshly ground black pepper
- 2 tablespoons peanut oil
- 2 tablespoons peanut oil
- 2 cups thinly sliced napa cabbage
- 2 carrots, shredded
- 1 Maui sweet onion, thinly sliced
- 1/4 cup chopped fresh cilantro leaves, plus sprigs for garnish
- 4 scallions, chopped
- Olive oil
- Salt
- Pepper

Directions

1. Preheat oven to 400 degrees F.
2. Combine macadamia nuts, flour and panko in a shallow baking dish. In another shallow baking dish, combine the buttermilk and chile paste and mix well. Lightly season the fish with salt and pepper. Dip the fish into the buttermilk-chile mixture and then into the nut mixture. Heat oil in a very large nonstick skillet over medium high heat; you will need to do this in 2 batches or have 2 skillets. Saute fish for 3 minutes, until golden brown. Turn the fish and place in the oven for 5 minutes, until cooked through and firm to the touch. Serve with Cabbage Stir-Fry.
3. Cabbage Stir-Fry:
4. In a large Wok over medium-high heat, add peanut oil until nearly smoking. Add cabbage, carrots, onions, and cilantro and cook until just wilted, about 3 minutes. Add the scallions, cilantro, olive oil, salt and pepper, and a touch of water and cook until tender but crisp. Garnish with cilantro sprigs.

Mackerel and Swiss Chard Stir-fry with Balsamic Vinegar

"This is a super delicious fish dish! Mackerel and balsamic vinegar are a great combination! Enjoy them with leafy greens :)"

Servings: 2 | **Time**: 45m

Ingredients

- 4 fillets mackerel
- 50 g leafy greens, I use mustard greens and Swiss chard
- 1 Tbsp balsamic vinegar
- 2 tsp soy sauce
- 1 Tbsp white wine
- 1 tsp sugar
- 1 tsp garlic powder
- 1 tsp powdered parmesan cheese
- 1 pinch salt and pepper

Directions

1. Remove the bones from mackerel and cut into smaller pieces. Put the soy sauce, wine, sugar, garlic powder, cheese, salt and pepper into a bowl and mix well. Add in the chopped mackerel pieces. Marinate for at least 30 min or half a day in the fridge.
2. Cut the greens into bite sized pieces.
3. Just before frying, coat each mackerel with flour, heat oil in a saucepan and fry the mackerel until it begins to crisp. Turn and fry until well cooked. Once cooked, place the fish on a plate with paper towels to soak up excess oil.
4. Using a clean frying pan, add 1 Tbsp of olive oil, and once heated, put in the vegetables and stir fry on medium heat for a minute, then add the fried mackerel. Shake the pan a little to mix it up, but not too much. Finally, pour in 1 Tbsp balsamic vinegar, season with salt and pepper if needed.

Mackerel, Broccoli and Garlic Stir-Fry

"This is a yummy fish dish with nutritious vegetables :) Eat well and be healthy!"

Servings: 2 | **Time:** 45m

Ingredients

- 300 g mackerel
- 50 g Broccoli
- 6 Mini tomatoes
- 2 Tbsp soy sauce
- 1 tsp garlic powder
- 1 Tbsp sake
- 1 Tbsp olive oil

Directions

1. Remove the bones from mackerel and cut into smaller pieces. Put the soy sauce, garlic powder, soy sauce, sake and the chopped mackerel pieces into a baggie and mix gently by hand. Leave to marinate for at least 30 minutes or half a day in the fridge.

2. Cut broccoli into pieces and put into a pan of boiled water with a pinch of salt. Cook for as long as you like (par boiled is ok) then drain water.
3. Heat oil in a sauce pan and fry the mackerel on medium heat with the lid on. Turn and fry until it is well cooked.
4. Then add the broccoli and stir fry on medium heat for a minute. Shake the pan a little to mix it up but not too much.
5. Finally, add the half cut mini tomatoes into the pan. Season with salt and pepper if needed, serve on a warmed plate and enjoy!

Malaysian Potatoes and Green Beans

Servings: 4 | Prep: 10m | Cook: 35m | Ready In: 45m

Ingredients

- 2 pounds large Red Bliss potatoes
- 1 tablespoon vegetable oil
- 1 tablespoon minced shallots
- 1 yellow onion, coarsely minced
- 2 garlic cloves, minced
- 1 tablespoon minced peeled fresh ginger
- 2 tablespoons Madras curry powder
- 1 cup coconut milk
- 2 cups vegetable broth
- 2 teaspoons salt
- 1 teaspoon freshly ground black pepper
- 1 pound fresh, young, green beans, trimmed

Directions

1. Wash the potatoes under cold running water. Peel and cut into 2-inch chunks.
2. In a carbon-steel Wok, heat the oil over medium heat until just smoking. Add the shallots, onion, garlic, and ginger, and stir-fry for 5 minutes, or until the onion is wilted. Add the curry and cook for 30 seconds, until aromatic. Add the coconut milk, broth, potatoes, salt, and pepper. Bring to a simmer and cook over low heat until the potatoes are tender, about 15 to 20 minutes. Add the green

beans and cook for another 10 minutes, or until the beans are just done.

Mediterranean Turkey With Swiss Chard Over Polenta

"Break out your Wok because the polenta, turkey and swiss chard in this Mediterranean dish can all be cooked one after the other in a single pan. Hooray!"

***Servings**: 4 | **Prep**: 25m | **Cook**: 12m*

Ingredients

- 3 teaspoons peanut oil, divided
- 1 (8-ounce) tube of polenta, cut into 12 slices
- 3/4 pound turkey cutlets, cut into 1/4-inch-thick strips
- 4 tablespoons fresh lemon juice
- 1 cup low-sodium chicken broth, divided
- 2 garlic cloves, minced and divided
- 1/3 cup currants
- 1/2 pound Swiss chard, finely chopped
- 1 onion, chopped
- 1 tablespoon pine nuts, toasted

Directions

1. Heat Wok or large skillet over medium heat. Add 1 1/2 teaspoons oil; cook polenta, turning halfway through, 3 minutes. Transfer to platter; cover.
2. Add remaining 1 1/2 teaspoons oil to Wok; cook turkey 3 minutes. Add lemon juice, 1/2 cup broth, 1 garlic clove, and currants. Cook, stirring, 1 minute more or until turkey is cooked through. Transfer to platter with slotted spoon, reserving liquid in Wok; cover.
3. Add Swiss chard and onion to Wok; cook, stirring, 3 minutes or until tender. Add remaining 1/2 cup broth and garlic; cook, stirring, 2 minutes more.
4. Spoon the chard mixture onto a platter; top with pine nuts.

Meditteranean Curry Stirfry

"In a moment of "there's nothing for supper!!!! AAAARRGGHH!"....this very yummy dish was created."

Ingredients

- 1 Medium Butternut squash, peeled and cut into "chips"
- 4 Filleted chicken breasts, cut into strips
- 1 Onion, sliced into semi circles
- 1/2 head Cabbage, shredded into bite sizes pieces
- 1 tsp Crushed garlic
- 30 ml Thick soya sauce
- 1 tsp Chicken spice
- 1 tsp Ground nutmeg
- 1 tsp Hot curry powder
- 1 tsp Ground Cumin
- 1 tsp Ground coriander
- 410 grams Chopped tomatoes (1 tin)
- 125 ml Cream
- 1/2 Lime
- 2 tbsp Coconut oil
- 2 tbsp Hot fruit chutney

Directions

1. Marinade the chicken strips in the soy sauce, crushed garlic, chicken spice and the juice of half a lime for 30 minutes or longer.
2. You can do your chopping now while the chicken is marinading ▢
3. Once the chicken is marinaded, in a hot pan, heat the coconut oil and put in the chicken strips. Stirfry for about 5 minutes or until cooked through. Remove from pan and reserve until later.
4. To the hot pan, add the onion strips and cook for about 5 minutes, stirring constantly.
5. Next, add the butternut squash strips to the pan and sprinkle the curry powder, nutmeg, coriander and cumin over them. Turn down the heat to a simmer and cook until the butternut is a little tender, but still crunchy. You may need to add a little water if the pan becomes too dry. Don't let it burn :-)!
6. Pour in the chopped tomatoes with juices and stir well.

7. Cook until the butternut is tender, but not too squishy, then add the cabbage. Stir through and simmer until the cabbage is heated through, but still crunchy.
8. Add the fruit chutney and stir through well.
9. Then add the cream and stir through well. Simmer for a couple of minutes, and then it's ready to serve!
10. Serve with rice or noodles or anything else you fancy

Mexican Stir Fry Fajita Veggies

"A spicy stirfried or fajita vegetable recipe. Great on tacos and burritos, or by itself as a side dish!"

Servings: 6 | **Time**: 30m

Ingredients

- 1 large Ziploc Bag
- 1 large white onion
- 1 Pack Small Sweet Peppers
- 3 tablespoons hotsauce
- 4 tablespoons olive oil
- 1 tablespoon lemon juice
- Seasonings of your choice (I recommend a blend with cumin or adding extra cumin to a different blend!)

Directions

1. Prepare the vegetable marinade by mixing together Lemon juice, Olive Oil and Hot Sauce (I suggest a Mexican blend like cholula or tapatio) in a large ziploc bag.
2. Slice the tops and bottoms off of your mini peppers, cut in half again, and wash and remove all seeds/ inner membrane. Slice up peppers lengthways and add to your bag of marinade.
3. Remove outer layer of onion. Cut onion into quarters and remove as many of the middle layers as you'd like. Slice the onions lengthways and add to the marinade bag. Shake the bag and store it in the fridge for 1-2 hours before cooking.
4. After letting the marinade soak into the vegetables, heat up a large stovetop skillet on medium heat. Once the skillet is heated, pour

your entire bag of veggies (marinade and all) into the pan. If you added enough olive oil you shouldn't need to add any more to the skillet.
5. Cook uncovered over medium to slightly above medium heat until veggies have reduced in size and are staring to brown. Cooking uncovered will take a little longer but you will not have to drain your skillet of liquids near the end of cooking like you would have to do with a covered skillet.

Mike's Mongolian Stir-Fry

"Let's clean out those crispers! If you have at least 1 item from each category and 3 from the vegetable section, you've got yourself an original stir fry tonight!"

Servings: 4 | **Time**: 30m

Ingredients

Start With This Basic Stir Fry Sauce

- 2/3 cup Soy Sauce
- 1 cup Chicken Broth
- 1/3 Rice Wine Or Rice Wine Vinegar
- 3 1/2 tbsp Sugar
- 1 tbsp Minced Ginger
- 1 tbsp Sesame Oil
- 1 tbsp Minced Garlic
- 4 dash Red Pepper Flakes
- 2 tbsp Corn Starch

Additional Sauce/Flavor Options

- 1 Sweet Chili Sauce
- 1 Szechuan Sauce
- 1 Sriracha Sauce
- 1 Teriyaki Sauce
- 1 Oyster Sauce
- 1 Hoisin Sauce
- 1 Fish Sauce

Noodle Options

- 1 Basic Ramen Noodles
- 1 Cellophane Noodles [use angle hair pasta as a replacement]
- 1 Hokkien Noodles
- 1 Egg Noodles
- 1 Rice Noodles
- 1 Rice Sticks
- 1 Wheat Noodles [use fettuccine as a replacement]

Meat & Meat Substitutions

- 1 Pork Strips
- 1 Beef Strips
- 1 Seafood [most types]
- 1 Chicken Strips
- 1 Tofu

Broth Options

- 1 Vegetable Broth
- 1 Chicken Broth
- 1 Beef Broth

Vegetable/Fruit Options

- 1 Water Chestnuts
- 1 Bean Sprouts
- 1 White Onions
- 1 Carrot Strips
- 1 Cabbage
- 1 Cilantro
- 1 Baby Corn
- 1 Thai Basil
- 1 Bok Choy
- 1 Broccoli Florets [blanched]
- 1 Green Onions
- 1 Garlic
- 1 Ginger
- 1 Jalapeños
- 1 Red Chili's
- 1 Bell Peppers
- 1 Diakon Radishes
- 1 Snap Or Snow Peas
- 1 Mushrooms

- 1 Squash
- 1 Egg Plant
- 1 Kimchi
- 1 Asparagus
- 1 Pineapple

Nuts And Seeds

- 1 Cashews
- 1 Peanuts
- 1 Sesame Seeds

Oil Options

- 1 Wok Oil
- 1 Sesame Oil
- 1 Peanut Oil

Directions

1. Create your basic stir fry sauce, mix all ingredients and set to the side. Double this recipe if need be.
2. Now, decide if you'd like any one of the additional sauces listed to incorporate into your basic sauce and add.
3. Note that if you do add more sauces, you'll need more cornstarch to thicken it. Mix 2 tablespoons cornstarch and 2 tablespoons water and set to the side. If you want your sauce thicker, slowly add to your heated Wok and stir quickly.
4. To a well heated Wok or pan, and I mean smokin', with Wok oil included, add your most dense foods. [if it's hard to bite it's harder to cook] These will be those foods that will take longer to cook. Meats, water chestnuts, broccoli, bamboo, carrots, onions, jalapeños, etc., and fry for 3 minutes or until meat or seafood is about 3/4 cooked.
5. Add your softer ingredients like cabbage and green onions and your basic stir fry sauce and cook 2 more minutes or until sauce has thickened.
6. Add noodles and fry as per manufactures directions. Usually about 2 minutes. Note: Noodles must be soft and ready for the Wok. Pre-cooked, if you will.
7. Serve hot and sprinkle with sesame seeds and red pepper flakes over rice.

Miso Stir-Fry with Eggplant & Green Bell Pepper

"The most important ingredients are eggplant and green bell pepper. And plus onion. If you have pork, add pork back ribs. They will be a good combination!"

Servings: 2 | **Time**: 10m

Ingredients

- 3 eggplants (remove the stem, cut into half and chop into chunks.)
- 3 green bell peppers (cut into half, seed and chop into chunks.)
- 1/2 onion (peeled and thickly sliced)
- pork back ribs (if you have, as much as you want)
- 2 Tbsp vegetable oil
- 2 Tbsp miso *
- 2 1/2 Tbsp sugar *
- 2 Tbsp each sake, mirin *
- Shredded shiso leaves (optional)

Directions

1. Combine the * ingredients in a bowl and mix well to make sauce.
2. Heat the oil in a pan over medium heat. Add pork (if you have), and when pork is slightly cooked, add eggplant and stir fry for 1-2 minutes. Add onion, next green bell pepper and sauté for 2-3 minutes.
3. Pour the sauce in and cook over the low heat until the liquid is almost gone (3-4 mins).
4. Top with shredded shiso leaves to finish (optional)

Moo Goo Gai Pan

"This Chinese dish translates to chicken with sliced mushrooms. This dish is great, light and very flavorful."

Servings: 3 | **Prep**: 25m | **Cook**: 15m | **Ready In**: 40m

Ingredients

- 1 tablespoon vegetable oil
- 1 cup sliced fresh mushrooms
- 2 cups chopped broccoli florets
- 1 (8 ounce) can sliced bamboo shoots, drained
- 1 (8 ounce) can sliced water chestnuts, drained
- 1 (15 ounce) can whole straw mushrooms, drained
- 1 tablespoon vegetable oil
- 2 cloves garlic, minced
- 1 pound skinless, boneless chicken breast, cut into strips
- 1 tablespoon cornstarch
- 1 tablespoon white sugar
- 1 tablespoon soy sauce
- 1 tablespoon oyster sauce
- 1 tablespoon rice wine
- 1/4 cup chicken broth

Directions

1. Heat 1 tablespoon of vegetable oil in a Wok or large skillet over high heat until it begins to smoke. Stir in the fresh mushrooms, broccoli, bamboo shoots, water chestnuts, and straw mushrooms. Cook and stir until all the vegetables are hot, and the broccoli is tender, about 5 minutes. Remove from the Wok, and set aside. Wipe out the Wok.
2. Heat the remaining tablespoon of vegetable in the Wok until it begins to smoke. Stir in the garlic, and cook for a few seconds until it turns golden-brown. Add the chicken, and cook until the chicken has lightly browned on the edges, and is no longer pink in the center, about 5 minutes. Stir together the cornstarch, sugar, soy sauce, oyster sauce, rice wine, and chicken broth in a small bowl. Pour over the chicken, and bring to a boil, stirring constantly. Boil for about 30 seconds until the sauce thickens and is no longer cloudy. Return the vegetables to the Wok, and toss with the sauce.

Tip

- Aluminum foil helps keep food moist, ensures it cooks evenly, keeps leftovers fresh, and makes clean-up easy.

Mushroom and Leek Spring Rolls

Servings: 4-6 | Prep: 15m | Cook: 3h25m | Ready In: 3h40m

Ingredients

- 2 cups sliced shiitake mushrooms
- 1 cup sliced button mushrooms
- 1 cup sliced cepes, chanterelles or oyster mushrooms (optional)
- 2 cups leek julienned
- 1 cup bean sprouts
- 1/2 cup hoisin sauce
- 2 minced serrano chile
- 1 tablespoon minced garlic
- 1 tablespoon minced ginger
- 2 tablespoons canola oil
- 1 cup chopped scallions
- 1/2 cup chopped cilantro
- 1 (4 ounce) package bean thread (rice vermicelli), blanched, refreshed and cut up
- Salt and black pepper to taste
- 1 package lumpia wrappers. Other types are egg roll and spring roll wrappers. I
- prefer lumpia.
- Eggwash (1 egg and 1/2 cup of water)

Directions

1. In a hot Wok or saute pan add the oil followed by the garlic, ginger and chile. Be careful not to burn. Add the hoisin and briefly saute to get the raw taste out. Add the shiitakes, leeks and bean sprouts. Check for seasoning. Let cool in a strainer and drain well. When cool, add the cilantro, scallions and bean thread. Lay out a lumpia wrapper with corner facing you. Place a small mound at the bottom, moisten edges with eggwash and roll bottom corner towards the middle. Fold in both sides and continue rolling. Finish roll and let rest. Deep fry at 350 degrees until golden brown, about 5 minutes. Serve with mint dipping sauce.
2. Mint dipping sauce
   Mix all ingredients in a small bowl.

My Mixed Up Veg Stir Fry

"Really lovely"

Servings: 4 | **Time**: 20m

Ingredients

- 2 tbsp Olive Oil
- 2 cloves Garlic Crushed
- 1/4 tsp Crushed Red Chilli Peppers
- 3 Shallots chopped
- 1 Red Onion chopped
- 200 grams Chestnut Mushrooms, sliced
- 2 medium Carrots peeled and sliced small longways
- 100 grams Green Beans boiled for 5 minutes first
- 1/2 can Chilli Beans
- 1/4 cup frozen Corn
- 1 tsp Dark Soya
- 1 tbsp Sweet Chilli
- 125 grams Bok Choy chopped in half
- 100 grams Grated Chedder Cheese
- 1 large Spring Onion chopped

Directions

1. Boil green beans for 5 minutes.
2. Strain off the green beans and pat dry on kitchen paper
3. Heat the oil in the Wok or fry pan, then add the shallots and chilli
4. Add the garlic and mix, then add mushrooms and mix. Add the carrots, cook for 5 minutes .
5. Add the green beans and the drained chili beans and mix
6. Add the chili peppers and the corn and mix.
7. After 3 mins add bok choy
8. Transfer into an oven proof dish and sprinkle the cheese on top and melt for a couple of minutes
9. All together it is frying for 10-15 mins and 2 mins in the oven
10. Sprinkle on top the spring onion on top to garnish.

No-Pain Lo Mein

Servings: 4 | **Prep**: 15m | **Cook**: 5m | **Ready In**: 20m

Ingredients

- 2 tablespoons (2 turns around the pan in a slow drizzle) vegetable or Wok oil
- 1 cup (2 handfuls) snow peas, halved on a diagonal
- 1 red bell pepper, seeded and cut into match stick size pieces
- 1/2 pound assorted mushrooms (shiitake, straw, enoki, or oyster), coarsely chopped, if necessary
- 4 scallions, thinly sliced on a diagonal
- 2 cups (about 4 handfuls) fresh bean sprouts
- 2 inches fresh ginger root, minced or grated with hand grater
- 4 cloves garlic, minced
- 1 pound lo mein noodles or thin spaghetti, cooked to al dente and drained well
- 1/2 cup aged tamari soy sauce
- 1 tablespoon toasted sesame oil, several drops
- Wok oil is infused with ginger and garlic and is widely available on the International Foods aisle of the market.
- Cooked shredded pork, chicken, or small de-veined shrimp may be added to this dish in any combination.

Directions

- Heat a Wok-shaped skillet or large non-stick skillet over high heat. When pan is very hot, add oil, (it will smoke a bit) then, immediately add the snow peas, pepper, mushrooms, scallions, and bean sprouts. Stir fry for 1 minute to flavor the oil, then add the ginger and garlic, and stir-fry 2 minutes. Add the cooked noodles and toss with to combine. Add the soy sauce and toss the ingredients to coat noodles evenly with sauce. Transfer the lo mein to a serving platter and garnish with a drizzle of toasted sesame oil.

Nue Pad Prik Namm Man Hoy Or Steak Stir Fry In Oyster Sauce.

"Steak is one of my family favourite food"

Servings: 4 | **Time:** 25m

Ingredients

- 400 grams of slices steak
- 1tb spoon of chopped garlic
- 1 slices onion
- 10 cut green onion
- half red and yellow sweet peppers slices
- 10 of thai basil leaves
- 2tb spoon of frying oil
- 4tb spoon of oyster sauce
- 1ts spoon of chicken stock powder
- 1/ 2 ts spoon of suga

Directions

1. In the heating pan add oil and garlic fry till golden brown
2. Add beef stir fry in oil till cook
3. Add in flavours by adding oyster sauce, chicken stock powder and sugar and keep stirring in the pan
4. Add onion, green onion and pepper then basil leaves for ended process

Orzo with Stir Fry Veggies

"Very light quick healthy side dish ...."

Servings: 6 | **Time:** 15m

Ingredients

- 1 cup Orzo
- 1 packages Chinese Stir Fry
- 1 tbsp Chicken Bouillon
- 2 tsp house seasoning
- 1 onion, chopped
- 1/4 tsp Vegetable Oil

Directions

1. Boil 1 cup of orzo as directed on box
2. Meanwhile saute veggies and onion in oil just for 2 mins then add orzo's and chicken bullion season well saute for 5 mins more you can add a teaspoon of water to steam veggies a little
3. Enjoy....

Pad Se Eew

"Thai-style rice noodle dish with chicken and a bit of a kick. It is a lot easier to make this if you cook it in the pan in two batches instead of one. That way you can customize it the way each person likes it (more chicken, more broccoli, no egg)."

Servings: 3 | **Prep**: 15m | **Cook**: 20m | **Ready In**: 35m

Ingredients

- 1 tablespoon dark soy sauce
- 2 tablespoons soy sauce
- 1 tablespoon white sugar, or more to taste
- 1 teaspoon chile-garlic sauce (such as Sriracha®), or more to taste
- 1 tablespoon olive oil
- 1 tablespoon chopped garlic
- 6 ounces chicken tenders, cut into bite-size pieces
- 1 (16 ounce) package frozen broccoli
- 1 pound fresh flat rice noodles
- 1 egg, beaten
- 1/4 teaspoon sesame seeds
- 1 pinch crushed red pepper flakes

Directions

1. Stir the dark soy sauce, soy sauce, sugar, and chile-garlic sauce together in a small saucepan and place over medium-how heat; simmer and stir until the sugar dissolves into the sauce, about 5 minutes. Remove from heat and set aside.
2. Heat the olive oil in a skillet over medium heat. Cook and stir the garlic and chicken in the hot oil until the chicken is no longer pink in the center, 7 to 10 minutes. Stir the broccoli into the chicken mixture; cook and stir until the broccoli is thoroughly heated. Add the noodles and stir until all the ingredients are evenly mixed. Pour the sauce over the mixture and stir until everything is evenly coated; continue cooking until the sauce begins to thicken.
3. Push the chicken mixture to the side of the skillet with a spatula. Add the egg to the skillet in the vacated space. Scramble the egg, cooking it through. Once egg is cooked, mix ingredients back in and heat thoroughly. Garnish with the sesame seeds and red pepper flakes to serve.

Tip

- Aluminum foil helps keep food moist, ensures it cooks evenly, keeps leftovers fresh, and makes clean-up easy.

Pad See Sahai Or 4 Friends Stir Fry

"The list of ingredients might be gone again but I will note them on my notes again again."

Servings: 2 |**Time**: 15m

Ingredients

- Half colriflower brunch cut full mouth side
- Alf zucchini slices
- Half of each red and yellow sweet peppers slices
- 1 ts spoon chopped garlic
- 1 tb spoon of oyster sauce

- 1 teaspoon of light soy sauce
- 1/2 ts of sugar
- 1 / 4 ts of black pepper
- 1ts spoon

Directions

- Ash all the vegetables and put in deep bottom plate top with chopped garlic, oyster sauce, light soy sauce, sugar, pepper and chicken stock powder on top of washed vegetables. In the deep bottom frying pan heat the oil till very hot and dump the vegetables that's been seasoning into the hot pan keep flipping the vegetables and in go the water. Do not stir just keep moving and flipping the vegetables in the pan 5 minutes move from heat. Pasta or rice good for serving.

Paleo Coconut Curry Stir Fry

"This paleo-style stir fry uses coconut milk and curry powder. Try it with shrimp!"

Servings: 4 | **Prep**: 15m | **Cook**: 20m | **Ready In**: 35m

Ingredients

- 1 1/2 cups coconut milk
- 1 tablespoon minced ginger
- 1 tablespoon lime juice
- 1 tablespoon fish sauce
- 1 teaspoon oyster sauce
- 2 teaspoons minced garlic
- 1/2 teaspoon chile-garlic sauce (such as Sriracha®)
- 2 tablespoons white sugar or sugar substitute
- 1 tablespoon avocado oil
- 1 pound chicken breast, cut into bite-sized pieces
- 1/2 onion, sliced 1
- 1/2 teaspoons curry powder
- 2 cups broccoli florets

Directions

1. Mix coconut milk, ginger, lime juice, fish sauce, oyster sauce, garlic, chile-garlic sauce, and sugar together in a small bowl.
2. Heat avocado oil in a large skillet or Wok over medium-high heat. Stir-fry chicken in the hot oil until no longer pink, 8 to 10 minutes. Remove from Wok and keep warm. Leave remaining avocado oil in skillet.
3. Stir onion and curry powder into hot oil in skillet; cook 2 minutes. Stir in broccoli; stir-fry 3 minutes. Add coconut milk mixture and bring to a boil. Reduce heat to medium and simmer sauce and vegetables for 3 minutes. Return chicken to skillet; cover and cook until chicken has heated through and vegetables are tender, about 3 minutes.

Cook's Note:

- Use olive oil in place of avocado oil; use sugar substitute if you don't eat sugar.

Paleo Teriyaki Stir-fry Zoodles

"Quick to make and tasty"

Servings: 3

Ingredients

- 1 T evoo
- 2 T coconut aminos teriyaki sauce
- 1 large carrot
- 1/2 large green bell pepper, thinly sliced
- 1/4 yellow onion, thinly sliced
- 1 head baby bok choy, chopped
- 1 large zucchini, spiralized
- 1 tsp garlic powder

Directions

1. In large skillet, heat oil and 1 T teriyaki sauce. Add carrot, green pepper and onion and cook until tender.
2. Stir in bok choy, zucchini and garlic powder. Drizzle on remaining teriyaki sauce.
3. Cook, stirring occasionally until zucchini is tender.

Pasta Stir-Fry

Servings: 4 | *Prep*: 25m | *Cook*: 5m | *Ready In*: 30m

Ingredients

- 1 (16-ounce) package whole-wheat linguine
- Salt
- 2 tablespoons canola oil
- 1 medium onion, sliced
- 1 red bell pepper, sliced
- 1 (1-inch) piece ginger, peeled and diced
- 1/2 small eggplant, sliced into small chunks, about 2 cups
- 2 cloves garlic, finely sliced
- 1 cup frozen broccoli florets, thawed
- 1 (15-ounce) can diced tomatoes
- 2 tablespoons soy sauce
- 1 chicken breast, cooked and sliced
- 2 scallions, sliced, for garnish

Directions

1. Cook the pasta in boiling salted water until al dente.
2. While pasta is cooking, heat canola oil in a large saute pan or Wok over high heat. Add onion, red pepper, ginger, eggplant and cook for about 1 minute. Add garlic, broccoli, tomatoes, and soy sauce and cook for another 2 minutes. Drain pasta. Add it and the chicken to the vegetable mixture, toss and cook for another minute.
3. Transfer to serving bowls and garnish with scallions.

Pierogy Stir Fry

"I was looking for meatless supper ideas for Good Friday, and got inspired from the Mrs. T's website."

Servings: 4 | **Cook**: 10m

Ingredients

- 1 packages frozen pierogies
- 2 tbsp vegetable oil
- 1 packages frozen stir fry vegetables
- 2 tbsp soy sauce (I used low-sodium)
- 1 tsp garlic powder
- 1 tsp onion powder
- 1 tsp dried parsley
- 1/4 tsp sesame oil

Directions

1. Cook vegetables according to the package directions. I used the microwave so I could concentrate on the pierogies.
2. Heat the vegetable oil in a 12" skillet.
3. Saute the frozen pierogies in the skillet over medium heat until golden brown.
4. Mix soy sauce, garlic powder, onion powder, parsley, and sesame oil in a small bowl and set aside.
5. When vegetables are cooked and pierogies are browned on both sides, add vegetables to the skillet.
6. Pour the sauce mixture over the vegetables and stir gently to coat.
7. Serve immediately. Goes well with a side of egg rolls, pot stickers, or rice!! Enjoy!

Piri Piri Bacon Stir Fry

Servings: 4 | **Cook**: 10m

Ingredients

- 4 slice bacon rashers
- 3 packages soft ready to Wok noodles
- 1 dash piri piri herbs/spices seasoning

Directions

1. Preheat Wok/frying pan and add olive oil. Let this heat up
2. Cut bacon strips into small pieces, stripping fat if desired.
3. Once the bacon is slightly cooked, add the noodles and stir for a couple of minutes.
4. Add the piri piri herbs to your desired intensity. Stir.
5. Add any other ingredients desired e.g onion, mushroom, pepper.
6. Once thoroughly cooked and hot, serve and enjoy!

Potato and Tuna Balsamic Vinegar Stir-fry

"A tasty trio of potatoes, onions, and tuna! Subtly flavored with balsamic vinegar, this dish is a nice accompaniment to any meal <3"

Servings: 2 | ***Time***: 40m

Ingredients

- Potatoes 2-3
- 1 Onion, thinly sliced
- 1 can Canned light tuna in oil
- 2 pinches salt and pepper
- 2 tsp Soy sauce
- 1 tsp Balsamic vinegar
- 1 Tbsp Dried herbs
- 1 clove Garlic, minced
- 1 Tbsp Olive oil
- Fresh basil, for garnish as desired

Directions

1. Without peeling the potatoes, cut them into 2cm cubes. Boil in a large pot of water until soft enough to poke with a toothpick.
2. While potatoes are boiling, saute sliced onions and minced garlic in olive oil with a frying pan.
3. Once onions are translucent and soft, sprinkle in some salt and pepper. Cook for a couple minutes longer then add in the tuna (lightly drained).
4. Add drained potatoes to the frying pan along with the soy sauce and balsamic. Sprinkle in a bit of dried herbs to taste at the end.
5. Divide into serving your dishes and garnish with fresh basil leaves for a nice touch <3

Prawn Stir Fry

"I slightly overcooked my vegetables here but it still came out tasting nice. It had a slight spicy mushroom flavour."

Servings: 4 | ***Cook***: 20m

Ingredients

- 1 red pepper (sliced)
- 4 baby sweetcorn (cut in half)
- 2 tat soi (leaves whole and stalks chopped)
- 1 onion (sliced)
- 2 garlic cloves (roughly chopped)
- 50 grams snow peas
- 1/2 tsp garlic salt
- 1 chicken stock cube
- 1 handful dried wild mushrooms
- 100 ml boiling water
- 1/4 tsp Cayenne chilli pepper
- 50 grams frozen prawns.
- 2 tbsp ground nut oil

Directions

1. First soak the dried mushrooms in the boiling water along with the chicken stock cube for 30 minutes.
2. Drain the mushrooms but reserve the liquid to be used.
3. Heat the oil in a Wok on a medium heat.
4. Add the onion and bay leaf when heated and fry for 2 minutes or until softened.
5. Add the garlic along with 4 tablespoon of the mushroom liquid and fry for a further 1-2 minutes.
6. Add the mushrooms and cook for 1 minute.
7. Next add the corn and peas and fry for 2 minutes. Add 4 tablespoons of the mushroom liquid.
8. Reduce liquid by cooking for a few minutes then add the prawns, pepper and stalks. Fry for 1 minute, then add 1 tablespoon of the liquid.
9. Add the salt and chilli.
10. Cook for a further 2-3 minutes.
11. Add the tat soi leaves and along with 1 tablespoon of liquid and fry for 1-2 minutes.
12. Check seasoning and serve.

Pressed Tofu, Roast Duck, and Broccolini Stir-Fry

"This marriage of Chinese ingredients and an Italian vegetable was inspired by a dish at Seattle's Ba Bar. Usually flavored with five-spice powder, brown-colored pressed tofu is sold at Chinese and Vietnamese markets, which often have a barbecue shop where you can pick up the roast duck or find char siu Chinese-style barbecued pork, which you can sub for the duck. If you'd rather not use duck fat for the stir-frying, substitute 2 tbsp. canola oil."

Servings: 4 | **Total time**: 1h

Ingredients

- 1 pound broccolini, cut into 3-in. lengths
- Salt
- 9 ounces brown (five-spice or smoked) pressed tofu
- About 1 tsp. sugar
- About 1/4 tsp. white pepper
- 1 tablespoon unseasoned rice vinegar

- About 1 1/2 tbsp. soy sauce
- 1 tablespoon toasted sesame oil, divided
- 6 ounces boned Cantonese roast duck, thinly sliced or shredded (include breast and leg/thigh meat and set aside fat and skin)
- 3 garlic cloves, finely chopped

Preparation

1. Boil broccolini in a pot of salted water until it's bright green, 2 to 3 minutes. Drain, rinse with cold water, and drain well. Set aside.
2. Cut tofu into very thin (1/8 in. thick) slices and put in a bowl. Stir together 1 tsp. sugar, 1/4 tsp. pepper, the vinegar, 1 1/2 tbsp. soy sauce, and 2 tsp. sesame oil in a small bowl. Put next to stove along with tofu, duck meat, and garlic.
3. Slice duck skin thinly and heat, along with fat, in a large Wok or frying pan over medium-high heat. Cook fat and skin, stirring 2 to 3 minutes, until most of the fat has melted and skin is crisp. Transfer skin with a slotted spoon to paper towels. Pour off all but about 2 tbsp. fat from pan (if you don't have that much fat, add canola oil to make up the difference).
4. Add garlic to pan and let sizzle just until fragrant, about 15 seconds. Add tofu and a pinch each of salt and sugar. Cook 30 seconds, then add duck meat and stir-fry 30 seconds to heat through. Add broccolini and stir-fry 2 minutes to heat.
5. Stir seasoning sauce again, then add to Wok. Cook until most of the liquid has been absorbed, about 1 minute. Season with extra salt or soy sauce if you like. Transfer to a plate or shallow bowl and sprinkle with remaining 1 tsp. sesame oil and white pepper to taste. Serve duck cracklings on the side so they stay crisp, for sprinkling on top.

Quick & Easy Shiitake Mushroom Stir-fry

"Recently there are so many fresh mushrooms at the super market. I got some big, "meaty" shiitake mushroom this week and made this easy (but yummy!) dish with them! It makes a side dish for dinner or lunch, or bento-box ♪"

***Servings**: 2-3 | **Time**: 15m*

Ingredients

- 8 large, fleshy shiitake mushrooms
- 1/2 tbsp sesame oil (or olive oil if you don't have it)
- 1 pinch salt
- 1/2 tsp soy sauce
- To taste ground black pepper

Directions

1. Separate the stems from the tops of the shiitake. Cut off the hard part from the bottom of the stem.
2. Cut the stems in half lengthwise. Cut the tops into about 1 cm thick slices.
3. Heat the sesame oil (or olive oil) on medium in a big frying pan. Lay out the pieces of shiitake mushrooms in the pan so one of the cut sides is facing the bottom. Sprinkle over a little salt.
4. Let the shiitake 'grill' for a few minutes until the bottom side is starting to soften and brown a little. Then, flip over (you can do it roughly) so the other side can cook.
5. Stir a few times if needed to cook any uncooked spots until shiitake slices are soft and juicy. Right at the end, quickly mix in the soy sauce and sprinkle with pepper. All ready to have as side dish or put in your lunch

Quick & Easy Stir- fry Ramen

Servings: 3 | Cook: 20m

Ingredients

- 3 packages ramen
- 3 envelope of ramen spice that comes with it
- 1/2 packages frozen or fresh shrimps, deveined
- 2 chicken breasts chopped into small square pieces
- 3 eggs
- 1/2 packages of frozen or fresh broccolis
- 6 green chillies sliced lengthwise
- 1 clove garlice chopped
- 2 small onions sliced thinly

- 3 tbsp low-sodium soy sauce
- 1 Sesame oil
- 1/2 tsp lime juice
- 1 Freshly ground black pepper

Directions

1. Heat oil in large skillet and fry the chicken pieces
2. Add shrimp and fry until meat turns opaque
3. Set chicken and shrimp aside
4. Add more oil in the skillet and fry broccoli and chillies until slightly tender (make sure it retains its crunch)
5. Boil the ramen
6. Soak the boiled ramen in ice cold water so that it doesn't get mushy
7. Fry the onions and garlic until tender
8. Add drained boiled ramen to the onions and garlic
9. Add chicken and shrimps
10. Sprinkle the spices from the envelope
11. Beat eggs and pour over the ramen
12. Add soy sauce and mix well
13. Add the broccoli in the end
14. Pour lime juice and toss
15. Add pepper, mix well and serve
16. Happy feasting!

Quick Grilled Steak Stir-Fry

"Very fast to make, it could be less than 30 min depends on time to cook steak. My family loves it hope you do to."

***Servings**: 6 | **Time**: 30m*

Ingredients

- 1/2 lb steak of your choice (round was our choice this time)
- 24 oz stir-fry vegetables of your choice
- 8 oz asparagus spears
- 2 tbsp olive oil, extra virgin
- 2 cup water
- 2 cup instant rice

Directions

1. Start grill while heating prepare steak
2. Grill steak to med rare
3. Add oil to Wok or skillet heat to 300° Add water to pan and boil. Add asparagus first stir for 5-7 min then add rest of vegetables. When water is boiling add rice cover set let set.
4. Slice steak add to vegetables during last 3-5 min of frying
5. Serve over rice (you can also use noodles ect.)

Quinoa Stir-Fry I

"Tastes like fried rice without the rice! :)"

Servings: 2

Ingredients

- 1/2 cup Quinoa
- 1/4 cup Water
- 1 cup Frozen/Fresh Mixed Vegies (I used a mix of frozen corn, peas & green beans)
- 1 Finely Chopped Carrot
- 1 Handful of Chopped Mushroom
- 2 Eggs
- 1/2 tbsp Olive Oil
- 1 Salt/Pepper to Taste
- 1/4 tsp Garlic Powder
- 1/4 tsp Oregano
- 1/2 tbsp Soy Sauce
- 1/4 tbsp Worcestershire Sauce

Directions

1. Cook Quinoa in water with an added pinch of salt until all the water has been absorbed
2. Once cooked, set aside and prep a skillet on med heat with only 1/2 tablespoon of the olive oil

3. Mix until all the veggies are cooked well and add in some salt and pepper to taste as they cook
4. Once veggies are cooked to your liking add in the garlic powder and oregano
5. Next (you can use the same skillet) push all the veggies to one side of the pan, add the remaining oil to the cleared out side and cook your two eggs here and add salt and pepper to taste (can also do this on a separate pan)
6. Once eggs are all scrambled and cooked, combine it with the veggies in the skillet
7. Once all combined add in cooked quinoa and mix in the sauces, once all incorporated taste and add any more salt, pepper or garlic powder you feel is missing
8. This is like fried rice expect without the rice! So this tastes best hot! Enjoy!

Quinoa Stir-Fry II

Ingredients

- 1/4 cup cooked quinoa
- 2 carrots
- 1/2 cup mushrooms
- bunch long green beans
- piece red pepper
- 1 ginger cut up into small units
- 4 almonds

Directions

1. Cook quinoa according to package directions and set aside.
2. Cut up carrots length wise and chop the rest of the vegetables up.
3. Add a dash of olive oil to a frying pan and add the ginger, carrots and green beans.
4. Leave for 5 minutes and add the mushrooms and red pepper. Add salt and pepper. Add the chopped almonds. Leave for 10 minutes on low heat.
5. When the carrots have softened add the quinoa. Cook for another 10 minutes and serve.

Ramen Stir Fry I

Ingredients

- 2 Packs Ramen Noodle
- 3 Eggs
- 1 Bell Pepper
- 1/2 Onion
- 1 Carrot
- 3 tbsp Vegetable Oil
- 1 Celery Stalk

Directions

1. Boil Ramen noodles in a saucepan until the loosen up, but don't let them get soggy.
2. Mix oil, and cut veggies in a skillet over high heat.
3. (I used a green bell pepper, and red, for color)
4. Once your veggies start to soften up and brown (just a little brown). Add noodles and just a little bit of oil.
5. Once your noodles start to darken (shouldn't be very long at all) add eggs to one side of your skillet and scramble them. Once they are firm, mix them right in with the noodles/veggies.
6. Pour in just a small amount of water, then mix in your ramen noodle sauce packs (waters helps them mix).
7. Let cool, then serve and enjoy!

Optional

8. Add chicken breast, shrimp, or pork, but make sure it's cooked first!

Ramen Stir Fry II

"got from betty crocker cookbook. may substitute chicken for beef"

Servings: 4 | **Cook**: 25m

Ingredients

- 1 lb beef sirloin
- 1 tbsp vegetable oil
- 2 cup water
- 1 packages top ramen
- 1 packages stir fry vegetables
- 1/4 cup stir fry sauce

Directions

1. Remove fat from beef. Cut beef into thin strips. In 12 inch skillet, heat oil over medium high heat. Cook beef in oil 3 to 5 minutes, stirring occasionally, until brown. Remove beef from skillet, keep warm
2. In same skillet heat water to boiling. Break up noodles from soup mix into water, stir until slightly softened. Stir in vegetables
3. Heat to boiling. Boil 5 to 7 minutes, stirring occasionally, until vegetables are crisp tender. Stir in contents of seasoning packet from soup mix, stir fry sauce and beef. Cook 3 to 5 minutes

Salmon & Cabbage Stir-Fry Miso Sauce

"This is stir-fry with miso sauce dish. I used salmon this time but chicken or pork are also good!"

Servings: 2 | *Ready In*: 10m

Ingredients

- 1 lb Salmon (or Chicken, Pork)
- 2 Cup Cabbage (Bite Size)
- 1 Tbsp Coconut Oil (or Olive Oil)

Sauce

- 1 Tbsp Miso Paste
- 1 Tbsp Sake (or Water)
- 1/2 tsp Soy Sauce
- 1 tsp Honey (or Sugar)

Directions

1. Cut salmon and cabbage with bite size.
2. All the ingredients of sauce into small bowl and mix it well.
3. Heat the oil in a skillet and saute them on middle heat few minutes.
4. Add mixed sauce and keep saute it.
5. Use the lid on the skillet and cook few more minutes.
6. If you wish, garnish with some chopped scallions. And ready to eat!

Sausage and Sweet Potato Stir Fry

"After watching all the recipes here and reading many more I realized it is about satisfying my own tastes hope someone else might like this mix"

***Servings**: 1 | **Time**: 15m*

Ingredients

- 1 cup sweet potato
- 1 medium onion, chopped
- 2 each Polish sausage
- 8 oz sauer kraut
- 2 tbsp molasses
- 4 oz dried cranberries
- 1 tsp cayenne pepper

Directions

1. Cook sweet potatoes and onions until soft
2. Add sausage heat through and tsp of cayenne
3. Add sauer kraut
4. Garnish with dried cranberries
5. I served with a horseradish cucumber pickle and a gluten free beer

Sauteed Green Beans with Soy, Shallots, Ginger, Garlic and Chile

Servings: 4-6 | Prep: 10m | Cook: 10m | Ready In: 20m

Ingredients

- 2 scallions, for garnish
- 1 pound green beans
- 2 tablespoons peanut or sesame oil
- 1 small shallot, finely chopped
- 3 teaspoons minced garlic
- 2 teaspoons grated fresh ginger
- 1/2 medium red chile, like jalapeno, thinly sliced
- 2 tablespoons soy sauce

Directions

1. Prepare the scallion garnish: Finely slice the scallions on an angle and drop them into a large bowl with ice and water - this will make the scallion threads curl up nicely so they look like ribbons. Set aside.
2. Wash green beans under cold running water. Cut off the root ends and discard. Bring a large pot of salted water to a boil over medium-high heat. Add the beans and blanch until bright green, about 2 minutes. Shock in ice water then drain in a colander.
3. Heat a large Wok over high heat. Add the peanut oil, then add the shallots, garlic, ginger and chile. Stir the mixture around so it fries in the oil and gets fragrant, about 30 seconds. Add the green beans and toss a couple of times to coat everything evenly. Saute for a couple of minutes so the beans get a little caramelization. Add the soy sauce and cook for 1 to 2 more minutes; the beans should still be nice and crisp. Transfer to a large platter and garnish with drained scallion curls.

Scallop Dumplings with Asian Slaw and Chili Butter Sauce

Servings: 6-8

Ingredients

- 1 pound fresh raw bay scallops, cleaned
- 1 large egg white
- 2 tablespoons chopped yellow onions
- 1 tablespoon chopped fresh cilantro leaves
- 1/2 teaspoon salt
- 1/8 teaspoon cayenne
- 2 teaspoons sesame oil
- 2 dozen round wrappers
- 15 romaine lettuce leaves
- 2 tablespoons olive oil
- 1 recipe Chili Butter Sauce, recipe follows
- 1 recipe Crunchy Asian Slaw, recipe follows
- 1 tablespoon chopped chives

Chili butter sauce:

- 1 tablespoon chopped shallots
- 1 tablespoon chopped garlic
- 1 cup dry white wine
- 1/2 pound butter, cold and cubed
- 1 tablespoon chili paste (found in Asian markets)

Crunchy asian slaw:

- 1 tablespoon olive oil
- 2/3 cup unsalted roasted peanuts
- 1/4 cup rice wine vinegar
- 2 tablespoons sesame oil
- 1 tablespoon honey
- 1 teaspoon chili paste
- 1/2 cup mayonnaise
- Salt
- Freshly ground black pepper
- 1/2 pound Napa cabbage, cored and shredded
- 1/2 pound red cabbage, cored and shredded
- 1/2 pound fresh spinach, cleaned, stemmed, and thinly sliced
- 2/3 cup thinly sliced red onions
- 1/3 cup chopped green onions, green part only
- 1/3 cup loosely packed fresh cilantro leaves

Directions

1. Put the scallops, egg white, onions, cilantro, salt, cayenne, and sesame oil in a food processor and pulse 2 or 3 times to finely chop. Do not puree. Working 1 dumpling at a time, place 1 tablespoon of the filling the center of each wrapper. Lightly wet the edges of the wrappers with water. Fold in 1/2, forming a semicircle and crimp the edges. Place the finished dumplings on a parchment-lined baking sheet and cover with a damp cloth. Fill half of the Wok with water. Place over medium-high heat and bring to a boil. Line the bottom of a medium bamboo steamer with lettuce leaves. Lay the dumplings on top of the lettuce leaves and cover with the lid. Place the steamer in the Wok and steam for 6 to 8 minutes. Carefully remove the steamer and remove the dumplings. Heat the oil in a large saute pan, over medium heat. When the oil is hot, add the dumplings. Cook for about 1 minute or until crispy on the first side. Remove from the pan. Spoon the sauce in the center of each plate. Mound the slaw in the center of the sauce. Lay the dumplings around the slaw. Garnish with chives.
2. Chili butter sauce:
In a small saucepan, over medium heat, combine the shallots, garlic and wine. Bring to a boil and reduce by half. Whisk in the butter, 1 cube at a time, until all of the butter is incorporated and the sauce coats the back of a spoon. Strain through a fine mesh sieve. Season with salt and pepper. Add the chili and mix well. Yield: about 1 1/2 to 2 cups
3. Crunchy asian slaw:
In a skillet, heat the oil over medium heat. Add the peanuts, stirring often, toast them for 3 to 4 minutes. Remove from the and set aside. In a mixing bowl, combine the vinegar, sesame oil, honey, chili paste, and mayonnaise. Season with salt and pepper. Mix well. In a large mixing bowl, combine the remaining ingredients. Mix well. Add the dressing and peanuts, toss to mix well and evenly. Season with salt and pepper. Keeps for 1 day before getting soggy. Yield: 6 to 8 servings

Seafood Mix Stir Frypasta

Ingredients

- 1/2 cup stir fry sauce

- 1/4 cup ponzu citrus sauce
- 4 cups mix vegetables (carrots, broccoli, celery, red/yellow peppers(
- 2 gloves garlic
- 1/2 onion
- 1 inch ginger
- 2 tbsp sesame oil
- 1/2 box pene pasta

Directions

1. Add 1 tbsp sesame oil to Wok
2. Add garlic, ginger & onion. Fry for 2 minutes
3. Add seafood mix , fry for 3-4 minutes, stirring frequently.
4. Add 1 tbsp sesame oil
5. Stir in mix vegetables
6. Cover for 4 minutes let steam, then add ponzu and stir sauce, replace cover for 3 more minutes
7. Stir in pene pasta. Toss and serve

Sichuan Steak and Asparagus

"The secret ingredient to this recipe is patience. By letting the meat brown slowly with minimal stirring, you get a crisp texture and caramelized flavor on each piece."

Servings*: 4 |* ***Total time****: 30m*

Ingredients

- 3 tablespoons vegetable oil
- 1 pound New York or flank steak, thinly sliced
- 3 tablespoons cornstarch
- 1 tablespoon plus 1 tsp. toasted sesame oil, divided
- 2 tablespoons minced fresh ginger
- 10 to 12 small dried hot (Thai) chiles
- 1 pound asparagus, ends trimmed, halved
- 2 tablespoons reduced-sodium soy sauce
- 1 teaspoon sugar

- 3/4 cup reduced-sodium beef broth
- Cooked Asian egg noodles (from 6 oz. dried)

Directions

1. Heat a large Wok or frying pan over high heat. Add vegetable oil, swirling pan to coat. Sprinkle steak with cornstarch, mixing to distribute evenly, then add to hot oil. Cook, stirring as little as needed for even browning, until meat is browned, 7 to 10 minutes. Transfer to a plate.
2. Add 1 tbsp. sesame oil to Wok, followed by ginger, chiles, and asparagus. Cook until fragrant, about 3 minutes. Stir in soy sauce, sugar, and broth. Cook until mixture comes to a simmer, about 4 minutes. Return steak to Wok, stirring once just to combine, and let sauce thicken slightly.
3. Put cooked noodles on a serving plate. Drizzle with 1 tsp. sesame oil; toss to coat. Spoon steak mixture over noodles.

Simple Broccoli Stir-fry

Servings: 4 | *Prep*: 5m | *Cook*: 5m | *Ready In*: 10m

Ingredients

- 1 large bunch broccoli (about 1 1/2 pounds)
- 2 tablespoons soy sauce
- 1 tablespoon cornstarch
- 1 teaspoon sugar
- 2 tablespoons plus 1 teaspoon vegetable or peanut oil
- 1 scallion, chopped
- 2 to 3 cloves garlic, chopped (about 2 teaspoons)
- 1 -inch piece ginger, peeled and chopped (about 2 teaspoons)
- Pinch to 1/4 teaspoon crushed red pepper flakes
- 1/4 teaspoon toasted sesame oil
- Cooked white or brown rice, for serving

Directions

1. Trim the florets off the broccoli, and cut into 1- to 1 1/2-inch pieces. Peel the broccoli stalks with a vegetable peeler to remove the tough outer skin, and slice 1/4 inch thick on the diagonal. Set aside.
2. Whisk together 1/2 cup water, soy sauce, cornstarch and sugar in a small bowl. Set aside.
3. Heat a large Wok over high heat. Add 2 tablespoons of the vegetable oil, and swirl to coat the Wok. Once the oil begins to smoke, add the broccoli florets and stems. Cook, stirring constantly, until browned around the edges, about 2 minutes. Add 2 tablespoons of water to steam the broccoli, and cook, stirring constantly, until tender, about 2 minutes more. Push the broccoli to the edges of the pan, forming an empty well in the center. Add the remaining 1 teaspoon vegetable oil, then the scallions, garlic, ginger and pepper flakes, and stir until aromatic, 30 to 45 seconds. Add the soy mixture, and stir until the sauce has thickened and the broccoli is coated, about 30 seconds. Remove from the heat, add the sesame oil and stir to coat. Serve with rice.

Note:

- If you don't have a Wok, use a large nonstick skillet. After the broccoli has steamed, push it to one side, tip the skillet slightly so the oil pools to one side, then add the remaining oil, scallions, garlic, ginger and pepper flakes to the oil and continue cooking according to directions.

Simple Sesame Stir-Fry (vegan)

"I used the leaves from two bok choy to line a terrine, so I was left with the succluent stems to make my lunch... This is what I made. It's that simple, I made it without a Wok, just a pan I had lying in the cupboard. Note to self...get a new Wok! :)
"

Servings: 1 | **Cook**: 5m

Ingredients

- 1 tbsp sunflower oil
- 1 tbsp ginger, thinly sliced into batons
- 1 clove garlic, finely chopped
- 1 long red chilli, sliced
- 1 packages 2 minute microwave basmati rice
- 2 bok choy, washed and sliced into one inch pieces
- 1/2 red bell pepper, sliced
- 1/2 yellow bell pepper, sliced
- 1 tbsp dark soy sauce
- 2 tsp toasted sesame oil

Directions

1. In a Wok or (as I used...a stainless steel pot) heat the sunflower oil.
2. Microwave the rice according to the instructions on the pack, and allow it to rest for one minute.
3. Add the garlic, chilli and garlic and stir. If the garlic catches and starts to smell like ut's burning, add a little water.
4. After about a minute, add the vegetables and stir fry for about another one to two minutes.
5. Add in the soy sauce, and get it mixed in all over the vegetables.
6. Add the rice to the Wok/pan and stir it in, breaking it up with your wooden spoon.
7. Put the stir fry on a plate to serve, then season with the sesame oil, and serve hot.

Simple Tofu Stir Fry I

"I'm just starting to learn how to cook, so I tried to throw together a stir fry, hope everyone enjoys! any tips are more than welcome :)"

Servings: 4 | **Cook**: 45m

Ingredients

- 1 packages tofu
- 2 tbsp Vegetable Oil
- 3 clove garlic

- 1 Onion
- 1 green bell pepper
- 1 yellow pepper
- 2 cup mushroom
- 2 tbsp honey
- 3 tbsp soy sauce
- 1 tbsp hoy sin sauce
- 2 tbsp white wine vinegar
- 2 tsp sesame seeds
- 1 tbsp corn starch
- 1/2 cup hot water

Directions

1. Preheat oven to 400°F Fahrenheit
2. Drain 16 oz tofu, set on cutting board. Wrap it in paper towels to rid it of extra moisture
3. Cut rectangular pieces about 1 inch big, place on baking sheet and bake for 20 minutes. Flip tofu after 10 minutes. This is to help dry up the tofu, that way it will absorb more flavor.
4. Dice up veggies (minus mushrooms) along with onion and garlic, and cook over medium heat.
5. Mix together vinegar, soy sauce, hoy sin sauce, and honey together. Set aside. Mix together water and cornstarch then add to mixture to thicken.
6. Put in tofu and mushrooms to cook and soften a bit, then mix in sauce mixture
7. Simmer for five minutes and you're done! Easy to make :) Serve over white rice if desired
8. Oh and feel free to add a tablespoon or two of your favorite chili sauce! I added some sriracha for an extra kick.

Simple Tuna Stir Fry II

"A dish that you can take out the chopsticks for."

Servings: 6 | **Time**: 1h30m

Ingredients

- 70 ml dark soy sauce
- 100 ml dark soy sauce
- 1/4 kg fresh tuna
- 2 tsp ground black pepper
- 30 ml olive oil
- 60 ml olive oil
- 1 large green bell pepper
- 1 large red bell pepper
- 1 large onion
- 2 tsp garlic, crushed
- 2 tsp fresh grated ginger
- 2 medium chillies
- 2 tbsp all-purpose flour
- 50 ml dry white wine
- 500 grams noodles
- salt and pepper

Directions

1. Cut the tuna into strips.
2. Mix together 70ml soy sauce with the black pepper. Mix with sliced tuna and leave in fridge to marinade for 1 hour.
3. Slice the green bell pepper, red bell pepper, onion and chillies.
4. In a heated frying pan or Wok (high heat), with 30ml olive oil, fry the green bell pepper, red bell pepper, onion, garlic, ginger and chillies. Until the onions turn lightly brown. Remove from the pan and set aside.
5. Mix the flour with the marinated tuna.
6. On a high heat in a pan or Wok, fry the tuna with 60ml olive oil. Only fry the tuna to your liking. You might have to do this in 2 or 3 stages, depending on the size of your pan. Don't worry if the tuna starts breaking up.
7. Deglaze your pan with white wine, for about 3 minutes. Then add 100ml soy sauce and simmer for another 3 minutes.
8. Cook your noodles according to the package instructions.
9. Mix your onion mixture together with the fried tuna in a heated pan for 5 minutes.
10. Mix your deglazed liquid with your noodles.
11. Serve the tuna on top of the noodles or mix them together.

Singapore Chile Prawns

*Servings: 4-6 | **Prep**: 15m | **Cook**: 20m | **Ready In**: 35m*

Ingredients

Sauce:

- 1 cup water
- 5 tablespoons tomato catsup
- 1 1/2 to 3 tablespoons sugar, or to taste
- 1 1/2 teaspoons corn flour
- 1 teaspoon pounded brown preserved soya beans or dark miso (optional)
- 1/4 teaspoons salt

Prawns:

- 1 pound large, whole prawns (unshelled)
- 3 tablespoons vegetable oil
- 8 cloves garlic, roughly chopped
- 8 fresh red chiles, roughly chopped
- 1 egg
- 2 scallions, cut into finger lengths
- 1 teaspoon freshly squeezed lime or lemon juice
- 1 small bunch cilantro, cut into 1-inch long pieces
- Serving Suggestions: loaf of French bread

Directions

1. Make the Sauce: Whisk together all the ingredients in a bowl and set aside.
2. Make the Prawns: Cut down the backs of the prawns and remove the black intestinal vein. Set aside.
3. Heat the oil in a Wok or shallow saucepan over high heat. Add the garlic and stir-fry for 1 minute. Add the chiles and stir-fry for another minute. Add the prawns and stir-fry until the shell turn slightly red, about 2 to 3 minutes. Add the sauce and stir-fry until the shells turn red.
4. Break the egg into the Wok and, using a fork, streak the egg through the sauce (this is an important step, as the egg has to be in

beautiful gold and white streaks). Simmer the sauce for a few seconds and remove from the heat. Stir in the scallions and lime juice.
5. Transfer the prawns to a platter, garnish with the cilantro, and serve with chunks of French bread.

Note

- This dish is also wonderful with mussels, crabs or lobsters; or you could mix all the seafood together. It's a Singapore version of a French seafood stew.

Sirloin-Snap Pea Stir-fry

Servings: 4 | *Prep*: 10m | *Cook*: 15m | *Ready In*: 25m

Ingredients

- 2 3 oz. packages ramen noodles
- 1 pound sugar snap peas
- 3 tablespoons vegetable oil
- 1 pound boneless sirloin steak, thinly sliced crosswise
- 1/4 cup chopped fresh ginger
- 3 garlic cloves, smashed
- 6 scallions, sliced
- 1 cup low-sodium beef broth
- 1/4 cup reduced-sodium soy sauce
- 2 tablespoons cornstarch
- 1 tablespoon toasted sesame oil

Directions

1. Cook ramen noodles as package label directs. Discard flavoring packets. Drain noodles. Boil snap peas for 2 minutes. Drain and rinse with cold water.
2. Warm 1 Tbsp. oil in a skillet over medium-high heat. Add steak, stir-fry for 2 minutes. Transfer to a plate. Add remaining 2 Tbsp. oil to skillet. Stir fry ginger, garlic and scallions for 1 minute.

3. Whisk together broth, soy sauce and cornstarch. Add to skillet; stir-fry for 1 minute. Add peas and steak; stir until hot. Stir in sesame oil. Toss in ramen noodles. Serve hot.

Sizzling Skirt Steak with Asparagus and Red Pepper

"The marinade of fish sauce and grated red onion gives intense flavor to the steak, tenderizes the meat, and results in a slightly caramelized crust. Use your largest sauté pan (preferably 14-inch so that the vegetables and steak have room to caramelize and cook quickly) or a large Wok."

Ingredients

Servings: 4 | ***Hands-on***: 20m | ***Total time***: 40m

Ingredients

- 1 pound skirt steak, halved crosswise
- 1 1/2 tablespoons fish sauce, divided
- 2 medium red onions, divided
- 12 ounces asparagus, trimmed
- 1 large red bell pepper, thinly sliced
- 2 tablespoons olive oil

Directions

1. Combine steak and 1 tablespoon fish sauce in a shallow dish. Cut 1 onion in half lengthwise. Grate half of the onion. Add onion pulp to steak; toss to coat. Cover and let stand at room temperature for 30 minutes.
2. Cut remaining 1 1/2 onions into 1/4-inch-thick vertical slices. Cut each asparagus spear diagonally into 3 pieces. Combine sliced onion, asparagus, bell pepper, and oil; toss to coat. Heat a large Wok or stainless steel skillet over high heat. Add vegetables to pan; stir-fry 5 minutes or until crisp-tender. Add remaining 1 1/2 teaspoons fish sauce to pan; stir-fry 30 seconds. Remove vegetable mixture from pan; keep warm.
3. Scrape onion pulp off of steak. Return Wok to high heat. Add steak to pan; cook 3 minutes on each side or until desired degree of doneness. Place steak on a cutting board; let stand at least 5

minutes. Cut steak across the grain into slices. Serve with vegetables.

Smoked salmon and broccoli stir-fry

Servings: 4 | **Cook**: 15 m

Ingredients

- 2 tbsp sweet chilli
- 2 tbsp fish sauce
- 2 tbsp rice vinegar
- thumb-size piece of fresh ginger, grated
- the juice of 1 lime
- 400g tenderstem broccoli
- a glug of vegetable oil
- 600g straight-to-Wok udon noodles
- 6 spring onions, finely sliced
- 1 red chilli, sliced
- 200g smoked salmon, torn

Directions

1. Mix the sweet chilli, fish sauce and rice vinegar with the ginger and lime juice.
2. Blanch the broccoli for 2 minutes, then drain. Over a high heat, pour the oil into a Wok, add the broccoli and stir-fry for 1 minute. Add the noodles and the spring onions. Stir-fry for 2 minutes.
3. Stir through half the lime dressing and the chilli. Top with the salmon, then pour over the rest of the dressing.

Soy Stir Fry

Servings: 3 | **Time**: 30m

Ingredients

- Soy
- Large potatos
- 1 garlic
- Medium onion

Directions

1. Large cut purple potatoes,cut carrots & oinons. Add 2 cooked chicken.
2. Put everything in fry pan, cook purple potatoes first, then add others to pan-then last

Spicy Cauliflower Stir-fry !

"If you're into spicy curry flavoured stir fry, then try this recipe! You won't regret it :)"

Servings: 4 | **Time**: 20m

Ingredients

- Pan
- 1 large Cauliflower cut into Pieces
- 1 medium Onion (sliced)
- 2 tbsp Olive oil

1 Salt

- Spices
- 3 Black cloves
- 1/2 tsp Cumin seed
- 1/2 tsp All spice powder (garam masala)
- 1 tsp Turmeric powder
- 1/2 tsp Cumin powder

Directions

1. Warm up the pan and add in the oil
2. Add sliced onions and fry until light brown (not burnt) on high heat
3. Add a pinch of salt while frying along with the cauliflowers
4. Fry the cauliflower until brown (a little bit tender on mid-high heat) don't burn em!
5. Add the spices and stir
6. Serve with a sliced lemon to the side and garnish with cilantro
7. Add the cloves and cumin seeds and continue frying. Stir every 30 seconds
8. You can serve it with rice or flat bread (roti)

Spicy Eggplant

Servings: 4 | ***Prep***: 20m | ***Cook***: 15m | ***Ready In***: 35m

Ingredients

- 2 tablespoons chicken broth
- 1 tablespoon hoisin sauce
- 1 tablespoon soy sauce
- 2 teaspoons Chinese black vinegar
- 2 teaspoons plum sauce
- 4 Chinese eggplants (about 1 pound), stems removed
- Vegetable oil, for deep-frying
- 2 teaspoons minced garlic
- 1 teaspoon minced ginger
- 4 dried whole chile peppers
- 2 green onions, cut into 2-inch lengths
- 1/4 pound ground pork
- Chopped cilantro leaves or sliced green onions

Directions

Sauce:

1. Combine sauce ingredients in a small bowl; mix well.
2. With a vegetable peeler, remove 1-inch strips of the eggplant skin, leaving a 1-inch strip of skin in between. Cut the eggplant into

fourths lengthwise, then cut each section crosswise into 3-inch pieces.
3. Pour enough oil into a 2-quart saucepan to fill 3 inches. Heat over medium heat to 350 degrees F. Deep-fry the eggplant batches until golden brown, about 3 minutes. Remove with a slotted spoon and drain well on paper towels.
4. Place Wok over a high heat until hot. Add 1 tablespoon of deep-frying oil and swirl to coat the sides. Add the garlic, ginger, dried chiles and green onion; cook, stirring, until fragrant, about 30 seconds. Add ground meat and cook, breaking up pieces with back of a spoon, until brown and crumbly. Add the sauce and bring to a simmer. Add the cooked eggplant and stir to coat. Scoop onto a warm serving platter. Serve, garnished with cilantro or green onions.

Spicy Lotus Root Kimpira Stir-fry

"Kimpira is a kind of slightly spicy stir-fried vegetables with mirin and soy sauce. Usually it's made with carrot and gobo root, but I LOVE making it with lotus roots ^^ You will love it too I think!"

Servings*: 2 | **Time**: 30m*

Ingredients

- 250 g lotus root (one large section)
- 1/2 red chili pepper (togarashi)
- 1 Tbsp sesame oil
- 2 Tbsp soy sauce
- 1 1/2 Tbsp mirin
- 1/2 Tbsp sugar
- Sesame seeds (optional)

Directions

1. This is what 1 section of lotus root looks like (I cut it in half).
2. Wash the lotus root well (leave the skin on) and slice into 7 mm rounds. Soak it in water for 5-10 minutes. Drain well and pat dry. If they are really big, cut in half.

3. Heat sesame oil in a frying pan. Add the lotus root and 1/2 red chili pepper. Stir fry until the lotus root is coated in oil. Cover the frying pan with a lid and "steam" for 4 minutes, stirring a couple times in between (this helps cook the lotus roots all the way through compared to just stir-frying)
4. Remove lid and add the soy sauce, mirin and sugar. Stir briefly then cover the pan with a lid again for about 3 minutes. Give it a stir in between.
5. Remove the lid and continuing cooking the lotus root until all the liquid has evaporating (make sure you stir it around while cooking so the flavor gets distributed).
6. I like to sprinkle on some sesame seeds at the end too. Serve immediately or used for your lunch boxes!

Spicy Stir-Fry Duck with White Pineapple

Servings: 6 | *Prep*: 30m | *Inactive*: 24m | *Cook*: 15m | *Ready In*: 1h9m

Ingredients

6 duck breasts

Brine:

- 1 gallon water
- 1/2 pound kosher salt
- 1/2 cup brown sugar
- 1 cup dry oregano
- 1/2 cup cumin seed
- 1 1/2 tablespoons chopped garlic
- 6 tablespoons ancho puree
- 1 cup apple cider vinegar
- 20 whole cloves

Stir Fry:

- 2 tablespoons olive oil
- 1 tablespoon Tequila
- 1/4 cup julienne red peppers
- 1/4 cup julienne green peppers
- 1/4 cup julienne carrots

- 1/3 cup asparagus tips
- 1/4 cup cleaned, blanched, and julienned Nopalitos, (Nopales found in Mexican markets)
- 1/3 cup scallions
- 1/2 piece jalapeno pepper, julienne
- 1 teaspoon hot chili sauce
- 1 teaspoon chopped garlic
- Salt and pepper
- 1 cup white pineapple circles or pineapple circles

Directions

1. Begin by making the brine. Combine all of the ingredients in a large pot. Warm slightly so salt and sugar dissolve. Remove from the heat and cool to room temperature. Add the duck breasts and marinate in brine, in the refrigerator, for 24 hours.
2. Once the duck is ready, cut the breasts into julienne strips and saute in a large skillet or Wok in olive oil. Add the Tequila and saute for a few minutes. Add all of the julienne cut vegetables, chili sauce and garlic except for the pineapple. Saute vegetables for approximately 5 minutes. Season, to taste, with salt and pepper.
3. Cut the pineapple into circles and add last, just before serving.
4. Serve stir-fry over pasta or rice.

Note

- This recipe was provided by professional chefs and has been scaled down from a bulk recipe provided by a restaurant. The FN chefs have not tested this recipe, in the proportions indicated, and therefore, we cannot make any representation as to the results.

Spicy Szechuan Stir-Fry

Servings: 4 | Prep: 15m | Cook: 12m | Ready In: 27m

Ingredients

- 1 tablespoon Szechuan peppercorns

- Salt
- 1 pound boneless, skinless chicken, pounded thin and cut into 1-inch thick strips
- 2 tablespoons canola oil
- 2 tablespoons ginger, minced
- 1 tablespoon garlic, minced
- 1 cup onions, julienned
- 1 cup broccoli florets
- 1/4 cup green peppers, julienned
- 1/4 cup red peppers, julienned
- 1/4 cup yellow peppers, julienned
- 1 cup shiitake mushrooms, sliced
- 2 tablespoons thin soy sauce
- 1/4 cup dry sherry
- 1 tablespoon chile paste
- 1/4 cup scallions, cut thinly on the bias

Directions

- Heat a small, dry saucepan. When the saucepan is hot, add the Szechuan peppercorns and, shaking the pan constantly, toast until the peppercorns are fragrant. Remove from the heat. Place the peppercorns in a spice grinder and grind. Season the chicken pieces with the peppercorns and salt and set aside. Heat a large Wok over high heat. When the Wok is hot, add the oil. Add the ginger, garlic and onions and stir fry for 1 minute. Add the chicken, broccoli, peppers, shiitake mushrooms, soy sauce, sherry and chile paste. Stir fry until the chicken is cooked through and the vegetables are cooked, but al dente, about 5 minutes. Add the scallions and stir fry for 1 more minute. T

Squid and mushroom stir fry

"I was cooking some dishes for a dinner and needed something showy for the table. I had some frozen squid in a diamond cut pattern. I soaked some dry shiitake mushrooms and used half a zucchini I had left. It turned out fantastic and my guests loved it."

Ingredients

- 300 grams frozen squid squares, diamond cut
- 6 medium size dry shiitake mushrooms
- 1 small green zucchini
- 2 tbsp oyster sauce
- 1 tsp. chopped fresh ginger
- 1 tsp finely chopped garlic
- 2 tbsp water
- 2 tbsp oil
- 1/2 Japanese leek sliced in 1/4 inch rings

Directions

1. Start the Wok with the oil and add the garlic and ginger, stir for 10 seconds.
2. Add the cubed zucchini, then the leeks and mushrooms
3. Mix the oyster sauce with the Water in a small bowl and then add it to the Wok, stir some more.
4. Add a bit more water if needed.
5. Lastly, add the squares of squid and stir well for about two more minutes and it is done!
6. The mushrooms have to be rehydrated before adding to the pan. Fresh mushrooms work well too.

Steak and Asparagus Stir-Fry

"Spring's favorite vegetable shines in this quick stir-fry. Serve with precooked jasmine rice, available in pouches on the rice aisle."

Servings: 4

Ingredients

- 1/4 cup unsalted chicken stock (such as Swanson)
- 1 1/2 tablespoons oyster sauce
- 1 1/2 tablespoons lower-sodium soy sauce
- 2 teaspoons grated peeled fresh ginger
- 2 teaspoons minced garlic
- 1 teaspoon cornstarch

- 5 teaspoons canola oil, divided
- 12 ounces boneless sirloin steak, cut into 1/4-inch strips
- 12 ounces medium asparagus, trimmed and cut into 2-inch pieces
- 1 medium red bell pepper, cut into strips
- 1/2 teaspoon crushed red pepper
- 3 green onions, chopped

Preparation

1. Combine first 6 ingredients in a small bowl, stirring well with a whisk.
2. Heat a large skillet over high heat. Add 1 tablespoon oil to pan; swirl to coat. Add beef; stir-fry until browned but not cooked through (about 1 1/2 minutes). Place beef on a plate; discard liquid in pan.
3. Return pan to high heat. Add remaining 2 teaspoons oil; swirl to coat. Add asparagus and bell pepper; stir-fry 2 minutes. Add crushed red pepper and green onions; stir-fry 30 seconds. Reduce heat to medium-high. Add stock mixture; cook 3 minutes or until sauce is slightly thickened. Return beef and any juices to pan, and cook for 1 minute.

Steak Stir Fry

Servings: 1 | **Cook**: 10m

Ingredients

- 1 bunch mixed veggies
- 1/4 onion
- 1 small potato
- 1 steak

Directions

1. Add butter to a warm saute pan.
2. Add your favorite mixed veggies once butter is melted (i used carrots, onions, corn and green beans)
3. Once veggies start to cook up add your sliced up steak and potato.

4. Season it to your liking (paprika, onion powder, garlic powder, salt and pepper)
5. Let it cook up for a minute then add 3 oz water (or chicken stock).
6. Let the water boil off and its ready to be served

Steak, Shiitake, and Bok Choy Stir-Fry

"Choose quick-cooking flank steaks for a speedy stir-fry dish packed with shiitake mushrooms and bok choy. These ingredients from the Orient combine to give the recipe high-impact flavor. Watch the video: How to Cook Steak, Shiitake, and Bok Choy Stir-Fry"

Servings: 4

Ingredients

- 2 tablespoons grated fresh ginger
- 1 tablespoon minced fresh garlic
- 3 tablespoons low-sodium soy sauce
- 4 teaspoons cornstarch, divided
- 1 teaspoon toasted sesame oil
- 1/2 teaspoon crushed red pepper
- 1 pound flank steak, trimmed and thinly sliced
- Cooking spray
- 2 cups thinly sliced shiitake mushrooms (about 1/2 pound)
- 1 cup thinly vertically sliced onion
- 1 cup red bell pepper strips
- 4 cups sliced bok choy (about 1 medium head)
- 1 cup less-sodium beef broth

Directions

1. Combine ginger, garlic, soy sauce, 2 teaspoons cornstarch, oil, and crushed red pepper in a large zip-top bag; add steak to bag. Seal and marinate in refrigerator 20 minutes.
2. Heat a large nonstick skillet over medium-high heat. Coat pan with cooking spray, and add mushrooms, onion, and bell pepper to pan. Cook 3 minutes or until crisp-tender; transfer to a large bowl. Add bok choy to pan; sauté 2 minutes or until slightly wilted; add to bowl; keep warm.

3. Recoat pan with cooking spray. Add half of steak mixture to pan; cook 3 minutes or until browned, stirring occasionally. Transfer to a large bowl; keep warm. Coat pan with cooking spray. Add remaining steak mixture to pan; cook 3 minutes or until browned, stirring occasionally. Add to bowl; keep warm.
4. Combine broth and remaining 2 teaspoons cornstarch, stirring with a whisk. Add to pan, scraping pan to loosen browned bits. Bring to a boil; cook 1 minute or until mixture thickens, stirring constantly. Return steak and vegetables to pan; toss gently to coat.

Steamed Bun Dough

Servings: 4 | *Prep*: 1h | *Inactive*: 4m | *Cook*: 25m | *Ready In*: 1h29m

Ingredients

- 1 tablespoon active dry yeast
- 3/4 cup warm water
- 2 tablespoons plus 1 teaspoon white sugar
- 1 3/4 cups flour
- 1/4 teaspoon salt
- 1 tablespoon lard or vegetable oil
- 1/2 teaspoon baking powder
- Shrimp and Green Onion Filling, recipe follows
- Lettuce or cabbage leaves, for lining steamer tray
- Shrimp and Green Onion Filling:
- 3 tablespoons vegetable oil
- 2 tablespoons ginger, chopped
- 6 green onions, chopped
- 1 pound raw shrimp, finely chopped
- 1/2 cup canned bamboo shoots, drained and chopped
- 1 1/2 tablespoons white sugar
- 1/4 cup soy sauce
- 1 teaspoon sesame oil
- 2 tablespoons cornstarch mixed with 2 1/2 tablespoons water

Directions

1. Dissolve the yeast in 1/4 cup warm water. Add 1 teaspoon sugar, 1/4 cup flour, and stir to mix well. Allow to stand for 30 minutes.
2. Mix in remaining warm water, remaining flour and sugar, salt, and lard or vegetable oil. Knead until dough surface is smooth and elastic. Roll over in a greased bowl, and let stand until triple in size, about 2 1/2 to 3 hours.
3. Punch down dough, and spread out on a floured board. Sprinkle baking powder evenly on surface, and knead for 5 minutes. Divide dough into 2 parts, and place the piece you are not working with in a covered bowl. Form each half into a log about 2 inches thick. Cut logs into 1-inch pieces and roll each into a ball. Cover with a damp towel.
4. Working with 1 piece of dough at a time, press into a thin disc shape. Place about 1 tablespoon of filling in center, and then gather up edges and twist to seal, using some extra drops of water to stick together as needed. Cover with a damp kitchen towel and repeat with remaining dough.
5. Line bamboo steamer tray with lettuce or cabbage leaves. Place buns, sealed side down, in bamboo steamer tray and let rise for 45 minutes. Meanwhile, heat water to boiling in a Wok to a level just below the bamboo steamer.
6. Place bamboo steamer in Wok and steam buns for 20 to 25 minutes, and then remove from heat. Remove lid before turning off heat, or else water will drip back onto bun surface and produce yellowish "blister".
7. Shrimp and Green Onion Filling:
Place a Wok over medium heat. Add the oil and, when hot, add the ginger, and green onion and stir-fry until aromatic, about 1 minute. Add the shrimp and bamboo shoots and cook for 1 minute. Add the sugar, soy sauce, and sesame oil and stir to combine. Combine the cornstarch and the water and add to the shrimp mixture, stirring frequently. The mixture should thicken immediately. Transfer mixture to a bowl and allow to cool before assembling the buns.

Steamed Clams in Butter and Sake

"This recipe is the best for seafood lovers. Clams are steamed with sake and mirin and a bit of green onion in this Japanese way of preparation. My husband likes it so much."

Servings: 4 | ***Prep***: 10m | ***Cook***: 10m | ***Ready In***: 20m

Ingredients

- 4 teaspoons sake
- 4 teaspoons mirin (Japanese sweet wine)
- 2 teaspoons rice vinegar
- 1/4 pounds clams in shell, scrubbed
- 3 tablespoons butter
- 1 teaspoon soy sauce
- 1 green onion, chopped

Directions

1. Scrub and rinse clams. Soak in a large bowl of cold water for 5 minutes. Drain thoroughly.
2. Heat a Wok or large saucepan over high heat. Quickly pour in the sake, mirin and rice vinegar. Add the clams; cover and cook until the clams open, 3 to 4 minutes. Discard any clams that do not open.
3. Remove any scum that forms on the surface using a spoon or paper towel. Stir in the butter, soy sauce and green onion, tossing to coat the clams as the butter melts. Arrange clams on a serving plate and drizzle the sauce over them. Serve immediately.

Steamed Dumpling Spoons with Special Sauce

Servings: 5 | **Prep**: 20m | **Cook**: 10m | **Ready In**: 30m

Ingredients

For the dumplings:

- 1/2 pound ground pork
- 1/2 cup finely chopped straw mushrooms (recommended: Polar)
- 3 scallions, green parts only, finely chopped
- 1 tablespoon minced ginger
- 1 tablespoon low-sodium soy sauce
- 1 teaspoon sesame seed oil
- 2 tablespoons hot and spicy Szechwan seasoning mix (recommended: Sun Luck)

- 21 gyoza or pot sticker wrappers

For the special sauce:

- 1/4 cup rice wine vinegar
- 1/2 teaspoon Asian Chili paste
- 1 teaspoon minced ginger
- 1 1/2 teaspoons honey

Directions

For the special sauce:

- Special equipment: bamboo steamer

For the dumplings:

1. In a large bowl, combine ground pork, chopped mushrooms, scallions, ginger, soy sauce, sesame seed oil, and seasoning mix. Stir thoroughly.
2. Place 1 tablespoon of filling on each wrapper and gather sides up to middle. Leave center of dumpling open. Tap bottom on counter so dumplings sit upright. To keep dumplings from drying out, cover with a damp paper towel until ready to steam.
3. Cut a piece of parchment paper to fit bamboo steamer. Lightly spray with cooking spray and fit into steamer.
4. Place dumplings in steamer and set on top of a Wok or medium pot of boiling water. Steam for 6 to 8 minutes or until filling is cooked through.

For the special sauce:

1. In a medium bowl, stir together all Special Sauce ingredients.
2. Serve dumplings on a Chinese soup spoon with a small amount of sauce.

Steamed Salmon with Savory Black Bean Sauce

"Look for dried wood ear (sometimes called cloud ear, tree ear, or silver ear) mushrooms and jars of black bean sauce in the Asian food aisles of large supermarkets. If you don't have a bamboo steamer, use a round cooling rack to support the pie plate in the Wok or skillet."

Servings: 4

Ingredients

- 2 dried wood ear mushrooms
- 4 (6-ounce) salmon fillets, skinned (about 1 inch thick)
- 2 teaspoons cornstarch
- 1/4 teaspoon salt
- 1/8 teaspoon ground white pepper
- 1/2 cup thinly sliced green onions
- 3 tablespoons sake (rice wine)
- 2 tablespoons black bean sauce
- 1 tablespoon minced fresh garlic
- 1 teaspoon sugar
- 2 teaspoons dark sesame oil
- 1 to 2 jalapeño peppers, thinly sliced

Directions

1. Soak mushrooms in hot water 20 minutes or until soft; drain and cut into thin strips.
2. Cut 3 (3/4-inch) deep lengthwise slits in each fillet. Combine cornstarch, salt, and pepper; sprinkle over fish. Let stand 10 minutes. Stuff mushroom strips and green onions into slits.
3. Place fish in a 9-inch pie plate. Combine sake and the remaining ingredients; pour over fish. Place a bamboo steamer basket in a large Wok, and add water to Wok to a depth of 1 1/2 inches below basket. Bring the water to a boil. Place pie plate in bottom of steamer basket; cover and cook 8 minutes or until fish flakes easily when tested with a fork.

Stir Fry Bacon With Brocoli In 10 Minutes

"My version

Easy and quick stir fry

Loving it"

Servings: 4 | *Cook:* 10m

Ingredients

- 2 cup dice bacon
- 6 cup brocoli
- 1 tbsp light soy sauce

Fried Shallot Oil

- 1 tbsp Lg Fried Shallot Oil

Directions

1. Quick blanch brocoli.....bring a pot of water to a boil then simmer down add salt and broccoli for 3 minute then drain under running water to cool it
2. In pan stir fry bacon till cooked and lightly crispy then toss in cooked brocoli, then add in the light soy sauce
3. Add light soy sauce and my simple recipe for SHALLOT OIL and mix well then serve

Stir Fry French Bean And Eggs With Onion Sambal

"Simple lightly spicy side dish that goes well with white rice"

Servings: 6 | **Time**: 10m

Ingredients

- 3 tbsp oil
- 4 cups French beans
- 1 cup onion
- 2 tsp sambal
- 1 tbsp light soy sauce
- 1 tbsp sugar

Directions

1. In an oiled pan, fry the French beans with sliced onion for few minutes, then add in the eggs and stir fry till well mixed.
2. Make a small cavity in the middle, add 1 tbsp of oil then the store bought sambal / sambal oelek together with light soy sauce and sugar. Mix well for 1 minute.
3. Then stir fry all the French beans and the sambal well for another 1 minute. Serve

Stir Fry Hallibut Fillet With Black Pepper

Servings: 4 | Cook: 20m

Ingredients

Any fish

- 2 halibut fillet or any fish
- 1 cup cornstarch (for coating the fish)

Seasoning

- 2 tbsp light soy sauce
- 1 tsp sugar
- 1/2 tbsp fresh fine grated Black pepper

Pounded paste

- 4 clove garlic
- 4 small shallot or onion
- 1 large onion

Cornstarch mixture (for thickening sauce)

- 1 tsp cornstarch
- 4 tbsp water
- 1 cucumber
- 3 small tomato

Directions

Cornstarch mixture

- Mix cornstarch with water and set aside

Pan fried fillet

- Coat fish with cornstarch
- With oil pan fried fillet then use a scissor and cut into bite size and set aside

Stir fry

1. With 2 tbsp of oil sauté pounded paste and onion till fragrance then add light soy sauce
2. Add fish and black pepper then top spring onion and gently stir fry to mix
3. Add 2 tbsp of cornstarch mixture and stir fry gently again and let sauce almost evaporated then off heat
4. Put cut up cucumber and tomato on the plate first then top cooked dish and serve immediately

Stir fry hotdogs and veggies

"Very delicious"

Servings: 6

Ingredients

- 2 lb hotdogs
- 1/2 cup sliced carrots
- 1/2 cup broccoli
- 1/2 cup cauliflower
- 2 tbsp vegetable oil
- 1 tbsp Heinz tomato ketchup
- 1/2 oz chicken broth
- 1 tbsp cornstarch
- 1 tsp yellow prepared mustard
- 1/4 cup water

Directions

1. Mix mustard, ketchup, and chicken broth together set aside
2. Cut hotdogs on a bias. Heat oil in a pan add hotdogs.
3. When hotdogs are crispy remove the hotdogs. Add veggies to oil and stir fry 3 minutes add chicken broth, mustard, and ketchup. Cook them till your desired doneness.
4. Add hotdogs back and add cornstarch solution of water and cornstarch. Cook 2 minutes let rest 7 minutes stir and serve

Stir Fry Mushroom and Omelette Ribbon

Servings: 4 | Cook: 10m

Ingredients

- 1 cup shimeji mushroom
- 1 cup spring onion or cilantro
- 2 tbsp oil
- 6 small cherry tomato
- omelette ribbon
- 3 eggs
- 1 tbsp oil
- kikomon tempura and base sauce
- 2 tbsp tempura sauce
- 1 tbsp water

Directions

1. Make omelette ribbon
2. Beat eggs and season with dash of salt and pepper then on oiled pan pour a layer of eggs then let eggs set
3. Let eggs cooled then roll up and thinly slice omelette
4. Stir fry mushroom
5. In pan with oil stir fry shimeji mushroom for 1 minute then add sauce mix well then add water and stir fry for half a minute
6. Off heat and add omelette ribbon and spring onion and mix well then serve immediately

Stir Fry Sugar Snap Pea

Servings: 4 | ***Cook***: 5m

Ingredients

- 2 tbsp oil
- 3 clove pounded garlic
- 1 large onion
- 2 cup slice sugar snap pea
- 1 deseeded red chili pepper slice
- 1 deseeded green chili pepper
- 1/4 cup any stock

Directions

1. In pan with oil saute pounded gaic and sugar snap pea and onion with red and green chili pepper
2. Season with a dash of salt
3. Add stock and bring it to a simmer and mix well then off heat and serve

Stir Fry I

"very good and easy"

Ingredients

- 3 lb boneless skinless chicken breasts or pork loin chops
- 1 bag of frozen oriental stir-fry vegetables with seasoning package
- 1 tbsp soy sauce
- 2 tsp vegetable oil

Directions

1. Cut meat into bit size pieces.
2. Coat large skillet with cooking spray. Heat to medium high temperature. Add meat cook till done
3. Add vegetables, cover cook 5 minutes.
4. Add 1/4cup of water, vegetable seasoning package, soy sauce and oil.
5. Cook, stirring until mixture is heated through. Serve over rice

Stir-Fried Bok Choy with Ginger and Garlic

Servings: 4 | **Prep**: 5m | **Cook**: 5m | **Ready In**: 10m

Ingredients

- 1 tablespoon olive oil
- 2 cloves garlic, minced
- 1 tablespoon minced fresh ginger
- 8 cups chopped fresh bok choy
- 2 tablespoons reduced-sodium soy sauce
- Salt and ground black pepper

Directions

- Heat oil in a large skillet over medium heat. Add garlic and ginger and cook 1 minute. Add bok choy and soy sauce cook 3 to 5 minutes, until greens are wilted and stalks are crisp-tender. Season, to taste, with salt and black pepper.

Stir-Fried Broccoli

Servings: 8 | **Prep**: 10m | **Cook**: 15m

Ingredients

- 2 tablespoons sesame seeds
- 2 tablespoons vegetable oil
- 1 tablespoon sesame oil
- 2 cloves garlic, minced
- 1/2 red bell pepper, cored, seeded and thinly sliced
- 2 pounds broccoli florets, cut into bite-size pieces (about 12 cups)
- 1 cup low-sodium chicken broth
- Salt and pepper

Directions

1. Spread sesame seeds in a small skillet over medium-high heat and cook, stirring constantly, until lightly toasted and beginning to release oil, about 1 minute. Remove to a plate to cool.
2. Warm vegetable oil with sesame oil in a large skillet over medium-high heat. Add garlic and sauté until fragrant, about 1 minute. Stir in bell pepper. Add broccoli and stir well until coated in oil. Cook, stirring, until broccoli is slightly softened, 2 to 3 minutes.
3. Pour in broth; bring to a simmer. Reduce heat to low, cover and cook, stirring once or twice, until broccoli is tender, about 5 minutes. Sprinkle with sesame seeds. Season with salt and pepper; serve warm.

Stir-fried Goya (Goya Chanpuru)

"This is known as the famous local food from Okinawa in Japan. And it's a kind of stir-fried vegetables, pork, and tofu. Goya is bitter gourd and is one of the most popular Okinawan foods."

Servings: 2 | **Time**: 15m

Ingredients

- 1/2 (20 cm) goya (cut in half lengthwise, remove the seeds, cut into 3~5mm slices)
- 200 g firm tofu (drained and cut into bite sized pieces)
- 100~150 g pork or ham (cut into bite sized pieces)
- 1/2 sliced onion

- 1/4 carrot (cut into thin strips)
- 1~2 beaten eggs

Seasonings:

- 1 tbsp sake
- 1 tbsp soy sauce
- 1/2~1 tbsp oyster sauce
- 1 tbsp vegetables oil or olive oil for frying tofu
- 1 tbsp sesame oil
- Dried bonito flakes for topping (optional)
- Salt and pepper for seasoning

Directions

1. Sprinkle salt on goya and rub, leave it for about 10 mins. Wash with water and drain well.
2. Heat the oil (vegetable or olive oil) in a pan over medium heat, stir fry tofu until browned. Remove tofu from the pan and set aside.
3. Heat the sesame oil in the same pan, add pork, onion, carrot, goya and stir fry for 1~2 mins(softened). Put tofu back in the pan and then add seasonings and combine.
4. Pour the beaten egg over and stir quickly to mix. Season with salt and pepper. Top with dried bonito flakes (optional).

Stir-Fried Mushrooms with Baby Corn

"Here is a Thai vegetable side dish with plenty of Chinese influences. Utilize whatever mushrooms are in season, such as straw, button, het kone or shiitake mushrooms. "

Servings: 4 | **Prep**: 10m | **Cook**: 15m | **Ready In**: 25m

Ingredients

- 2 tablespoons cooking oil
- 3 cloves garlic, minced
- 1 onion, diced
- 8 baby corn ears, sliced
- 2/3 pound fresh mushrooms, sliced

- 1 tablespoon fish sauce
- 1 tablespoon light soy sauce
- 1 tablespoon oyster sauce
- 2 teaspoons cornstarch
- 3 tablespoons water
- 1 red chile pepper, sliced
- 1/4 cup chopped fresh cilantro

Directions

1. Heat the oil in a large skillet or Wok over medium heat; cook the garlic in the hot oil until browned, 5 to 7 minutes. Add the onion and baby corn and cook until the onion is translucent, 5 to 7 minutes. Add the mushrooms to the mixture and cook until slightly softened, about 2 minutes. Pour the fish sauce, soy sauce, and oyster sauce into the mixture and stir until incorporated.
2. Whisk the cornstarch and water together in a small bowl until the cornstarch is dissolved into the water; pour into the mushroom mixture. Cook and stir until thickened and glistening. Transfer to a serving dish; garnish with the chile pepper and cilantro to serve.

Stir-Fry Cabbage

Servings: 4 | Prep: 5m | Cook: 6m | Ready In: 11m

Ingredients

- 2 teaspoons canola oil
- 1 small onion, sliced
- 1 clove garlic, minced
- 1 teaspoon minced ginger
- 1 head napa cabbage, cleaned and sliced
- 2 tablespoons soy sauce
- 1 tablespoon rice vinegar
- 2 teaspoons toasted sesame oil

Directions

- In a large saute pan over medium-high heat, add the canola oil and heat. Add the onion, garlic and ginger and saute, stirring, for 1 minute. Add the cabbage and cook until just starting to wilt, about 2 minutes. Add the soy sauce and rice vinegar and stir well and cook just until cabbage is wilted, about 3 minutes. Remove from heat and drizzle with the sesame oil.

Stir-Fry in a Bun

Servings: 4 | **Prep**: 15m | **Inactive**: 15m | **Cook**: 5m | **Ready In**: 35m

Ingredients

- 1 tablespoon canola oil
- 1 tablespoon minced garlic
- 1 tablespoon minced ginger
- 1 pound top sirloin, slightly frozen, then cut into 1/4-inch slices, cut against the grain
- 2 carrots, peeled and cut on the bias into 1/4-inch pieces, approximately 1 cup
- 3 celery stalks, cut on the bias into 1/4-inch pieces, approximately 1 cup
- 1 red bell pepper, cut into 1/2-inch strips, approximately 1 cup
- 1 red onion, cut into 1/4-inch pieces, approximately 1 cup
- 1/4 cup sake
- 3 tablespoons soy sauce
- 1 tablespoon hoisin sauce
- Cornstarch slurry (mix 1/2 teaspoon cornstarch with 1/2 teaspoon water)
- 1 cup bean sprouts
- 1/4 teaspoon sesame oil
- 1 package Hawaiian sweet dinner rolls (12 to 16 rolls)
- 1/2 bunch green onions, julienned for garnish

Directions

1. In a large saute pan, or Wok, add oil over high heat. Add in garlic and ginger, cook for 10 to 15 seconds. Add sirloin and saute,

stirring frequently until just cooked through, approximately 1 minute. Stir in carrots, celery, red bell peppers and red onions sauteing briefly, 1 minute. Add in sake to deglaze, then add in soy, hoisin and cornstarch slurry. Continue to stir on high heat for about 30 seconds. Stir in bean sprouts and sesame oil to combine and remove from heat.
2. Steam or heat rolls in a warm 250 degree F oven, tightly wrapped in foil for 8 minutes.
3. Take rolls, 2 at a time, and leaving them attached, gently split open and fill with approximately 3/4 cup of stir-fry mixture. Garnish with green onions and serve immediately.

Stirfry of Goodness

"delicious"

Servings: 6

Ingredients

Seasonings

- 1 teaspoon seasoned salt
- 1/2 teaspoon ground paprika
- 1/3 teaspoon granulated garlic powder
- 1/4 cup chopped parsely
- 1/4 pound smoked hog jowlsor bacon

Vegetables

- 1 head cauliflower
- 1/4 cup water
- 1 medium onion
- 1 pound carrots

Eggs

- 4 large eggs
- 1/3 stick butter

Directions

1. Slice the smoked hog jowls. let them render the fat
2. While that is happening slice the carrots and onions add them to the rendered fat and smoked pork
3. Let it saute for 10 minutes covered, stir occasionally, add cauliflower and the rest of the seasonings.
4. While that is going on add the eggs to heated butter. Cook till done and set aside. Add water to stirfry and simmer covered till liquids disappear.
5. Add eggs and stir them in cover remove from heat. Let rest 3 minutes
6. Serve i hope you enjoy!

Stir-Fry Sugar Snap Peas & Mushrooms

"I like peas, and sugar snap are better for you, and better for diabetics than regular peas. Working doesn't always leave a lot of time to cook, so I like tasteful, easy to make side dishes such as this. I hope you think so also."

Servings: 3 | **Time**: 15m

Ingredients

- 2 tbsp butter
- 1 tbsp vegetable oil
- 3 clove garlic
- 8 oz sliced mushrooms
- 12 oz sugar snap peas
- 1/4 tsp red pepper flakes (optional)
- 1/4 tsp ground black pepper
- 1/2 tsp salt or to taste

Directions

1. In a stir-fry pan/Wok/skillet melt butter over medium heat
2. Add oil and diced garlic
3. Add red pepper if using.
4. Stir for 1 minute so the garlic imparts some flavor into the oil

5. Add sliced mushrooms, stir until about half way cooked to your liking.
6. My wife liked me to tip the peas first, so I do, but it is not required if you don't care. Add peas to pan.
7. Stir constantly until peas take on a bright green color, about 5 minutes.
8. Add black pepper and salt, stir for about 2 or 3 more Minutes
9. Serve hot.

Stir-Fry Veggie Medley

Servings: 1 | **Time**: 20m

Ingredients

- 1/2 packages snow peas
- 1/2 can canned corn
- 1/2 cucumber (slices)
- 7 mushrooms
- 4 bunch broccoli

Directions

1. Sauteed all veggies with garlic, onion, salt, and pepper
2. Add grilled chicken, tofu, or beef for protein.

Stir-Fry Your Way

Servings: 4 | **Prep**: 40m

Ingredients

- 1/2 cup low-sodium chicken broth
- 2 tablespoons cider vinegar
- 1/2 tablespoon light soy sauce

- 2 tablespoons brown sugar
- 3 tablespoons canola oil
- 1 pound boneless, skinless chicken breast, cut into bite-size pieces
- 4 cups of your favorite vegetables (broccoli cut into bite-size pieces, shredded carrots, thinly sliced red bell peppers, chopped onion or thin green beans)
- 1 tablespoon minced garlic
- 1 8-oz. can pineapple chunks, canned in juice, drained, optional
- 2 teaspoons cornstarch mixed with 2 Tbsp. cold water
- 2 cups cooked brown rice or whole-grain noodles

Directions

1. Preheat a Wok or large skillet on low. In a bowl, combine chicken broth, vinegar, soy sauce and brown sugar. Turn heat up to high. Pour in 1 Tbsp. canola oil and, once hot, add half of chicken and sauté until cooked through, about 5 minutes. Remove to a plate. Repeat with 1/2 Tbsp. oil and remaining chicken.
2. Add vegetables and 1 1/2 Tbsp. oil to Wok; sauté until tender, about 3 minutes. Add garlic; sauté 1 minute.
3. Return chicken to Wok; add pineapple, if desired. Pour in chicken broth mixture and stir well. Add cornstarch and stir until sauce thickens and becomes shiny. Serve over brown rice or whole-grain noodles.

Stir-Fry II

"The success of this recipe is the 'foundation' mixture. It makes for quick and easy meals that you can chop and change as you please. Add and change to the foundation mixture to keep it exciting. You can keep it vegetarian or carb-free too."

Time: 20m

Ingredients

- 1 whole garlic
- 4 chili's
- 30 ml fresh ginger
- 30 ml lemongrass, grated

- 20 ml olive oil
- 1 onion, chopped
- 1 mixed vegetables
- 1 protein
- 60 ml soy sauce
- 1 noodles or rice
- 1 lemon
- 1 bunch fresh coriander

Directions

1. Chop chili & garlic, grate lemongrass & ginger.
2. Combine chili, garlic, lemongrass, ginger & add olive oil. This will serve as your foundation, this mix can be kept in the fridge for a fair amount of time.
3. From here everytime you cook, fry off the onion & add the 'foundation' mixture.
4. To this add protein of your choice, when half way cooked add vegetables of your choice.
5. Season with soy sauce.
6. While this is cooking, boil, noodles/rice and combine with stri-fry mixture.
7. Finish with lemon juice & fresh chopped coriander.

Super Easy Stir-Fried Cabbage

"A very simple stir-fry dish. The reason for using only soya sauce for stir-frying cabbage is that it brings out the natural sweetness in the cabbage itself."

Servings: 4 | **Prep**: 10m | **Cook**: 5m | **Ready In**: 15m

Ingredients

- 1 tablespoon vegetable oil
- 2 cloves garlic, minced
- 1 pound shredded cabbage
- 1 tablespoon soy sauce
- 1 tablespoon Chinese cooking wine (Shaoxing wine)

Directions

1. Heat the vegetable oil in a Wok or large skillet over medium heat. Stir in the garlic, and cook for a few seconds until it begins to brown. Stir in the cabbage until it is coated in oil; cover the Wok, and cook for 1 minute. Pour in the soy sauce, and cook and stir for another minute. Increase the heat to high, and stir in the Chinese cooking wine. Cook and stir until the cabbage is tender, about 2 minutes more.
2. Stir chicken into cabbage mixture. Pour chicken broth mixture over chicken mixture, reduce heat to medium, and simmer until sauce thickens, about 1 minute. Reduce heat to low; add cashews and cook until heated through, 1 minute. Sprinkle with paprika.

Sweet and Sour Stir Veggie fry

"Get the boys to eat veggies"

Servings*: 4 | **Time***: 20m

Ingredients

- 1 can Pineapples in juice
- 1/3 Red bell pepper
- 1/3 tbsp Brown sugar
- 2 tbsp Soy sauce
- 1 tbsp Corn starch
- 2 tbsp Olive oil
- 1 envelope Frozen stir fry

Directions

- Place oil in pan until hot ,add the stir fry ,red pepper and cook until tender,add the sugar ,soy sauce,corn starch,pineapples with the juice ,then simmer untill it thickens or add a little more starch if it's too watery.u done

Sweet Chili Stir Fry I

***Servings*: 6 | *Time*: 15m**

Ingredients

- 2 boneless chicken breast chopped
- 8 oz Fettuccini noodles
- 4 tbsp sesame oil
- 1/2 cup Thai sweet chili sauce
- 3 tbsp soy sauce
- 1 tsp crushed red pepper
- 1/4 cup minced garlic
- 1/4 cup minced cilantro
- 1 white onion quarter chopped
- 1 small red pepper thinly sliced
- 1 bunch green onions finely chopped
- 1 head broccoli chopped
- 1 cup chopped mushrooms

Directions

1. In a medium pan bring water to a bowl and add Fettuccini noodles. Bowl for 10 minutes or until noodles are al dente. Set aside in a bowl of cold water for later.
2. Bring a Wok to high heat, add sesame oil, garlic, white onions and crushed red pepper. Saute for 3 minutes or until onions begin to soften. Then add chicken and soy sauce. Saute for another 8 minutes.
3. Then add mushrooms, peppers, broccoli and chili sauce. Saute for another 5 minutes or until sauce thickens.
4. After sauce thickens add noodles and cilantro and saute for another 2 minutes and then set aside to cool for 2 minutes and then serve.

Sweet Chili Stir-Fry II

***Servings*: 1 | *Time*: 25m**

Ingredients

- 6 oz chicken breast
- 1/3 cup white rice
- 1/4 cup broccoli
- 1/8 cup water chestnuts
- 8 slice red pepper
- 1 portabella mushroom
- 1/2 tsp ground cumin
- 1/8 tsp ground black pepper
- 1/8 tsp cayenne pepper
- 2 pinch salt
- 3 tbsp sweet chili sauce

Directions

1. Take rice, add to water, and bring to boil. Reduce to simmer and cover. Stir occasionally.
2. Season chicken breast with cumin, cayenne pepper, black pepper, and salt.
3. Take broccoli, and cut into thirds. Slice 2-inch section of red pepper, and cut into 8 even strips. Slice mushroom into even slices.
4. Steam broccoli, water chestnuts, red pepper, and mushroom.
5. Place chicken breast in frying pan on high heat, sear outside, and reduce heat. Cover and flip occasionally, cook until internal temperature is at least 165°F.
6. Drain remaining water from rice when at desired texture. Plate rice, veggies, chicken, and then evenly spread sweet chili sauce.

Sweet Chilli and Lime Prawn Stir fry

Servings: 2 | Time: 15m

Ingredients

- 1 packages Sweet Chilli and Lime Stir fry Sauce
- 1 packages Udon Noddles

- 400 grams Stir fry Vegetables, carrots, green beans, Broccoli, peppers etc.
- 300 grams Cooked peeled prawns

Directions

1. In a Wok, sear the prawns in a dash of oil for a few minutes
2. Add vegetables and stir fry for 3 or 4 minutes
3. Pour over sauce and then add sauce and stir fry for a further 5 minutes

Sweet Potato and White Potato Spinach Stir Fry

Servings: 4 | Time: 10m

Ingredients

- 2 tbsp coconut oil
- 4 small white potatos
- 1 medium sweet potato
- 1/2 medium white onion
- 1/2 medium red onion
- 3 clove garlic
- 1/2 tbsp olive oil
- 1/2 tsp chives (dried or fresh)
- 3 tsp garlic salt
- 1/2 tsp basil
- 1 tsp Italian seasoning
- 1 tsp black pepper
- 1 cup frozen spinach

Directions

1. Set stove top to medium, add coconut oil. Cut potatoes into bite size pieces. I leave the skins on, you can peel them if you prefer. Cover while you cut the rest of the ingredients and stir occasionally.
2. Dice and add the onions. Mince and add the garlic. Stir.
3. Add the olive oil, and the rest if the ingredients. Mix well.

4. Keep an eye on them and stir every few minutes. Reduce heat to low once potatoes begin to soften.

Sweet Sour Stir Fry

Ingredients

- 1 cabbage
- 1 red pepper
- 1 onion
- 1 carrot
- 1 chicken
- 1 rice
- 1 sweet sour sauce
- 1 pineapple

Directions

1. Finely slice carrot , cabbage, onion and red pepper
2. Sweat veg
3. Cook chicken with veg
4. Add sauce
5. Add pineapple
6. Cook rice
7. Simmer stir fry while rice cooks

Szechwan-Marinated Flat Iron Steak

Servings: 4 | *Prep*: 25m | *Inactive*: 12h | *Cook*: 15m | *Ready In*: 12h40m

Ingredients

Chili Oil Vegetables:

- 1 tablespoon chili oil
- 2 tablespoons peanut oil
- 1 tablespoon jalapeno, sliced thinly

- 1 tablespoon shallots, julienned
- 1 tablespoon cilantro leaves
- 1 tablespoon green onions, cut into 1-inch lengths
- 1 tablespoon ginger, julienned

Marinade:

- 1 cup Worcestershire sauce
- 1 cup mirin, or sweet sake
- 2 cups soy sauce
- 3 pieces whole ginger, smashed
- 1/2 cup ketchup
- 1 cup chopped garlic
- 1 3/4 cups honey
- 1 cup chopped shallots
- 1/2 cup lemon juice
- 1/2 cup sambal (garlic chili paste)
- 3 tablespoons freshly ground black pepper
- 4 (8-ounce) flat iron steaks

Szechwan Deglaze:

- 1/4 cup blanched garlic
- 2 tablespoons sambal
- 1/4 cup sugar
- 1/4 cup shaohsing, or Chinese rice wine
- 2 cups oyster sauce
- 3 cups chicken stock

Sauteed Vegetables:

- 2 tablespoons peanut oil
- 1/2 cup shiitake mushrooms, quartered
- 1/2 cup blanched asparagus, cut into 1/2-inch lengths
- 1/2 cup scallions, cut into 1/2- inch lengths
- 1/2 cup bok choy
- 1/2 cup red onion, sliced
- Chopped cilantro leaves, for garnish
- Chopped scallions, for garnish

Directions

Chili Oil Vegetables:

- In a small saute pan, heat the chili and peanut oils. Add the jalapeno, shallots, cilantro, green onions, and ginger and cook until slightly tender. Remove from the heat and set aside.

Marinade:

- Combine the marinade ingredients in a medium bowl and whisk together until thoroughly combined. Place the steaks in the marinade and refrigerate for 12 hours.
  Heat the grill to high heat. Remove steaks from the marinade and season with a little salt and pepper. Grill to desired temperature, about 2 to 3 minutes per side. Remove the steaks from the grill and allow to rest. Slice the steaks on a thin bias and set aside.

Szechwan Deglaze:

- In a medium bowl, whisk together all the ingredients. Set aside.

Sauteed Vegetables:

- Heat the peanut oil in a Wok or hot saute pan over high heat. Add the mushrooms, asparagus, scallions, bok choy, and red onions, and cook until tender. Deglaze the vegetables with the Szechwan Deglaze until almost all the liquid is absorbed.

To Serve:

- Place some of the Chili Oil Vegetables on individual serving plates. Arrange the steak slices on top of the vegetables. Place the Sauteed Vegetables over the top. Garnish with cilantro and scallions. Serve immediately.

Teriyaki Stir Fry

"Great for anyone that loves teriyaki!"

Servings: 4 | ***Time***: 20m

Ingredients

- 1 lb pork loin, steak, or chicken
- 1 cup sugar snap peas
- 1/2 cup sliced onion

- 1/2 cup sliced carrot
- 1 can water chestnuts
- 1/2 cup sliced peppers
- 1/2 cup Teriyaki sauce

Directions

1. Saute all ingredients except meat for about 3 minutes.
2. Add meat and continue cooking until cooked through
3. Serve over rice or in a tortilla shell

Tilapia Stir-fry with Ginger Honey Sauce

"This is one of my favorite dishes to cook and enjoy. The crispy fried tilapia with its tender texture, together with a delicious ginger honey glaze that is both spicy and sweet tastes, is certainly a dish that will please any picky eater. (Contributed by Heina Phuong)"

Servings: 3 | **Time**: 30m

Ingredients

- 2 whole tilapia or 4 fillets
- 1 piece fresh ginger root
- 3 cloves garlic
- 1 bird's eye or Thai chili
- 1 small lemon
- 3 teaspoons fish sauce
- 5 teaspoons honey
- 1 teaspoon black pepper
- 1 small pinch salt
- 1 small bowl water
- 3 sprigs fresh dill

Directions

1. Fillet the tilapias, rinse, pat dry.

2. Dice the fillets into 3 cm cubes. Coat the fish with a little salt and black pepper and let sit about 15 minutes.
3. Heat a good amount of cooking oil in a frying pan. When hot, place the fish in the pan and fry until golden brown on all sides.
4. The tilapia tends to fall apart easily when fried, so gently use chopsticks to turn over cubes when frying.
5. When both sides of fish are evenly fried, remove and drain the oil.
6. Prepare the sauce: Peel off the skin of the ginger and pound. De-seed the bird's eye chili and slice. Add to a bowl and stir well with honey, water, fish sauce, lemon juice, black pepper.
7. Pound garlic and stir-fry until aromatic. Add the mixed sauce and bring to a boil.
8. When the sauce thickens, drop the fried fish and chopped dill in. Shake the pan to let the sauce coat the fish or gently use chopsticks to stir thoroughly. Be gentle in order not to break apart the fish.
9. Use a pair of tongs to pick out the fish and lay on serving platter. Sprinkle the remaining ginger and garlic left in the pan onto the fish. It's very tasty to serve this dish with rice or use the leftovers to fry with rice

Tofu Mushroom Stir Fry

"High protein, low calorie dish"

Ingredients

- 1 tofu cutlet or extra firm tofu ,cut into cubes
- 1 cup sliced oyster mushroom
- 2 tbsp marsala wine
- 1 red chili, sliced
- 1 spring rosemary
- to taste salt
- Oil

Directions

1. Heat oil in a pan on medium heat, add tofu and fry till golden brown and add the mushrooms to the pan and cook for 3 mins and add marsala wine, red chili and rosemary.
2. Simmer on low heat for few mins and add salt accordingly.

3. Enjoy with any salad

Tofu, Asparagus, and Red Pepper Stir-Fry with Quinoa

"Quinoa packs iron, fiber, and potassium into this meatless main dish."

Servings: *6*

Ingredients

Dressing:

- 2 tablespoons rice vinegar
- 2 tablespoons low-sodium soy sauce
- 2 teaspoons dark sesame oil
- Dash of crushed red pepper

Stir-fry:

- 1 1/2 cups water
- 1 1/2 cups uncooked quinoa
- 1 tablespoon dark sesame oil
- 1 cup chopped onion
- 2 garlic cloves, minced
- 2 cups red bell pepper strips
- 2 cups sliced mushrooms
- 2 cups (1-inch) sliced asparagus (about 1 pound)
- 1/2 teaspoon salt
- 1 (12.3-ounce) package reduced-fat firm tofu, drained and cubed
- 2 tablespoons sesame seeds

Directions

1. To prepare dressing, combine first 4 ingredients in a small bowl; stir with a whisk. Set aside.
2. To prepare stir-fry, bring water to a boil in a small saucepan. Stir in the quinoa; cover, reduce heat, and simmer 10 minutes. Remove from heat. Let stand, covered, 10 minutes; fluff with a fork.
3. Heat 1 tablespoon oil in a large nonstick skillet over medium-high heat. Add onion and garlic, and stir-fry 5 minutes. Add the bell

pepper, mushrooms, asparagus, salt, and tofu; stir-fry 3 minutes. Stir in dressing. Serve over quinoa, and sprinkle with sesame seeds.

Tomato and Egg Stir Fry

"This is an easy protein."

Servings: 3 | **Prep**: 10m | **Cook**: 5m | **Ready In**: 15m

Ingredients

- 2 tablespoons avocado oil, or as needed
- 6 eggs, beaten
- 4 ripe tomatoes, sliced into wedges
- 2 green onions, thinly sliced

Directions

1. Heat 1 tablespoon avocado oil in a Wok or skillet over medium heat. Cook and stir eggs in the hot oil until mostly cooked through, about 1 minute. Transfer eggs to a plate.
2. Pour remaining 1 tablespoon avocado oil into Wok; cook and stir tomatoes until liquid has mostly evaporated, about 2 minutes. Return eggs to Wok and add green onions; cook and stir until eggs are fully cooked, about 30 more seconds.

Triple-Mushroom Stir-Fry with Tofu

"This recipe gives you a complete meal. Be sure to have all the ingredients prepped before you heat the skillet--once you start cooking, things move quickly."

Servings: 5

Ingredients

Sauce:

- 1 1/4 cups organic vegetable broth (such as Swanson Certified Organic)
- 1/4 cup low-sodium soy sauce
- 1 1/2 tablespoons cornstarch
- 2 tablespoons water
- 2 tablespoons hoisin sauce
- 1 1/2 teaspoons sugar
- 1 teaspoon grated peeled fresh ginger
- 1/2 teaspoon crushed red pepper
- 1/2 teaspoon dark sesame oil
- 3 garlic cloves, minced

Stir-fry:

- 1 1/2 tablespoons canola oil, divided
- 1/2 pound extrafirm tofu, drained and cut into 1-inch cubes
- 2 cups presliced button mushrooms
- 2 cups sliced shiitake mushroom caps (about 3 ounces)
- 1 cup snow peas, trimmed
- 1/2 cup red bell pepper strips
- 1 (8-ounce) can sliced water chestnuts, drained
- 2 cups sliced oyster mushroom caps (about 4 ounces)
- 3/4 cup (1-inch) slices green onions

Remaining ingredient:

- 5 cups hot cooked long-grain rice

Directions

1. To prepare sauce, combine first 10 ingredients, stirring well with a whisk.
2. Heat 1 tablespoon canola oil in a large nonstick skillet over medium-high heat. Add tofu; cook 8 minutes or until lightly browned, turning occasionally. Remove from pan. Add the remaining 1 1/2 teaspoons canola oil, button mushrooms, and shiitake mushrooms to pan; sauté 3 minutes or until almost tender. Add peas, bell pepper, and water chestnuts; sauté 1 minute. Stir in broth mixture, tofu, oyster mushrooms, and onions; cook 2 minutes or until slightly thick. Serve over rice.

Tuna and Scrambled Egg Stir Fry

"A quick and easy breakfast for busy person. You can try some of the variations or come up with your own creative twists. Bon appétit!"

Servings: 3 | **Time**: 15m

Ingredients

- 1 can tuna (in oil or in water)
- 1 egg scrambled
- 1 tomato sliced
- 1/2 onion sliced
- 1 tbsp cooking oil
- Salt and pepper
- Lamb's lettuce for garnishing

Directions

1. Use a frying pan or skillet and add about 1 tbsp of cooking oil to it. Warm it over medium heat.
2. Put the sliced tomatoes and onions and stir fry. Add salt and pepper to taste.
3. Add the tuna and stir fry.
4. Add the scrambled egg and stir fry.
5. Put the lamb's lettuce for garnishing. Serve and enjoy.

Tuna Ginger Stir-Fry. (First Allotment Crop Stir Fry)

"This morning I spent a couple of hours at my plot mainly amazed at the lovely surprises it held for me. Hidden courgettes, pepper, broad beans, purple sprouting broccoli, peas, some strawberries for dessert...

So I thought of using it all up in a warming stir fry"

Servings: 2 | **Time**: 20m

Ingredients

- 1 green pepper chopped fine
- 1 red pepper chopped finely
- 1 courgette/zucchini spiralized
- 100 g purple sprouting broccoli
- 2 handfuls broadband podded and boiled for a minute
- 280 g tuna chopped in bite size pieces
- Sesame oil
- Fresh ginger to grate finely
- Dried chilli flakes
- Soya sauce

Directions

1. Heat some sesame oil in Wok and stir fry pepper and broccoli
2. Boil beans and add to the rest of vegetables
3. Spiralize courgette or finely chopped it and add to Wok.
4. Add tuna chunks and season with finely grated fresh ginger. Add a few flakes of dried chilli if you like a bit of a spice.
5. Add a dash of soya sauce. serve piping hot

Tuna Stir-fry

Servings: 1 | *Time*: 20m

Ingredients

- 4 oz tuna
- 1/3 cup rice
- 1/4 cup shredded pepper jack cheese
- 1/4 cup broccoli
- 2 tbsp green onion
- 2 tbsp tomato
- 1 tbsp peanut oil
- 1/2 tbsp low sodium soy sauce
- 1/2 tbsp honey
- 1 tsp sesame oil

- 1/2 tsp garlic powder
- 1/4 tsp cayenne pepper
- 1/4 tsp ground black pepper
- 1/8 tsp salt

Directions

1. Bring pot of water to a rolling boil. Add rice, and let boil for 15-20 minutes.
2. Wash all veggies and chop. Combine with tuna in frying pan. Add oil, and bring to medium heat. Cook for 8-10 minutes.
3. When veggies are soft and tuna is at 150°F, season with black pepper, cayenne pepper, salt, and garlic. Reduce heat and cover.
4. When rice has reached desired texture, drain water. Stir in honey, soy sauce, and sesame oil. Add cheese and stir til melted.
5. Plate veggies and tuna on top of rice.

Veggie Tofu Stir-fry (Lactose free)

Ingredients

- 1 medium handful Sliced carrots
- 1 small handful broccoli florets
- 1 small handful cauliflower
- 3 Bok Choy leaves
- 3 Napa Cabbage leaves
- 1 small handful Snap Peas
- 1 small handful Snow Peas
- Onion Powder
- 2 tbsp Earthbalance vegan butter
- 1/2 cup Vegetable Broth
- soy sauce (I used La Choy low sodium)
- 1 packages Melissa's Extra Firm Tofu
- RealLemon Juice

Directions

1. Tofu prep: cut tofu into strips and press for 45 minutes to drain excess water out. (Afterwards.. ya can either use plain, or marinate it for several hours. the longer it sits in marinate the stronger it

tastes.) After done prepping tofu - cube it to size ya like.. Set aside for now.
2. Chop up Carrots, Cauliflower, Broccoli. Cut ends off snap peas and snow peas. Group up and set aside in a bowl for now. (the picture is carrots, snow peas, and snap peas - see picture in step 3 for the broccoli and cauliflower)
3. Chop up Napa Cabbage and Bok Choy. Group up and Set side in another bowl. (The picture is of broccoli florets, Bok Choy, Napa Cabbage, and Cauliflower)
4. Preheat Wok and add earthbalance butter and onion powder.
5. Slowly add the chopped up vegetables (from step 2) to the Wok. Stir them around. When they are hot, add the leafy vegetables (from step 3) and tofu. When vegetables are close to al dente, add vegetable broth, Real lemon and soy sauce.
6. Remove from heat and enjoy :)

Veggie and Tofu Stir-Fry

"Veggie and Tofu Stir-Fry gives you that delicious seared, slightly smoky taste that you enjoy in a good Chinese restaurant but are the results from your own Wok."

Servings: 4 | Hands-on: 19m | Total time: 49m

Ingredients

- 1 (14-ounce) package water-packed extra-firm tofu, drained
- 1 tablespoon canola oil, divided
- 1/4 teaspoon black pepper
- 3 1/2 teaspoons cornstarch, divided
- 3 large green onions, cut into 1-inch pieces
- 3 garlic cloves, sliced
- 1 tablespoon julienne-cut ginger
- 4 small baby bok choy, quartered lengthwise
- 2 large carrots, peeled and julienne-cut
- 1 cup snow peas, trimmed
- 2 tablespoons Shaoxing (Chinese rice wine) or dry sherry
- 1/4 cup organic vegetable broth
- 2 tablespoons lower-sodium soy sauce
- 1 tablespoon hoisin sauce

- 1 teaspoon dark sesame oil

Directions

1. Cut tofu lengthwise into 4 equal pieces; cut each piece crosswise into 1/2-inch squares. Place tofu on several layers of paper towels; cover with additional paper towels. Let stand 30 minutes, pressing down occasionally.
2. Heat a large Wok or skillet over high heat. Add 1 1/2 teaspoons canola oil to pan; swirl to coat. Combine tofu, pepper, and 2 teaspoons cornstarch in a medium bowl; toss to coat. Add tofu to pan; stir-fry 8 minutes, turning to brown on all sides. Remove tofu from pan with a slotted spoon; place in a medium bowl. Add onions, garlic, and ginger to pan; stir-fry 1 minute. Remove from pan; add to tofu.
3. Add remaining 1 1/2 teaspoons canola oil to pan; swirl to coat. Add bok choy; stir-fry 3 minutes. Add carrots; stir-fry 2 minutes. Add snow peas; stir-fry 1 minute. Add Shaoxing; cook 30 seconds, stirring constantly. Stir in tofu mixture.
4. Combine remaining 1 1/2 teaspoons cornstarch, broth, and remaining ingredients in a small bowl, stirring with a whisk. Add broth mixture to pan; cook until slightly thickened (about 1 minute).

Veggie Stir Fry

"Filling up those Bellies one fork full at a time! This meal is so good it'll become a weekly favorite oh n did I mention soooooo easy!? Please do enjoy!"

Servings: 4 | **Time**: 10m

Ingredients

- 1 bunch fresh green beans
- 1 clove fresh garlic
- 1 zucchini
- 1 bunch fresh broccoli
- 2 red bell peppers
- 2 onions
- 1 bunch fresh kale

- 1 bunch shredded carrots
- 2 tbsp olive oil
- 1 sea salt
- 1 ground black pepper
- 4 tbsp kikkoman soy sauce
- 1 cup water

Directions

1. In a large skillet, add olive oil, kikkoman soy sauce, water, and diced cloves of garlic under low to medium heat.
2. Dice all veggies into large chunks...and no worries, they'll shrink a bit. The larger they are, the easier it is to pick them up with chopsticks.
3. Reduce the heat and while the skillet is on, add the onions, fresh broccoli, fresh green beans, and red bell peppers.
4. After 10-15 minutes, turn off the heat and add the fresh kale, zucchini, and shredded carrots and cover skillet. These are softer veggies and they don't need as much heat to be edible.
5. Stir, and after 10-15 minutes, add sea salt and ground black pepper to taste.

Vickys Quick Salmon Rainbow Stir-fry, Gluten, Dairy, Egg & Soy-Free

"I call this the rainbow because of all the different colours. Healthy and delicious!"

Servings: 4 | **Cook**: 20m

Ingredients

- 1 tbsp olive oil
- 1 tbsp Vickys Soy-Free Soy Sauce recipe from my profile
- 1 orange bell pepper, deseeded & sliced
- 1 yellow bell pepper, deseeded & sliced
- 300 grams baby plum tomatoes, halved
- 240 grams mange tout
- 12 baby sweetcorns, thickly sliced

- 1 cabbage, sliced
- 4 salmon fillets
- 80 ml thai sweet chilli sauce

Directions

1. Preheat the oven to gas 6 / 200C / 400°F
2. Place the salmon fillets skin side down on a foil lined baking tray and bake uncovered for 15 minutes
3. Meanwhile, mix together the oil and soy sauce in a frying pan
4. Fry off the peppers, tomatoes, mange tout & baby corn for 3 minutes then add the cabbage and stir-fry for a further 2 minutes
5. Split the stir-fry between 4 pre-warmed plates
6. Take the salmon out of the oven, remove the skin and flake the flesh over the top of the vegetables
7. Serve with a drizzle with sweet chilli dipping sauce over the top

Walnut Stir-Fry Bok Choy

"Greens are good for you, bok choy is pretty consistent in the stores around me, so I am always looking for better ways to make it. I used a middle size bok choy here, you may want to ramp it up for more."

Servings*: 2 | **Time***: 15m

Ingredients

- 1 medium size Bok Choy
- 4 (or to taste) garlic cloves
- 1 inch piece of fresh ginger
- 1/2 tsp salt
- handful walnuts
- to taste hot sauce
- 1 Tbl. acid like vinegar, lemon juice (optional)
- 2 Tbl. oil for stir-fry

Directions

1. Clean your bok choy breaking off each stem and making sure tops and stalks are clean. Grit sucks!
2. chop your bok choy into about 1 - 2 inch pieces
3. Add oil to pan, set on medium high heat (I'm using sesame here, but any works)
4. chop onion, garlic and ginger
5. When pan is hot, add onion, garlic and ginger. Stir fry until onion is translucent, about 2 minutes
6. Add bok choy to pan, stir all the time until wilted. Sometimes you have to add the thicker stems first, then add the tops after a couple minutes for even cooking.
7. Once bok choy is wilted add walnuts
8. Add salt and hot sauce, acid if using. Stir constantly until done, 3 minutes
9. Serve. Shown here with a pan fried tenderized lightly breaded steak with pan gravy.

Wok Seared Scallops in Teriyaki Tabasco Butter Sauce

Servings: 8 | Prep: 10m | Cook: 25m | Ready In: 35m

Ingredients

- 1/2 sticks butter
- Hot pepper sauce (recommended: Tabasco)
- 24 large scallops
- Kosher salt and freshly ground black pepper
- 1 pound sugar snap peas, trimmed and cleaned of stems and blanched
- 2 red bell peppers, diced
- Peanut oil
- Store-bought teriyaki sauce

Directions

1. Heat Wok over high heat. Working in batches, add two tablespoons butter and melt. Add a generous splash of hot pepper sauce, or to taste. Add four scallops to sizzling butter mixture and sear both

sides until nice and golden brown, about one minute per side. Season with salt and pepper. Remove scallops from Wok to plate. Repeat until all the scallops are cooked.
2. To the Wok add the sugar peas and bell pepper and stir-fry for about 2 to 3 minutes until slightly soft yet still crunchy. If they are sticking you may need to add a dash of peanut oil to help out. Pour a large dash of your favorite teriyaki sauce into the Wok and return the scallops to the Wok. Give them a final toss and serve.

Wok-Fried Prawns with Broccoli And Bok Choy

Servings: 2

Ingredients

- 1 kg peeled prawns
- 1/2 cup Teriyaki Marinade
- 1 tsp garlic flakes
- 2 tsp cornflour
- 1/2 cup Chicken Stock
- 1 tbsp Olive Oil
- 1 bunch bok choy
- 1 bunch baby broccoli
- 2 cup steamed rice

Directions

1. Combine prawns, teriyaki marinade and sweet chilli sauce in a bowl. Mix well and save some mix for next step
2. Combine cornflour, chicken stock and reserved marinade in a jug
3. Defrost prawns in boiling pot. Heat a Wok over high heat until hot. Add half the oil and half the prawn mixture. Stir-fry prawns for 2 minutes. Remove to a plate.
4. Use boiling pot (that defrosted prawns) to cook rice. Add bok choy and broccoli to Wok. Stir-fry for 1 minute. Add prawns and stock mixture. Stir-fry for 1 to 2 minutes or until sauce thickens. Serve with steamed rice.

Yoboi Stir Fry

"I've experienced with this with rice, but never told anyone about it..hope it's clearly understandable. Thanks and enjoy"

Servings: 4 | **Time**: 30m

Ingredients

- 4 eggs
- 2 Packages Ramen
- 1 Package kikkoman Fried Rice Seasoning Mix
- 1 some cheese "quantity doesn't matter"
- 1 some shrimp, you judge
- 1 birds eye Steamfresh, Asian Medley

Directions

1. Saute shrimp until pink, I used medium cooked.
2. Do your 4 eggs and add the cheese
3. Boil water for the ramen noodles
4. Read the direction for the for the Fried Rice Seasoning.
5. Put the veggies in the microwave
6. After the noodles were done, I added a little veggy oil to a Wok I have, then added the Fried Rice Seasoning so it wouldn't stick so much
7. Add, after the seasoning is the the Wok, add the stemmed veggies and eggs along with the shrimp..and enjoy.

Zucchini Stir Fry

"Absolutely Delicious! Great for breakfast, lunch, or dinner. If you are new to the vegan lifestyle, I recommend trying this first! It's hearty and nutritious. It's easy to make and you can substitute the vegetables for the kind you like best. If you do not like zucchini you may like it after this! ;)"

Servings: 2 | **Cook**: 30m

Ingredients

- 2 cup Chopped Zucchini (about 1 large)
- 1 cup Broccoli Florets
- 1 large Tomato
- 2 clove Garlic
- 1 large Onion
- 2 tsp Cajun Seasoning
- 2 tbsp Sodium Free Soy-Sauce (braggs)
- 1 cup Water
- 1/2 packages Firm Tofu
- 1/2 cup Salsa

Directions

1. Heat 1/2 cup of water in a large nonstick skillet.
2. Add onion & garlic. Cook over high heat, stirring often, until soft about 5 minutes.
3. Add zucchini, tofu, and Cajun powder. Reduce heat and cook, stirring often cook for about 3 min then add broccoli and cook for an additional 2 min or until zucchini is tender.
4. Add small amounts of additional water if needed to prevent vegetables from sticking.
5. Stir in soy sauce and tomatoes.
6. Top with salsa if desired.
7. Serve with English muffins, warm tortillas, or roasted French bread.

Conclusion

Thank you again for downloading this book!
I hope you enjoyed reading about my book!
Finally, if you enjoyed this book, please take the time to share your thoughts and post a review on Amazon. It'd be greatly appreciated!
Write me an honest review about the book – I truly value your opinion and thoughts and I will incorporate them into my next book, which is already underway.

Leave your review of my book here:
http://www.amazon.com/dp/B01N0G9HIL/

Thank you!
If you have any questions, feel free to contact at
contact@smallpassion.com

An Awesome Free Gift

For You

Download Gift
http://www.smallpassion.com/awesome-gift

I want to say "**Thank You**" for buying my book so I've put together a few, awesome free gift for you **Tips and Techniques for Cooking Like a Chef & Delicious Desserts!**
This gift is the perfect add-on this book and I know you'll love it.
So click the link to go grab it.

Read more my book here:

http://www.amazon.com/author/anniekate
http://www.smallpassion.com/my-cookbooks

Annie Kate

Founder of www.SmallPassion.com

* * *

Made in the USA
Lexington, KY
30 June 2019